KU-520-358

The Transformation of
English Provincial Towns
1600–1800

for W. G. *Hoskins*

The Transformation of English Provincial Towns 1600–1800

Edited by Peter Clark

Hutchinson

London Melbourne Sydney Auckland Johannesburg

Hutchinson & Co. (Publishers) Ltd

An imprint of the Hutchinson Publishing Group

17–21 Conway Street, London W1P 6JD

Hutchinson Group (Australia) Pty Ltd
30–32 Cremorne Street, Richmond South, Victoria 3121
PO Box 151, Broadway, New South Wales 2007

Hutchinson Group (NZ) Ltd
32–34 View Road, PO Box 40–086, Glenfield, Auckland 10

Hutchinson Group (SA) (Pty) Ltd
PO Box 337, Bergvlei 2012, South Africa

First published 1984

Photoset in 10 on 12 Times Roman by
Kelly Typesetting Limited
Bradford-on-Avon, Wiltshire

Printed and bound in Great Britain by
Anchor Brendon Ltd,
Tiptree, Essex

British Library Cataloguing in Publication Data
The Transformation of English provincial towns
    1600–1800.
    1. Cities and towns—England—History
    I. Clark, Peter
    942'.009'732   HT133
ISBN 0 09 154610 9

710100124-9

Contents

Figures and illustrations

Figures

Illustrations

(between pages 96 and 97, 128 and 129)

Acknowledgements

The editor and publishers would like to thank the copyright holders below for their kind permission to reproduce the following material:

Plate 1 reproduced from a photograph probably of *c.* 1860 in the Dryden Collection by permission of the Northampton Public Libraries Committee.

Plates 4, 7, 11, 12, 13 and 14 reproduced by permission of the Royal Commission on Historical Monuments (England).

Plate 5 is reproduced from a pencil sketch by R. P. Spiers in the Victorian and Albert Museum.

Plate 8 is copyright the Trustees of the British Museum.

Plates 9 and 10 are from *Ancient Chester: a series of illustrations of the Streets of this Old City . . . Drawn and Etched by George Bateman*, edited by Thomas Hughes (London 1880) and reproduced by permission of the British Library.

Plate 15 is copyright Hallam Ashley, FRPS.

Abbreviations

Agric. Hist. Rev.	*Agricultural History Review*
AO	Archives Office
APC	*Acts of the Privy Council*
Bodl.	Bodleian Library, Oxford
BL	British Library
C	Proceedings in the Court of Chancery, Public Record Office
CSPD	*Calendar of State Papers, Domestic*
E	Exchequer Records, Public Record Office
EcHR	*Economic History Review*
EHR	*English Historical Review*
HMC	*Historical Manuscripts Commission*
P. and P.	*Past and Present*
PP	*Parliamentary Papers*
PRO	Public Record Office
PROB	Probate Records, Public Record Office
RO	Record Office
SP	State Papers Domestic, Public Record Office
St Ch	Star Chamber Records, Public Record Office
TRHS	*Transactions of the Royal Historical Society*
VCH	*Victoria County Histories*

Notes: In the dates the Old Style has been used, except that the year has been taken to begin on 1 January; the original £ s. d currency has been retained.

All publications cited in the Notes and references sections are British unless stated otherwise.

Contributors

Peter Borsay has been Lecturer in History at St David's University College, Lampeter since 1975. He completed his doctoral thesis on 'The English Urban Renaissance. Landscape and leisure in the provincial town, *c*. 1660–1770', and is now preparing a book on the same theme for Oxford University Press.

C. W. Chalklin is a graduate of the University of New Zealand. Since 1965 he has been successively a Lecturer and Reader in the Department of History, University of Reading. He has published books on *Seventeenth-Century Kent* (1965) and *The Provincial Towns of Georgian England* (1974). He is at present working on the subject of non-residential building in England, *c*. 1650–1835.

Peter Clark is Reader in Social History at the University of Leicester. His publications include *Crisis and Order in English Towns 1500–1700* (edited with P. Slack, 1972), *English Provincial Society from the Reformation to the Revolution* (1977); and *The English Alehouse: A Social History* (1983).

Joyce Ellis is Lecturer in Economic and Social History at Loughborough University of Technology. She is a graduate of Oxford and has taught at Newcastle and Leicester Universities and Trinity College, Oxford. Her research has concentrated on North-East England in the seventeenth and eighteenth centuries, with publications on the salt industry, popular protest and local enterprise.

Michael Laithwaite is a researcher and lecturer on vernacular architecture, specializing in studies relating buildings to social and economic history. He has published an important study of the town of Burford in A. Everitt (ed.), *Perspectives in English Urban History* (1973). He began the Totnes project while Senior Research Fellow in the Department of English Local History, Leicester University.

Peter Large undertook post-graduate research at Oxford under the supervision of Dr Joan Thirsk. He was a Research Fellow at Wolfson College, Oxford and is now an investment analyst with a London firm of stockbrokers.

Ian Mitchell read modern history at Wadham College, Oxford. He completed his doctoral thesis on markets and shops in Cheshire towns in 1974 and his main interests are in eighteenth-century inland trade and urban economies, on which he has published several articles. He is a Principal with HM Customs and Excise.

C. B. Phillips has lectured in Economic History at Manchester University since 1969. His research interests centre on North-West England in the early modern period and he has written articles on Cumbria during the Civil War, on the region's iron industry and on Kendal. He was editor of the *Lowther Family Estate Books 1617–1675* which was published by the Surtees Society in 1981.

David Souden was an undergraduate at Cambridge and subsequently a Research Fellow at Emmanuel College. He completed his doctoral thesis on seventeenth-century migration in 1981 and has published a series of articles on physical mobility in the early modern period.

Preface

In the 1960s a band of younger historians, mostly friends at Oxford and students of Professor W. G. Hoskins, became interested in the early modern town, then a relatively neglected field. One outcome of their research and lively debates was a collection of essays on urban history, *Crisis and Order in English Towns, 1500–1700*, which Paul Slack and I edited in 1972. Over the last few years a growing number of monographs, surveys, articles and dissertations have been written on the English town, looking mainly at the period from the late Middle Ages to the Civil War. But much remains to be discovered about urban development, not least for the seventeenth and eighteenth centuries.

Like *Crisis and Order* the present collection has been very much a co-operative exercise and we have all learnt a great deal from one another. The purpose however has not been to produce a monolithic, collectivist view of the English town between 1600 and 1800, but rather to open up and further discussion of a number of major aspects of urban development in an era which was increasingly dominated by industrialization. It is testimony to the way that urban studies have advanced in recent years that this volume makes use of the approaches and techniques not only of social and economic history, but of agricultural, demographic and building historians as well. The prime concern is with English provincial towns. This is partly because of the unique scale and character of metropolitan expansion which clearly deserves systematic treatment in a separate work. But it also reflects the fact that many of the changes and innovations which will be discussed here – economic, social, political and cultural – were increasingly centred in the traditional and new towns of provincial England.

Any student of the early modern town relies heavily on archivists and their staffs and we are grateful to those at Gloucester, Chester, Kendal, Carlisle, Newcastle-upon-Tyne, Preston, Exeter, Norwich, and the Huntington Library, California. Drs J. Chartres,

K. Grady, D. S. O'Sullivan, M. H. Smith, and J. Longmore kindly allowed us to refer to their unpublished dissertations or other work. The Nuffield Foundation assisted with a grant towards publication. Claire L'Enfant and Sarah Conibear of Hutchinson have made the business of publication more enjoyable and less troublesome than it can often be. Jenny Clark with her usual fortitude has helped with the myriad of editorial tasks and so kept those crises which are conventionally associated with collections of this kind largely at bay.

P.A.C.

1 Introduction

Peter Clark

Between 1600 and 1800 England's cities and towns were in the throes of transformation. At the death of Elizabeth I just under one in ten of the population lived in urban centres of over 2500 inhabitants; two centuries later the figure was about 31 per cent – making England one of the most urbanized nations on earth. For much of the period London remained the principal growth point, its population rising from 200,000 in 1600 to 948,000 in 1801. But provincial towns increasingly entered the running too. While there were no centres other than London with 20,000 people or more at the start of our period, and only two in 1700, by 1801 fifteen provincial communities had reached that level. To quote Dr Corfield: 'the urban world was becoming notably multi-centred rather than focused upon a single city'.[1]*

A large part of the impetus for urbanization came, of course, not from the South and East of the country, as in the past, but from the Midlands and the North. These areas, once relatively backward in the size and density of their towns, now acquired important clusters of new, large centres as a result of expanding industrial activity. By 1800 the Bradfords and Boltons, the Sheffields and Salfords, industrial cities which were to leave an indelible imprint on the Victorian consciousness, were already prominent on the urban horizon. However, well into the late eighteenth century many of the ancient incorporated towns retained their importance. In 1801 just five of the fifteen largest provincial centres (with over 20,000 inhabitants) could be classed as 'new' towns: only after 1831 was the proportion greater than a half.[2]

During the last decade or so there has been considerable debate about how far towns contributed to economic growth during the seventeenth and eighteenth centuries. To what extent were they themselves engines of expansion, generating new industrial

---

* Superior figures refer to the Notes and references which appear at the end of chapters.

products and processes, changing patterns of consumer demand, mobilizing capital resources, helping to modernize social attitudes? And how far were they, conversely, parasites, or at best camp followers in the onrush of economic development, benefiting from vital changes in the country as a whole? Frequently the expansive element in urban society has been viewed as limited to the newer industrial towns with their absence of old-style regulatory and corporate structures. (London might qualify here as a new town because the Georgian metropolis had dramatically outgrown the old political city.) Only very recently has there been any recognition of the positive, even dynamic changes affecting the established towns of provincial England in the eighteenth century.[3]

The argument of this collection is that the seventeenth and eighteenth centuries were a time of accelerating innovation and adaptation in provincial towns, that in many ways radically modified their economic, social and other structures. As we shall see, both older and newer towns not only gave significant, if sometimes indirect impetus to economic growth: they were a vital lead sector in the wider modernizing process affecting English society. Our approach is necessarily selective, determined by the inevitably slow-moving and erratic carthorse of current research. The Northern industrial cities are not discussed, nor are the dockyard towns. Poverty, religion and the professions deserve more attention than they receive in this volume. None the less, by examining migration (the life-blood of the urban community), economic specialization, marketing, social relationships, elites, civic and popular ritual, and the townscape, the following papers help to bring into focus some of the most important aspects of urban development in the early modern period.

I

There is no intention in this introduction of painting a general picture of English towns in the seventeenth and eighteenth centuries. Rather the purpose is to concentrate attention on a number of key questions and themes related to the transformation of urban society, looking in particular at the later Stuart and Hanoverian periods. An obvious starting point is demographic growth, which is conventionally regarded as the principal defining characteristic of urbanization. Before the late eighteenth century, however, population growth and urban expansion were by no means synonymous: demographic increase might occur when towns were in the economic doldrums and vice versa. Much remains to be discovered about the demographic performances of English towns in the early modern period. In their otherwise admirable work on *The Population History of England, 1541–1871*, Wrigley and Schofield have little to say on towns, with the exception of London.[4] To a considerable extent, this is because of the serious problem of parish register evidence for urban communities. The registers themselves are more vulnerable to the underrecording of vital events than their country counterparts. In the earlier period there is the difficulty caused by high inflows of poor migrants outside the pale of orthodox parish life; from the seventeenth century the problem of the concentration of dissenters in certain towns, limiting the comprehensiveness of Anglican registers. Some compensation is afforded by census listings and population estimates which survive in random fashion from the Tudor period. But in general we must be wary of dogmatism about urban population figures, especially before the Civil War.

So far as one can judge, the overall demographic trend for English provincial towns in the sixteenth and early seventeenth centuries was broadly similar to that delineated by Wrigley and Schofield for the national population, though with higher rates of growth in the smaller urban centres than in the larger communities. The substantial urban growth before 1640 was all the more remarkable given the subsistence crises and incidence of endemic and epidemic disease, with plague progressively confined to towns.[5] The post-Restoration era saw some deceleration in demographic expansion. Many small- and medium-size towns may have marked time or advanced more slowly. Major growth tended to be limited to the more important cities (including most of the provincial capitals), a number of the ports (including Liverpool, Hull and Whitehaven), several spa towns (such as Bath and Scarborough), industrial towns like Birmingham and Manchester, and dockyard centres like Portsmouth. Most striking, however, there is little sign of the absolute demographic contraction which Wrigley and Schofield have computed for the whole kingdom from the 1660s until the 1690s, and in real terms the urban population grew markedly, fuelled after 1700 by provincial centres rather than London.[6] Continuing immigration played an important part in keeping town populations reasonably buoyant, a point we must return to shortly.

After the third and fourth decades of the eighteenth century there is substantial evidence that many larger and medium-size provincial towns were growing rapidly in size. The increase was most spectacular in the case of the emergent manufacturing towns. Birmingham had a population of about 24,000 people in 1751 and nearly 74,000 fifty years later; Sheffield about 12,000 in 1755 and 31,000 in 1801. Manchester, Blackburn, Bolton, Oldham, Leeds, Bradford, Stockport and Walsall doubled or more than doubled their populations in the last quarter of the century. But older towns also grew, in many cases outstripping the national rate of increase (approximately 48 per cent between 1751 and 1801). Among the industrial centres, Nottingham trebled its population between 1739 and 1801; Leicester doubled its size between 1750 and 1801. Bath, the leading resort town, moved up from 8000 inhabitants in 1750 to over 33,000 in 1801. Fuelled by massive naval expenditure Plymouth and Portsmouth also achieved striking growth. The upturn was more modest in the case of older-style regional centres and county towns, but it was not unimportant. Waking from its earlier demographic slumbers, York pushed its population up from about 11,400 in 1750 to 17,000 in 1801; Maidstone had about 5000 people in 1750 and 8000 half a century later; Gloucester had 5500 in 1750 and 7265 in 1801. Over the same period most of the small market towns of Bedfordshire and Dorset increased their populations more speedily than the neighbouring countryside. As one might expect, the pattern was not uniform. Most of the provincial capitals, for instance, hardly grew at all and Norwich actually lost population at the close of the period. But in many ways these were the exceptions to prove the general rule of accelerating urban growth.[7]

By the late eighteenth century natural population increase may have contributed more significantly to the growth of towns than in the past. We find an excess of baptisms over burials in a number of towns; Exeter, Nottingham and Leeds. But just how vigorous or widespread natural growth was in English provincial towns before 1800 remains uncertain. The causes of such growth are even more contentious. Mortality rates in towns almost certainly retained their traditional dreadful premium over those in the countryside, as a consequence of the persistence of epidemic and endemic diseases. New evidence has been presented to resurrect the old view that the spread of town hospitals may have had a beneficial effect on mortality. Certainly the thirty general hospitals established between 1736 and 1800 in most of the major provincial centres were impressive manifestations of town improvement and capital investment in the Hanoverian period. But the influence on mortality of the hospital movement and other medical advances was probably modest in comparison to the more traditional role of rising fertility rates. Here the critical variable was the falling age at marriage. Earlier marriage may have been linked with improvements in job and housing opportunities in many towns before 1800; it also probably reflected the decline of apprentices and journeymen living in their masters' houses, encouraging young people to set up home on their own. Urban birth rates may also have been boosted by the greater volume of immigration for conventionally a high proportion of movers are always likely to be younger persons.[8]

None the less, much of this discussion must be speculative in the absence of detailed demographic studies of provincial towns in the early modern period. Generally it would be premature to overstate the novel importance of natural population growth for eighteenth century urbanization. For the great majority of cities and towns throughout the early modern period, immigration was the principal locomotive of demographic expansion. Immigration was heavy in the sixteenth and early seventeenth centuries when recurrent population deficits in towns and surplus labour and housing shortages in the countryside combined to create a flood of newcomers to urban communities, notably in the South and East. There were significant flows of poorer migrants travelling long distances from the impoverished uplands.[9] During the later Stuart period, as David Souden argues in his essay, the aggregate level of movement into towns remained high (higher than in the countryside). On the other hand, longer distance movement waned. To some extent, this was the effect of fewer and less violent demographic crises in towns. It was also influenced by the abatement of subsistence pressures in the countryside as populations stagnated or fell, real wages advanced, and the rural poor enjoyed more generous parish relief. No less important, Souden shows that the composition of migrational flows altered during the course of the seventeenth century, with growing numbers of women coming to find work in the enlarged service and market trades – the so-called tertiary sector – of English towns.[10]

By the mid eighteenth century the volume of migration to town was rising rapidly. In 1765 Dr Ash declared: 'more than half the manufacturers [workmen] of the town of Birmingham are not parishioners of it. . . . Many of them are foreigners, but the greatest part belong to the parishes of the neighbouring country'. Renewed population pressure in the villages and the decline in some areas of rural industry, as well as higher urban wage rates and large-scale house building in towns (providing cheap accommodation), were among a concatenation of forces propelling people into urban centres. Regrettably, quantifiable evidence for physical mobility in this period is lacking except for certain categories of poor movers. It seems likely however that the broad pattern of movement to town continued along the lines established by 1700. Most newcomers to the industrializing centres and older towns of Hanoverian England had travelled fairly short distances, commonly, as Ash noted for Birmingham, from the adjoining countryside. This was one important factor helping to minimize the social trauma of the new surge of urbanization.[11] Again female migration must have predominated: in 1801 the sex ratios of virtually all the major towns, irrespective of economic complexion, reveal a continuing bias against males. If the Bradfords and Sheffields were the frontier towns of eighteenth-century England they never suffered from that paucity of womenfolk which afflicted their American counterparts. This high sex ratio may indicate the important traditional aspects of the urban economy, even in industrializing centres, with the tertiary sector maintaining its relative significance. Again the job opportunities for women doubtless increased in some of the new industries, while those in arable husbandry diminished. Demographic inertia and the national surplus of women also contributed.[12]

What about the reception of migrants in town? By the end of the seventeenth century apprenticeship, the old access route to urban economic and political power, was in decline. But there was an increasing array of informal agencies that helped the newcomer to find work and a place to live: alehouses, artisan clubs, registry offices, religious bodies, voluntary societies and, more important than in the past, the extended family. These mechanisms enabled the urban community to absorb the growing tide of immigration in the late eighteenth century without enormous disruption.[13] Looking at the general demographic performance of our provincial towns the abiding impression is one of major changes, increasingly rapid towards the end of the period, taking place within a fairly stable and traditional framework.

II

Fundamental to the transformation of English provincial towns between 1600 and 1800 were economic developments, including (not least) industrialization. At the start of the period numerous old established towns, like the county towns of Canterbury, Coventry,

Gloucester and Salisbury, faced economic setbacks and uncertainty. Along with particular local difficulties, many communities suffered from a number of common problems: the decline of their old staples (principally textiles) as industries drifted to the countryside; the challenge to their marketing role from growing numbers of small, open, market towns; and competition in the luxury trades from London and the largest regional centres.[14] Colin Phillips shows how the Kendal old drapery industry suffered increasing strains by the early seventeenth century, confronted as it was both by a sharp decline in overseas demand (due to fashion, war and protectionism), and by competition from rural producers. There were exceptions to this scenario of urban distress. Towns which acquired a more specialist role as industrial, distributive or service centres were able to ride out the worst economic storms, among them most of the provincial capitals like York, Norwich and Bristol. But these were a distinct minority before the English Revolution.[15]

As the seventeenth century progressed, however, economic specialisms became more widespread. Kendal, for instance, moved over to the new draperies, concentrating on stuff-weaving; later it became a stocking knitting centre. Plenty of other medium-sized towns followed suit, acquiring or expanding a craft speciality, and so consolidating their economic role. By 1700 at least half the established urban centres specialized industrially to some degree. Vital now was the multiplying number of types of goods produced. At the start of the eighteenth century Nehemiah Grew spoke of the great profusion of kinds and sizes of metal wares: 'Needles of 12 [types], iron-wire of 14, brass wire of 24. Files from 5 lbs weight to the smallness of a sewing needle.' Product diversification was very much an urban phenomenon. Other specialist towns also grew up. Almost perpetual naval warfare with the Dutch and then the French gave a boost to dockyard towns and fleet stations like Portsmouth, Plymouth, Rochester, Chatham, Harwich and Falmouth.[16] With the rise of leisured professional and landed classes, there was a proliferation of spas and spa towns. Early spas were often primitive places with little more than the reputation of their springs and the fashionable fame of royal visits to grace them. At Tunbridge Wells in the 1690s we hear:

> For did you ever see in any town
> So many inconveniency go down
> The sun appearing, we with dust are choked,

> And with the least of rains our feet are soaked;
> Both weathers keep us in a shed that stinks. . . .

But luxury shops, purpose-built assembly rooms, churches, walks, and a string of lodging-houses soon distinguished the successful spa towns, such as Scarborough, Tunbridge Wells and, of course, Bath, from the other spas (often close to London) whose renown quickly evaporated. By 1749 Bath may have had 12,000 visitors a year.[17]

Less specialist were the so-called gentry towns that developed in the later Stuart period and which catered for the entertainment and service needs of landowners in the district, offering a choice of good inns, clubs, playhouses, libraries and the chance to consult reputable attorneys and physicians. Bury St Edmunds, Preston, Shrewsbury, Stamford, Lichfield, Beverley and Warwick were all prosperous examples of this type of town.[18]

The rise of more specialized urban economies during the later Stuart period is now well established. It was accompanied by an equally important development – the rationalization of economic functions between towns. During the Tudor and early Stuart periods when most towns in an area had basically mixed economies (combining craft, marketing and service activities), their functions frequently overlapped, causing debilitating competition. By George I's reign one can identify a growing measure of specialization within regional networks of towns. In the West Riding, Leeds became known as a cloth-finishing centre; Halifax and Bradford for weaving worsteds; Huddersfield for kerseys; Sheffield for cutlery; Barnsley for wire-making and later linens; Knaresborough as a spa; Pontefract for market gardening; and Doncaster as a smart gentry town. There was a similar trend in the West Midlands with the industrial roles of Birmingham, Walsall and Wolverhampton complemented by Lichfield as a social centre and Stafford as an administrative town.[19]

Specialization and rationalization had a negative effect on many minor towns. If the eighteenth century saw the decline of the small landowner, it also witnessed the relative decline of numerous small urban communities. Prosperous farmers and gentry preferred to travel further to bigger centres with a better range of shopping, professional and other facilities. At the same time, the small town faced growing competition from the villages, many of which could boast a range of trades and several shops by the start of the Georgian period. As early as 1681 it was said: 'in every country village, where is . . . not above ten houses, there is a shopkeeper', often dealing in substantial commodities. There were plenty of exceptions to this picture, where a small town was favoured by improvements in communications or acquired a manufacturing or marketing specialism. Even urban decline did not entail economic indigence; rather, as at Totnes, a lower level of prosperity. However the number of market towns did fall sharply in the eighteenth century. According to John Chartres, the overall contraction in England between 1690 and 1792 was about 18 per cent. The downturn was especially marked in the West.[20]

The reduction of numerous lesser market centres to village status was only one aspect of the reworking of town and country relations that occurred during the period. The conventional model of 'proto-industrialization' by which rural industry was subsidized by the involvement of its workforce in part-time subsistence agriculture and competed head-on with urban crafts in wider markets, hardly seems applicable to England during the late seventeenth and eighteenth centuries.[21] Here earlier rivalries between urban and rural trades were diminishing by 1700. From Phillips's paper we can see how the new relationships that developed in regard to industrial specialization were often highly complex. Later Stuart Kendal and its hinterland prospered by going their own separate ways, cultivating particular trades. Elsewhere, as in the case of metalworking in the Sheffield region or hosiery in and around Leicester, there was a division between skilled production in town and cruder output in the neighbouring villages.[22] No less vital for long-term industrial and urban expansion, was the growth of agricultural specialization. Peter Large demonstrates in Chapter 5 how by the start of the eighteenth century, Birmingham's hinterland was increasingly polarized between spreading industrial activity and intensive farming, mainly of corn to feed Birmingham's inhabitants. In North Worcestershire the old dual economy of pastoral farming and metalworking was swept away. The point is not simply that intensive farming was vital for sustaining the growth of towns – the argument deployed by Professor J. de Vries to explain the high level of urbanization in the Netherlands during the seventeenth century. Improvements in agricultural productivity permitted the release of at least some labour from the land. And, most important, farming specialization helped define the geography of accelerating industrial growth, growth which (in contrast to the Continent) was usually closely linked with urban centres, whether old or new. Even less dynamic towns frequently had extensive market gardens in the vicinity by the eighteenth century, helping to improve the diets of citizens. At the same time, agricultural activities within towns continued to decline in importance. This more sharply focused nature of the relationship between towns and their hinterlands may well have contributed towards the rise of a romantic picturesque vision of the countryside which became fashionable in Georgian England.[23]

In sum, it is evident that, compared with their condition a century before, English provincial towns were by Queen Anne's reign increasingly prosperous communities, particularly the larger centres. Behind this prosperity and the growth of economic specialization were a series of factors. One was the improvement of living standards for the mass of people as the national population contracted, prices fell and wages advanced. This generated greater demand for urban products, especially consumer wares and services. Answering that demand was a progressively sophisticated system of inland trade. Old style open markets and fairs were complemented now by tribes of respectable chapmen, traders and carriers (both short and long distance), who commonly operated out of major town inns. These, as Professor Everitt has described, functioned as commercial exchanges, shopping and transport centres and stores all rolled into one. In more important towns permanent specialist shops also began to appear by 1700.[24] At this time overseas demand was probably less crucial in stimulating economies, though the West Country clothing towns exported extensively to the Mediterranean and Far Eastern markets in the early part of the eighteenth century, and Birmingham had a mounting trade in guns and other metal products with Africa.[25]

A second factor aiding urban prosperity, and helping in fact to turn the terms of trade between town and country more in favour of towns, was the growing custom for members of the rural élite and their wives to spend weeks or months of the year in an urban milieu. The gaiety and excitement of London's social season bewitched the landed classes. But the great majority of gentry could never afford more than the occasional, brief visit to the metropolis. They opted instead for a longer stay in a county or resort town – if they were lucky at a smart spa. Flush with the income from their landed estates, the gentry were welcome visitors and townsmen pandered to their presence: by offering a growing selection of shops and professional services; by staging entertainments, firework shows and ceremonies; by building more classical, brick and tiled houses; by initiating improvement schemes, making the streets passable for carriages and providing piped water supplies; and last, but not least, by encouraging the participation of county magnates in town politics.[26]

Essential for the expansion of urban commerce and gentry traffic was a third factor: the advance in transport and communications. River transport had been important for the prosperity of towns in East Anglia and parts of the Home Counties for many years. In the 1590s it was said that a number of East Anglian towns had up to 300 boats apiece since 'all their living stands by the water . . . they travel and trade from country to country, mill, market and fairs, by their boats'. But it was river navigation, mostly from the late seventeenth century, that enabled large numbers of inland towns, old and new, to develop a galaxy of specialist manufactures and to find markets for them in London, other leading cities, or abroad. Improved roads also had their part to play. Better bridges and the spread of turnpikes (from the 1690s), facilitated the movement of thousands of chapmen and carriers and brought flocks of landowners to town.[27]

A further variable affecting town economies was the influence of London. The impact of metropolitan growth was less direct or extensive than for agriculture. There is only patchy evidence of substantial London investment in manufacturing activity in either the old or newer towns. London producers were regularly in conflict with their colleagues in provincial towns before the early eighteenth century, though this subsequently disappeared. Nevertheless, the scale and sophistication of metropolitan demand (generated by enormous population increase and high wages) together with the capital's emergence as one of the world's premier international ports, almost certainly gave a boost to urban industrial specialization. It may also have encouraged the development of more fashionable, up-market products with a wider marketing potential. On occasion London's technical innovations and equipment were translated to the provinces. In the early eighteenth century, Newcastle-under-Lyme and the North Staffordshire pottery industry benefited from contact and exchange of personnel with the London china manufacturers of Chelsea and Bow. During the same period part of the London hosiery industry moved to Nottingham. London remained the central market and distribution point for many provincial industries well into the late eighteenth century.[28]

Finally, there may have been the positive effects of economic liberalization. Though much more work needs to be done on this question, there are signs of an increased influx of outside traders and craftsmen into corporate towns. Some came as a result of the Civil War and the Great Fire of London; others took advantage of the political instability of the 1680s and the mass production of freedoms for electoral purposes after the Glorious Revolution. Gilds survived in certain towns and trades (particularly the luxury sector where there was a continuing concern with quality and a desire to prevent skilled workers using their new economic muscle to maximize wages). But in the majority of trades, gilds disappeared or turned into drinking clubs. One consequence was that established towns may have been able to respond somewhat more flexibly to changing patterns of consumer demand. Market and fair tolls were likewise increasingly difficult to collect by the early eighteenth century, helping to reduce one of the burdens on inland trade.[29]

Many of the advances of the post-Restoration period came to fruition in the late eighteenth century. By then urban economic specialization was in full spate. This was in marked contrast to the Dutch experience where specialization, once a cardinal feature of a flourishing urban system, was retreating after 1750, precipitating a century of de-urbanization. In England industrial specialization was a crucial feature of most of the newer urban centres. Birmingham became famous for its guns, toys and glass, Sheffield for fine cutlery, Manchester and Bolton for cotton fustians, calicoes and muslins, Halifax and Bradford for worsteds and Burslem for chinaware.[30] In a number of industries output was given powerful new impetus by technological innovation: silver plating at Sheffield; spinning inventions (Hargreave's 'jenny', Arkwright's waterframe, Crompton's 'mule') for the cotton and worsted towns of Lancashire and the West Riding; and on a lesser scale (before 1800), Boulton and Watt's steam engine for spinning and china-making. Of course, technological change was not confined to newer towns. Nottingham was an important pioneering centre for textile innovation, while technical changes were also influential in the countryside.[31] At the same time, production in the new industries was increasingly geared towards overseas demand. Josiah Wedgwood led the way in opening up European markets for his potteries; in the 1780s Manchester cottons were pouring into France; and Birmingham and other West Midland towns depended heavily on American trade by 1800.[32]

Supply and distribution was facilitated by continuing transport improvements including the new canal network, largely opened by the 1790s, connecting many industrial towns with international ports like Liverpool and Hull. In South Lancashire the topography of industrial expansion was heavily influenced by canal developments with iron, glass, pewter and heavy engineering works thriving at St Helens, Warrington, Wigan and Liverpool, located near waterways. Economic differentiation within the urban network, already visible by 1750, was taken a stage further in some areas. A number of the small industrializing centres in the Birmingham region began to concentrate on different types of metal products that were then sold through Birmingham: one or two places started to evolve as component towns, making metal items for assembly in Birmingham workshops.[33]

Yet the industrial progress of the new or embryonic manufacturing towns must be seen in perspective. Before the 1790s most production continued in traditional channels, based on small workshops, though with greater reliance in certain areas on the putting-out system. Factories were growing in number and scale during the second half of the century, but they were exceptional and by no means monopolized by the new centres. There was a general reluctance (even in Birmingham) to use steam power. Rising industrial output after 1750 built upon and owed a good part of its momentum to the efflorescence of crafts and trades in post-Restoration towns.[34]

Moreover, while industrial specialization acted as the cutting edge of economic advance in the new towns, both large and smaller places quickly assumed or expanded the more basic functions of marketing and service activities. Already in the early eighteenth century Birmingham's significance as a metal-making town was buttressed by its role as a distribution and commercial focus for South Staffordshire and as a purveyor of services, including printing, bookselling, banking and leisure facilities. By 1800 the town was not only one of the kingdom's leading manufacturing towns, but a powerful regional capital with an economic influence embracing a good part of the West Midlands. Manchester may have been less significant as a regional centre than Birmingham before 1800 but it too was acquiring numerous service activities in the late eighteenth century with large numbers of professional men, theatres, concert rooms, subscription libraries and educational institutions. The parallel growth of the tertiary sector is also apparent in smaller centres. Indeed, it might be argued that it was the vitality and responsiveness of other elements in the town economy as much as industrial specialization which made possible rapid urbanization during the second part of the century. In 1755 John Clayton noted the recent rise in Manchester of 'retailing milk, butter, coals and so forth'. Ian Mitchell reveals in his paper on Cheshire towns how small-scale street traders and retail shop-keepers multiplied alongside older distributive channels like markets, fairs and inns, and performed an essential role in feeding and clothing the workmen of industrializing Macclesfield and Stockport.[35]

At the same time, economic specialization and prosperity was not confined to the newer towns. Some major industrial growth points were located in old-established corporate towns. Leicester hummed as a stronghold of the hosiery trade; Nottingham added lace manu-facture to its hosiery speciality; in the West Country the fine cloth industry, languishing in mid century, prospered in the last decades and brought wealth to towns like Frome, Devizes and Trowbridge; and the late eighteenth century was a buoyant time for the Gloucester pin-industry. There were some notable casualties it is true. The Norwich worsted industry was badly hit by wars in the 1790s; Tiverton faded as a new draperies town. In general, how-ever, many traditional towns retained quite flourishing specialist industries until the close of the century, their success frequently consolidated by the movement of craft activity from the adjoining countryside.[36]

Some of the established towns shared in the growth of overseas markets. At home enhanced agricultural prosperity, fed by rising prices and output, gave them a bedrock of regional demand. Manu-facturers could also take advantage of the relative accessibility of finance in older towns. In the early eighteenth century and after, urban attorneys were leading money-lenders, often mobilizing capital and savings from the nearby countryside. In the later period the older towns also had a high incidence of country banks, exploit-ing both landed profits and commercial prosperity. While Smith's of Nottingham were probably exceptional in the scale of their lending to local industry, most banks provided some help to manufacturers through short-term bills and overdrafts. The capital resources of the older towns also contributed handsomely to canal and river naviga-tion schemes – helping urban industry indirectly.[37]

Overall, it would be wrong to exaggerate the contrasts in the economic structures and performance of the established and newer

towns of Hanoverian England. Where there were differences, they
were differences of degree rather than of a qualitative nature. Table
1 sketches a rough outline of the occupational pattern of a cross-
section of nine provincial towns in the 1790s, including the more
traditional county centres of Chester, Colchester and Maidstone,
the provincial capital and port of Bristol, the industrializing old
town of Nottingham, and newer resort, dockyard and industrial
centres like Bath, Plymouth, Bolton and Wolverhampton. The
analysis is based on the listings in the *Universal British Directory*
(1790–8). The limitations of this type of source are well known.
Directories are incomplete, covering only a varying portion of the
working population of towns, and are biased towards the economic
élite.[38] However, the picture presented here is not implausible in
the context of the late eighteenth-century urban economy. Several
conclusions are suggested. First, all the towns, including
Nottingham, Bolton and Wolverhampton, had substantial groups
of inhabitants engaged in the distributive and dealing trades; the
highest proportion was in the luxury town of Bath. Second, industrial activity, even in the specialist manufacturing towns, never
exceeded much more than half the listed occupations, and at
Wolverhampton, for instance, it included sizeable numbers
engaged in traditional crafts like woodworking and dressmaking.
As for professional and public services, all the towns had some
people in this sector, though the proportion was marginally lower in
the industrial towns. Gentlefolk and rentiers were predictably most
numerous in county towns like Chester, but they were also present
elsewhere (except at Bath where they seem to have been omitted
from the listing). If the directory evidence is any guide, there was
clearly a considerable degree of convergence in the occupational
order and possibly economic functions of both traditional and
newer provincial towns in the late eighteenth century.

From the 1790s problems began to mushroom for industry in
older urban centres. The war with revolutionary France disrupted
overseas markets. Harvest failures led to violent fluctuations in
home demand. The banking crisis of 1793 disproportionately
affected the country towns. Meanwhile, smaller producers suffered
increasingly fierce competition from the great manufacturers of the
new towns. Even so, it would be wrong to exaggerate the threat to
traditional urban economies before 1800. As we shall see, many
provincial towns had been actively engaged in civic improvement in
the last part of the eighteenth century, widening streets, building

Table 1   *Occupations in nine provincial towns in the 1790s from the* Universal British Directory *(percentages)*

Occupational group	Bath	Bolton	Bristol	Chester	Colchester	Maidstone	Nottingham	Plymouth (inc. Dock)	Wolverhampton
Agriculture	1.2	0.8	0.9	1.2	7.8	0.4	1.1	0.3	1.4
Building	5.3	3.5	5.3	5.2	6.4	6.4	6.3	3.6	4.0
Manufacturing	23.6	49.3	29.7	27.7	30.7	39.1	48.5	25.6	53.2
Transport	1.0	0.4	0.8	2.3	3.6	0.0	0.1	5.1	0.4
Dealing	54.4	30.9	36.1	27.1	28.2	44.4	23.4	40.0	28.8
Professional and public	12.4	10.1	12.2	15.1	13.6	7.7	9.7	14.8	7.0
Domestic service	1.9	0.5	1.6	2.2	2.3	1.2	2.9	2.7	1.2
Proprietors and independents	0.2	4.5	13.0	18.5	7.4	0.8	8.0	6.6	3.6
Miscellaneous	0.0	0.0	0.4	0.7	0.0	0.0	0.0	1.3	0.4
Number	1 197	596	3 134	1 200	528	248	728	1 483	771
Approximate 1801 population	33 000	18 000	61 000	15 000	12 000	8 000	29 000	40 000	13 000

new market halls, and so on. In this way they sought to strengthen their functions as distributive and service centres. When their industries came under pressure older towns like Tiverton, Norwich and Colchester had the flexibility to shift their economic emphasis towards the lucrative gentry and farming trade which was bolstered by agricultural expansion and the war.[39]

All in all, economic specialization first forged in the post-Restoration period remained the driving force behind urban change in the late eighteenth century. Among the ports there was a progressively sharp distinction between the leading havens and the medium and small centres. The former, including Hull, Liverpool and Glasgow had extensive, improved dock facilities, were linked by canals and river navigation to major industrial regions, and enjoyed a large share of international trade. The second-rank ports confined their energies mainly to coasting traffic. Thus Yarmouth, which was deprived by the 1780s of its once profitable trade to the Netherlands in corn and Norwich worsteds, turned with some success to shipping grain to London. As for 'leisure towns', fashion was increasingly fickle. Several of the smaller 'gentry' centres lost some of their social glitter; Preston turned into a gloomy industrial town.[40] Some county towns such as Lincoln became more overtly 'farming towns' catering still for gentle visitors but also assuming a major importance in agricultural marketing, increasingly commercialized by 1800. Old established spa towns including Bath, Scarborough and Tunbridge Wells faced new rivals. As Bath was taken over by smaller gentry and the professional classes, many of whom like Sir Walter Elliot found it a comfortable place to which to retire (Bath was probably our first 'retirement town'), the fashionable élite floated away to more private spas like Cheltenham. There was also competition from the new-style watering places, including Weymouth, Southampton and Brighton (aided by road improvement), and less select, from Margate and Bangor.[41]

Essential to the growth of economic specialization was the division of labour. This was by no means confined to industry. Equally striking was the proliferation of specialist processes and practitioners in the tertiary sector. We can see this in marketing. Mitchell's paper (Chapter 8) charts the rise of permanent luxury shops at Chester – lineal forerunners of the late-Victorian department stores. At the same time, there was the development of various types of basic shop for the lower classes selling food, clothing or other wares, usually on extensive credit. The food and drink trade was an obvious example of the new commercial differentiation. By the start of the nineteenth century we can recognize in larger towns not only different classes of public house with their own core clienteles, but also a host of competing businesses – spirit shops, licensed and unlicensed, oyster shops, chop-houses, pastry shops, confectionery shops and so on.[42] Greater occupational definition is also evident in the professions, with town attorneys abandoning some of their less remunerative or more technical work to surveyors, auctioneers, estate agents and land stewards. The multiplication of new specialist trades and the decline of old-style multiple occupations was one of the more radical and modern aspects of urban development during the late eighteenth century, affecting most larger provincial towns.

III

In spite of the accelerating pace of urbanization and the powerful economic changes we have just described, the seventeenth and eighteenth centuries did not witness any great upsurge of social instability in towns, any traumatic breakdown of the urban social order. Part of the explanation for this may be the nature of the demographic and economic changes before 1800, evolutionary rather than revolutionary, frequently retaining a traditional format. But the success of urban society in absorbing potentially disruptive pressures, notably during the late eighteenth century, may also testify to the increasing coherence and flexibility of the social system within towns. Two advances deserve particular attention: the containment of poverty; and the advent of a more sectored, multilinear and diffuse social hierarchy in provincial towns.

At the start of the seventeenth century, poverty figured among the most urgent preoccupations of town magistrates. At Oxford in 1611 the university complained that 'the number of the poor is very much increased in and about the said city within these 30 years last past'. Crowds of migrant paupers compounded local unemployment and created levels of poverty that exceeded 30 per cent on occasion and nearly overwhelmed traditional relief mechanisms. The situation was often critical during trade slumps or plague outbreaks. Town rulers endeavoured to combat the problem with a medley of local measures: workstocks, bridewells, beadles against beggars, purges of immigrants, transportation of the poor, new almshouses, on occasion elaborate municipal enterprise schemes. None of these was very effective. More useful probably was the growing volume of statutory or parish relief. By 1640 this may have been making a more significant contribution to the support of the urban poor.[43]

In the later Stuart period, parish relief became the main agency for assisting the indigent. Although detailed evidence is patchy, it seems likely that more people were relieved and *per capita* expenditure was increased; in addition, the range of relief became more sophisticated. This was a major achievement. A principal factor was the effectiveness of the parish poor rate, one of the few instruments of urban finance which actually worked and which could raise growing amounts of money. Another may have been the increased participation of town leaders in parish administration after the Restoration, as we can see at Gloucester. Arguably this gave poor relief a new dynamic and direction.[44]

The level of urban poverty was certainly still high in the 1660s if the exemptions from the Hearth Tax are any guide. No comparative data are available for the early eighteenth century. One has a sense though that the long-term problem may have been easing or stabilizing in the later Stuart period under the influence of a reviving urban economy, better living standards for the lower classes and the diminished influx of poor immigrants. Plague outbreaks disappeared from the 1660s and subsequent epidemics had a far less disruptive social and economic impact.[45]

In this sunnier climate, expanded parochial relief was able to bring the poverty problem under control. The financial cost was high and from the 1690s a number of larger towns attempted to contain expenditure by centralizing relief through Corporations of the Poor. In most of these schemes a prime component was the workhouse where the able-bodied were set on labour; only inmates received relief. Most of the corporations failed, however, partly because of administrative problems, partly because, while a prime objective was saving money, establishments of this sort required considerable capital investment. But in the late eighteenth century workhouses became a more important conduit of relief. The Leeds workhouse, established in 1726, quickly fell into debt and closed down after 1729. Re-opened in 1732, it was by the 1780s an extensive institution with a variety of offices and accommodation for 120 persons. It also had a more specialist function: its inmates were mostly the elderly and sick, tramping labourers and the homeless.[46]

All the indications are that as the eighteenth century advanced, the increase of town populations, higher levels of immigration, and rapid but volatile economic growth created a rising tide of urban poverty. Of vital significance was the way that the decline of the dual economy and the onset of industrial (and agricultural) specialization enhanced the vulnerability of workers to recession. Parish overseers continued to act as the most important source of relief (aided to a lesser extent by the workhouse). At Leeds £3693 was disbursed on parochial relief in 1775–6; £4397 in 1785 and £19,274 in 1802–3. At Coventry expenditure rose from £4256 in 1775 to £9764 in 1802. Parish relief broadly doubled in the larger provincial towns in the last quarter of the eighteenth century with no clear divergence between corporate and non-corporate towns. But neither the parish overseers nor the workhouse could cope with the emergencies precipitated by the severe commercial crises which recurred towards the end of the period when hundreds of working families required relief. On these occasions help came from special subscription funds which were patronized by town and county notables, advertised in local newspapers and organized systematically to mobilize middle-class support. Funds of this sort can be traced back to the late sixteenth century, but they became a major feature of Hanoverian efforts to alleviate distress and prevent social disorder. They were particularly important in the 1790s. On a lesser scale, a host of middle-class voluntary societies appeared to assist particular groups of indigent, while friendly societies may have helped sizeable numbers of artisan families over short-term crises. In some towns like Coventry, traditional charities still made a significant contribution to relieving the poor and needy.[47]

The middle classes, so important by the late Hanoverian period in containing social distress, were themselves a manifestation of the changing shape of the social order in provincial towns during the early modern period. In 1600 the urban social hierarchy, if we accept the orthodox view, resembled a pyramid with a narrow, mostly mercantile élite at the apex and large numbers of poor people at the base. The middling ranks of the community gained at best only a mild improvement in their social position before the Civil War; they clearly did not make the running in urban society. A century later, however, the social order appears much less polarized. At the top the ruling class was reinforced by an influx of professional men, notably lawyers and physicians, who had strong personal, political and economic ties with the countryside, and by landowners who took up residence in town for part of the year. One effect was that the urban élite became more outward-looking, orientated towards county society and to some extent towards London. To match the new fashionable interests of the well-to-do all kinds of societies and clubs sprang up, musical, literary, philo-sophical, botanical and antiquarian, usually meeting in inns or coffee-houses. These helped meld together the old and new élite groups which attended them.[48]

At the other end of the social spectrum the lower ranks displayed enhanced social differentiation, as we can see from Joyce Ellis's analysis of social relations in Newcastle. While ordinary labourers benefited from some advance in real wages, skilled workers or those in privileged positions like the keelmen did well and started to acquire an increased social self-confidence. Like the upper classes, they frequently had their own trade, benefit and convivial clubs, normally based at the alehouse. They saw themselves as a cut above labourers, and where possible restricted entry to their trades.[49]

During the same period, the social 'middle' of towns began to fill out. Modest shopkeepers and tradesmen exploited the growth of business and celebrated their success with larger and improved houses, while their domestic furnishings, as itemized in probate inventories, reveal a greater material affluence. They too had their own clubs and societies; they filled the congregations of dissenting chapels; and they dabbled in old-style antiquarianism. The late Georgian period saw the flowering of these middling social groups. The prosperity of masters-cum-manufacturers, the rise of specialist shopkeepers, the emergence of secondary professional men – auctioneers, schoolmasters, surveyors, accountants – blurred status divisions with the élite. The middle classes threw themselves enthusiastically into the new wave of voluntary societies from the 1780s. They were active in parish vestries and the religious awaken-ing. They flocked to scientific lectures, patronized subscription libraries and purchased the growing spate of published town histories.[50]

As for the urban upper classes, the old professional groups that had become prominent in the post-Restoration period strengthened their power. Lawyers and medical men became influential figures not only in older county towns, but also in some of the newer industrial centres. At Gloucester, as we shall discover below (Chapter 10), attorneys were busy on the corporation, in improve-ment schemes and in banking.[51] Such men were well-educated and increasingly conscious of professional standards of behaviour (Norwich lawyers had their own society from the 1780s; Colchester doctors one about the same time). They had wide connections and interests in national society. As such they were a powerful modernizing force in local society. William Gray, a leading York attorney, was a supporter of the anti-slavery movement, established local Sunday schools, was a director of the York dispensary and treasurer of the county hospital, a founder of the York Savings Bank, and also served as secretary of the Yorkshire Reform Association from 1778.[52] By contrast with the professional men, the gentry were less conspicuous in the larger or medium-size towns by 1800, discouraged perhaps by the economic bustle and attracted back to their estates by the profits of farming and fears of rural unrest. Leading manufacturers started to replace them. Whether urban élites were more open, recruiting from lesser groups in some of the new industrial towns, than was the case in the established corporations, remains uncertain at present. In Manchester and other cotton towns manufacturers were often from wealthy backgrounds; in Birmingham too upward social mobility by smaller men may have been less common than has been supposed. The real division in terms of élites may be less between old and new towns than between large and small ones. It was in the latter that men with modest fortunes tended to hold sway.[53]

In the major urban centres there are clear signs that town leaders were becoming more integrated into national society. They co-operated in trade lobbies with colleagues from other towns.[54] But the urban élite did not turn their backs on their home community. As we shall see, there was a strong commitment to the town as a vehicle of economic, moral and cultural improvement. No less important, by 1800 upper- and middle-class groups were frequently acting together in defence of the established urban order against the threat of disruption from below.

Economic growth in the late eighteenth century seems to have caused further differentiation among the lower orders, though the picture is muddied by variations between towns and trades. Skilled workers (some in new factories) may have experienced a longer-term boost in their standard of living. They had better housing and more domestic comforts. They had greater educational opportunities, joined trade clubs and unions and not infrequently espoused radical politics. On the other hand, by 1800 their advance was repeatedly threatened by short-term commercial crises and in certain trades by industrial obsolescence. Labourers and the semi-skilled were also attracted to town by the promise of higher wages, especially in the rapidly expanding centres. But with rising food prices and costly housing their position in the community was often precarious. During the economic slumps of the 1790s many labouring families were thrust into destitution.[55]

Popular protests and disturbances erupted sporadically in English provincial towns during the seventeenth and eighteenth centuries. There were riots over food prices and shortages, over wages and trade innovations, over military levies, turnpikes and other grievances. Though there was often a broad correlation between disorders and times of economic distress it is difficult to identify long-term trends. Thus there was no great upsurge of disorders in the second half of the eighteenth century. Only after 1790 does one find a rash of rioting, especially in 1792–3, 1795–6 and 1800–1, as a result of harvest failure and trade slumps. Between 1795 and 1801 there were twelve food riots in Birmingham and its vicinity; the Lancashire towns had about two dozen over the same period. As well as old-style riots there was a growing incidence of strikes, mostly in better-off trades. But, in general, one is struck not by the frequency and scale of the disorders in Hanoverian towns but by the fact that they were not more serious and numerous, given the accelerating pace of urbanization and industrial growth. Urban disturbances only rarely got out of control before 1800 and then it was mainly at the behest or with the tacit consent of members of the upper classes (as in the Priestley riots at Birmingham in 1791).[56]

The absence of large-scale social instability in our towns before 1800 was testimony to the way that agricultural expansion and specialization and the advances in marketing and food provisioning helped sustain urban growth. It was also linked with improvements in poor relief and the more complex and segmented social order that was evolving by the eighteenth century. As Ellis indicates in Chapter 6 traditional neighbourhood and occupational sanctions also had their effect, while the authorities could call on growing numbers of constables and watchmen, and, in crises, on the military. This is not to be complacent. At Newcastle social tension and conflict was frequently bubbling to the surface, but it only sporadically erupted into organized violence.[57] Certainly, class warfare was not an inevitable consequence of industrial and urban growth – at least before the nineteenth century.

IV

From time to time, as during the 1590s, 1620s and 1790s, social tension in provincial towns overlapped with political and party conflict. The growth of political factionalism was in fact one of the most corrosive developments in urban communities during the seventeenth century. A root cause in the early Stuart period was middle and lower order opposition to the growth of civic oligarchy. Though élite rule had been a feature of the urban polity since the Middle Ages, everything suggests there was a general tightening of control during the sixteenth century and after. Sometimes it occurred through alterations in old corporate structures, with council and commonalty losing power and rights to the aldermanic bench. This was not the only path to greater oligarchic domination. More important was the short-circuiting of the traditional civic constitution through the bench resorting to their extensive and unilateral authority as justices of the peace.[58]

In the later Stuart period the oligarchic trend may have been reversed temporarily by the rapid turnover of personnel arising from Crown interference, particularly during the 1680s. But in the long run political power continued to be concentrated in the hands of town magnates, leading to a chorus of complaint against corruption and abuse. At the same time the fire of political dissension was fanned by other influences: religious divisions exacerbated and institutionalized by the Civil War and the later persecution of dissenters; growing intervention by the gentry in parliamentary elections, encouraged after the Restoration by their residence in towns; and linked with both these pressures, the infiltration of national political issues into the urban arena, with local factions divided by 1700 along Whig and Tory lines. Political conflict in towns was particularly heated and contagious during the 1620s, the 1640s, the 1660s and 1680s, coming to a crescendo during the two decades after the Glorious Revolution. It was at this time that the mass creation of freemen became an accepted party manoeuvre at elections, with the result that in many towns the freemen were effectively detached from civic government and oligarchic power was confirmed.[59]

The Septennial Act of 1716, government pressure, and a sense among the ruling élite in Parliament and on the bench that political conflict needed to be kept within bounds seems to have led to a reduction in the party political temperature in many boroughs from the 1720s or 1730s. This period of compromise lasted until the 1770s. Then once again political and party dissension reared its head, mostly, but not wholly, centred on parliamentary elections.

The reasons are not hard to find. Oligarchic rule remained the norm in most corporate towns and there may in fact have been a further consolidation of élite control during the second half of the eighteenth century. Allegations of corruption were commonplace. Other factors included: recurrent commercial disruption; the grievances of dissenters; the influence of American and later French radical ideas; the relative prosperity and social consciousness of the middle classes and artisans; national political criticism of government abuse in the late 1770s and 1780s; the rapid expansion of towns and the numerous administrative, financial and other problems this caused. In the 1780s we find civic and parliamentary reformist movements, as at Gloucester. In the following decade there was an upsurge of radical clubs and organizations in many of the larger provincial towns, among them new towns like Manchester, Birmingham, Sheffield and Leeds, and old corporations like Norwich, Nottingham, Leicester and Maidstone.[60]

And yet the scale and impact of political and party conflict in early modern towns should not be exaggerated. During the late seventeenth century and much of the eighteenth, conflict tended to be associated mainly with parliamentary elections. In most cases it had only a marginal effect on urban administration. Corporate crises could still occur. In the early decades of the eighteenth century several towns like Scarborough and Bewdley were ruled by two rival corporations and in some cases (thus Maidstone and Colchester) towns lost their charters altogether for a number of years. In 1735, fifteen towns faced *quo warranto* actions in the courts disputing their legal status. But despite these crises town administration did not break down. There was no explosion of public disorder.[61]

Part of the explanation may be that as the seventeenth century progressed town government assumed its own institutional momentum, in some measure insulated from the rough and tumble of corporation and electoral politicking. In the first place administration became more bureaucratic. By the reign of George II, the town clerk, usually with a bevy of minions, was a prosperous and influential townsman, a leading local attorney with important county connections. He was able to raise loans for the town, was in charge of a great range of business in and out of the corporation, and served for years at a time, possibly as one of an official dynasty. Compared with their predecessors, Hanoverian town clerks had considerably greater authority, autonomy and administrative experience. Other permanent salaried officials also began to appear. Stewards or receivers took over much of the responsibility for day-to-day financial management, rent collection and the like, from annually elected members of the corporations, thereby ensuring greater administrative continuity. By the late eighteenth century equally valuable officials were salaried town surveyors, who advised on and implemented improvement schemes. Thomas Baldwin who served at Bath from 1776 to 1792 presided over much of the expansion of the city. At Liverpool John Foster, 'superintendant of all the public buildings' from 1789, organized the extension of the docks, laid out much of the corporation estate, and designed a succession of public edifices.[62]

The rise of a small bureaucracy not only gave town administration more coherence and stability but may also have led to greater efficiency. Recent work on town finances at Nottingham, York and Boston in the late seventeenth and eighteenth centuries has concluded that corporations ran their town estates with growing skill, professionalism and a sense of public responsibility. There was mounting vigilance in the rent of town property with leases put up for competitive bidding through newspaper advertisements; a reduction in the term of leases; and a valuable increase in rents. Town income from rents and tolls rose threefold at Nottingham between 1700 and 1800, and fivefold at York. The most spectacular increase was at Bath, where municipal revenue expanded twenty times. Not all towns were so fortunate. A number of smaller places, for instance Stratford-on-Avon, suffered from financial negligence and abuse. But generally speaking the upsurge of corporate indebtedness towards the end of our period, which caused serious problems in the early decades of the nineteenth century, was mainly the result not of corruption and profligacy (as critics alleged), but of high expenditure on town improvement funded by heavy borrowing on bonds and annuities. There were other innovations in town administration. Corporation business was dealt with more expeditiously through the systematic use of *ad hoc* and standing committees. York had an active lease committee in the eighteenth century; from 1779 Gloucester had an influential committee of secrecy to introduce reforms and to plan longer-term civic strategy.[63]

No less important, the practice in many chartered towns whereby the mayor and aldermen met regularly as a permanent inner committee of town government was institutionalized. Using their wide range of statutory powers as Justices of the Peace, the aldermanic bench set themselves up as an omnicompetent sessional body distinct and superior in many areas to the corporation as a whole. At York aldermanic Justices meeting virtually every day in petty or special sessions executed a great deal of summary justice, maintaining social order. Bath's mayor and Justices dealt summarily with over 700 cases in 1770. At Coventry a wide range of corporate powers passed to the mayor and aldermen acting as Justices. Overall it can be argued that the principal rulers of English provincial towns by the eighteenth century were JPs. In corporations aldermanic Justices might be joined by county Justices who in some cases were allowed to exercise their power in town. In non-corporate towns the Justices were usually a mixture of local notables, professional men and landowners. At Manchester when the court leet declined in the eighteenth century, the Justices' courts of sessions took over the old manorial powers. As JPs, magistrates could mobilize the help of parish officers and constables; by 1800 there were often contingents of watchmen under their command as well. The Justices of the Leeds Rotation Office (set up in the 1770s on the London model) had a posse of police at their disposal.[64]

There was then a growing trend towards decentralization in town administration. This is noticeable in other areas too. By the later Stuart period social problems were mostly dealt with at the parish level by overseers of the poor and the vestry, which might well include members of the corporation. With the amalgamation of small parishes during and after the English Revolution, the parish was a reasonably effective unit for dealing with the problems of the local poor and migrants. The parochial rate was, as we have said, one of the most flexible devices for raising revenue in the urban community. Attempts at the start of the eighteenth century to co-ordinate parish relief and funds through Corporations of the Poor were only partially successful. Parish administration was an important pillar of governmental stability in towns up to 1800. This was particularly the case in newer towns where parish vestries were an active focus of political power.[65]

Though the Corporations of the Poor had a chequered career in the field of poor relief, they did help pioneer another important administrative development of the period – quasi-governmental town bodies. The Webbs called these 'new statutory authorities', but not all of them were sanctioned by Parliament. There were many different types fulfilling a variety of specialist administrative

functions. Among them we find watch, lighting and cleansing commissions, rebuilding and general improvement boards, turnpike
and infirmary trusts and harbour commissions. Frequently the
personnel of the new bodies overlapped with that of the corporation, but other members were drawn more widely and might
include county landowners, professional men and middle-class
citizens not on the town council. These new bodies were generally
empowered to raise their own finance, either through rates,
borrowing or subscriptions. They played a significant role in the
expansion of town government during the late eighteenth century to
meet the social and other difficulties generated by population
increase. In the non-corporate towns such bodies evolved as one of
the principal machines of administration. At Dudley the town
improvement commissioners, mostly prominent local men, acted
swiftly to improve public highways and lighting. In Birmingham the
commission appointed under the 1769 Improvement Act moved
several of the markets out of the town centre (an indispensable
reform) and provided lighting and cleansing. Leadership was in the
hands of a core group of commissioners, including gentry, attorneys
and manufacturers. The commission's powers were much enlarged
in 1801. Improvement bodies had less impact at Manchester,
although a powerful Police Board was finally established in 1792.[66]

Towards the end of the eighteenth century townspeople found
themselves ruled by a miscellany of official agencies, sometimes
conflicting with, but mostly complementing one another. In chartered towns there was the corporation, Justices of the Peace, parish
vestries and quasi-governmental bodies; in non-corporate towns
everything but the first. Nor was this all. The cause of public order
was also furthered by numerous informal organizations, frequently
dominated by the middle classes: vigilante groups against criminals;
semi-private police forces (paid for by subscription); anti-radical
societies in the 1790s (notably the Reeves Associations); and armed
volunteer forces.[67]

Hanoverian town government may have looked rather chaotic.
Decentralized it increasingly was. But it was not ineffectual. There
was a growing sense among the established citizenry of the need for
a civic improvement, for reforms to withstand the pressures of
urbanization. And there were positive achievements. By the late
eighteenth century numerous larger provincial towns had built up a
range of utilities (lighting and piped water) and facilities (police,
numbered houses, pavements and drained streets, market halls and

planted walks), which we identify with the modern municipality. By late Victorian standards the provision of services was socially selective and generally inadequate. In the largest centres it failed to keep pace with accelerating urban growth and the cascade of problems that it spawned. Urban administration was slow-moving, under-funded and dominated still by political oligarchy. But in the historic context of the early modern town, civic government took a major step forward during the eighteenth century.

V

The image of the provincial town was remodelled before 1800 by civic improvement. Public building was small-scale during the sixteenth and early seventeenth centuries, in part because of a lack of money in civic treasuries, but also because of a greater emphasis on private housing. In the twelve main towns of the West Riding in 1600 there were only fifty public buildings altogether, although the number was somewhat higher further south. New edifices were mostly confined to market houses, guildhalls, grammar schools, and occasionally large almshouses.[68] By 1700, however, there was burgeoning interest in improvement, in street widening, the building or rebuilding of parish churches, and the erection of grander town halls. In some places, this was to repair damage left by the Civil War. Elsewhere, magistrates hoped to emulate the latest London building fashions (after the Great Fire) in order to attract county landowners to town. But most of the improvements were piecemeal. More extensive reconstruction was limited to towns like Northampton and Blandford Forum that had suffered major conflagrations.[69]

From the middle of the eighteenth century civic improvement became the rage. The number of improvement measures enacted rose from an average of about eight a decade in the first half of the century to forty a decade in the second half. Town gates, long derelict, were demolished for instance at Salisbury in the 1770s and 1780s, and Norwich in the 1790s. Streets and bridges were widened. Some markets were removed from congested central areas and spacious covered market halls erected to bring traders off the street. Sheffield's new market building cost over £11,000 in 1786; Gloucester's over £4000 in the same year. Towns revamped or enlarged their almshouses and founded impressive new infirmaries.[70]

One of the most visually interesting and also expensive aspects of urban improvement was church building. After languishing in the century after the Reformation, with many parish churches falling into decay and sizeable numbers being pulled down, building activity rose significantly after the Glorious Revolution, as Christopher Chalklin shows in his paper (Chapter 9). About 130 Anglican churches were reconstructed or newly built in provincial towns between 1700 and 1800. Many of them were large buildings, often costing between £4000 and £8000 and sometimes much more. Dissenting chapels also proliferated after the Toleration Act, with a further surge in the late eighteenth century; their size and cost was usually rather more modest. In many cases the initiative came from prosperous townsfolk who were concerned to provide more space for growing congregations and to have more congenial and fashionable places in which to worship. However, the financial burden of building was spread very widely so that it never became a major strain on local inhabitants.[71]

The visitor to the larger late Georgian town would have been struck by the great variety of other specialist, quasi-public buildings. Earlier assembly rooms were joined by theatres, libraries, concert and newsrooms. In some places new industrial material like iron was incorporated in classical designs, uniting innovation and tradition. The average cost of erecting a public building in the West Riding towns rose tenfold between the seventeenth and late eighteenth centuries. By 1800 improvement had outgrown the desire to please the county gentry or to imitate London fashion. It reflected now the enhanced prosperity of numerous towns and a considerable supply of capital for building schemes; a growing sense of civic self-esteem; a preoccupation with the more efficient use of urban space as towns rapidly filled with people; and, above all, a resolve to try and get to grips with the problems and also the opportunities presented by accelerating urbanization. At the start of the nineteenth century most provincial towns, old and new, had a panorama of public buildings that proclaimed an enthusiastic belief in the city as a progressive force in English society.[72]

Visual changes were not limited to public improvement. The period was one of growth and innovation in private building as well. In the century or so before the English Revolution there was a great wave of house construction or reconstruction for the urban élite. Michael Laithwaite's study of the small but prosperous commercial town of Totnes reveals that the merchant class lived in increasingly large and impressive houses (Chapter 2). These were taller and deeper than their medieval predecessors with ebullient, carved, usually jettied timber frames, oriel windows and vaulted ceilings; there was an extraordinary variety of building plans. At the same time, the architectural inspiration remained essentially traditional and conservative, though leavened by important regional and possibly continental influences.[73]

After the Restoration brick houses came into vogue, frequently with simple, austere fronts, deeper interiors, large frame staircases, kitchens and basements. With a growing gentry presence in towns, the ascendancy of metropolitan fashions in cultural matters, and increased urban affluence, there was clearly a desire to emulate the new upper-class houses of London's West End, themselves influenced by the latest French and Dutch styles. The dissemination of London building types was aided by architectural pattern books. By George II's reign, English Baroque styles were giving way to Palladianism, while provincial towns also began to acquire squares and terraces on the London model. Even so, architectural fashions imported from the capital did not swamp the provincial scene. Laithwaite emphasizes the important survival and vitality of regional traditions, exemplified by plastering, pargetting, tile or slate hanging, which helped to moderate the shock of the new classicism.[74]

During the seventeenth century purpose-built lower-class housing was rare in provincial towns. But the next hundred years were marked by the sustained if fluctuating expansion of the building industry, linked in the provinces with local economic swings. By the late Georgian period urban construction was not only more or less keeping pace with demographic expansion but there was a growing range of house types to meet the differing needs of the middle classes, respectable artisans, and factory operatives. Some of the impetus for this growth came from building societies; the one founded at Dudley in 1779 included leading professional men among its trustees. The rise of the construction industry, in the field both of private and public building, not only reflected urban economic buoyancy but had a dynamic multiplier effect on economic activity, helping to promote a virtuous circle of economic and urban growth.[75]

Another important development changing the face of the provincial town was the advent of respectable suburbs. Many English towns had displayed ribbon development outside their walls since the Middle Ages, but these suburban districts were usually dominated by the poor. From the eighteenth century, however, there was a considerable extension of the suburban area, marking a major breakthrough in the physical expansion of towns. In place of the poor, merchants, manufacturers and professional men flocked to the more attractive or congenial suburbs and also to villages close to town. Contributory factors were the worsening density of population in the old town centres, the heavy traffic and pollution associated with commercial and industrial growth, road improvements, sharper class awareness among the well-to-do, the increased differentiation of private and business life, and new planned housing developments on the urban periphery. The seeds of suburbia were already sown before 1800.[76]

While the changing physical shape and appearance of towns was one of the most important developments affecting the urban cultural image and identity, other changes were equally vital, though less well known. Towns were important centres of literacy and education throughout the early modern period, but the precise pattern of educational progress is still rather obscure, especially from the mid seventeenth century. It may well be, however, that the marked upturn in upper-class literacy observable during the sixteenth and seventeenth centuries was paralleled by falling illiteracy among the middling ranks of urban society during the seventeenth and eighteenth centuries. The trend lower down the urban scale was probably more confused, with significant variations between trades and between skilled and unskilled workers. Further differences are found between larger and smaller urban centres. None the less most of the signs would indicate that illiteracy among artisans declined slowly but steadily in the post-Restoration period.[77]

Certainly the argument for educational stagnation in towns after the English Revolution (compared with quite fast growth in the preceeding period), a view to which Paul Slack and I subscribed several years ago, seems much less valid now. Admittedly new grammar school foundations declined in number, but private schools and academies, as well as charity schools, were on the increase and even some of the older schools were prospering. Chapbooks and other forms of popular literature were pouring from the presses on an unprecedented scale. Book distribution became highly organized with clusters of booksellers in all the larger centres and a good sprinkling in many of the market towns too. Provincial newspapers enjoyed a growing circulation after 1700. Demand for education was boosted by the continuing increase of inland trade and by rising living standards for many ordinary townsmen.[78]

For the later eighteenth century the impression is one of a sophisticated, literate urban culture stretching down to embrace the ranks of skilled workers. This was at least the case in some of the larger old towns. The high volume of labouring immigrants into industrial centres and the first impact of factory employment may have depressed overall literacy rates in the short term, but even so recovery was on the way prior to 1800. By then endowed and private schools were being joined by a multiplicity of Sunday schools and new voluntary establishments. Catering for a growing urban readership were numerous subscription libraries, a smaller number of public libraries, and newspapers. The later eighteenth century saw the provincial newspaper come of age. In 1793 Manchester had several newspapers; the *Manchester Chronicle* had a circulation of almost 5000 in and around the town. At that time smaller county towns frequently supported two or more competing journals. Newspapers were a powerful force in the formation of a new urban identity. They applauded a town's economic, social and physical achievements; helped focus attention on urban problems; served as a communication channel for the respectable classes; and acted as spokesmen in town for the region, helping to integrate the two.[79]

The intellectual vitality of the provincial town was very much in evidence by the close of our period. Two developments are notable: the widespread interest in science and the growth of urban antiquarianism. From the mid eighteenth century a succession of well-known scientific and related societies were established at Lichfield, Birmingham, Manchester, Leeds, Derby, Newcastle and elsewhere. They were, in part, a product of the post-Restoration movement for élitist clubs and learned societies. But they were also strongly influenced by the growing wave of industrial and urban expansion during George III's reign. Members included manufacturers, gentry and the ubiquitous professional men. Frequently participants were active in town improvement projects, and as often as not they had lively contact with other provincial societies, with London and abroad. Such societies published scientific books and organized exhibitions and lectures. But there was also a small army of freelance lecturers criss-crossing the country, expounding on a great number of scientific or pseudo-scientific subjects to audiences in market, county and industrial towns. At Worcester in the 1740s there were talks on electricity and optics and in the 1780s lectures on chemistry, anatomy and astronomy. Isaac Thompson, one of over sixty professional lecturers in the North in the eighteenth century, gave courses in Durham and Newcastle that covered mechanics, hydrostatics, pneumatics and optics, as well as astronomy. Rivalry among lecturers might be intense but attendances were high, attracting not only the upper classes but growing numbers of middle-class townspeople.[80]

By 1800 there was a strong belief in the town as a civilizing agency in the land. The same pride in urban learning and culture stimulated a wide concern with the past. Large numbers of town histories were published – as many as fifty-one between 1781 and 1800. These were frequently written by professional men and tradesmen. As well as chronicling earlier times, the volumes recorded the recent demographic and economic progress of towns and applauded the impact of improvement. Published inexpensively, sometimes put out in cheap, truncated versions, these antiquarian works had an obvious appeal to the growing middle-class readership in provincial towns, even perhaps to some skilled workers.[81]

But new-style science and antiquarianism were only one side of the cultural coin. More traditional themes such as ceremony and ritual continued to play their part in urban life into the late eighteenth century. Undoubtedly the Reformation and later Puritanism, together with the accentuation of town oligarchy, created serious problems for traditional urban rituals in the century or so before the Civil War. Many civic processions, plays and pageants were suppressed or suffered an abrupt change of timing and function. Civic ceremony was now largely centred on the activities of the ruling élite. Craft rituals often suffered from the declining vitality of the gilds. Popular neighbourhood games and rites tended to be pushed out of their traditional venue in parish churches and forced to take refuge in alehouses. By the later Stuart period, however, it is clear from Peter Borsay's contribution (Chapter 7), that there was a broad revival of urban ritual. Along with older oligarchic celebrations we find a flurry of entertainment rituals to amuse the new influx of landowners. Meantime, popular rituals recovered much of their former ebullience, in smaller centres encouraged by local gentry. Lawrence Lee of Godalming described how, on Easter Monday 1686, the townspeople had made 'that which we call Jack a Lent which is the image of a man set upon a wild colt taken out of the common and turned loose', subsequently being led in procession to the lord of the manor. Urban ritual was boosted by the diminished impact of dissent, the mounting prosperity of many townsmen, and the growth of commercialization. Innkeepers and alehousekeepers were prominent in promoting a great variety of wakes, feasts and other functions, including new ritualized spectator sports like horse-racing, cricket and boxing.[82]

In the course of the eighteenth century social differentiation in the pattern of ritual activity may have become more marked. Among skilled workers, for instance, trade, benefit and convivial clubs became an important forum for ritual activity with fortnightly drinkings and annual feasts and processions. By the later part of George III's reign there are signs that respectable townspeople were becoming less enthusiastic supporters of urban ceremonies and rites. Civic ritual may have stagnated.[83]

By the end of the period urban rituals were starting to come into conflict once again with religion. The evangelicals, the Methodists, and the revived Nonconformist sects, all growing in strength from the 1780s were generally hostile to most forms of urban ritual, criticizing the disorder and heavy drinking associated with them. Not only were the upper and middle classes encouraged to divert themselves instead with involvement in a second generation of respectable voluntary societies, mostly dedicated to moral reform or other public or religious works, but there was a concerted attack on lower-class recreations such as wakes, fairs and sports. The alehouse, long a popular neighbourhood centre, was a prime target, with growing regulation of the kinds of social activity that went on there. The attack on popular festivities and entertainments was only partially successful, but religion and urban rituals and recreations were increasingly on opposite sides of the fence.[84]

The religious awakening in many provincial towns in the last decades of the eighteenth century can be regarded as a move by the well-to-do to consolidate their own position and control the lower classes at a time of considerable economic upheaval. But this was not the whole explanation. While the religious revival was very much an urban phenomenon, more stable, slower-growing old towns were often affected as much as the more volatile, rapidly expanding new centres. The evangelicals and other religious groups were able to take advantage of the enhanced social confidence of the respectable classes in towns, including even some artisans. These people were buoyed up by increased affluence, educational improvement, and a strong sense of the late-Georgian town, with its array of churches, chapels and other public buildings, as a major cultural stronghold.[85]

This is not to imply that the church was unimportant in town life in the preceding period. As is well known, towns and particularly their rulers were frequently committed supporters of Puritanism before the Civil War; separatists found numerous recruits among townsmen and women in the seventeenth century. After the Restoration a sizeable number of county towns and provincial capitals became sanctuaries for the broken religious army of the Good Old Cause, and ecclesiastical antipathies, as we noted earlier, infected party politics. But in the decades after 1700 urban dissent was on the wane, discouraged by the influential presence in town of the country gentry and the stultifying impact of Toleration. Dissenting congregations were frequently torn apart by theological controversy. Some turned into rather select family clubs with affinities to the secular societies that multiplied in early eighteenth-century towns. It was only towards the end of our period that urban religion regained its earlier dynamic influence. It was, of course, a more specialist impact than in the past with religious denominations competing for particular social or class markets in a new, more socially segregated urban world.[86]

Thus, during the seventeenth and eighteenth centuries English provincial towns experienced a major transformation. There were numerous and cumulative breaks with the past which were to have powerful repercussions for the future. To name but a few: towns learnt how to adjust to large-scale immigration; economic (principally industrial) specialization became the driveshaft of urban expansion; there was a crucial shift in the balance of trade and wealth between town and country, to the advantage of the former; the social order within communities became more differentiated but also possibly more stable; effective municipal government began to emerge; provincial cities gained a new intellectual vitality and started to challenge London as cultural centres; towns started to sprawl physically, often breaking out of the corset of medieval ground-plans. Technological innovation, growing access to overseas markets, the growth of the tertiary sector, urban investment in industry, infrastructure and building, enabled provincial towns to make a significant if never overwhelming contribution to eighteenth-century economic growth. The rise of the professions, the development of more cosmopolitan urban élites, the proliferation of societies and other interest groups, helped in the creation of a more integrated, sophisticated and progressive society.

Yet, as we have seen, many of the changes took place over an extended period. There was never an 'Urban Revolution' (at least not before the nineteenth century), any more than there was an 'Agricultural Revolution'. Some of the most interesting and dynamic advances took place in long-established corporate towns. Indeed, so far as one can judge, contrasts in the economic, social and political functions of so-called new and old towns were relatively unimportant in the eighteenth century. The urban advance before 1800 was on a wide front, a point which has too often been underestimated by historians. The next great period of crisis for the ancient cities and country towns of provincial England was to come in the early decades of the nineteenth century, with the impact of war, and the agricultural and industrial depression and financial instability which followed the return of peace in 1815.

Acknowledgements

Research for this paper has been generously supported by the Twenty-Seven Foundation and the Leicester University Research Board. I am also grateful for discussions with Penelope Corfield and Brian Outhwaite.

Notes and references

1 P. Clark and P. Slack, *English Towns in Transition 1500–1700* (1976), p. 83; P. J. Corfield, *The Impact of English Towns 1700–1800* (1982), pp. 8–10.

2 B. R. Mitchell and P. Deane, *Abstract of British Historical Statistics* (1962), pp. 24–6.

3 See the discussion in P. Abrams and E. A. Wrigley (eds.), *Towns in Societies* (1978), chs. 9–10, 12. For recent positive views of old established towns see P. Borsay, 'The English urban renaissance: the development of provincial urban culture c.1680–c.1760', *Social History*, no. 5 (1977), pp. 581–98; A. Everitt, 'Country, county and town: patterns of regional evolution in England', *TRHS*, 5th series, **29** (1979), pp. 90–105; also Corfield, *The Impact of English Towns*.

4 E. A. Wrigley and R. S. Schofield, *The Population History of England 1541–1871* (1981).

5 ibid., pp. 531–2. For high rates of growth in market towns see, for example, J. R. Taylor, 'Population, disease and family structure in

early modern Hampshire with special reference to the towns' (unpublished PhD thesis, University of Southampton 1980), esp. pp. 220–1; D. Fleming, 'A local market system: Melton Mowbray and the Wreake Valley 1549–1720' (unpublished PhD thesis, University of Leicester 1980), fig. 1. For slower expansion in some larger centres see Clark and Slack, *English Towns*, p. 83; D. M. Palliser, 'Tawney's century: brave new world or malthusian trap?', *EcHR*, 2nd series, **35** (1982), p. 351. P. Slack, 'Mortality crises and epidemic disease in England 1485–1610', in C. Webster (ed.), *Health, Medicine and Mortality in the Sixteenth Century* (1979), pp. 14–59; D. Palliser, 'Dearth and disease in Staffordshire, 1540–1670', in C. W. Chalklin and M. A. Havinden (eds.), *Rural Change and Urban Growth 1500–1800* (1974), pp. 58–71.

6   P. Clark (ed.), *Country Towns in Pre-industrial England* (1981), p. 16; C. W. Chalklin, *The Provincial Towns of Georgian England* (1974), pp. 18–25; Wrigley and Schofield, *The Population History of England*, pp. 532–3.

7   Population estimates based on: C. M. Law, 'Some notes on the urban population of England and Wales in the eighteenth century', *Local Historian*, **10** (1972–3), pp. 22–6; Corfield, *The Impact of English Towns*, p. 183; Chalklin, *Provincial Towns*, pp. 321–2, 338–40. Wrigley and Schofield, *The Population History of England*, p. 577. For Norwich, P. J. Corfield, 'The social and economic history of Norwich 1650–1850: a study in urban growth' (unpublished PhD thesis, University of London 1976), pp. 23, 456, 500.

8   Corfield, *The Impact of English Towns*, p. 109, 111; J. D. Chambers, 'Population change in a provincial town 1700–1800', in L. S. Presnell (ed.), *Studies in the Industrial Revolution* (1960), pp. 110–20. cf. S. Cherry, 'The role of English provincial voluntary general hospitals in the 18th and 19th centuries' (unpublished PhD thesis, University of East Anglia 1976), p. 33 *et passim*. For a useful discussion of causation see Corfield, *The Impact of English Towns*, pp. 107–23; see also in a national context: Wrigley and Schofield, *The Population History of England*, ch. 10.

9   P. Clark, 'The migrant in Kentish towns 1580–1640', in P. Clark and P. Slack (eds.), *Crisis and Order in English Towns 1500–1700* (1972), pp. 122–31; P. Slack, 'Vagrants and vagrancy in England 1598–1664', *EcHR*, 2nd series, **27** (1974), pp. 368–73, 379.

10 See below, pp. 158 *et seq.*; see also P. Clark, 'Migration in England during the late 17th and early 18th centuries', *P. and P.*, no. 83 (1979), p. 68 *et seq.* on the decline of longer distance movement to town.

11 C. Gill, *History of Birmingham: I* (1952), p. 121; E. J. Buckatzsch, 'Places of origin of a group of immigrants into Sheffield 1624–1799', *EcHR*, 2nd series, **2** (1949–50), pp. 303–6; E. G. Thomas, 'The poor law migrant to Oxford 1700–1795', *Oxoniensa*, **45** (1980), pp. 301–5; A. Redford, *Labour Migration in England*, 2nd edn (1964), pp. 183–7.

12 *1801 Census*, vol. 1; I. Pinchbeck, *Women Workers and the Industrial Revolution* (1969), pp. 162–5, 272–4, 293–300; K. D. M. Snell, 'Agricultural seasonal unemployment, the standard of living and women's work in the South and East', *EcHR*, 2nd series, **34** (1981), pp. 420–3.

13 P. Clark, 'The reception of migrants in English towns in the early modern period' (forthcoming). On registry offices: B. Walker, 'Birmingham Directories', *Trans. Birmingham Archaeolog. Soc.*, **58** (1934), p. 2.

14 Clark, *Country Towns*, pp. 12–14; on the prosperity of market towns see Alan Everitt's account in J. Thirsk (ed.), *The Agrarian History of England and Wales: IV* (1967), pp. 467–505; also Taylor, 'Population, disease and family structure', p. 183 *et seq.*

15 See below, pp. 113, 115; D. M. Palliser, *Tudor York* (1979), ch. 10; J. F. Pound, 'Tudor and Stuart Norwich 1525–1675', (unpublished PhD thesis, University of Leicester 1974), p. 81 *et seq.*; J. M. Vanes, 'The overseas trade of Bristol in the sixteenth century' (unpublished PhD thesis, University of London 1975), pp. 131, 290, 391–2.

16 See below, pp. 115–16; also J. D. Marshall, 'Kendal in the late 17th and 18th centuries', *Trans. Cumberland and Westmorland Antiquarian and Archaeol. Soc.*, 2nd series, **75** (1975), pp. 188–257; Huntington Library, California, HM MS 1264, p. 62; Chalklin, *Provincial Towns*, pp. 23–4.

17 S. McIntyre, 'Bath: the rise of a resort town 1660–1800', in Clark, *Country Towns*, pp. 199–222; J. Barrett, 'Spas and seaside resorts, 1660–1780', in J. Stevenson *et al.*, *The Rise of the New Urban Society* (Open University English Urban History course 1977), pp. 42–69; Huntington Library, Ellesmere MS 8770, p. 200; R. S. Neale, *Bath 1680–1850: A Social History* (1981), p. 46.

18 J. Macky, *A Journey Through England* (1724), vol. 1, pp. 5–6; Borsay, 'The English urban renaissance', pp. 583, 585; H. Fishwick, *The History of the Parish of Preston* (1900), pp. 61–2, 66; A. McInnes, *The English Town 1660–1760* (1980), pp. 17–21; A. Rogers (ed.), *The Making of Stamford* (1965), pp. 72–3, 83–5; H. Thorpe, 'Lichfield: a study of its growth and function', *Staffordshire Historical Collections* (1950–1), pp. 189–95; BL, Lansdowne MS 896, fol 6–7; *VCH*, Warwickshire, **8**, pp. 507–8, 511–13.

19 K. Grady, 'The provision of public buildings in the West Riding of Yorkshire c. 1600–1840' (unpublished PhD thesis, University of Leeds 1980), pp. 14–27; Thorpe, 'Lichfield', pp. 185–6; K. R. Adey, 'Seventeenth-century Stafford', *Midland History*, **2** (1973–4), pp. 166–7.

20 *The Trade of England Revived* (1681), p. 42; Clark, *Country Towns*, pp. 17, 29; see below, pp. 86–7; J. Chartres, 'The marketing of agricultural produce', in J. Thirsk (ed.), *The Agrarian History of England and Wales: V* (forthcoming).

21   For the original theory of 'proto-industrialization' see F. Mendels, 'Proto-industrialization: the first phase of the industrialization process', *Journal of Economic History*, **32** (1972), pp. 241–61; recent glosses have made the thesis so flexible as to be able to embrace virtually every economic eventuality in the eighteenth century: see F. Mendels 'Proto-industrialisation: theory and reality', in *Eighth Internal Economic History Congress: Budapest 1982: 'A' Themes* (Budapest 1982), pp. 69–105.

22   See below, pp. 115–24; D. Hey, *The Rural Metalworkers of the Sheffield Region* (1972), pp. 9–10; *VCH*, Leicestershire, **4** pp. 168–70; Clark, *Country Towns*, p. 17.

23   See below, p. 176 *et seq.*; J. de Vries, *The Dutch Rural Economy in the Golden Age 1500–1700* (1974); N. and R. Crafts, 'Income elasticities of demand and the release of labour by agriculture during the British Industrial Revolution', *Journal of European Economic History*, **9** (1980), pp. 153–68; J. Thirsk, 'Seventeenth-century agriculture and social change', in J. Thirsk (ed.), *Land, Church and People* (1970), p. 163; F. Beavington, 'Early market gardening in Bedfordshire', *Trans. Institute of British Geographers*, 1st series, no. 37 (1965), pp. 91–3; J. Goodacre, 'Lutterworth in the 16th and 17th centuries' (unpublished PhD thesis, University of Leicester 1977), pp. 205–6, 302. Most towns had enclosed their common fields by 1800.

24   D. C. Coleman, *The Economy of England 1450–1750* (1977), pp. 101–3; J. Thirsk, *Economic Policy and Projects* (1978), esp. chs. 5–7; J. A. Chartres, *Inland Trade in England 1500–1700* (1977), pp. 47–55; M. Spufford, *Small Books and Pleasant Histories* (1981), ch. 5; Huntington Library, Stowe-Temple MSS, Parl. Box 3, item 29; A. Everitt, 'The English urban inn 1560–1760', in A. Everitt, (ed.), *Perspectives in English Urban History* (1973), pp. 104–9; *Trade of England Revived*, p. 34.

25   J. de L. Mann, *The Cloth Industry in the West of England from 1640 to 1800* (1971), pp. 24–36; W. H. B. Court, *The Rise of the Midland Industries 1600–1838* (1938), pp. 145–6.

26   Borsay, 'The English urban renaissance', pp. 582–91; Clark, *Country Towns*, pp. 19–24, 176–84; see below, pp. 323–4.

27   Huntington Library, Ellesmere MS 1126 (unfol.); see also Henley about the 1580s: Inner Temple Library, Petyt MS 538/10, fol. 39. For the navigation to Bedford: T. S. Willan (ed.), *The Navigation of the Great Ouse . . . in the Seventeenth Century* (Bedfordshire, Historical Record Society, **24** 1946), pp. 15–18, 26–7. E. Pawson, *Transport and Economy: The Turnpike Roads of Eighteenth Century Britain* (1977), esp. chs. 5–6.

28   For the classic account of London's impact on the provinces see E. A. Wrigley, 'A simple model of London's importance in changing English society and economy 1650–1750', *P. and P.*, no. 37 (1967), pp. 45–70;

VCH, Leicestershire, **4**, p. 169; P. J. Bemrose, 'Newcastle under Lyme: its contribution to the growth of the North Staffordshire pottery industry 1650–1800' (unpublished MA thesis, University of Keele 1972), p. 62 *et seq.*; J. D. Chambers, *Nottinghamshire in the Eighteenth Century* (1966), pp. 92–4; Mann, *The Cloth Industry in the West of England*, p. 79 *et seq.*; S. D. Chapman, *The Early Factory Masters* (1967), pp. 21–2.

29 Clark, *Country Towns*, pp. 19, 120–2; Huntington Library, Stowe-Grenville MSS, Manorial Box 3 (Buckingham). For the survival of gilds at Chester see M. J. Groombridge, 'The city gilds of Chester', *Journal of the Chester and N. Wales Architect., Archaelog. and Historic. Soc.*, **39** (1952), p. 100. *Ancient Canterbury. The Records of Alderman Bunce* (1924), p. 22; R. W. Goulding, *Louth Old Corporation Records* (1891), p. 52.

30 For the Dutch experience see de Vries, *The Dutch Rural Economy*, pp. 100, 113 *et seq.*; also H. Diederiks, 'Leiden in the 18th century' (unpublished paper). I am greatly indebted to my friends Herman Diederiks and Peter Jansen of the universities of Leiden and Amsterdam for their advice here. Court, *The Rise of the Midland Industries*, pp. 142–7, 222–4, 244–5; Hey, *Rural Metalworkers*, pp. 9, 50–2; A. P. Wadsworth and J. de L. Mann, *The Cotton Trade and Industrial Lancashire 1600–1780* (1965), p. 255 *et seq.*; R. G. Wilson, *Gentlemen Merchants: The Merchant Community in Leeds 1700–1830* (1971), pp. 55, 95; P. Mantoux, *The Industrial Revolution in the Eighteenth Century* (1937), pp. 243, 395–6.

31 Grady, 'The provision of public buildings', pp. 20–1; Wadsworth and Mann, *The Cotton Trade*, ch. 23; Chapman, *The Early Factory Masters*, chs. 3–4; Mantoux, *The Industrial Revolution in the Eighteenth Century*, pp. 220–33, 334–43; Mann, *The Cloth Industry in the West of England*, p. 139 *et seq.*

32 N. McKendrick, 'Josiah Wedgwood: an eighteenth-century entrepreneur in salesmanship and marketing techniques', *EcHR*, 2nd series, **12** (1959–60), pp. 408–33; Mantoux, *The Industrial Revolution in the Eighteenth Century*, p. 263; Court, *The Rise of the Midland Industries*, pp. 206–7.

33 J. Langton, *Geographical Change and Industrial Revolution* (1979), pp. 161–80; D. C. Flint, 'Industrial inertia in Halesowen 1700–1918' (unpublished MA thesis, University of Birmingham 1975), pp. 49–50.

34 W. G. Rimmer, 'The Industrial Profile of Leeds 1740–1840', *Miscellany XIV* (Thoresby Society, **50**, 1965–8), pp. 147–8; S. R. H. Jones, 'John English and Co., Feckenham: a study of enterprise in the West Midlands needle industry in the 18th and 19th centuries' (unpublished PhD thesis, University of London 1980), p. 31 *et seq.*; Flint, 'Industrial inertia in Halesowen', pp. 6–12; E. P. Duggan, 'The impact of industrialization on an urban labor market: Birmingham England 1770–

1860' (unpublished PhD thesis, University of Wisconsin 1972), p. 38; for factories at Worcester and Northampton see V. Green, *The History and Antiquities of the City and Suburbs of Worcester* (1796), vol. 2, pp. 19–21; L. Weatherill, *The Pottery Trade and North Staffordshire 1660–1760* (1971), p. 52.

35   M. J. Wise, 'Birmingham and its trade relations in the early 18th century', *University of Birmingham Historical Journal*, **2** (1949–50), pp. 53–79; J. Money, *Experience and Identity: Birmingham and the West Midlands 1760–1800* (1977), chs. 1–3; W. E. A. Axon, *The Annals of Manchester* (1886), pp. 97–125; Weatherill, *The Pottery Trade*, pp. 114–16, 127–9; J. Clayton, *Friendly Advice to the Poor* (1755), p. 25; see below, pp. 259–78.

36   *VCH*, Leicestershire, **4**, p. 173; Chapman, *The Early Factory Masters*, p. 29; Mann, *The Clothing Industry in the West of England*, pp. 62, 139, 336; see below, p. 313; Corfield, 'Norwich', pp. 317–33; W. G. Hoskins, *Industry, Trade and People in Exeter 1688–1800* (1935), pp. 75–6. For another instance of traditional urban prosperity see T. Rath, 'The Tewksbury hosiery industry', *Textile History*, **7** (1976), pp. 146–9.

37   B. L. Anderson, 'The attorney and the early capital market in Lancashire', in J. R. Harris (ed.), *Liverpool and the Merseyside* (1969), pp. 51–74; L. S. Pressnell, *Country Banking in the Industrial Revolution* (1956), ch. 2; Chapman, *The Early Factory Masters*, pp. 22–3; G. Jackson, *Hull in the Eighteenth Century* (1972), pp. 225–32; Jones, 'John English and Co.', p. 94; see below, pp. 332, 336; also Goulding, *Louth Old Corporation Records*, p. 62.

38   For a discussion of the problems of trade directories as a source see J. E. Norton, *Guide to the National and Provincial Directories of England and Wales . . .* (1950), pp. 16–24. The *Universal British Directory* is generally regarded as one of the more reliable early directories, though the coverage is of variable quality (see C. W. Chilton,' "The Universal British Directory" – a warning', *Local Historian*, **15** (1982), pp. 144–6). The occupational classification in Table 1 broadly follows W. A. Armstrong (based on Charles Booth) in 'The use of information about occupation', in E. A. Wrigley (ed.), *Nineteenth-Century Society* (1972), pp. 284–310. However, because of small numbers Armstrong's mining category has been combined with miscellaneous, and industrial services (mainly banking) with professional and public services.

39   Hoskins, *Industry, Trade and People in Exeter*, pp. 81–2; Corfield, 'Norwich', p. 325 *et passim*; Pressnell, *Country Banking*, pp. 457–8, 460; Neale, *Bath 1680–1850* pp. 261–2; M. Dunsford, *Historical Memoirs of the Town and Parish of Tiverton* (1790), pp. 56–7, 245–6, 295–8; A. F. J. Brown, *Colchester in the Eighteenth Century* (1969).

40   Corfield, *The Impact of English Towns*, pp. 35–44; for the growth of Hull see Jackson, *Hull in the Eighteenth Century*, esp. ch. 3; for

Liverpool see F. E. Hyde, *Liverpool and the Mersey* (1971), esp. ch. 3; J. D. Murphy, 'The town and trade of Great Yarmouth 1740–1850' (unpublished PhD thesis, University of East Anglia 1979), p. 35 *et passim*. Stamford for instance seems to have begun to fade as a gentry town by 1800. H. W. Clemesha, *A History of Preston in Amounderness* (1912), pp. 214–19.

41   F. Hill, *Georgian Lincoln* (1966), pp. 100–1, 139–40; S. McIntyre, 'Towns as health and pleasure resorts: Bath, Scarborough and Weymouth 1700–1815' (unpublished DPhil thesis, University of Oxford 1973), pp. 58, 294–320; B. Little, 'The Gloucestershire spas: an eighteenth century parallel', in P. McGrath and J. Cannon (eds.), *Essays in Bristol and Gloucestershire History* (1976), pp. 180–99; A. Temple Patterson, *A History of Southampton 1700–1914: I* (Southampton Record Series, **11** 1966), pp. 39–60; S. Farrant, *Georgian Brighton 1740–1820* (University of Sussex Centre for Continuing Education, no. 13 1980), pp. 3–6, 13–60; J. Whyman 'A Hanoverian watering place: Margate before the railway', in Everitt, *Perspectives in English Urban History*, pp. 138–56; P. E. Jones, 'Bathing facilities in Bangor, 1800 to the present day', *Transactions Trafodion*, **36** (1975), pp. 124–7. See also J. K. Walton, *The English Seaside Resort: A Social History 1750–1914* (1983), pp. 6–21.

42   See below, pp. 272–8; P. Clark, *The English Alehouse: A Social History 1200–1830* (1983), pp. 296, 313; also D. Davis, *A History of Shopping* (1966), ch. 12.

43   Huntington Library, Ellesmere MS 1950; A. L. Beier, 'The social problems of an Elizabethan country town: Warwick, 1580–90', in Clark, *Country Towns*, pp. 54–60; P. Slack, 'Poverty and politics in Salisbury 1597–1660', in Clark and Slack, *Crisis and Order*, pp. 176–94; P. Slack, 'Social problems and social policies', in C. Phythian-Adams *et al.*, *The Traditional Community under Stress* (Open University English Urban History Course 1977), pp. 93–5.

44   R. V. H. Burne, 'The treatment of the poor in the eighteenth century in Chester', *Journal of the Chester and N. Wales Architect., Archaeolog. and Historic. Soc.*, **52** (1965), pp. 35–8. At Norwich the average annual charge for each poor 'collectioner' relieved rose from £1 10s. in the 1620s to £2 3s. in the 1660s and £4 5s. in the 1710s: over the same period the number of pensioners trebled (Corfield, 'Norwich', pp. 289–9). See below, p. 325.

45   J. Patten, *English Towns 1500–1700* (1978), pp. 34–5; Chambers, *Nottinghamshire in the Eighteenth Century*, pp. 113–14.

46   D. Marshall, *The English Poor in the Eighteenth Century* (1926), pp. 47–51; E. E. Butcher (ed.), *Bristol Corporation of the Poor* (Bristol Record Soc., **3** 1932); P. W. Anderson, 'The Leeds workhouse under the old poor law 1726–1844' (unpublished MPhil thesis, University of Leeds 1977), pp. 4–10, 50–9, 70; also P. W. Anderson, 'The Leeds

workhouse under the old poor law 1726–1834', *Miscellany XVII* (Thoresby Soc., **56** 1980), pp. 88, 94–5.

47   See below, pp. 184–5; J. Marshall, *A Digest of all the Accounts . . . of the United Kingdom of Great Britain and Ireland* Part 1 (1833), p. 41; Northamptonshire RO, Northampton Borough Records, 4/1, p. 173; Anderson, 'The Leeds workhouse', p. 75; M. H. Smith, 'Conflict and society in late 18th century Birmingham' (unpublished PhD thesis, University of Cambridge 1977), pp. 266–7, 272–3, 276–7; P. Searby, 'The relief of the poor in Coventry 1830–1863', *Historical Journal*, **20** (1977), pp. 356–7.

48   See below, pp. 323–4; Everitt, 'Country, county and town', pp. 93–6; for urban lawyers see, for example, R. Stewart-Brown, *Isaac Greene: A Lancashire Lawyer of the Eighteenth Century* (1921); for medical men see R. A. Cohen, 'Documents concerning Dr William Johnston . . . of Warwick', *Trans. Birmingham Archaeolog. Soc.*, **78** (1962), pp. 55–7; E. Hobhouse (ed.), *The Diary of a West Country Physician* (1934), pp. 11–15, 18–19, 27, 39–42. For the general rise of the professions at this time see the excellent account by G. Holmes, *Augustan England: Professions, State and Society 1680–1730* (1982). For urban societies see Norfolk and Norwich RO, Rye MS 78, vol. 2, p. 218; also W. C. Lukis (ed.), *The Family Memoirs of the Rev. William Stukeley* (Surtees Soc., **73, 76** 1882, 1883) *passim*.

49   See below, p. 207 *et seq.*; C. R. Dobson, *Masters and Journeymen* (1980), p. 38 *et passim*; Dunsford, Historical Memoirs, pp. 205, 229–31, 238.

50   Clark, *Country Towns*, pp. 106, 110, 131, 182; J. D. Marshall and C. A. Dyhouse, 'Social transition in Kendal and Westmorland c.1760–1860', *Northern History*, **12** (1976), pp. 132 *et seq.*; E. M. Hunt, 'The anti-slave trade agitation in Manchester', *Trans. Lancashire and Cheshire Antiquarian Soc.*, **79** (1977), pp. 46–52.

51   K. A. MacMahon (ed.), *Beverley Corporation Minute Books (1707–1835)* (Yorkshire Archaeolog. Soc., Record series, **122,** 1958), p. x; W. G. Rimmer, 'William Hey of Leeds, surgeon 1736–1819', *Proceedings Leeds Philosophical and Literary Soc.*, **9** (1959–62), pp. 192–213; R. E. Leader, *Sheffield in the Eighteenth Century* (1905), pp. 114, 190–2; see below, p. 330 *et seq.*

52   Corfield, 'Norwich', p. 410; W. Radcliffe, 'The Colchester medical society 1774', *Medical History*, **20** (1976), pp. 394–401. A similar organization for schoolmasters existed at Newcastle: F. J. G. Robinson and P. J. Wallis, 'The association of Protestant schoolmasters in the North of England', *Trans. Architect. and Archaeolog. Soc. of Durham and Northumberland*, 2nd series, **3** (1970–2), pp. 87–90. E. Gray (ed.), *Papers and Diaries of a York Family 1764–1839* (1927), p. 34 *et passim*.

53   Hill, *Georgian Lincoln*, p. 269; Marshall and Dyhouse, 'Social transition in Kendal', pp. 131–2; K. Honeyman, *Origins of Enterprise*

(1982), p. 61 *et seq.*; Duggan, 'The impact of industrialization', pp. 50, 74, 242; see also at Leeds, Wilson, *Gentlemen Merchants*, pp. 19–20; comments on small town élites based on preliminary work on Gloucestershire market towns.

54   cf. the short-lived General Chamber of Manufacturers discussed in D. Read, *The English Provinces c.1760–1960* (1964), pp. 24–33; also Money, *Experience and Identity*, pp. 33–47; for brewing lobbies: Clark, *The English Alehouse*, p. 265.

55   The complexities of the data are admirably discussed in M. W. Flinn, 'Trends in real wages 1750–1850', *EcHR*, 2nd series, **27** (1974), pp. 395–411; see also E. H. Hunt, *British Labour History 1815–1914* (1981), pp. 62–73. For more recent figures see P. H. Lindert and J. G. Williamson, 'English workers' living standards during the Industrial Revolution: a new look', *EcHR*, 2nd series, **36** (1983), pp. 2–25.

56   D. G. D. Isaac, 'A study of popular disturbances in Britain 1714–1754' (unpublished PhD thesis, University of Edinburgh 1953); R. F. Wearmouth, *Methodism and the Common People of the Eighteenth Century* (1945), pp. 19–76; J. Stevenson, 'Food riots in England, 1792–1818', in R. Quinault and J. Stevenson (eds.), *Popular Protest and Public Order* (1974), pp. 35–67; Smith, 'Birmingham', pp. 1–4, 19–23, 161; A. Booth, 'Food riots in the North-West of England 1790–1801', *P. and P.*, no. 77 (1977), p. 90; Neale, *Bath 1680–1850*, pp. 69, 92; Dobson, *Masters and Journeyman*, pp. 154–70.

57   See below, p. 212 *et seq.*; for the growing forces at the disposal of the authorities see J. Stevenson, 'Social control and the prevention of riots in England', 1789–1829, in A. P. Donajgrodski (ed.), *Social Control in Nineteenth Century Britain* (1977), p. 31 *et seq.*

58   P. Williams, 'Government and politics in Ludlow 1590–1642', *Trans. Shropshire Archaeolog. Soc.*, **56** (1957–60), pp. 284–8; J. T. Evans, *Seventeenth-Century Norwich* (1979), pp. 30–1, 53–4, 65–78. C. Hammer's 'Anatomy of an oligarchy the Oxford town council in the fifteenth and sixteenth centuries', *Journal of British Studies*, **18** no. 1 (1978–9), pp. 4–10, 25–6, misses the point when he emphasizes the continuity of fairly open conciliar institutions in Tudor Oxford, failing to see the growing power of the aldermen *qua* justices: for oligarchic abuses at Oxford under James I see Huntington Library, Ellesmere MSS 1945–6, 1956.

59   See below, p. 324 *et seq.*; Evans, *Seventeenth-Century Norwich*, chs. 3, 5–7; Huntington Library, Ellesmere MS 8435 (Aylesbury); R. Muir and E. M. Platt, *A History of Municipal Government in Liverpool* (1906), pp. 101–15; L. A. Vidler, *A New History of Rye* (1934), pp. 82–6; R. East (ed.), *Extracts from Records . . . Portsmouth* (1891), pp. 207 *et seq.*, 224; A. Gray, *The Town of Cambridge* (1925), pp. 130–1, 136–8; see also generally, W. A. Speck, *Tory and Whig: The Struggle in the Constituencies 1701–1715* (1970), esp. ch. 4.

60   Lichfield Joint RO, Lichfield Hall Book, vol. 1, fol. 200; vol. 2, fol. 61;
      D. S. O'Sullivan, 'Politics in Norwich 1701–1835' (unpublished MPhil
      thesis, University of East Anglia 1975), p. 79 *et seq.*; S. and B. Webb,
      *English Local Government from the Revolution to the Municipal Cor-
      porations Act: The Manor and the Borough Part II* (1908), p. 469;
      Clemesha, *A History of Preston*, p. 210; Gray, *The Town of
      Cambridge*, pp. 157–62; M. J. Smith, 'Politics in Newark in the 1790s',
      Trans. Thoroton Soc., **84** (1980), pp. 59–65; M. I. Thomis, *Politics and
      Society in Nottingham, 1785–1835* (1969), pp. 115–24; Corfield,
      'Norwich', p. 232. For the growth of party conflict generally in towns at
      this time see J. A. Phillips, *Electoral Behaviour in Unreformed
      England* (Princeton 1982). See below, pp. 334–5; W. Holmes, *Tract on
      Bodies Corporate* . . . (1799) pp. 9, 15; O'Sullivan, 'Politics in
      Norwich', p. 108 *et passim*; A. Goodwin, *The Friends of Liberty* (1979),
      pp. 139 *et passim*, 513.

61   S. McIntyre, 'The Scarborough Corporation Quarrel 1736–1760',
      Northern History, **14** (1978), pp. 208, 211–23; J. M. Russell, *The
      History of Maidstone* (1881), pp. 203–5.

62   Bedford Town Hall, Minute Book 1729–34 (unfol.); E. J. Dawson,
      'Finance and the unreformed boroughs: a critical appraisal of corpor-
      ate finance 1660 to 1835 with special reference to the boroughs of
      Nottingham, York and Boston' (unpublished PhD thesis, University of
      Hull 1978), pp. 77–9, 109–11; see below, pp. 324, 327; Clark, *Country
      Towns*, pp. 229, 231–3; J. Longmore, 'Docks and drains: the role of the
      Liverpool corporation surveyors in the development of the port and
      town of Liverpool 1789–1835' (Paper at 1981 Economic History Con-
      ference).

63   Dawson, 'Finance and unreformed boroughs', pp. 69, 98 *et passim*,
      242; Clark, *Country Towns*, p. 226; L. Fox, *The Borough Town of
      Stratford upon Avon* (1953), pp. 122–3; see below, p. 334.

64   York City RO, E 92; Neale, *Bath 1680–1850*, pp. 86–7; Webb and
      Webb, *English Local Government*, p. 432; Huntington Library, Stowe-
      Temple MSS, Manorial Box vol. 5 (Buckingham); A. Redford, *The
      History of Local Government in Manchester: I* (1939), pp. 43, 45–6;
      Webb and Webb, *English Local Government*, p. 419.

65   H. Peet (ed.), *Liverpool Vestry Books 1681–1834: I* (1912), pp. xxviii–
      xlvi; Muir and Platt, *Municipal Government in Liverpool*, p. 122;
      Anderson, 'The Leeds workhouse', pp. 79–80; Gill, *History of
      Birmingham*, pp. 70–3.

66   Webb and Webb, *English Local Government*, pp. 394–6, 433–4,
      459, 463–4; J. S. Roper, *Dudley: The Town in the Eighteenth
      Century* (1968), pp. 22, 25; C. Gill, 'Birmingham under the street
      commissioners', *University of Birmingham Historical Journal*, **1**
      (1947–8), pp. 257–68; Redford, *Local Government in Manchester*, pp.
      200–22.

67 'Bradford in 1759', *Bradford Antiquary*, **2** (1895), pp. 216–17; Gill, 'Birmingham under the street commissioners', p. 266; Smith, 'Birmingham', pp. 66–73, 90, 98, 103; also Stevenson, 'Social control', pp. 36–8.

68 Grady, 'The provision of public buildings', p. 28; M. Aston and J. Bond, *The Landscape of Towns* (1976), pp. 121–2.

69 M. Turner, 'The nature of urban renewal following fire damage in late-seventeenth-century and eighteenth-century English provincial towns' (paper at Conference of the Institute of British Geographers 1981); smaller fires were also crucial for piecemeal rebuilding and improvement: E. L. Jones, 'The reduction of fire damage in southern England 1650–1850', *Post-Medieval Archaeology*, **2** (1968), pp. 141–9.

70 Clark, *Country Towns*, p. 21; *VCH*, Wiltshire, **6**, p. 89; B. Green and R. M. R. Young, *Norwich: the growth of a city* (1972), p. 29; Grady, 'The provision of public buildings', pp. 72, 194; see below, p. 335.

71 See below, pp. 284–306.

72 Grady, 'The provision of public buildings', pp. 35, 88, 193–213; M. M. Rix, 'Industrial archaeology with special reference to the West Midlands', *Trans. Birmingham Archaeolog. Soc.*, **79** (1960–1), p. 86.

73 See below, pp. 62–86.

74 Aston and Bond, *The Landscape of Towns*, pp. 120–1, 165–6; P. Borsay, 'Culture, status and the English urban landscape', *History*, **67** (1982), pp. 2–12; A. Henstock, 'County-House, High Pavement, Nottingham', *Trans. Thoroton Soc.*, **78** (1974), pp. 55–6, 58; Rogers, *The Making of Stamford*, pp. 83–4; see below, pp. 87–92.

75 F. Sheppard, V. Belcher and P. Cottrell, 'The Middlesex and Yorkshire deeds registries and the study of building fluctuations', *London Journal*, **5** (1979), pp. 179–80; Chalklin, *Provincial Towns*, ch. 8 *et seq.*; Roper, *Dudley*, p. 15.

76 Aston and Bond, *The Landscape of Towns*, pp. 153–4, 156; F. M. Eden, *The State of the Poor*, edited by A. G. L. Rogers (1928), p. 189; see below, p. 333; T. R. Slater, 'Family, society and the ornamental villa. . .', *Journal of Historical Geography*, **4** (1978), pp. 130–44.

77 A. D. Dyer, *The City of Worcester in the Sixteenth Century* (1973), pp. 248–9; R. A. Houston, 'The development of literacy: Northern England, 1640–1750', *EcHR*, 2nd series, **35** (1982), pp. 206, 208–13, 215.

78 cf. Clark and Slack, *English Towns*, p. 155; Holmes, *Augustan England*, pp. 44–80; A. Smith, 'Endowed schools in the diocese of Lichfield and Coventry 1660–99', *History of Education*, **4** (1975), pp. 5–20; Spufford, *Small Books and Pleasant Histories*, p. 98 *et seq.*; J. Fawcett, 'Eighteenth-century Norfolk booksellers', *Trans. Cambridge Bibliographical Soc.* **6** (1972–6), pp. 1–18; G. A. Cranfield, *The Development of the Provincial Newspaper 1700–1760* (1962), esp. chs. 1, 8–9.

79   V. A. Hatley, 'Literacy at Northampton 1761–1900', *Northampton-shire Past and Present*, **5** (1977), p. 347; M. J. Campbell, 'The development of literacy in Bristol and Gloucestershire 1755–1870', (unpublished PhD thesis, University of Bath 1980), pp. 21, 112, 143–4, 147, 155, 206, 223. For an optimistic view of urban trends see T. W. Laqueur, 'Literacy and social mobility in the industrial revolution in England', *P. and P.*, no. 64 (1974), pp. 96–107; for pessimistic pictures: W. B. Stephens, 'Illiteracy and schooling in the provincial towns, 1640–1870', in D. Reeder (ed.), *Urban Education in the Nineteenth Century* (1977), pp. 30–4; M. Sanderson, 'Social change and elementary education in industrial Lancashire, 1780–1840', *Northern History*, **3** (1968), pp. 144–53. H. M. Hamlyn, 'Eighteenth-century circulating libraries in England', *The Library*, 5th series, **1** (1946–7), pp. 197–222; Green, *History and Antiquities of the City and Suburbs of Worcester*, vol. 2, pp. 23, 26; D. Clare, 'The local newspaper press and local politics in Manchester and Liverpool, 1780–1800', *Trans. Lancashire and Cheshire Antiquarian Soc.*, **73–4** (1963–4), pp. 102–10.

80   A. E. Musson and E. Robinson, *Science and Technology in the Industrial Revolution* (1969), chs. 3–4; R. E. Schofield, *The Lunar Society of Birmingham* (1963); F. Nicholson, 'The literary and philosophical society, 1781–1851', *Memoirs and Proceedings of the Manchester Literary and Philosophical Soc.*, **68** (1923–4), pp. 97–8, 103, 130; F. M. Martin, 'Cultural and social life in Worcester in the second half of the eighteenth century, 1740–1800' (unpublished BA thesis, University of Birmingham 1962), p. 10; F. J. G. Robinson, 'A philosophic war: an episode in 18th century scientific lecturing in North-East England', *Trans. Architect. and Archaeolog. Soc. of Durham and Northumberland*, 2nd series, **2** (1970), pp. 101–7; I. Inkster, 'The development of a scientific community in Sheffield 1790–1850', *Trans. Hunter Archaeological Soc.*, **10** (1971–7), pp. 100–19.

81   P. Clark, 'Visions of the urban community: antiquarians and the English city before 1800', in D. Fraser and A. Sutcliffe (eds.), *The Pursuit of Urban History* (1983), pp. 106, 118–24.

82   C. Phythian-Adams, 'Ceremony and the citizen: the communal year at Coventry, 1450–1550', in Clark and Slack (eds.), *Crisis and Order*, pp. 79–80; L. M. Clopper (ed.), *Records of Early English Drama: Chester* (Toronto 1979), pp. lii–lv, lviii–lx; see below, pp. 228–53; Martin, 'Cultural and Social life in Worcester', pp. 46–9; H. Jenkinson, 'A late Surrey chronicler', *Surrey Archaeological Collections*, **27** (1914), p. 11; for more popular rituals in Norwich see, BL, Additional MS 27, 966, fol. 241–2; R. W. Malcolmson, *Popular Recreations in English Society 1700–1850* (1973), pp. 71–4.

83   Clark, *The English Alehouse*, pp. 234–5; Money, *Experience and Identity* pp. 110–17; D. Cannadine, 'Civic ritual and the Colchester oyster feast', *P. and P.*, no. 94 (1982), p. 112.

84   Malcolmson, *Popular Recreations*, pp. 120–52; also H. Cunningham, *Leisure in the Industrial Revolution* (1980), p. 41 *et seq.*; Hunt, 'Anti-slave trade agitation', pp. 46–53; C. P. Darcy, *The Encouragement of the Fine Arts in Lancashire 1760–1860* (Chetham Soc., 3rd series, **24** 1976), pp. 7–41.
85   T. W. Laqueur, *Religion and Respectability: Sunday Schools and Working Class Culture 1780–1850* (1976), pp. 2–5, 21 *et passim*.
86   W. J. Sheils, 'Religion in provincial towns: innovation and tradition', in F. Heal and R. O'Day (eds.), *Church and Society in England Henry VIII to James I* (1977), p. 168 *et seq.*; A. Brockett, *Nonconformity in Exeter* (1962), pp. 2–3, 23–116; D. Hey, 'The pattern of nonconformity in south Yorkshire 1660–1851', *Northern History*, **8** (1973), pp. 88–113.

2 Totnes houses 1500–1800

Michael Laithwaite

Totnes is a small town on the River Dart in South Devon, about 16 kilometres upstream from Dartmouth. Its most conspicuous historic buildings are the Norman motte-and-bailey castle which dominates the top of the town and the fifteenth-century church half-way down the main street. Less obvious under a modest coating of eighteenth- and nineteenth-century plasterwork and slate-hanging are its private houses. Yet these are basically one of the finest collections of sixteenth- and seventeenth-century urban domestic architecture in the country, comprising not just small-town architecture but also houses that would not look out of place in the main streets of Chester, Exeter or York.

The primary object of the essay is to analyse these houses and to attempt to explain the special historical and topographical conditions that brought them into existence. It is suggested that they belong principally to the short period *c.* 1570–1640: a visual, highly urban expression of the final phase of Totnes as a rich merchant town. A secondary aim is to discuss the ways in which the houses were adapted, and new ones built, between the middle of the seventeenth century and *c.* 1800. By then Totnes seems to have been fading into an ordinary, if still prosperous market town, and this is reflected in the quality of its architecture. Good work was still being done, but interest centres more on the strong regional character that set it apart from the fashions emanating from contemporary London.

Town houses are notoriously difficult to analyse from a structural point of view. Even in the most decayed town pressures of architectural fashion will ensure that out-of-date features are plastered over or boarded in, often to be replaced by work of greatly inferior quality. A successful study requires at least a proportion of the houses to be closely examined either while being demolished or in the course of alteration, preferably during a slow and careful restoration. Fortunately Totnes falls into this last category, strongly protected by conservation legislation and with building repair work encouraged by central and local government grants. The present essay is to a great extent the result of observing this work over a period of sixteen years.

I

Totnes originated as a defended site, situated at the lowest crossing-point on the Dart and at the head of its navigable reaches. These three topographical features were crucial to the development of the town in the sixteenth and seventeenth centuries. For although its defensive role had almost ceased by the fourteenth century, the tightly constricted site continued to limit its physical growth. At the same time its pivotal position in the area south-east of Dartmoor, combined with the ability to move goods by river to and from the seaport of Dartmouth, made it the centre for an important merchant community. The port of Dartmouth in the early seventeenth century was still of national importance, ranking ninth behind London in terms of Customs revenue in 1614–20.[1]

The interrelationship between pairs of towns like Totnes and Dartmouth was well understood by the Cornishman, Richard Carew, writing in the 1580s:

at the top of a creek, Penryn town hath taken up his seat, rather passable than notable for wealth, buildings, and inhabitants, in all which, though near the haven's mouth, it giveth Truro the pre-eminence: the like whereof I observe touching divers other towns of the same situation in Devon, as Salcombe and Kingsbridge, Dartmouth and Totnes, Topsham and Exeter: amongst which, those that stand highest up in the country afford therethrough a fitter opportunity of access from all quarters, and so a speedier and larger vent of their commodities.[2]

In the seventeenth century Carew's observation was becoming less true as Dartmouth increased its trade with the Newfoundland fisheries and used the proceeds to import highly profitable commodities from Spain, Portugal and Southern France.[3] But in 1600 the relationship between the two towns remained much as it had been throughout the sixteenth century. Totnes, through its river-port, operated a lucrative trade with France, exporting cloth and Dartmoor tin in return for linen and canvas, while Dartmouth concentrated on shipping and the still-modest fish trade. In 1576–7 only fifteen Dartmouth men traded overseas through their port compared with forty-one from Totnes; the Dartmouth men, more-over, were concerned only with the import trade and exported nothing at all.[4]

The economic result of this activity is to be seen in the lay subsidy returns for 1523–5, when the relative wealth of the town can be satisfactorily quantified. Totnes was then valued at three or four times as much as Dartmouth and ranked (according to W. G. Hoskins's estimate) an almost incredible fifteenth among all the English provincial towns.[5] After that date there are no reliable figures, but there is evidence of a considerable expansion of the town quays between 1565 and 1611.[6] Also the population seems to have been increasing, from an estimated 1700 in the 1570s to a fairly steady figure of around 2500 in the early decades of the seventeenth century.[7] But this period before the Civil War saw the beginning of Totnes's decay as a merchant town. The tin trade had fallen from its peak in the 1560s to practically nothing in 1600, while the cloth trade began a more gradual decline from the 1620s onwards. The causes of this commercial failure are by no means clear.

The size and wealth of the merchant community enabled it to dominate the town up to the middle of the seventeenth century: 'this our Towne of Totnes which wholie dependeth upon the trade of merchandize', wrote an official in about 1620.[8] All but two of the mayors between 1550 and 1649 were merchants or gentlemen of merchant origin, and those two, a clothier and a woollen draper, were also engaged in overseas trade.[9] In the lay subsidy returns between 1571 and 1623, merchants, ex-merchants and merchants' widows formed the overwhelming majority of taxpayers and invar-iably made up the fifteen to twenty people most highly assessed on personal estate.[10] What is most striking is the impression (supported by the evidence of wills and port books) of considerable wealth spread among a large upper class, the ideal conditions, in fact, for the creation of a high-class housing stock.

The weakness of the Totnes economy was its lack of a specialized industry. The cloth manufacture that was so important to the town's export trade seems to have taken place mainly in the neighbouring small towns and villages. References to clothworkers in Totnes are uncommon, and there was certainly no clothier of the stature of Peter Blundell of Tiverton.[11] As a market centre, however, Totnes seems to have been strong. By the early seventeenth century there were markets for cattle, meat, fish, fruit and vegetables, corn, wool, yarn and cloth, together with three annual fairs.[12] Moreover, there were signs of growth. A new meat-market hall was built in the last decade of the sixteenth century, and a new fruit-market house in 1611.[13] In its best year, 1616–17, the former had ninety-six butchers renting stalls.[14]

II

While exceptional wealth encouraged the building of high-class houses, the constricted site ensured that they were built in crowded conditions comparable to those in the centres of larger towns. Totnes lies on a narrow, steeply-rising ridge which was originally surrounded by marshes on the north, south and east sides. Although these appear to have been drained by the end of the sixteenth century, they continued to form a barrier against the physical expansion of the town. A further limitation was that the borough was small, about 800 metres from east to west and 600 metres from north to south.[15]

The town plan (Figure 1), which is still relatively unaltered, was based on one long main street (now Fore Street and High Street) running up the spine of the ridge, fanning out only at the top, where the ridge was wider and the ground firmer, to form what are now Castle Street, Collins Road, Cistern Street and Leechwell Street. Most of the High Street lay within the old, probably Saxon, walled town, with gates on the east, west and north, and the Fore Street suburb was also walled on the south side. The town walls were already 'clene downe' when Leland visited Totnes in *c.* 1535–43,[16] but the roads encircling them (now South Street, North Street and Victoria Street) survived and provided an early back access for the properties fronting the main street. Otherwise the side-roads were mere passages, except for Ticklemore Street and its continuation, Warland, which are believed to represent the line of a former causeway across the marshes.[17]

Most of the surviving sixteenth- and seventeenth-century houses front on to Fore Street and High Street, with Castle Street, Cistern Street, Leechwell Street and the west side of Warland containing nearly all the rest. Documentary evidence suggests that these, together with Ticklemore Street, were the only streets to be built up to any extent before 1700. The best-quality houses (with very few exceptions) are in Fore Street and High Street, the very best being mainly those that originally had rear access from one of the back streets. Only at the bottom of Fore Street does the quality fall off, no doubt because this end of town was subject to regular flooding.[18]

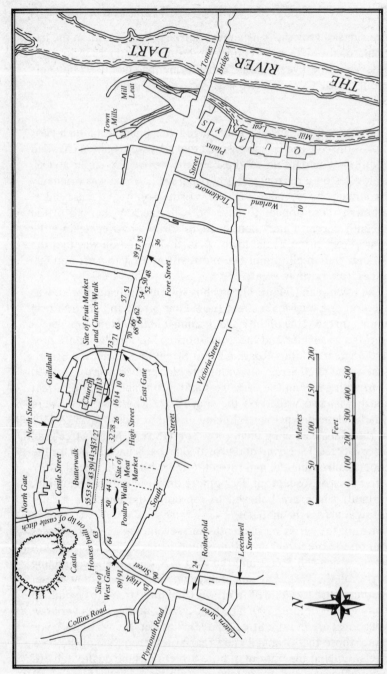

Figure 1 Street plan of Totnes, showing the position of buildings and other features mentioned in the text The numbers are the modern street numbers of the houses discussed.

The housing pattern, as with other old towns, was of long, narrow-fronted plots, with the buildings crammed at one end and occupying the whole of the street-frontage (the side-alley shown in Figure 2a is a rare exception). Where Totnes differed from most small towns was in the extreme narrowness of many of its plots: widths 4.6 to 7.6 metres (15 to 25 feet) were typical. In length they were equally remarkable, extending to 90 or 120 metres (300 or 400 feet) on the south side of the main street. What mattered, clearly, was frontage to this street where the markets were held, a point sharply emphasized by the quality of 11–13 High Street (Plate 5), which backed straight on to the churchyard and had no space even for a yard behind it. The markets may have mattered little to the great merchants of the sixteenth and seventeenth centuries, but the pattern of plots had undoubtedly been set much earlier. Already in the thirteenth century pressure on frontage was such that plots were being laid out in the narrow space between High Street and Castle Street on one side and the lip of the castle ditch on the other.[19]

From taxation and property records it would appear that the suburbs outside the east and west gates were already well developed in the early fifteenth century.[20] Thereafter only marginal suburban development seems to have taken place before the early nineteenth century, when modest groups of stuccoed houses were put up in Plymouth Road and the Plains. Where the sharply increased population of the late sixteenth and early seventeenth centuries was housed is far from clear. Some of it must have been taken up in larger families living in bigger, newly built houses. Possibly, also, existing houses were being subdivided. In 1594, for example, 57 Fore Street was described as 'the tenement which Grace Kelly widow and Christofer Brodridge of Totnes . . . ther now dwell in'.[21] A house in Ticklemore (or Pricklemore) Street seems to have been still further split up in 1635, when Richard Macy, merchant, bequeathed to Elizabeth Tippett 'the roome in the house in Pickell Streete where nowe Gabriell Gousen dwells', to Peternell Venard 'the roome in the said house that John Brocke dwells in', and to Zachery Perett 'the roome in the said house wherein nowe dwells Nicholas Docke'.[22]

In the late eighteenth and early nineteenth centuries population growth was accommodated to a considerable extent by building on the backs of the plots. But for earlier periods there is only the slightest evidence of this from surviving structures, and little more from documents. A carefully detailed view of the neighbouring town of Kingsbridge, dated 1586, actually shows the rear of the plots completely empty.[23] Totnes, as a more successful town, may have been quicker to build over its gardens, yet the first reference to this practice is not until 1617, when a lease of 26 High Street mentions 'those houses or roomes of newe erected and builded . . . in and upon the backer part of the herbe garden belonginge to the saide messuage or tenement'.[24] Such evidence, however, is fortuitous, since buildings on the rear of plots never seem to have been owned independently of the houses on the street frontage before the eighteenth century, and hence receive little mention in title deeds.

III

The general refacing and encasing of Totnes houses, both externally and internally, in the eighteenth and nineteenth centuries makes it difficult to divide them into neat groups by period. Some sixteenth- and seventeenth-century houses cannot be identified until the interior is inspected and others will be discovered only when stripped for building work. All that can be done, therefore, is to assess them on the date of their earliest visible architectural details, strengthened with the knowledge that a reasonable proportion have been examined more closely.

On this basis at least sixty-six houses can confidently be dated to before 1700, if fifteen examples identifiable only by their prominent 'jetties' or overhanging upper storeys are included. Some very shallow jetties seem to have been built in the early eighteenth century, but the deeper ones appear to have gone out of fashion at the end of the previous century: 52 Fore Street, firmly dated to 1692, was probably among the last of them.[25]

What is most striking about this large group of houses is the almost total absence of medieval forms or detail, which in Devon lasted until around 1560. The original single-storeyed houses with smoke-blackened roof-timbers of the pre-chimney era, common in rural Devon,[26] are not to be found, except for one possible example (10 Warland) on the edge of the old town. The single-storey, open halls with two-storeyed end-sections that were to be found in Exeter until recently[27] are also absent. One did exist in Totnes, for as early as 1310 a house outside the east gate was described as '*totam aulam meam cum solar' & celar' de novo levat' ad eandem adiacent*'; a 'cellar' was a ground-floor storage-room and 'solar' a first-floor chamber.[28] Open halls were probably already out of fashion by the early sixteenth century. A grand mid sixteenth-century house like 43 High Street was two-storeyed throughout with a fireplace not only in the hall but also in the chamber over it.

However, it is not just open, or formerly open halls that are missing in Totnes. Medieval carved mouldings are known only in two houses (14 and 35 High Street) and the multiple mid sixteenth-century mouldings at 43 High Street are unique. There is no sign of the very late medieval Gothic chimney-pieces that have been found in several Exeter houses.[29] Nor are there now any medieval roofing features such as arch-braced collar-beams and windbraces to be seen, except in the roof at 53 High Street which has clearly been moved from elsewhere.

Only three houses in the old centre and the one in Warland are thus datable to the period before the major rebuilding of the late sixteenth and early seventeenth centuries. The enormous wealth indicated by the 1523–5 lay subsidy returns is virtually unrepresented, especially if 43 High Street is accepted as dating from around 1550 or 1560. The contrast with Exeter is quite remarkable. The latter's economic fortunes largely matched those of Totnes up to the early seventeenth century and greatly exceeded them thereafter. Yet a substantial group of its late medieval to mid sixteenth-century houses outlasted even the bombing raids of 1942.[30]

It is not clear why Totnes was so different. The earlier houses are unlikely to have been destroyed in a great fire: 'myschaunce of fyar' was one of the reasons given for establishing a piped water supply in 1553 and a recent disaster would surely have been mentioned.[31] Nor is it really conceivable that the rich early sixteenth-century generation were not interested in house building. This was a period when wealth was usually given a visual expression and the Totnesians were still enlarging their parish church, a fine late Gothic structure, in the 1540s.[32] It can only be that the prosperous and self-confident Elizabethan and Jacobean townsmen were rebuilding their houses with an unusual thoroughness, presumably to conform with new standards of housing. A general heightening by one storey would explain the lack of medieval roofs and a desire for loftier ceilings could be the reason why so few early moulded ceiling-beams survive.

Allowing for the four late medieval to mid sixteenth-century houses and the fifteen that are not closely datable, there are at least forty-seven houses assignable roughly to the period from 1570 to 1700. The problem is to subdivide this long time-span. Only five

houses bear dates from before 1700 – too few to allow any conclusions to be drawn from them. Unfortunately stylistic changes
within the period can rarely be pinpointed with any accuracy: for
example, 52 Fore Street of 1692 is not distinguishable in date
externally from its neighbour, number 54 of 1607 (Plate 2). In this
Totnes is like other towns in the region: both Dartmouth and Bristol
have houses with decorative timber-framed fronts provably of the
1660s yet not obviously different in style from known Elizabethan
or Jacobean town houses.

The one point at which architectural fashion altered quite dis-
tinctly before the mid seventeenth century was in the design of
ornamental plaster ceilings. The earliest dated examples, which
consist of simple geometrical designs marked out by thin moulded
ribs, start in Devon about the 1570s and last until approximately
1640, although the main period seems to end soon after 1600. By
1610 a more ornate range of designs was coming in, basically similar
but with double-moulded or broad enriched ribs; it seems to have
been primarily a fashion of the 1620s and 1630s with examples as
late as the 1660s (Plates 3 and 4).[33]

Totnes has twenty-two single-rib ceilings compared with one
double-rib and two broad-ribs. Admittedly these are all contained
in a mere fifteen houses, but the contrast is impressive none the less.
Moreover, the double-rib and one of the broad-rib ceilings are in a
pair of houses (48 and 50 Fore Street) which also have identical
single-rib ceilings on the second floor and may be regarded as early
examples within their group. The second broad-rib ceiling, at 64
Fore Street, bears the Prince of Wales' feathers and the initials CP,
placing it presumably between 1616–25 or *c.* 1638–49. Within the
single-rib group at least ten ceilings seem likely to date from before
1600,[34] but it cannot be assumed that the same applies to the rest. A
particularly interesting fact is that plaster of Paris (the main
ingredient of the ceilings) suddenly started to be imported through
Dartmouth in the second decade of the seventeenth century, the
trade being dominated by Totnes merchants up to the 1630s. At this
time, moreover, Totnes imports of fine building stone from Caen
were also substantial, reinforcing the impression that a significant
phase of building was in progress.[35]

After the middle of the seventeenth century plasterwork in the
town declined considerably, both in quantity and in interest. There
is an excellent ceiling of 1692 at 52 Fore Street, consisting of sprays
of foliage enclosing winged cherub-heads, and two very simple

ceilings have the shaped panels framed by mouldings in high relief, characteristic of the end of the seventeenth and beginning of the eighteenth centuries.[36] But the wide, deep, enriched ribs of many late seventeenth-century ceilings are totally absent as are the *putti* and other figures of the early eighteenth century.

Evidence from so few ceilings may seem a fragile basis by itself for dating a whole chunk of the town's building fabric. But set against a known background of prosperity at the same period it provides a convincing argument for a major rebuilding between about 1570 and 1640. These dates, of course, will come as no surprise to those familiar with W. G. Hoskins's essay on 'The Great Rebuilding', but that theory has recently come under attack, particularly from those who see rebuilding as a continuous process, often occurring in sudden bursts but at different times in different places.[37] Medieval houses are rare in all Devon towns; Barnstaple, Dartmouth, Exeter and Plymouth show impressive evidence of late sixteenth- and seventeenth-century house-building, but it is not at present clear how much of this really belongs to the second half of the seventeenth century.

Regrettably, the designers of the 1570–1640 rebuilding at Totnes are unknown, as are most of the leading craftsmen. Some of the latter were clearly more than local figures, however. Andrew Langmeade acted as master mason at Kingswear in the late sixteenth century and in 1622 Edward Hawkings was supplying Purbeck stone for Dartmouth church, while Totnes plumbers worked as far afield as Cullompton and Plymouth in 1615–16.[38] But only Langmeade and the plumber, Daniel Hole, were assessed for the lay subsidies and then at the lowest level.[39] The local plasterers apparently ranked even lower, the rating list for 1602 referring almost disparagingly to 'Nyc° the playsterer' and 'Milles the playsterer'.[40] There is only one hint of a skilled craftsman coming in from outside, when the Totnes burial register for 1589 mentions 'Richard Slyngsbery a free mason honyton'.[41]

A Chancery deposition of 1595 provides a solitary glimpse of the cost of house building. A carpenter testified that about twelve years previously Henry Every, merchant:

buylded a howse in Totnes wherein he nowe dwelleth . . . and sayeth that ther was a booke made of the chardge of the buyldynge . . . which chardge amounted to the some of cxxj[li] . . . in which chardge was contayned the buyldynge of the walls partycons wyndowes dowres and coveryadge, but for glasse seelynge and other chardge was not contayned as he thynkethe within the seid booke which buyldynge contynewed by the space of three quarters of a yeare.[42]

Another carpenter estimated the cost at £200, perhaps including the glass, panelling and other fittings. Judged by the little that is known of housing costs elsewhere this seems fairly realistic. In the early seventeenth century, for example, a Tiverton cordwainer claimed to have spent at least £100 rebuilding his house, while in 1618 a London mercer contracted with a carpenter to build him 'one great fayre messuage or tenement of fower storeyes highe' in Fenchurch Street for £310, although the finishings may not have been included in this price.[43]

It is clear that the larger Totnes houses, however grand they may have seemed, represented quite a modest investment by the merchant community. Several late sixteenth-century wills include bequests totalling £3000–£4000 and this, of course, excludes the residue of the estate and an often substantial amount of property.[44] Henry Every himself belonged to one of the leading families and paid the fifth highest tax on personal estate for the 1592 lay subsidy return.[45]

IV

The most important building material in Totnes, right down to the beginning of the nineteenth century, was wood. Internally it provided the floors and partitions, and externally in most cases the front and back walls as well. Stone was used mainly for the party walls, except in the poorer streets such as Castle Street, Cistern Street, Leechwell Street and Warland, where all the external walls were usually of stone.

The reason was clearly a combination of economy and fashion. The local stone is a particularly rough, unshapeable slatestone and better material had to be brought in from a distance: granite from Dartmoor, red sandstone from Torbay and fine limestone from Beer in East Devon, or even (as has been suggested) from Caen in Normandy. As a result it was used mainly for small items such as corbels and chimney-pieces. 16 High Street, with its fine classical stone façade dated 1585, and 70 Fore Street, with its stone rear wall full of mullioned windows of limestone, were the houses of very rich men who must have seemed architecturally adventurous even to their merchant contemporaries.

Wood, on the other hand, was available closer at hand and when used in timber-framed construction with wattle-and-daub panels must have been much more economical. It was also more easily carved and could be used to dramatic effect in jettying and in building long ranges of oriel windows. But above all it was the fashionable urban building material in other English towns up to at least the middle of the seventeenth century, not only in areas where timber-framing was general for rural houses but also in those where stone predominated – as in the Cotswolds. In Devon the rural houses were exclusively of stone or cob, apart from the occasional entrance-porch, and the contrast is striking. Timber-framing in Totnes can only have been used for reasons of architectural display, partly, no doubt, in imitation of larger towns and partly because a degree of exhibitionism was essential to a commercial community living in close-packed urban conditions. A man had to be seen to be doing well and his house reflected his status: in 1621, for example, Matthew Came claimed that he had 'on ffaire messuage or dwellinge howse fitt and convenient for a marchaunt to inhabite & dwell in'.[46]

Perhaps it was because of the high quality of building in the town that only one example of cob construction survives and that right at the far end of Warland. Some of the smaller Devon towns, such as Ashburton and Bovey Tracey, retain it for houses in the town centres, and it remains in considerable quantity even in Barnstaple, though mostly in boundary walls, back-street houses and lower-class cottages in the backs of plots. Possibly Totnes had similar cottages, prior to their being rebuilt in stone in the eighteenth and nineteenth centuries.

The absence of early brickwork is less surprising because brick was uncommon throughout Devon, even at the end of the eighteenth century. The earliest brick-fronted building in Totnes seems to have been the upper storey of the Church Walk (just visible in the distance in Plate 1), rebuilt in 1718,[47] but it remained one of a very small group until brick terrace-housing began to appear at the end of the nineteenth century. In the late seventeenth and early eighteenth centuries the small yellow and pink bricks believed to be of Dutch origin were quite often used for chimney-stacks, as at 52 Fore Street. They may even have come in earlier, since brick stacks were being built in Dartmouth as far back as 1527 and Dutch brick was being imported by 1618.[48]

Slate, accompanied by clay ridge-tiles, seems to have been the usual roofing material rather than thatch, although the latter was common in the countryside and even in towns as considerable as Tiverton down to the early eighteenth century.[49] In Totnes, however, slate was available from local quarries and was being shipped from the town quay to Southampton as early as 1180–1.[50] It was being used on Totnes guildhall by 1561 and on small houses owned by the town in 1647–8 at the latest;[51] Dartmouth was already slating its houses in the 1530s.[52]

It is difficult now to visualize the houses as they must have appeared before the middle of the seventeenth century. Judging from the surviving evidence, houses of two and a half or three storeys (a half storey being one with low side-walls and a ceiling extending into the roof-space) were the commonest, especially in the main part of the High Street and at the top of Fore Street. Only one house, 73 Fore Street, is taller at four storeys, and that was almost certainly heightened in the late seventeenth or early eighteenth century. Houses of one and a half or two storeys seem to have been more usual at the lower end of Fore Street and in the area around the Rotherfold, but the contrast with the fashionable part of town may originally have been less noticeable. Scraps of structural evidence suggest there was a general levelling up from two to three storeys from the late sixteenth century onwards. A well-documented example is 52 Fore Street (Plate 2), which remained a 'little old low house' of two storeys, dwarfed by its neighbours, until late in the seventeenth century.[53]

At their best the houses create a considerable architectural effect with their tall, timber-framed fronts set between side-walls of stone, the latter corbelled out to match the jetties (Plate 5). The dramatic effect is increased by the use of gables, which are sometimes also jettied, although many were hipped back in the eighteenth and nineteenth centuries; the chemist's shop on the left in Plate 1, and the house opposite, behind the lamp-post, demonstrate the point. It was not just the narrow-fronted houses that were gabled, but often the wider ones also, using a pair of gable-ended roofs in place of the more logical arrangement of a single roof with its ridge parallel to the street.

What is almost totally lost, except at the restored museum building (70 Fore Street), is the garish effect of the exposed timber-framing, carved, patterned and with projecting oriel windows. Old drawings occasionally show the latter (Plate 5), but the framing is usually seen only when briefly exposed for repair. Most of this seems to relate to the traditions of the West Midlands rather than those of South-East England: small rectangular panels with moulded or chamfered edges, close-studding with a middle rail, and one example (54 Fore Street) of quatrefoils and star-pattern.[54]

The best houses, with jetties in each storey and matching corbels at either end, are admirably symmetrical, but the realities of urban building mar the effect in many cases. For most houses had only one side-wall of their own (that containing the chimneys) and leant up against their neighbour on the other, the result being lop-sided façades with corbels of different design at different heights.

Unjettied timber fronts seem more often to have been a feature of the late seventeenth, eighteenth and early nineteenth centuries, apart from the remarkable series of arcaded houses at the upper end of High Street (Plate 1). Rows of houses of the latter type are common on the Continent, where they can date from at least the thirteenth century, but they are rare in England. Moreover, only Totnes, Chester and (before a great fire in 1743) the small Devon town of Crediton[55] are known to have had them on both sides of the street. At Totnes the earliest reference to building an arcaded house is in 1532, when the specific purpose was to have stalls underneath 'for stondyngs on market days'.[56]

The arcades seem to have evolved piecemeal rather than as a unified architectural feature, and in three cases (44, 50 and 51 High Street) the corbels of the former jettied fronts can be seen at the rear of the walk. They may have originated from building over market stalls in the street, which in Totnes could be owned separately from the house behind them. Thus in 1590 Richard Bogan bequeathed to his eldest son certain property in the town, together with 'all the standinges and comodyties thereunto belonginge whiche are before the house wherein William Averie nowe inhabyteth and dwelleth'.[57]

V

The narrow plot-frontage imposed a distinctively urban layout on Totnes houses. Whereas other prosperous Devon towns like Cullompton and Tiverton had space in the town centre for the traditional rural plan of three rooms and a cross-passage, all in a row along the street-frontage, Totnes rarely had such houses and then only on its outskirts. Most of its plots allowed for no more than one or two ground-floor rooms and a cross-passage towards the street. Further rooms had to be accommodated at the rear, arranged so as to give them as much light as the narrowness of the plot and the proximity of the adjacent houses would allow.

Even a one-room-wide plan could produce a considerable range of variants, as can be seen from Figure 2. The addition of a further room at the back (Figures 2a, b, c, d, e, f) could double the floor area of the house, and a detached block, separated from the main house by a courtyard, could transform an externally modest-looking house into one of considerable size (Figures 2b, c, d, g). There are grounds for thinking that the largest version of the plan had a second detached back block and this has been reconstructed (on evidence from 70 Fore Street) in Figure 2a.

A typology of plans is, of course, only one way of looking at the range of housing available in the town. The same design can vary considerably in quality of accommodation according to the size of the room, as can be seen by comparing Figures 2b and c. Lofty ceiling-heights can give a house of one-room ground plan an extremely imposing aspect and a three-storeyed house of this type can actually be grander than one of two-rooms-deep plan that is only two-storeyed. Plate 1 shows three houses (from the left, 51, 53 and 55 High Street) of closely similar external aspect; number 53, however, has a two-rooms-deep plan while numbers 51 and 55 were originally only one-roomed. An attempt has been made in Table 2 to tabulate the variants in terms of the number of rooms they seem likely to have contained, although it would be unwise to compare the results closely with, say, those from a series of probate inventories. The 'rooms' are in some cases merely units of the plan, which could have been subdivided by partitions of which no trace now remains; also closets, often tucked into odd corners, have been ignored.

Turning to the plans in more detail it is important to note that in the two-rooms-deep houses the rear room is invariably the same width as the front one, if side-passages on the ground floor are included with the rooms. In this it contrasts with the sort of plan found, for example, in King's Lynn and Oxford, where the rear room is narrower, forming an L-shaped house with a slip of court-yard alongside the back part.[58]

Because of this design feature, combined with their narrow internal frontage-widths of between 4.04 and 6.86 metres (13 feet 3 inches and 22 feet 6 inches), the Totnes houses were able to develop their characteristic, single gable-ended roofs with the ridges running at right angles to the street (Figure 3). Nearly all the

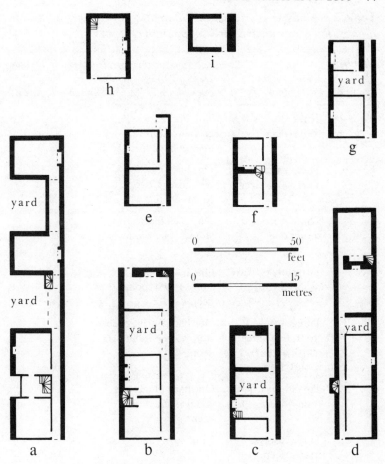

Figure 2   *A reconstructed typology of one-room-wide plans of the sixteenth
and seventeenth centuries The plans are based roughly on actual houses, but
sometimes incorporate features from more than one example. Staircases are
shown only when their original position is reasonably certain.*

Table 2　*Analysis of rooms in different types of one-room-wide houses: late sixteenth and early seventeenth centuries*

Number of examples	Description of front block	Description of back block	Number of rooms	Plan type (see Figure 2)
2	Three storeys. Two rooms deep.	Two back blocks, each two storeys, one room deep.	10	a
1	Three storeys. Two rooms deep.	One back block, two storeys, two rooms deep.	10	d
8	Three storeys. Two rooms deep.	One back block, two storeys, one room deep.	8	b, c
1	Two storeys. Two rooms deep.	One back block, two storeys, two rooms deep.	8	d
1	Three storeys at front, two at rear (catslide roof). Two rooms deep.	One back block, two storeys, one room deep.	7	c
3	Two storeys. Two rooms deep.	One back block, two storeys, one room deep.	6	b, c
3	Three storeys. Two rooms deep.	None surviving.	6	e, f
2	Three storeys. One room deep.	One back block, two storeys, one room deep.	5	g
1	Two storeys. One room deep.	One back block, two storeys, one room deep.	4	g
1	Two storeys. Two rooms deep.	None.	4	e, f
7	Two storeys. One room deep.	None.	2	h, i

Note: Adjustment has been made as far as possible to allow for later additions and demolitions.

one-room-wide houses had this kind of roof, right down to tiny two-storeyed, one-room-deep houses like that in Figure 2h. A few were roofed with the ridge parallel to the street, but these were exceptional and the smallest of their respective categories. 62 Fore Street (Figure 2c) was so shallow that a single parallel roof could cover its two-rooms-deep plan, while at 71 Fore Street the rear section was covered with a catslide roof. A group of one-room-deep houses (Figure 2i) also had parallel roofs, and these were noticeably shallower and wider-fronted than the rest, occupying inferior positions, such as around the Rotherfold or in front of the church-yard.

Another characteristic of the houses is the practice of building the chimney-stacks in the side-walls. It is a logical arrangement where stone side-walls are usual and is employed in other western towns such as Bristol and Taunton.[59] The two-rooms-deep plan with a central stack (shown in Figure 2f) survives in only two houses. It seems to be an alien design associated with more easterly towns like King's Lynn and Oxford and perhaps with the tradition of timber-framed side-walls, although in the case of King's Lynn these were already being replaced by brick in the late Middle Ages.[60]

Detached back blocks (which were always two-storeyed) belonged mostly to houses with a two-rooms-deep front part, although two, and possibly originally three, of the grander one-room-deep houses also had them. Two-rooms-deep back blocks, however, seem to have been rare, despite their obvious conven-ience, and only two examples are known. No clear rules apply to back blocks: they may or may not extend the full width of the plot, and their roofs can be parallel with or at right-angles to the street. The great problem is to know whether their absence implies that they never existed, for in later and poorer times they could be left to decay as warehouses or cottages and then demolished.

A similar difficulty exists with another remarkable feature, the wooden gallery that in many cases spans the courtyard to link the front and back blocks (Figure 3). Only the one (much altered) at 66 Fore Street is probably of the late sixteenth to mid seventeenth century, although galleries are known to have existed in similar houses elsewhere at this date and in Totnes the presence of others can be deduced from external doorways surviving at first-floor level. An early gallery recorded at 38 North Street, Exeter, had mullioned windows the full extent of the courtyard,[61] and this was also orgin-ally the case with the gallery of 1692 at 52 Fore Street, Totnes.

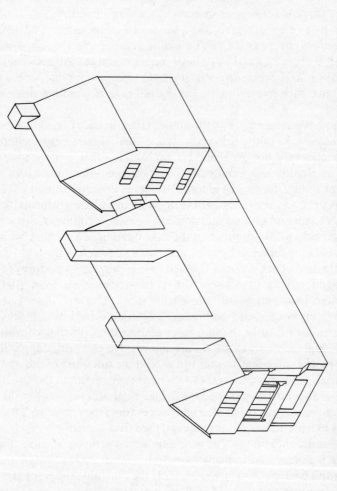

Figure 3 *Isometric reconstruction of a one-room-wide, two-room-deep, gallery-and-back-block house of the sixteenth and seventeenth centuries For the plan of a similar house see Figure 2b.*

The internal arrangements of the one-room-wide houses are best discussed separately in their two main categories of two-rooms-deep and one-room-deep front blocks. The former follow roughly a single pattern, with a side-passage on the ground floor running from front to back and giving separate access to the two rooms. This was certainly an original feature at 70 Fore Street (Figure 2a), where the rooms are divided from the passage by a fine timber-framed partition, but in some houses there was possibly a passage only alongside the rear room and in others none at all. The staircase invariably appears to have been a winding newel, placed usually between the rooms on the fireplace-wall; only one such now remains, at 32 High Street, but the hollows in the wall where others stood can still be seen. They must have been totally dark, for the carefully contrived light-well shown in Figure 2a is unique to the two houses in that group.

The scarcity of probate inventories in Devon makes it difficult to generalize about how the rooms were used, but fortunately the only surviving Totnes inventory to give the names of rooms seems to relate to a two-rooms-deep house of this type. It is that of Henry Beare, merchant, made as late as 1673 but using terms that are familiar from earlier wills. References to the 'fore chamber' and 'higher fore chamber' certainly imply a one-room-wide house three storeys high, and the house is known to have stood at the western end of Fore Street, on the south side, where a group of such houses still remains. It may be inferred, on grounds to be discussed, that the front block contained the shop and the hall on the ground floor, with the study and three of the chambers (all with beds in them) on the two upper floors. The kitchen and the bedchamber over it were presumably in the back block, perhaps with the buttery fitted in either here or in the hall. The 'middle chamber', occupied only by a bed and a press, may have been in the gallery. The brewhouse and the stable, both with chambers over them, were probably placed still further down the plot.[62]

The shop, as might be expected, was most likely to have been at the front of the ground floor in these houses, since that room, when stripped, never has an early fireplace and sometimes no fireplace at all. Clearly, also, the hall, or dining-room, tended to lie behind the shop, with the kitchen across the courtyard in the back block. This is implied in the will of Walter Kellond in 1592 when he speaks of 'the chamber over the haull and the gallerie adioninge to the same chamber, and the chamber over the kitchen which adionethe to the same gallerie'.[63]

Casual evidence from wills supports the idea that the upper floors were mainly given over to bedrooms, the master of the house tending to sleep in the first-floor back room and the servants in the room or rooms over the kitchen. A study is not mentioned in earlier documents, but a counter or counting chamber, which may have served the same purpose, occurs in wills of 1572, 1628 and 1633.[64] Also mentioned on three occasions, in 1557, 1598 and 1621, is the 'forehall', the second reference distinguishing carefully between 'the fore hale & the lower hale wherein I nowe dwell'. No doubt, as in Exeter, this was the first-floor front room, combining the functions of parlour and bedroom.[65]

The lack of any room other than the hall for dining and recreation purposes would seem to have been a deficiency in these houses, and perhaps explains why some occasionally deviate from the general pattern. Thus 66 Fore Street has a room over the kitchen with an unusually good fireplace and evidence of a former oriel window looking on to the garden, while at 32 High Street the ground-floor room of the back block has a great hooded chimney-piece of granite and a single-rib ceiling, the cooking functions having apparently been moved to a new kitchen built on behind. At 68 Fore Street (Figure 2d) a new two-rooms-deep back block provided a parlour, or perhaps a separate dining-room in front of the kitchen.

Turning to the internal arrangements of the one-room-deep houses (Figures 2g, h, i) these cannot, of course, have been complicated, but they are difficult to interpret because every one has been considerably altered, usually added to, and sometimes (Figure 6) completely engulfed in a larger building. Most were probably too narrow to have a side-passage, although 55 High Street, which has an unusually wide internal frontage of 6.19 metres (20 feet 4 inches) had one (now occupied by a staircase) with a very fine stud-and-panel partition. Staircases are now normally in one of the rear corners, this being the most convenient position, and an original example survives at 51 High Street.

There is little evidence of the practice, noted in Bristol in 1472, London in 1581 and Taunton in 1669, of placing a shop on the ground floor with the hall or main living accommodation on the first floor and bedchambers (if there were more than two storeys) above that.[66] Totnes examples tend to have large fireplaces on the ground floor, 64 High Street having quite an impressive hooded one dating from the sixteenth or seventeenth century. Two small houses in the upper quarter, 1 and 24 Leechwell Street, did have unheated ground-floor rooms, however, and both have rooms with hooded fireplaces on the first floor. Leases of 1599 and 1612 refer to still humbler versions of this design in the part of the High Street backing on to the churchyard, each with a cellar or storage-room on the ground floor and a single chamber above.[67]

A final point worth making about the one-room-wide houses is their enormous social range. One might have thought that the richest citizens would want to build on the wider-fronted plots, but in many cases this was not so. Perhaps one-room-wide houses were fashionable because leading citizens of places like Exeter had of necessity to live in them. Thus of the two houses represented by Figure 2a, 70 Fore Street was occupied by Geoffrey Babb (d. 1604), twice mayor and taxed on the largest personal estate in 1592, and 44 High Street by Richard Wise (d. 1670), mayor in 1640 and the leading Totnes merchant in the 1640–1 Dartmouth port book.[68] The lowest social level is hard to determine, but a house of the type shown in Figure 2h, 90 High Street, was occupied in the late sixteenth and early seventeenth centuries by the Pitford family, who appear in none of the national taxation returns and only get into the more extensive rating list of 1602 at the bottom level, along with joiners, tailors and other craftsmen.[69]

Although most of the best-preserved houses are of the one-room-wide type, there is also a substantial group that are two rooms wide. They cover a much greater variety of frontage-width, from 6.4 to 12.8 metres (21 to 42 feet) and naturally include a larger number of subtypes. Unfortunately they have also undergone far more alteration, perhaps because they offered better scope for remodelling. Only 35–37, 39–41 and 43 High Street are really well enough preserved to be discussed in any detail. Seven broad categories of plan are shown in Figure 4, some of them so little understood that even the position of the original front door is uncertain. The front range was almost always one room deep, although the use of a pair of right-angled roofs could produce a roughly square plan (Figure 4b). The double-depth house (Figure 4g), of which 35–37 High Street is the only example, is a rare precursor of a type that did not come into general use in the town until the eighteenth century. Before that the most common method of enlarging the house was by adding an L-wing at the back, usually containing only one ground-floor room (Figure 4c). 43 High Street (Figure 4d) is the exception, having originally four ground-floor rooms, though three of these were added during the sixteenth or seventeenth centuries. The

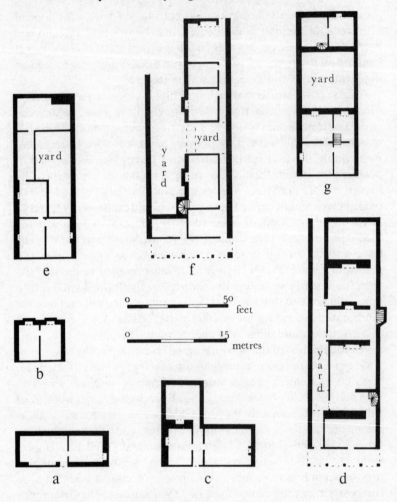

Figure 4   *A reconstructed typology of two-room-wide plans for the sixteenth and seventeenth centuries Plans b, e and g are shown at first-floor level. Plan d, shown at ground-floor level, is two rooms wide on the first floor.*

alternative to a longer wing was a gallery and back block, the latter either extending the full width of the plot (Figure 4e) or forming a kind of interrupted extension of the wing (Figure 4f). 35–7 High Street also had a back block (Figure 4g), but in this it was once again unique in having it set well back, 8.33 metres (27 feet) behind the main house, almost certainly without a gallery.

As with the one-room-wide houses, chimney-stacks tended to be in the side-walls, although with some notable exceptions. 43 High Street (Figure 4d) had them in the rear walls of all three heated rooms in the wing, and two houses that were originally roofed with a pair of symmetrical gables, 27 and 89–91 High Street, had stacks in the rear wall corresponding to each gable (Figure 4b). Evidence of entrance-passages is rare, and only at 97 High Street was there certainly the medieval arrangement of a passage separating two rooms of unequal size, traditionally the hall and 'service' room (Figure 4c). At 43 High Street (Figure 4d) there was only one ground-floor room at the front with the passage at one end, leading directly into the side courtyard, while 39–41 High Street (Figure 4f) had a similar passage through most of the house, though not provably through the front-range. The original position of stair-cases is rarely detectable. Surprisingly, little use seems to have been made of a stair turret in the angle of the L, although it has been conjectured that 39–41 High Street (Figure 4f) had one. At 43 High Street (Figure 4d) the original newel stair survives and is tucked, quite needlessly, into the darkest corner of the wing.

Only at 11–13 High Street (Figure 4a; Plate 5) is it possible to get some impression of how the simplest two-rooms-wide house functioned, the ground-floor rooms being of low status, perhaps a shop and a kitchen, while the two upper floors were of high quality. Each first-floor room had a fine oriel window and a single-rib ceiling, while the eastern room on the second floor had a finely carved chimney-piece. 43 High Street (Figure 4d) seems to have followed the pattern of the one-room-wide houses, with an unheated shop at the front and a grand room behind it that must have been the hall. The kitchen occupied the next to rearmost room in the wing and the two first-floor front rooms were of high quality, one with a single-rib ceiling and the other with a carved limestone chimney-piece. 39–41 High Street (Figure 4f), though larger, was somewhat similar, with two low-quality rooms, perhaps shops, on the street frontage. The ground-floor room in the wing and the larger first-floor front room both had fine quality single-rib ceilings (Plate 3), appropriate to a hall and combined bedroom and parlour, while the kitchen (with an enormous fireplace) occupied the ground-floor rear room of a three-rooms-deep back block. The unheated middle room of the latter was perhaps a buttery and the front room, which had a single-rib ceiling, possibly a dining-room.

The social status of the occupiers of these two-rooms-wide houses seems to have been more select than in the case of the one-room-wide houses. Even the smaller types, like 11–13 High Street (Figure 4a) and 39 Fore Street (Figure 4e), were the homes of minor merchants, Thomas Every (in 1599) and Geoffrey Barber (in *c.* 1646).[70] The biggest ones, 43 and 39–41 High Street, appear (on the evidence of title deeds, combined with initials on the ceilings) to have been occupied by two of the greatest Totnes merchant families, the Bogans and the Dowses.

VI

After the Civil War the merchant trade of Totnes fell rapidly. There were prosperous merchants in the town right down to the end of the eighteenth century, but their numbers became fewer and fewer: while thirty had traded through Dartmouth in 1633–4, and twenty-nine in 1640–1, only twelve or fourteen were left in 1682–3.[71] By the beginning of the eighteenth century it was possible for Defoe to describe Totnes as 'a very good town; of some trade but has more gentlemen in it than tradesmen of note'. He goes on to remark that the cheapness of provisions 'makes the town of Totness a very good place to live in; especially for such as have large families, and but small estates, and many such are said to come into those parts on purpose for saving money, and to live in proportion to their income'.[72]

In fact, however, there is little evidence of this sort of person moving into the town, or even a marked growth in the professional classes. John Gilbert, esquire, of Compton did live in Totnes for a while and became mayor in 1726. From the 1760s Farmery Epworth maintained his home in the town while pursuing his career from lieutenant to rear admiral (retired), becoming mayor in 1785.[73] But these were exceptions. Much more typical were Richard Norris (d. 1702) and John Adams (d. 1771),[74] descendants of Totnes merchant families living off the wealth accumulated in the sixteenth and seventeenth centuries.

The population was also falling. Baptisms dropped sharply, recovering only at the very end of the eighteenth century. In 1801

Totnes had a population of 2503, just about equal to the estimate for the early seventeenth century. In the 1690s, when the validity of the baptism figures can be cross-checked to some extent,[75] the population may have been as low as 1600. The character of the town was also changing. While the markets seem to have remained prosperous and the number of clothiers increased,[76] the leading figures were becoming much more the mixture of tradesmen that one would expect in a small place. In sharp contrast to the years 1550–1649 when all but two mayors were merchants, fifteen non-merchant mayors can be identified between 1650 and 1699. In the eighteenth century only two merchants became mayor, the office increasingly being filled by tradesmen such as butchers, saddlers and soapboilers.[77]

VII

The effect of this economic decline, or rather this subsidence to a lower level of prosperity, shows clearly in the town's buildings. It was not that new building ceased: the sale of town properties on 2000-year leaseholds in 1719 may actually have stimulated building. Eighteen houses in the town centre were sold, including 8, 44 and 63 High Street, all of which were heavily altered or rebuilt about this time.[78] It was really the relative architectural quality that declined in national terms. This has already been noted with regard to moulded plaster ceilings: it was equally true of other interior fittings. Moreover, there was no thorough attempt to sweep away the architecture of the late sixteenth and early seventeenth centuries, absurdly outdated as it must have seemed by the eighteenth century. At 51 Fore Street, for example, John Adams (d. 1771), esquire, a quite considerable property-owner, was content to live in a three-storeyed, late sixteenth- or seventeenth-century house like that shown in Figure 4e.[79] All that seems to have been done to update its plan was the insertion of an early or mid eighteenth-century staircase in the angle of the L (Figure 5g).

Others were quite prepared to rebuild part of a house, leaving the rest largely unaltered. At 65 Fore Street, the front section of a one-room-wide, two-rooms-deep house was almost totally, if not wholly rebuilt and heightened in the early eighteenth century. Yet the rear part was left with its single-rib ceiling and wide mullioned window, the former merely cut back a bit to intrude an eighteenth-century staircase. Then in the late eighteenth or early nineteenth century this rear part was heightened to match the front, again without altering the ground floor.

The most important change was external: the cladding of patterned timber-framing with wooden panelling, plaster and slate-hanging, and the replacement of wide, low, mullioned windows with tall, narrow, mullioned and transomed ones, followed, in the course of the eighteenth century, by vertically sliding sashes. The change must have been less startling because of the resolute region-alism of Totnes builders, who remain as anonymous as those of the earlier period. One Mr Farwell was described as 'ye main contriver' of 52 Fore Street, but nothing more is known of him.[80]

It was the continued use of timber-framed front walls, still jettied in some cases in the early eighteenth century, that produced façades contrasting sharply with the severe brick architecture that became fashionable in London after the Restoration. Timber-framing was being erected in Totnes right up to the end of the eighteenth century, and was only finally superseded in the early nineteenth century by rough stone walls faced with stucco. 35 and 37 Fore Street, for example, were rebuilt with timber-framed, slate-hung fronts somewhere between 1789 and 1809.[81] When timber-framed fronts are covered with cladding, the basic date, if not entirely concealed, is much less obvious to the casual observer, and in Totnes this served to blend the old with the new.

Another feature that helped to blur the change-over from the essentially medieval façades of the late sixteenth and early seven-teenth centuries to post-Restoration classicism was the survival of the gable-end on the street-frontage. The extreme conservatism of 52 Fore Street has already been noted. 26 and 28 High Street, probably built soon after 1700, show the next step forward (Plate 6). The gables remain, but the second and third storeys are subjected to classical discipline with a straight entablature below the gable and (at number 26) giant pilasters to support it.

28 High Street, in particular, demonstrates the kind of ebullient design that plasterwork laid on a timber frame could produce: fantastic mask 'keystones', scrolls flanking the windows and foliage on the coved cornice. At 8 and 10 High Street bolection-moulded panelling of *c*. 1700 has a similar, if less dramatic effect. Possibly slate-hanging also contributed to the street-scene in this way. What now remains in Totnes is the austere late eighteenth-century type (Plate 1), occasionally enlivened with some modest patterning (Plate 5), but the rare survival of *c*. 1660 at the Tudor House, Exeter, is full of vigorous detail.[82]

Brick has already been mentioned as a rare material in Totnes. It also tended to be used for prestigious buildings with a national rather than a purely regional flavour, and the people for whom they were built were probably those with more extensive outside contacts. Thus the upper storey of the Church Walk was rebuilt in 1718 at the instigation of a local gentleman, Nicholas Trist. 36 Fore Street, a great double-fronted mansion looking wholly out of place in the narrow main street, was built between 1795 and 1808 for Giles Welsford, a considerable entrepreneur engaged in supplying bread for the army at Plymouth and post-horses for the whole of the South-West.[83]

Internally the houses were finished with panelling, chimney-pieces and staircases little different from their London contemporaries. The exceptions were the stud-and-panel partitions, lighter versions of those used in the late sixteenth and early seventeenth centuries and (outside Totnes) in the late Middle Ages; 52 Fore Street has one in its side-passage, as does the slightly later 26 High Street. Also the regional technique, widely employed in Devon in the second half of the seventeenth century, of decorating the fireplace-back with black and white sgrafitto plasterwork was used in at least two houses, 27 High Street and 70 Fore Street.

In plan the houses altered or rebuilt at this period are a curious mixture of national styles and local traditions (Figure 5). The one-room-wide, two-rooms-deep plan with a framed staircase in the centre (Figures 5a, d) was particularly popular. It had appeared in London by 1658 and in Bristol by the early 1660s.[84] In Totnes the first example seems to have been at 52 Fore Street in 1692, but thereafter it became the common type. 26 High Street has a reduced version, lacking the room behind the staircase (Figure 5f), and there was even a two-room-wide variant (Figure 5b). Older houses were converted simply by ripping out the old newel stair and replacing it with a framed one, often, as at 65 Fore Street, cutting away earlier plasterwork in the process. Smaller houses were also enlarged for the same purpose. At 24 Leechwell Street an early eighteenth-century staircase and an extra room were tacked on behind an existing one-room-deep house, while at 14 High Street a similar house with a detached back block was converted by infilling the courtyard with a staircase in the late eighteenth century (Figure 6).

The other common London house-type from the late seventeenth century onwards, in which the staircase is placed to one side of the back room, rarely occurs in pre-Victorian Totnes. The earliest example is at 37 Fore Street and is of the period between 1789 and

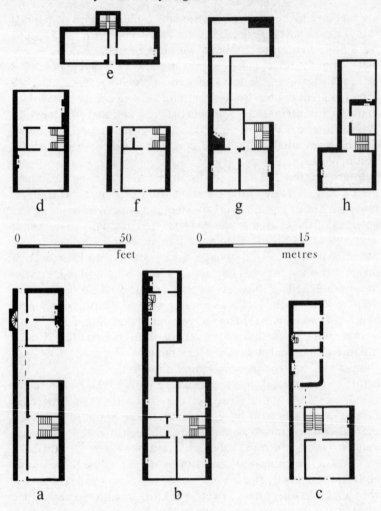

Figure 5   *A reconstructed typology of late seventeenth- and eighteenth-century plans Houses b, d, g and h are shown at first-floor level.*

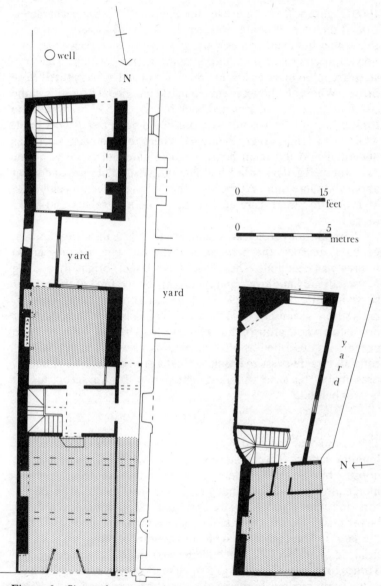

Figure 6 *Sixteenth- and seventeenth-century houses remodelled in the eighteenth century. The earlier parts of the house are stippled* Left: *14 High Street, ground-floor plan (note that it has its own side-walls on the east, but is built-up against the adjoining house on the west).* Right: *24 Leechwell Street, first-floor plan.*

1809 (Figure 5c), although even this has a side-passage uncharacter-
istic of the type. Probably the central staircase was better suited to
the narrow but deep Totnes house-plots, particularly since the older
houses already had their newel stairs in this position. The side-
staircase fitted more easily into the angle of an L-plan, as at 51 Fore
Street. Where the houses retain a marked regional flavour is in the
continued use of galleries and back blocks. At 52 Fore Street the
former back block was not only preserved but a new gallery built,
while at 14 High Street (Figure 6), where the old back block was
absorbed into the main house in the eighteenth century, a new
two-storeyed gallery or link building and a back block were added at
about the same time. At the very end of the eighteenth century 35
and 37 Fore Street were entirely newly built as gallery-and-back-
block houses.

There was, nevertheless, a tendency to reduce the size of houses,
probably because the number of really rich men needing grand
houses was declining. Thus 39–41 High Street, originally one big
house, already had two separate owners by the time of the earliest
surviving title deed in 1694. 26 High Street of *c.* 1700 (Plate 6),
magnificent as it looks from the street, can only have been the front
house to a whole group of humbler dwellings behind, for in 1678 the
property is described as 'now divided into severall habitacions'.[85]
Indeed, its side-passage has never had a door into the front house,
presumably because its sole function was to give access to the
houses behind.

VIII

The essay so far has tried to distinguish two quite separate phases of
building among Totnes houses. On the one hand, there are the
houses of the late sixteenth- and early seventeenth-century
merchant town, almost totally replacing their medieval predecessors and with a range of size and quality appropriate to a much
larger place. On the other hand, there is the more modest work of
the late seventeenth and eighteenth centuries, often just a superficial adaptation of earlier building and matching the decline of
Totnes to its basic function as a small market centre. Encasing it all
is the early medieval topography, resisting expansion and forcing
new houses into ancient, narrow-fronted plots. Some attempt has
been made to compare the houses with those in other towns, but
generalization is difficult because of the paucity of published
material. The front blocks appear to fit in a recognizable tradition,

though the one-room-wide, gable-ended houses seem to have predominated in few other towns. Detached back blocks, however, are
rarely to be found elsewhere in England. Were they an archaic local
feature, descended from the detached kitchens of the Middle Ages,
or is it that conditions in Totnes have favoured their preservation
better than in other towns?

There are strong arguments in favour of the second alternative.
The Devon towns of Barnstaple, Dartmouth, Exeter, Plymouth
and Tiverton, where a few houses with detached back blocks
survive or are known to have existed, have all suffered heavily from
demolition. Kingsbridge and Topsham, with one example each, are
small places where only isolated pieces of grand urban architecture
would be expected.[86] Outside Devon, the only three towns known
to have contained any early examples at all, Bristol, Chester and
Taunton, have all been much altered.[87] Mid or late seventeenth-
century examples are also known in York and London[88] together
with eighteenth- and early nineteenth-century ones in Gosport
(Hampshire), Newton Abbot (Devon) and Alexandria in Virginia.[89]
Strictly speaking, however, these have link buildings like that added
to 14 High Street, Totnes, in the eighteenth century (Figure 6),
rather than galleries. They may have been designed from pattern-
books instead of developing from an earlier local tradition. This
certainly seems to be true of the house at York and one of the
London houses, in which the link building is occupied by a staircase,
a design available in an English pattern-book by 1670.[90]

The reason Totnes retains so many examples is that it is a small,
architecturally stagnant place, whereas the other towns (except, of
course, Kingsbridge and Topsham) are larger centres that have
retained their strong commercial position. Consequently they have
undergone much more rebuilding, especially in the rear of the plots
where the back blocks would have stood. At the Leche House in
Chester, for example, the gallery survives but the back block has
been removed in order to build a wholly separate eighteenth-
century house. Unfortunately English inventories (unlike those of
Paris) rarely distinguish between blocks of building: a Chester
reference to 'the court betweene the hall and the kitchin' is so far
unique.[91] Exeter inventories do refer to galleries, but their connection with back blocks could not be understood without the surviving
structural evidence.[92]

A quite different dimension appears when the gallery-and-back
block house is considered in a European context. For here, as with

the arcaded walks, the English examples look like poor relations. In France, Belgium and parts of Switzerland the type is common: French historians call it *une maison à deux corps de logis*. Beyond this area there are fewer examples, with no more than a scattering in Germany and the Netherlands. The only country outside the obvious range of French influence to have them in any numbers is, rather curiously, Poland, which before the eighteenth century is usually associated architecturally with Germany.[93]

There is obviously an argument for regarding the English examples as the fringe of a French architectural fashion, particularly since they are modest in scale and post-medieval in date, whereas the French ones begin earlier with some very grand late medieval examples. One has only to look at the trading links between English and French towns in the sixteenth and seventeenth centuries, especially in the South-West, to see how the plan-type could have been diffused. At Rouen, where many such houses have been recorded, the English merchants had special privileges and even their own hall for the sale of cloth.[94]

By 1623, moreover, French plans were available in pattern-book form in Pierre Le Muet's *Maniere de Bien Bastir*, which shows a whole range of gallery-and-back-block plans, from a single-fronted terrace-house to a small palace. Particularly interesting is the plan which has a closet-wing exactly like the late sixteenth- or early seventeenth-century example at 65 Fore Street, Totnes (Figure 2e), clearly seen here as a vestigial gallery. The whole of Le Muet's plan is in fact good evidence of the influence of French design on English town houses. In other respects it is unlike the Totnes houses, except, to some extent, 35 and 37 Fore Street (Figure 5c), but it is exactly like that other house-type common in London and usually thought to have been introduced in the late seventeenth century: the one with a room front and back, the rear room being reduced in width to accommodate a dog-leg staircase beside it.

It is conceivable, therefore, that Totnes presents a view of late sixteenth- and early seventeenth-century urban domestic architecture that cannot be paralleled in any other English town, that its detached back blocks are not just a local oddity but a feature that was once widespread. Unfortunately so much has been demolished that the hypothesis can no longer be tested from surviving buildings. Archaeological excavation may possibly help fill the gap, but it is really documentary sources that offer the greatest scope for further study.

Notes and references

1   W. B. Stephens, *Seventeenth-Century Exeter* (1958), p. 8.
2   Richard Carew, *The Survey of Cornwall*, 1602, edited by F. E. Halliday (1969), p. 226.
3   P. Russell, *Dartmouth* (1950), p. 84.
4   References throughout the essay to overseas trade are drawn mainly from the Dartmouth port books, especially a selection of those from 1566 to 1641: PRO, E 190/925/13, 930/23, 935/15, 936/1, 935/7, 937/8, 944/2, 947/1, 949/1, 951/8, and E 122/201/16.
5   W. G. Hoskins, *Local History in England* (1959), p. 177. L. M. Nicholls, 'The lay subsidy of 1523', *University of Birmingham Historical Journal*, **9** no. 2 (1964), pp. 113–29.
6   Devon RO, 1579A/3/47 and 103; TD 166, Deeds Misc. Devon.
7   Based on the number of baptisms per decade, using the multiplier suggested in Hoskins, *Local History*, p. 143.
8   Devon RO, 1579A/16/35.
9   The mayors' names come from E. Windeatt, 'Totnes: its mayors and mayoralties', *The Western Antiquary*, **9** (1889–90), pp. 149–53, 190–2; **10** (1890–1), pp. 3–5, 123–6, 146–9; **11** (1891–2), pp. 73–5; *Transactions of the Devonshire Association (hereafter TDA)*, **32** (1900), pp. 111–28. Their occupations have been gleaned from many sources.
10 Based on the returns for 1571, 1592, 1610 and 1623/4 (PRO, E 179/100/368, 101/409, 101/450, 102/463). Occupations have been identified from a variety of sources.
11 W. G. Hoskins, *Devon* (1954), p. 127.
12 Devon RO, 1579A/3/1 and 14; 6/11; 7/1, nos. 6 and 27; 7/9. BL, Additional Charters 27, 282–3. *TDA*, **32** (1900), p. 128.
13 Devon RO, 1579A/3/7–10; 7/1, no. 39. Inscription on pillars of fruit-market house.
14 Devon RO, 1579A/7/1, no. 7.
15 *PP*, 1831–2, **37** *Reports from Commissioners on . . . Boundaries of Boroughs*, p. 131.
16 L. T. Smith (ed.), *The Itinerary of John Leland* (1964), vol. 1, p. 218.
17 P. Russell, *The Good Town of Totnes* (1963), p. 27.
18 Devon RO, Manuscript volume by John Swete, 'Picturesque Sketches of Devon', **2** (November–December 1792), pp. 182–4.
19 Devon RO, 1579A/2/1.
20 For taxation records see H. R. Watkin, *History of Totnes Priory and Medieval Town*, (1914) vol. 1, pp. 321–30.
21 Deed in possession of Mr J. L. Hamshere of Dartington in 1974.
22 PRO, PROB 11/168, 87 Sadler.

23   Engraved in the *Gentleman's Magazine*, **69** (1799), p. 369.
24   Devon RO, 1579A/3/6.
25   PRO, C 7/332/1. Also date and initials on plaster overmantel.
26   N. W. Alcock and M. Laithwaite, 'Medieval houses in Devon and their modernization', *Medieval Archaeology*, **17** (1973), pp. 100–25.
27   D. Portman, *Exeter Houses, 1400–1700* (1966), pp. 6–7.
28   Devon RO, 1579A/2/5.
29   198 High Street; The Ship, St Martin's Lane; The White Hart, South Street.
30   Portman, *Exeter Houses*, pp. 3–22.
31   Devon RO, *TD* 166, Deeds Misc. Devon.
32   PRO, E 305/B.56; PROB 11/29, 1 and 18 Spert, wills of Henry Dottynge and William Hokmor.
33   K. and C. French, 'Devonshire Plasterwork', *TDA*, **89** (1957), pp. 124–44.
34   11–13, 16, 32, 39–41, 43 High Street. The ceilings are either in dated houses or carry sets of initials that can be tentatively identified.
35   PRO, E 190/944/2, 949/1, 950/1.
36   8 and 55 High Street.
37   W. G. Hoskins, 'The rebuilding of rural England', in W. G. Hoskins, *Provincial England* (1963), pp. 131–48. R. Machin, 'The great rebuilding: a reassessment', *P. and P.*, no. 77 (1977), pp. 33–56.
38   PRO, C 21/E.16/18. *TDA*, **82** (1950), p. 286. Devon RO, Cullompton PW1. E. Welch (ed.), *Plymouth Building Accounts*, (Devon and Cornwall Record Society, new series, **12** 1967), pp. 85, 88. I am indebted to Mr T. Falla for the Cullompton reference.
39   PRO, E 179/101/450, E 179/102/463.
40   Devon RO, 1579A/17/18.
41   Devon RO, Totnes PRI.
42   PRO, C 21/E.16/18.
43   PRO, C 2/James I/D.10/2, C 2/James I/H.2/42.
44   For example, PRO, PROB 11/62, 28 Arundell (Walter Dowse); PROB 11/100, 49 Montague (John Wyse).
45   PRO, E 179/101/409.
46   PRO, St Ch 8/86/24.
47   *TDA*, **34** (1902), p. 333.
48   H. R. Watkin, *Dartmouth*, (1935), vol. 1, p. 339. PRO, E 190/944/2.
49   Samuel Smith, *An Account of the Late Dreadful Fire at Tiverton* (1732), p. 1.
50   Pipe Roll Society Publication, **30** (1909), *Pipe Roll – 27 Henry II*, p. 28.
51   Devon RO, 1579A/7/4; 1579 A/7/1, no. 77.
52   Watkin, *Dartmouth*, pp. 340–1.
53   PRO, C 7/332/1.
54   Devon RO, Deckemant Collection, vol. 12 p. 135. J. T. Smith, 'Timber

Right Fore Street, Totnes, looking east From the right: numbers 54, 52, 50 and 48.

Below High Street Totnes, looking east, *c.* 1860 The Butterwalk is on the left, the Poultry Walk on the right.

Above   Single-rib ceiling in the first-floor front room of 39 High Street, Totnes

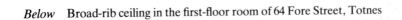

Below   Broad-rib ceiling in the first-floor room of 64 Fore Street, Totnes

framed building in England', *Archaeological Journal,* **122** (1965), pp. 133–58.
55 Devon RO, 2065/add. 3.
56 Devon RO, 1579A/3/50.
57 PRO, PROB 11/88, 90 Drake.
58 V. Parker, *The Making of King's Lynn* (1971), pp. 81–94. W. A. Pantin, 'The development of domestic architecture in Oxford', *Antiquaries Journal,* **27** (1947), pp. 120–50.
59 R. Taylor, 'Town houses in Taunton, 1500–1700', *Post-Medieval Archaeology,* **8** (1974), pp. 63–79.
60 Parker, *King's Lynn,* pp. 102–3.
61 Stripped and recorded by the Exeter Archaeological Field Unit before demolition in 1972.
62 PRO, PROB 4/6660; PROB 11/342, 89 Pye (Beare's will). Most Devon inventories were destroyed by bombing in 1942.
63 PRO, PROB 11/80, 83 Harrington.
64 PRO, PROB 11/57, 13 Pyckering (William Powell); PROB 11/154, 99 Barrington (Nicholas Wise); PROB 11/165, 63 Seager (Samuel Wise).
65 PRO, PROB 11/39, 5 Wrastley (William Giles); PROB 11/138, 81 Dale (Richard Newman). Devon RO, 48/14/98/13. Portman, *Exeter Houses,* p. 30.
66 L. F. Salzman, *Building in England down to 1540* (1967 edn), p. 598. PRO, Req 2/173/50. Taylor, 'Town houses in Taunton', p. 75.
67 Devon RO, 1579A/3/54; TD 166, Deeds Misc. Devon.
68 PRO, E 179/101/409; E 190/951/8. Devon RO, 1579A/6/11, no. 160.
69 Devon RO, 1579A/6/11, no. 259; 1579A/17/18.
70 Devon RO, 1579A/3/54; 1579A/7/2, no. 71. PRO, C 7/332/43.
71 PRO, E 190/949/1; 951/8; 962/1.
72 D. Defoe, *A Tour Through the Whole Island of Great Britain* (1962 edn), vol. 1, pp. 224–5.
73 Title deeds of 2–4 North Street, Totnes. National Trust, *Compton Castle* (1975), p. 18. Totnes baptism and burial registers.
74 Totnes burial register.
75 By comparing the 1698 census of the neighbouring town of Buckfastleigh (Harl. MS 6832, fols. 107–18) with their baptism register.
76 The meat market was partly rebuilt in 1652–3 (Devon RO, 1579A/7/113), a new sheep and pig market was established in 1677 (*TDA,* **33** (1901), p. 537), and a corn market house built in 1720 (Russell, *Totnes,* p. 77). The names of clothiers have been gleaned from many sources.
77 Windeatt, 'Totnes: its mayors and mayoralities'; *TDA* **32** (1900), pp. 128–41; **33** (1901), pp. 535–51; **34** (1902), pp. 325–43; **36** (1904), pp. 487–505. The mayors' occupations come from a variety of other sources.
78 Devon RO, 46/1/1/3a-b.
79 Title deeds of 51 and 53–5 Fore Street. Devon RO, 466M/Z1.
80 PRO, C 7/332/1.

81   Title deeds of 37 Fore Street in possession of Mrs L. P. Bennett in 1969.

82   Portman, *Exeter Houses*, plates 31, 32. The house is dated from evidence in the title deeds.

83   Devon RO, 1579A/2/124–5, 133. *Exeter Flying Post*, 3 February 1803, and 26 November 1811.

84   A. F. Kelsall, 'The London house plan in the later 17th century', *Post-Medieval Archaeology*, **8** (1974), pp. 80–91. The Bristol houses are in King Street: I am grateful to Miss B. C. May for documentation about their date.

85   PRO, C 7/547/22.

86   Portman, *Exeter Houses*. J. Barber, 'No. 4, Vauxhall Street, Plymouth', *TDA*, **105** (1973), pp. 17–35. The other houses are 98 High Street and The Three Tuns, Barnstaple; 27 Lower Street, Dartmouth; Coronet Place, Kingsbridge; 74 Fore Street, Topsham. The Tiverton evidence comes from a probate inventory of 1630 (Devon RO, 2723M/ unlisted: I owe this reference to Mrs S. M. Laithwaite).

87   Taylor, 'Town houses in Taunton'. W. A. Pantin, 'Medieval English town-house plans', *Medieval Archaeology*, **6–7** (1962–3), pp. 228–31. Also for Chester, the Deva Hotel and probate inventory of 1609 (cited below, note 91). The Bristol information was kindly provided by Dr R. Leech.

88   19 The Shambles, York (kindly shown to me by Dr E. A. Gee), the Hoop and Grapes, London (for which I am grateful to Mr J. Schofield), and a house in King Street, Covent Garden (PRO, C 10/511/7, C 10/281/55).

89   Royal Commission on Historical Monuments, *Monuments Threatened or Destroyed* (1963), p. 40. The Newton Abbot houses are in Wolborough Street. D. Davis, S. P. Dorsey and R. C. Hall, *Alexandria Houses, 1750–1830* (1946), pp. 17, 112, 114 (I am indebted to the late Mr S. E. Rigold for this reference).

90   P. Le Muet, *Maniere de Bien Bastir* (Paris 1623). English translation, *The Art of Fair Building* (1670).

91   M. Jurgens and P. Couperie, 'Le logement à Paris aux XVIe et XVIIe siècles', *Annales E-S-C,* **17** (1962), pp. 488–500. Cheshire County RO, inventory of Thomas Fletcher (1609).

92   Portman, *Exeter Houses*, p. 34. The inventories are in the Court of Orphans collection in Devon RO.

93   The sources for this paragraph are too vast to be cited here, but will be found in my PhD thesis, to be submitted to the University of Exeter.

94   R. Quenedey, *L'Habitation Rouennaise* (Rouen 1926). Lewes Roberts, *The Merchants Mappe of Commerce* (1638), p. 29.

3 Town and country: economic change in Kendal *c*. 1550–1700

C. B. Phillips

I

The relationship between a town and the countryside around is a complex one, extending back in time to that geographical common sense which first recognized a good bridging point, route centre or defensive position. Kendal was all of these things by the time that William de Lancastre granted burgage tenure to his market town early in the thirteenth century. The cloth industry in the town may date from about the same time; there was a fulling mill there by 1256 and a dyehouse by 1310. References to fulling mills show that a rural cloth industry was established by at least the second and third decades of the fourteenth century.[1] In later medieval England many towns had complained loudly of the ruin that followed the growth of rural textile industries, although other rural industries associated with minerals, leather and the service crafts of the smiths, wrights and carpenters had long existed. In Kendal those late medieval centuries appear to have passed quietly, and in the sixteenth and seventeenth centuries the town's ancient manufacturing and marketing roles, and the long distance trade in Kendal cloth, continued. The town also functioned as a minor centre of secular and ecclesiastical government. These roles too rested on medieval foundations, and strengthened the ties between Kendal and its surrounds, established by communications, the market and cloth. It is the relationships between town and country arising from manufacturing and associated trade that form the substance of this essay.

The medieval tensions between rural industries and urban centres persisted, and contemporary consciousness of them in the sixteenth century is obvious in both statutory and local attempts at control. Under Mary and in the early years of Elizabeth's reign statutes dealt with manufacturing, retail sales, labour, wages and prices.[2] By the end of the Tudor dynasty the policy that industry should be located in towns, and not in the countryside which should concentrate on agriculture, had given way to an acceptance of rural industry.[3] Nevertheless, virtually all corporate towns, through the privileges of the freedom and controls on labour, tried to protect themselves against outside competition. Kendal did not have such powers until it was incorporated in 1575.[4] Braudel has argued that the 'countryside did not give up all its industrial activities in favour of nearby towns, it had its share of them, although they were generally those activities the towns were glad enough to leave to it'.[5] Dr Thirsk has suggested that town and country did not compete, for where they produced the same product the town version was of higher quality aimed at different consumers.[6] How did Kendal conduct its competitive affairs? What was the outcome for the town: development or decay?

II

Where is Kendal and what sort of town was it? Both questions would have confounded the Royal Commission on the cloth industry in 1640, which placed Kendal in Yorkshire.[7] The town in fact lies in a Westmorland valley on the south side of the mountainous core of the Lake District. Historians have classified towns by complexity of economic function and size of population. Kendal enjoyed enough economic and governmental functions to be ranked as a county centre, but with a population never far from 2500 in our period it always came near the bottom of the second level of English towns – those with between 2000 and 5000 inhabitants.[8] To the north, in Westmorland, the decayed town of Appleby clung to the county assizes as its only seventeenth-century claim to county status, but it was commercially weak and small in numbers. In Cumberland, Carlisle was twice as big as Kendal by 1700 although it may not always have enjoyed this superiority. In the later seventeenth century the port of Whitehaven grew to about Kendal's size.[9] To the south of Kendal the nearest town of comparable importance was Lancaster.[10] A ring of small market towns, Dalton, Ulverston, Hawkshead, Sedbergh and Kirkby Lonsdale surrounded Kendal; they were joined by Ambleside and Burton after 1650. These towns are shown on Figure 7. To the north of the area covered by Figure 7 were Cockermouth, Keswick and Penrith, and to the west Egremont. There were good roads from the South and Lancaster via Kendal to Penrith and between Kirkby Lonsdale and Kendal; these were Kendal's two routes to London. There was also a road from Kendal via Grasmere to Keswick and Cockermouth.[11]

When he came to Kendal about 1540 Leland was aware of the town's commercial reputation in textiles.[12] Disputes over seigneurial jurisdiction in and around the town involving, first, the Duke of Richmond and the Earl of Cumberland in the 1530s, and in the next decade William Parr, Marquis of Northampton, make it clear that the town was wealthy enough to be worth fighting over.[13] Some at least of this prosperity came from cloth, and given the Parr family's connection with the Court, it is not surprising that some found its way on to the king's back.[14] There are, however, enough literary references to the wearing of Kendal cloth to justify two conclusions: that Kendal's textile industry was down-market, and that it was healthy. Most of the product was aimed at the lower end of the domestic market in the sixteenth century, and export statistics are not a helpful guide to production.[15] At the same time, we should note that Kendal cloth was the name for cloth manufactured both in the town and in the surrounding countryside; traders from South Westmorland who distributed the cloth also came from town and country. At the turn of the sixteenth century Camden noted the new borough's prosperous and vital textile industry, and in 1698 Celia Fiennes also described the town as a flourishing textile centre and a big market for leather.[16] The only note of doubt about the town's good fortune comes from Richard Braithwaite, a local gentleman poet, who noted that the textile slump of the 1620s and 1630s had made into paupers some cloth-workers who used to give alms themselves.[17] This picture of relative economic stability which the literary evidence amounts to is reinforced if we look at the structure of the town's economy using breakdowns of the occupations of the townsmen as a guide.

In numerous corporate towns it is possible to calculate the number of freemen in various gilds and such evidence has been used to shed light on the urban economy. Some historians, however, have argued that the data can be misleading. First, inaccuracies in compilation and the incompleteness of the records may distort the picture. Second, it has been argued that membership of a particular gild does not guarantee that an individual followed that trade, or continued to follow it through his working life. Furthermore a townsman often had more than one occupation and source of income. In Kendal the armourer and hardwareman, Thomas Sandes, was also a wool-trader. Concurrent with these activities he was treasurer for sequestrations in Westmorland during the Interregnum and, after the Restoration, a receiver for Crown lands.

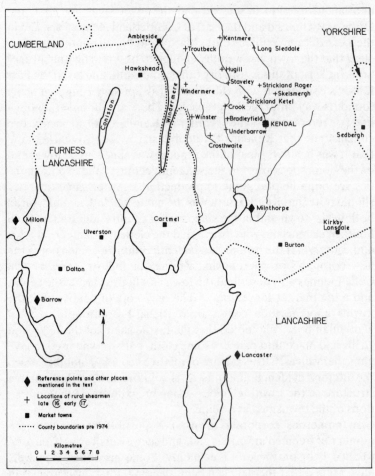

Figure 7   *Westmorland cloth-making (location of rural shearmen)*

We have no way of knowing precisely how Sandes amassed his fortune, but later in life he prospered from money-lending and mortgages.[18] At the other end of the social scale, there were few if any in Kendal who were full-time brewers, because many ale-sellers brewed their own drink, frequently in conjunction with some other occupation. Third, there were inhabitants who traded in the market who are not listed in the freeman records. Finally, of course, the source provides no information on those important members of a town's working population who were not enfranchised – journeymen, apprentices and other servants.[19]

In the light of these criticisms what can the Kendal data tell us? The corporation's freemen records only allow us to count the numbers in different trades at one point, in 1578, when they are listed in their gilds. The evidence of 1578 is categorized in Table 3 and provides the basis for an analysis of the occupational structure of the town.[20] No list was made of building workers in 1578, although by 1590 there were eight freemen in that gild. The first of them was in the town by 1580, the second by 1583.[21] The various professional men in Kendal never had distinct gilds of their own and joined the scriveners' gild. Counting the vicar and his curates, the schoolmaster, and the attorneys in the court of record, there was a small group of professionals in 1578.[22]

Another useful source is the 1576 list of contributors to the cost of Kendal's incorporation. Payment entitled a townsman to the freedom. 658 men are listed, as against only 399 in 1578. Part of the discrepancy can be ascribed to mortality: forty-two townsmen were buried 1576–8.[23] Others, such as Brian Garnett of Stramongate, were minor gentry or yeomen with no urban trade to follow; also absent in 1578 were labourers or paupers. So far as we can judge the 1578 list of freemen is reasonably accurate for the most important groups of tradesmen. By comparing the two lists we can measure the number of townsmen who were householders but not gildsmen.

The 1695 census of Kendal, taken under the Marriage Duties Act, records occupations for many inhabitants. Clearly, there are some problems of comparison with the 1578 freemen list. Most of the occupational terms in 1695 are the same as earlier, but there are some new trades like limeburner and farrier. The apprenticeship registers indicate however that such trades might be followed by freemen.[24] The census does omit occupational data for some fifteen people known to be following trades, but correlation of the census with the sole surviving gild list for the shoemakers indicates no

Table 3 *Occupational order in Kendal*

c. 1578 Freemen		Occupational grouping	1695 census				1690–9 freemen All sources*	
			Freemen		Freemen plus servants			
Number	Per cent		Number	Per cent	Number	Per cent	Number	Per cent
204	51.0	Textiles	134	41.2	254	41.2	170	43.0
82	20.5	Leather	69	21.2	118	19.2	81	20.5
28	7.5	Metals	25	7.7	36	5.8	28	7.1
44	11.0	Distributive (except food)	30	9.2	76	12.3	33	8.4
22	5.5	Food	6	1.9	14	2.3	9	2.3
18	4.5	Services	27	8.3	65	10.6	36	9.1
1	—	Professions	12	3.7	19	3.1	13	3.3
—	—	Building trades and woodworking	22	6.8	34	5.5	25	6.3
399	100.0	Totals	325	100.0	616	100.0	395	100.0

* Includes freemen who died 1690–5 and apprentices who became free 1695–9. See Appendix, p. 124 for occupational classification.

significant under- or over-recording of masters in that trade. Taking a wider sample of freeman data for 1690–9 as a check (see Table 3, final column), the census would seem to present a generally convincing view of Kendal's occupational structure.

The 1695 source lists the male and female servants in each family, so that it is possible to measure the scale of resident wage labour in particular trades. Apprentices comprised 39 per cent of resident male servants, most of the rest were probably journeymen. The combined number of freemen and male servants was 487; in addition there were 129 female servants (important in the distributive and service trades). As we can see from Table 3 the rank order for each trade in percentage terms is the same for freemen and servants as for freemen only. Pound has observed a similar correlation in late sixteenth-century Norwich.[25]

Our freemen evidence for 1578 and 1695 has obvious limitations then for the study of the town economy. It does not tell us how freemen made their money. It underplays the contribution of the distributive sector and the economic role of women. But the sources seem reasonably accurate and provide comparable data for studying economic trends. We come to appreciate the value of the Kendal material when we try to estimate the numbers following a particular occupation in the adjoining countryside. Probate records, court cases, marriage bonds and parts of the 1695 census of Lonsdale ward in Westmorland indicate the presence of rural tradesmen, cloth-workers and leather and metalworkers.[26] But we never discover the scale of craft or trade activity in a parish at one time. In the case of shearmen, for example (see Figure 7), we cannot be sure of pinpointing all the places where they worked. There are thus considerable difficulties in detecting and evaluating rural developments.

At first sight the occupational evidence for the town seems to confirm the impression of stability afforded by the literary sources that we looked at above. Over the period the textile, leather, distributive and metal groups retained their relative importance. Yet this stability conceals not only a decline in the proportion of freemen in textiles, but, and most importantly, changes in the composition of all three manufacturing industries as Tables 4, 5 and 6 show. Production of the old draperies continued, but alongside them developed the manufacture of stuffs. In the leather industry the glovers and saddlers diminished in importance, although tanning continued and shoemakers thrived. The iron-based

Table 4   *Cloth-makers in Kendal*

c. 1578 Freemen	Occupational grouping	1695 Census freemen	1690–9 Freemen all sources*
165	Shearmen/ shearmen dyers	51	65
—	Stuffweavers	61	76
—	(Wool-combers)	3	3
—	(Stockiners)	2	3
165	Totals	117	147

* See note to Table 3.

hardwaremen declined in number and importance, while by 1695 pewter emerged to dominate the metalmen. We need now to establish the chronology of change between the late sixteenth and late seventeenth centuries and to try and explain the pattern of development.

III

Historians used to see economic change in sixteenth- and seventeenth-century towns as a balanced process in which some towns declined while others improved their position or even sprang up from nowhere. Most recent work has emphasized that the two centuries were a period of difficulty, summarized in Clark and Slack's epithet, 'Crisis and Order', although by no means all

Table 5   *Leather trades in Kendal*

c. 1578 Freemen Number	Per cent	Occupational grouping	1695 census Freemen Number	Per cent	1690–9 freemen: all sources* Number	Per cent
13	15.9	Tanners	9	13.0	12	14.8
—	—	Curriers	3	4.4	4	5.0
38	46.3	Cordwainers	40	58.0	44	54.3
8	9.8	Saddlers	3	4.4	3	3.7
23	28.0	Glovers	14	20.2	18	22.2
82	100.0	Totals	69	100.0	81	100.0

* See note to Table 3.

Table 6   *Metal trades in Kendal*

c. 1578 Freemen number	Occupational grouping	1695 census Freemen number	1690–9 freemen: All sources* number
8	Card-makers	4	4
—	Hook-maker	1	1
11 plus 2 foreign	Hardwaremen and armourers incl. whitesmiths (edges)	2	4
7	Blacksmiths	8	8
2	Pewterers, braziers, incl. whitesmiths (tinmen)	10	11
28 plus 2 foreign	Totals	25	28

* See note to Table 3.

scholars accept that misery was general and widespread.[27] Both sides of the current argument accept that population change both around and within towns was an important influence on urban prosperity.

The demographic history of Cumbria shows marked differences between the north and south of the region (see Table 7). In Cumberland a comparison of the population indicated by the 1563 diocesan enumeration with that given for each parish by Thomas Denton in 1688 points to an increase of 50 per cent.[28] The protestation returns for Cumberland parishes in the diocese of Carlisle demonstrate that this level had been reached by 1642, and fragmentary parish register evidence suggests that population growth was at its most vigorous before the last quarter of the sixteenth century.[29] For Westmorland and Furness no 1688 returns exist and the 1563 population count has to be compared with hearth tax data. In North Westmorland the hearth tax survey of 1675 indicates that the population had increased by 41 per cent since 1563, a trend parallel with that in Cumberland.[30] The picture in South Westmorland was much different, for here there may have been a decline of 16 per cent compared with 1563. Using the 1664 hearth tax records, Furness exhibits a rise of 3.5 per cent.[31]

Table 7   *Population of Cumbria*

	1563		1664		1674-5		1688	
	Households	Inhabitants*	Households	Inhabitants*	Households	Inhabitants*	Households	Inhabitants*
Cumberland**	8 935	42 441	—	—	—	—	13 277	63 066
Westmorland								
North	2 688	12 673	—	—	3 500	17 955†	—	—
South	4 121	19 575	—	—	3 208	16 457†	—	—
whole county	6 789	32 248	—	—	6 708	34 412†	—	—
Furness	2 091	9 932	2 157	10 246	—	—	—	—

* Numbers of inhabitants calculated by use of 4.75 multiplier.

** Excludes Alston.

† Adjusted upwards (by 8 per cent) to take account of tax exemptions.

The contraction observed in South Westmorland was marked in the area around Kendal.[32] The evidence for population change in the town of Kendal itself is more difficult to interpret. The 1695 census gives a reliable figure of around 2200[33] and the hearth tax returns of 1669–73 and 1675 point to a similar total shortly after the Restoration. This compares with estimates of a town population of between 2300 and 2600 for the last decade of the sixteenth and first decade of the seventeenth century, based on town lists of householders and muster returns. Somewhat earlier, a town tax return of 1576 suggests a figure as high as 3300.[34] This is a difficult source to construe and there is no supporting evidence, but the marked contraction of population which this implies for the end of the sixteenth century is not implausible.

Overall the population figures for Kendal argue that, during the seventeenth century, the demographic growth that occurred in the town was only just able to compensate for the ravages of famine and plague in 1597–8 and for the crisis mortality of 1623 (possibly caused by famine). Natural population growth probably played some part in the limited recovery after these crises. Unfortunately Kendal parish register is missing between 1631 and 1679 and, though there was a surplus of baptisms over burials from 1608 to 1622, it is unclear whether a surplus was maintained long afterwards: in 1629 and 1631 there were small deficits with burials exceeding baptisms. For the period 1679 to 1700 the total surplus of baptisms over burials was marginal.[35] What about immigration? In 1607 and 1615 immigration rates of 0.8 per cent and 1.4 per cent are indicated by a comparison of town lists, in addition to the admission of new apprentices. During the seventeenth century, however, immigration was restricted. The corporation tried to control the letting of rooms to poor tenants. Views of town wards of 1607 and 1615 and a poor law list in 1658 note strangers and suggest continuing vigilance against poor newcomers.[36] There does not seem to have been any campaign to restrict the number of apprentices taken and some traders and craftsmen were admitted to the freedom by special composition throughout the period.[37] But from evidence in 1670 it is clear that the town had been imposing settlement controls on immigrants.[38] Meagre natural growth and selective immigration may well help to explain the lack of population expansion in the seventeenth century. This scenario is accentuated if we place the town's population at 3300 in 1576, for in that case the long-term stability between c. 1590 and 1700 was preceded by a one-third fall in population in the last quarter of the sixteenth century.

A demographic reduction of this order could have important economic consequences, though the precise impact on the urban community might depend on the extent to which particular social groups were affected. There are signs at Kendal that the poorer classes suffered most from the demographic decline. Different records provide varying definitions of poverty so that changes in the proportion of inhabitants who were poor are not easy to determine. A survey of rents paid by those receiving alms in 1597–8 lists 182 heads of poor households[39] and there were other pauper families no doubt who were not rent-payers. In 1660 about sixty-four households (264 people) were in receipt of alms.[40] Even allowing that recipients of relief represented only a portion of the needy poor, the figures do suggest a possible decline in the incidence of poverty, though it has to be remembered that the 1597–8 evidence is affected by the economic crisis at that time. Another, cruder comparison can be made between those households who contributed nothing to the incorporation levy of 1576 (50 per cent),[41] and those householders listed as poor in the 1695 census (only 30 per cent);[42] in neither year were there any special economic difficulties at Kendal. If there was a reduction in the numbers of poor in the town, the economic impact may have been beneficial. Looked at in harsh economic terms, demand from the poor for craft products of the town was low, though poor relief in kind, for instance in the form of clothing, may have led to some sales of cloth and shoes. No less important, the declining numbers of poor decreased the supply of labour and perhaps improved the economic position of those who remained. Cloth-making in particular employed a considerable number of poor and to that industry we must now turn.

IV

Kendal and its hinterland in the later sixteenth century produced the same range of cloths, and were famed for their cottons, a cloth made from wool with a raised nap which gave it a frizzy or cottoned finish. In 1576 Kendal's new corporation established the town's gilds and there were no independent royal charter companies. The only cloth-making gild was the shearmen's company. Its ordinances were purely concerned with the dressing of cloth, that is preparation for fulling (but not fulling itself), stretching on tenters, and finishing. Between 1575 and 1636 the shearmen had control over all finished cloth in the town; and only they were entitled to finish cloth in the town. The preparation of wool and yarn, and the weaving of cloth were not regulated, and anyone could undertake them. There was no control over the quality of this work, except in so far as the shearmen had a general overview of the quality of finished cloth, and might then reject gross faults of workmanship in spinning or weaving. After 1636 the mayor was entitled by the town's new charter to appoint a searcher to check the quality of all cottons offered for sale in the town;[43] in practice this only made explicit the right of search in the shearmen's company ordinances approved by the corporation under the 1575 charter. The shearmen played almost no part in the national and international distribution of Kendal cloth, which was part of the trade of the town's mercers and chapmen. Finally the town's card-makers provided specialist tools for the textile industry.

Because spinning and weaving were not regulated by the corporation we have no indication from the lists of freemen of the number of townspeople who produced yarn and webbs for the market. The best evidence for such production comes from the content of probate inventories. To allow for production for household use, the surest guides to spinning and weaving for market are the presence in inventories of more than one wheel or pair of looms (discounting old and broken machines) and greater than average stocks of yarn or raw webbs. A few non-shearmen were cloth weavers on a large scale: the chapman Anthony Pearson with two looms and four spinning wheels comes to mind;[44] most tanners and glovers had substantial spinning and weaving interests. Outside the ranks of the freemen there were some widows and spinsters whose spinning and weaving capacity betokens production for market. The poet Richard Braithwaite, whose father had been recorder of Kendal from 1576 to 1610, wrote of 'poore men' who sold yarn or raw webbs to 'get one bit to eat or drop [to] suppe'.[45] In 1576 there may have been plenty of people in Kendal who could have fitted this description, but they would have been from a social stratum rarely illumined by our most useful sources, probate records and law suits.

Such workers created important employment for the shearmen; for example, the spinster Margaret Washington contracted the shearman Robert Carus to full, dress and sell her cloth.[46] But the shearmen themselves were rarely only cloth finishers; their inventories show that they also carded, spun and wove, and the non-freemen may therefore have represented competition for them.[47]

This was especially so for the small proportion of shearmen who were specialist weavers and not finishers at all. Table 8 summarizes this evidence. For specialist or non-specialist shearmen fixed costs were low for machines and tools; burgages provided room for workshops, storage and some tenters; common land on the fell provided more tentering. The Kendal shearmen seldom invested in fulling mills. Many seem to have worked on their own, although most took an apprentice at least once in their career; a few employed journeymen, for example John Potter, who owned a number of wheels, looms and shears, referred in his will to his four 'servants'.[48] This varied scale of activity was revealed in the wider range of wealth of shearmen compared with other town trades, as is attested by probate inventories.

The rural element of the Westmorland cloth industry at the end of the sixteenth century was composed of shearmen who, as lawsuits and probate records tell us, had work habits much like their Kendal counterparts; Figure 7 shows the main centres of rural manufacture about 1600.[49] Four important differences between the rural and urban industries are apparent. The first and fundamental difference was that the rural areas contained fulling mills,[50] but there were none in Kendal. Furthermore, between 1575 and 1700 only three instances can be documented of Kendal shearmen with an interest in fulling mills, while there is evidence of Kendal shearmen paying fullers to work their cloth. Here the rural industry had an important

Table 8   *Activities of shearmen from wills and inventories 1578–1700*

Activities	Number
Carding, spinning, weaving	9
Carding, spinning, weaving, dressing	34
Carding, spinning, weaving, dressing, dyeing	5
Weaving, dressing	12
Dressing	14
Dressing, dyeing	1
Dyeing	4
Weaving, dressing, dyeing	2
No details	20
Sample	101

Note: There is no chronological variation, except perhaps that the specialist dyers are a late seventeenth-century phenomenon.

advantage. Second, the town contained the specialist dyers. Evidence of rural dyeing is sparse, but if a century later the habits of the Fells of Swarthmore are an accurate guide, while the rural dyers were good enough to dye cloth for servants to wear, the gentry sent their goods to the skilled dyers of Kendal.[51] Third, rural shearmens' inventories are not characterized by the ownership of numbers of wheels or looms such as appear in Kendal probate data. The concentration of the urban shearmen's wealth was in their trade tools and goods, and few had significant agricultural interests to divert them from the workloft or shop. Cattle and crops represented a much larger proportion of the rural shearman's inventoried wealth, and occupied more of his or his family's time and effort. Finally, there is no evidence of the employment of apprentices or journeymen by rural shearmen.

Town and rural elements were therefore complementary. The town dominated dyeing, and the countryside controlled fulling. The townsmen had another advantage because the rural manufacturers came to sell their unfinished and finished cloth in Kendal. Kendal shearmen purchased unfinished cloth from rural weavers, and Kendal chapmen bought finished cloth from rural shearmen as well as, in both instances, from townsmen. Rural shearmen and chapmen also bought from townsmen. The rural shearmen thus enjoyed the reputation of the town's name and market when selling finished cloth provided they met the town's requirements of quality. From Kendal, town and country chapmen sold cloth throughout Britain, while chapmen from Scotland, Durham, Lancashire and Yorkshire (especially from Wakefield and Wensleydale), came to buy in the town. The details of Kendal's trade will be analysed on another occasion; for the present, Figure 8 shows where Kendal cloth was fed into the national and international markets.[52]

However by the late sixteenth century there were growing difficulties in Kendal's cloth markets. All but two of these markets can be shown to have declined in the course of our period. First Spain, then the home market (so far as literary evidence suggests, for there are no figures), then the Baltic, then France, all fell away. War, foreign competition and protectionism, and fashion struck at foreign markets. At home too, fashion was a major cause of change in demand. Sales to Scotland and Ireland, by contrast, appear to have persisted. Only one new market developed after the mid seventeenth century, and became important in the eighteenth century: the West Indies and North America. By the eighteenth

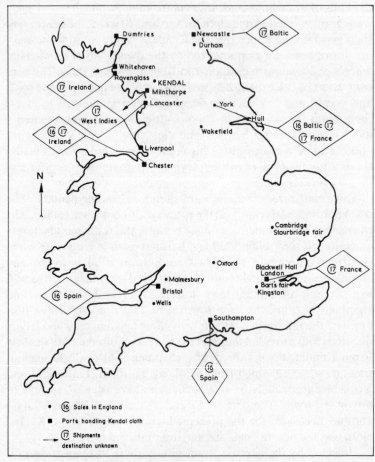

Figure 8 *Internal and foreign trade in Kendal cloth*

century Kendal and its surrounds were the specialists in cottons. But a century earlier, when pressure on the old draperies was at its greatest, Kendal cottons competed with 'Manchester cottons' and Welsh cottons. Welsh cottons, produced by a system that involved a clear division of labour (unlike in Westmorland), were of no better quality and more costly. The Lancashire industry was organized much like the Westmorland one, and until the industry moved over to the new draperies in the seventeenth century it posed a considerable threat.[53]

Competition in a contracting market meant that the old draperies could support fewer carders, spinners, weavers and shearmen. If Braithwaite was correct, poor migrants were most likely to work as carders and spinners for the old draperies. We have already seen that some of the non-freemen in the town who depended on cloth weaving were widows and spinsters, most of whom would be the first to feel any squeeze on the markets. Perceptive parents of migrant apprentices would not place their sons as shearmen. At three points, the 1590s, the 1620s and the 1630s, high food prices made the effects of this contraction more severe, and especially so for the poor. If famine was the main killer in 1597 and 1623, the numbers of poor would have fallen, and remained low since, as we have seen, the town did its best to keep out poor migrants.[54] New admissions to the Company of Shearmen declined more markedly in the first two decades of the seventeenth century than admissions to the town's other numerically larger trades. Those other trades recovered in the third decade, but admissions to the shearmen continued to plummet.[55] The essential structural links between urban and rural cloth-makers could not easily be changed, yet in a contracting market rural production of cloth, as opposed to finishing, meant more pressure on town producers. It is not surprising, therefore, that the townsmen developed a new cloth which did not depend on the rural locality either for raw materials or for finishing. The innovation was slow in coming, but by 1624 two of the shearmen were weaving linens. By 1637 there were enough of these new weavers to warrant the corporation listing separately those men who worked in linen or long staple wool.[56] Thirty years later even the local gentry recognized that something had changed in Kendal, and that new textiles were produced there. By the end of the century Kendal's new products were in demand in London. In 1710 the town's entrepreneurship was extolled by an anonymous Blackwell Hall factor who told how the high priced monopoly of the

Kidderminster weavers had let the Kendal men into the market. Kendal now produced good quality 'Kidderminster' at much cheaper prices.[57]

These new stuffweavers produced linsey-woolsey, all linen and all wool cloth. Hemp rather than flax was grown in Kendal's hinterland and certainly flax was brought to the town from Newcastle-on-Tyne by mercers and linen-drapers. This flax trade does not preclude the import of linen yarn, and there was a yarn market in the town. It does suggest that flax-dressing generated work for unskilled labour, and that women were needed to spin linen yarn. Town inventories such as that of Richard Stephenson, husbandman (d. 1676), show this dressing being carried out; the grocer John Mitchell (d. 1676) also dressed flax, or more likely his household did, as a by-employment.[58] Long staple wool was also used in the stuffs, but I have found no evidence of wool-combs in inventories. However, it is unlikely that the three wool-combers in the town in 1695 supplied all the stuffweavers and the worsted stocking knitting industry in the town. Those townsmen in the 1695 census (Table 3) not given an occupation and listed as poor, together with widows and single women, would have welcomed work as flax-dressers and spinners. Certainly the stuffweavers' inventories show that they bought their yarns. If the stuffweavers did not weave coloured yarn then coloured cloth was dyed in the piece. A few of the stuffweavers did their own dyeing, but others resorted to the shearmen-dyers, and indeed by the end of the century there were one or two men in the town who appeared to have concentrated on dyeing. The specialized stuffweavers severed two ties between Kendal and its surrounds: their new draperies were not fulled, and their raw materials came from outside the region. Stocking knitting was another new venture, but the knitters are more shadowy figures compared to the stuffweavers whose trade is revealed in their inventories. According to a visiting clergyman in 1692, the town's poor children were stocking-makers.[59] The rise of stocking knitting to commercial importance in Kendal was definitely an eighteenth-century phenomenon.[60]

The extent to which the new draperies had succeeded in diversifying Kendal's cloth-making industry by 1695 is measured in Table 4. The new stuffweavers ensured that textiles remained the dominant industry of the town. Some stuffweavers were listed as poor in 1695, but probate records show others to have been modestly successful. Inventories suggest that among the shearmen wealth was polarized at the end of the century compared to the beginning: in the later part of the seventeenth century there were poor shearmen and wealthy shearmen, but fewer in between.

Two questions immediately come to mind about rural cloth-making in the period after the appearance of stuffweaving in Kendal: how did the manufacture of cottons fare, and were stuffs made in the countryside too? Evidence to answer both questions is scarce. Cottons continued to be made throughout the seventeenth century but we can only speculate about the numbers of shearmen, and the level of output. A possible clue is the number of fulling mills which appear to be decayed; other mills became bloomery forges.[61] Is this necessarily evidence of surplus fulling capacity and therefore of contraction? If it is, did the loss of rural or Kendal business cause it? 'Country stuffs', 'linseys' and 'druggets' were subject to toll in Kendal between 1685 and 1690, but the chamberlains' accounts reveal nothing of the nature of these cloths. The tolls, together with complaints from the Kendal stuffweavers to Parliament in 1702 that unapprenticed labour outside the town made low quality goods, suggest that cloths other than the old draperies were made in the countryside.[62] A search of the probate records of known rural weavers, and a sample survey of probate records for Kendal and Furness Deaneries suggests very strongly that these 'country' cloths were, however, quite different from the products of the Kendal stuffweavers. The variety of fibres and colours characteristic of Kendal was lacking. Cloth seems to have been woven in very small amounts, not for market but for domestic use. Harden sheets and sacks made from hemp predominate (for farm and industrial uses, for example, in the iron industry). These coarse hemp-based products were not an innovation for they can be traced in the sixteenth and early seventeenth centuries.[63] Nor were they the origins of the town's stuffs, since the first Kendal stuffweavers did not come from the town's hinterland. 'Country' stuffs do not, therefore, appear to have compensated the countryside for any contraction in the rural production of old draperies, though some recompense may have come from the developing yarn trade between Westmorland and Norwich.[64]

V

The number of freemen cloth-workers in 1578 and 1695 exceeds those in the leather and metal industries put together. Nevertheless, as we can see from Tables 3 and 4, the proportion of freemen involved in leather and metal occupations was marginally greater in the late seventeenth century and there are signs that the two trades were becoming relatively more important in the town's economy. If we look at the leather industry first, we can see a marked decline in the numbers of saddlers and glovers. On the other hand, there is independent evidence of an increase in leather-working in the town. In 1684 Kendal petitioned for a new charter and asked for a new market toll on hides:[65] the following decade Celia Fiennes remarked that 'a great deale of leather is tanned here'.[66] Leather was the only commodity (besides textiles) which she thought important enough to note and she was the earliest commentator on Kendal to mention it. In 1695 the tanner, alderman William Wilson, was a wealthy townsman and only one of the other Kendal tanners was classed as poor.[67] There were rural tanners in the well-coppiced Furness Fells and in droving centres such as Killington.[68] But if, as in the past, they sold in Kendal, they do not appear to have harmed their urban counterparts, while the town shoemakers may have benefited from the extra supplies of country leather.

Kendal had forty shoemakers in 1695 (only a minority of whom were poor) and the Cordwainers' company sought to limit competition from foreigners in the market. Among their rural competitors were three shoemakers at Killington, while Sir Daniel Fleming's household accounts make frequent reference to the Rydal shoemaker. On the other hand, Fleming had his own shoes made in Kendal, not Rydal, so the town triumphed over the country opposition at least at the top end of the market.[69] Nevertheless, the village shoemaker William Denney appears from his inventory to have enjoyed much the same standard of living as his urban counterparts.[70]

Rural competition may account for the declining number of saddlers in Kendal, for important customers such as the carriers were not based in the town but in the country. The number of town glovers had sunk to seven in 1687; in that year they had to call on the mayor to support their claim to the best standings in the market. The less skilled art of leather dressing by which the glovers prepared their leather was suitable for a dual economy, and may have been followed in the countryside.[71] Those town glovers who sold by retail were competing with the town mercers who also sold purses and gloves. If the number of saddlers and glovers declined because of rural competition, the better survival of tanners and shoemakers may witness the recognition by Kendal men of a direction in which to specialize.[72]

VI

As for the metal trades, the activities of the freemen, if not their numbers, had changed noticeably by 1695. In the sixteenth and early seventeenth centuries Kendal had an important distribution trade throughout South Westmorland in bar iron and iron artefacts, which chapmen brought to the town from outside the region. The Kendal hardwaremen's inventories show that they were distributors as well as artisans; they had to compete for the retail trade with their chapmen suppliers, with merchants who landed cargoes of iron and ironware at West Cumbrian ports, and with specialists such as the Hornblower family of scythesmiths from Worcestershire who sold in the town.[73] Even so, in the early seventeenth century the Kendal hardwareman Edward Adamson was sufficiently confident of his position to have shops in the smaller market towns of Penrith and Kirkby Lonsdale.[74] His confidence was widely shared for the hardwaremen admitted to their gild a number of foreigners who lived outside Kendal but kept a shop there.[75] The Cumbrian iron smelting industry rose rapidly after the first decade of the seventeenth century, and its competition greatly reduced the Kendal trade. Until the last quarter of the century no Kendal metalmen had any controlling interest in the smelters.[76]

The smelting industry struck at the hardwaremen's trade because it sold bar iron direct to customers, from blacksmiths to gentry, who previously had purchased their iron in Kendal. The smelters enabled the early establishment in Kendal's hinterland of plant to manufacture and sell artefacts such as edge tools, hitherto an important part of the hardwaremens' stock in trade. Not until 1661 was a scythe mill for edge tools built in Kendal, by which time the decline of the old draperies had depressed demand for edge tools such as shears.[77] As the smelters prospered the Kendal men's shops in the outlying smaller market towns gradually disappeared. Instead, by the later seventeenth century in market towns like Burton-in-Kendal, Kirkby Lonsdale and Cockermouth, all towns at some distance from the concentration of smelting sites, hardware shops were owned by local men.[78] Not only did these shops compete in areas of Cumbria where Kendal men might still have hoped to trade in iron, they effectively took over the trade in the supply of iron and artefacts hitherto dominated by Kendal.

Yet the difficulties of the hardwaremen were compensated for in the town's economy by the growing number of pewter and brass workers, especially pewterers; in the last quarter of the seventeenth century the hardwareman Richard Washington even diversified into pewter. While Wigan remained the prime provincial centre of the pewter industry, Kendal men developed a modest expertise with the alloy which was recognized throughout Cumbria.[79] There were two pewterers in Kendal in *c.* 1578 who joined with most of the other metalmen in a common gild; the card-makers were the only metalworkers to enjoy a separate gild. The number of pewterers may have increased gradually, but the admission to the freedom of Kendal in 1619, by special composition, of Richard Forth a pewterer from Wigan, marked the start of a wealthy magisterial dynasty in the town. We can see from the debts in the probate inventory of Richard's son James how a trade over the whole of Cumbria had developed; many of his customers were gentry. In 1683 when he died the wealthy pewterer William Cookeson owned a shop in Penrith as well as one in Kendal.[80] The pewter/brass trades, which in Kendal as in other provincial towns were clearly intertwined, appear to have included a large share of the wealthy metalworkers in town. The Kendal pewterers of course had to compete with London pewter, and with the work of men in Penrith and Carlisle. The prosperity demonstrated by Kendal inventories and the rise in the number of masters suggests a thriving trade. That this was so was confirmed in 1662 when a separate pewterers gild with sixteen members was established by Kendal corporation.[81]

VII

Metal manufacturers and distributors such as Edward Adamson and William Cookeson were not the only group of Kendal traders with shops in the market towns around Kendal. In the late sixteenth century a number of Kendal chapmen and mercers owned such establishments. We may surmise that these shops had two uses for Kendal men: first, they secured trade with rural customers who might otherwise have been lost to retailers and wholesalers based outside the towns; second, such shops gave them a presence in the smaller markets. Those chapmen and mercers based outside Kendal and engaged in the long distance cloth trade no doubt distributed their return cargoes of wine, dyestuffs and luxury goods wholesale through the smaller market towns, as well as in Kendal itself. The trade of such men as the Lockey family of Strickland Kettel, *habitués* of the Brokerage Hall in Southampton in the later sixteenth century,[82] or of the early seventeenth century chapman

Miles Dawson of Crosthwaite,[83] represented considerable competition for the Kendal men. Itinerant pedlars sold goods door to door through the dales which the countryfolk might otherwise have bought in Kendal. It has to be said that some pedlars were supplied by Kendal shopkeepers, but others, especially Scotsmen, seem to have operated independently.[84] Rural tradesmen did not only represent competition for townsmen by sales in the countryside, direct to country customers, they also sold in the town. Miles Dawson sold frequently both retail and wholesale in Kendal. Such sales by countrymen were a longstanding problem, which Parliament had tried to legislate for in 1555 with 'An Act that persons dwelling in the Countrye shall not sell divers wares in Cities and Towns corporate by Retaile.'[85] Kendal's second charter of 1636 included a new provision to prevent pedlars selling in the borough.[86] But the 1555 Act specifically permitted rural men to sell wholesale in towns, including market towns, and exempted any who were free of a corporation or gild. Miles Dawson was just such a person, a freeman of Kendal who had served as one of the town's chamberlains but who later resided outside it.[87] The woollen draper William Jennings of Stricklandfield may be cited as a later seventeenth-century example.[88]

The withdrawal of Kendal-owned shops from the small market towns may represent a loss of opportunity for Kendal traders and a gain for their competitors. On the other hand, by the 1650s Kendal men were beginning to supply goods to traders in small market towns such as Hawkshead.[89] This may mark the emergence of Kendal as a wholesale distribution centre for surrounding towns in a move towards more sophisticated marketing arrangements. But the small market towns still retained direct connections with London. Egremont on the West Cumberland coast had a London carrier in the 1670s who did not pass through Kendal.[90] Penrith was on the Carlisle–London road. Kirkby Lonsdale sat astride Kendal's main route to London and made use of it. The shop stock of the mercer James Backhouse of Kirkby Lonsdale, who died in 1578, or of the apothecary John Baynes, who died in 1696, were as comprehensive in range and quality as any Kendal shop. Baynes used the Kendal carrier to obtain his goods from London.[91]

If the evidence of outside visitors is taken, Dalton, Ulverston, Kirkby Lonsdale and Penrith seem to have retained and enjoyed prosperity within Kendal's region during our period.[92] Among the small market towns we have seen Kendal men supplying shops at

Hawkshead in the later seventeenth century; Blome described the market there as 'little'.[93] The refounding of the market at Flookburgh near Cartmel in 1663 to add to that of Cartmel itself, and the grant of new charters to Orton and Ambleside (1650s) and Burton-in-Kendal (Charles II) may have posed a threat to Kendal's trade. Even in tiny Burton there was one well-stocked shop, that of Thomas Greenhud.[94] Ambleside's market for wool and yarn appears to have been successful. Yet none of these places were really of a size to merit the term town, and their futures were shaky. Flookburgh failed very quickly, Cartmel was only significant for food and fish. In 1695, thirty years after the grant of its charter, Burton was still a hamlet. Further away from Kendal the rise of Whitehaven, which was not well connected by road to Kendal, probably did Kendal no harm, and Egremont and Cockermouth remained prosperous. Keswick, a small market in Leland's time, benefited from the copper works but they had closed by 1640, and Blome found the town decayed in 1673.[95] In the long term Kendal survived unscathed by these innovations.

VIII

Manufacturers comprised a major proportion of Kendal's freemen in our period, and widows and spinsters made up an additional group in cloth-making. The whole manufacturing sector was proportionately larger than those of the more important Gloucestershire towns in the early seventeenth century. Like them Kendal also had important distribution and service sectors.[96] The relationship between the manufacturing and trading sectors of Kendal's economy and the countryside around the town changed as the town specialized in new products in response to pressure on its ancient products and trade. In the sixteenth century there had been co-operation between the town and country in textiles. In part this co-operation was a relationship determined by manufacturing and trading needs: the town depended on the country for wool and fulling; the rural shearmen on the town's market and reputation as well as the town's skilled dyers. But co-operation extended beyond these technical and commercial needs. The 1575 charter of incorporation did not signal an attempt by the town to discriminate against countrymen. Townsmen and countrymen combined to beat the aulnager's exactions, when either could easily have tried to obtain advantage by supporting the aulnager.[97] The harmony between town and country did not stem from a qualitative difference in their product; urban and rural cottons were of the same quality. If they had differed in standard then town and country could have aimed at different consumers and thus avoided competition. In fact rural and urban men bought and sold from each other in Kendal market, demonstrating a sameness of quality.

The contraction of the market for old draperies brought hard times. The townsmen were specialist craftsmen and traders who certainly had little agricultural involvement beyond a cow although some richer traders had landed estates. The rural shearmen could fall back on their agricultural resources: in the later seventeenth century sales of Cumbrian wool outside the region grew, and the demand for cattle, which suffered a setback with the destruction of the Irish livestock trade in the 1660s, was maintained by a rising trade in Scottish cattle.[98] The old relationship survived this period of contraction, cottons were still made in the nineteenth century, and town and country continued to co-operate in old draperies throughout our period. There is no doubt that the mortality crises between 1587 and 1623, and the downturn of population associated with these crises, eased the economic difficulty. When fewer cloths were wanted, there were fewer people to make them. Nevertheless, the 1636 Kendal charter, with its provisions for a searcher of cottons made outside Kendal, might have signalled an attempt to discriminate against rural cloth. If so, nothing seems to have come of it.

Instead, the townsmen developed new products, and in the later seventeenth and early eighteenth centuries their innovations in textiles involved little interrelationship with Kendal's hinterland. The raw materials of the stuffs came from outside the region, and no finishing at fulling mills was needed. Nevertheless, in the long run this weakening of town and country bonds proved short-lived. Already in the later seventeenth century stocking knitters were at work in the town. The rapid growth of this industry reforged the relationship between town and country, through the use of rural labour. When Arthur Young visited Kendal he noted the use of wage-earners from outside the town in the industry.[99]

Pressure from country leather-workers, especially on glovers, may have led to a reduction in leather dressing in the town. But shoemaking and tanning thrived. The urban shoemakers provided for the high class demand in the rural market. They could not survive on this alone and must have made shoes for peasants in competition with village shoemakers as well. Any impact of rural leather-work on the town is much less clearly demonstrated than the effect which the growing Cumbrian iron smelting industry had on the town's craftsmen–traders in metals. After the rise of the smelters the dominant group of town metalmen worked and traded in pewter.

A number of metal traders were among those Kendal tradesmen whose shops in the market towns of the region passed into local hands. There is evidence in the case of Hawkshead of Kendal men supplying shops in that town, and developing a market hierarchy. However, it is not clear that the long-established market towns had begun to decline before 1700 in response to Kendal's development as a centre for trade, professional services and social intercourse.[100] On the other hand, those places granted a new market in the last half of the century never posed a serious threat to Kendal's economic well-being.[101] To paraphrase Braudel, in the late six-teenth century the townsmen let rural traders get on with their trade, just as they allowed the country craftsmen to manufacture. When adverse conditions in national and international cloth markets changed rural colleagues into something more akin to competitors, when rural shopkeepers, retailers and wholesalers appeared, and when rural iron works threatened the town's place in the regional iron trade, economic decline in Kendal was avoided not by attempts to disadvantage rural craftsmen, but by the develop-ment of manufacturing specialisms which were not duplicated outside the town.

Appendix   Occupations in 1578 and 1695**

Occupations are grouped together in Table 3 as set out in Tables 4–6, with the addition of tailors and *hatters* to the textile group. Occupations not specified in Tables 4–6 were grouped as follows:

Distributive: Chapmen,† mercers, merchants, *petty-chapmen*, *chandlers*, *wool-staplers*.

Food:‡   Butchers, *maltsters*.

Services: Innkeepers,+ alehousekeepers, *barbers*, *wig-makers*,* *farriers*,* *tobacco spinners*,* *coopers*, *fletchers*,* *musicians*, *apothecaries*.

Professions: *Clergy*, lawyers, *physicians*, *surgeons*, *govern-ment officials* (for example, excise officer), *town officials* (for example, bailiff).

Labourers	i.e., day-labourers, exempt from the duty; perhaps poor.
Building trades:	Slaters, glaziers, plumbers, joiners, carpenters, masons, wallers, limeburners.

Notes

** The classification for the 1690s follows the same principles.

‡ Two women bakers listed in the census were not free.

⁺ Includes women free.

* There was only one practitioner in these trades.

† In the North of England in the sixteenth and early seventeenth centuries chapmen were substantial merchants, whereas in the South they were pedlars. The term chapman is replaced by merchant and/or mercer in the course of the seventeenth century in so far as it relates to a man of substance. The chapmen in the 1695 census were akin to pedlars.

Trades indicated in italics not found *c*. 1578.

Acknowledgements

Some of the ideas behind this paper were first ordered in a short paper to the Northern History Conference at Leeds in 1981 and were further developed in a paper to the Pre-Modern Towns Group at London. The present version was given to seminars at the universities of Adelaide and Oxford. I have benefited greatly from those four discussions and also from the comments of my fellow authors in this volume. I should also like to thank the Cumbria County Record Offices for their help, and also the Cumbria County Library Service. The Lancashire Record Office greatly facilitated my work on probate records. Part of the material used in this paper was collected with the aid of a grant from the Social Science Research Council.

Notes and references

1 William Farrer, *Records . . . of Kendale*, edited by J. F. Curwen, (Cumberland and Westmorland Antiquarian and Archaeological Society (hereafter CWAAS), record series, **4–5** 1923–4) (vol. 1), pp. 2, 6, 9, 15, 319, 357. There is no full history of the Westmorland cloth

industry, but see the present author's forthcoming work on Kendal. See the pamphlet by M. Davies-Shiel, *Wool is my bread* (1975); and M. L. Armitt, 'Fullers and freeholders in Grasmere', *Trans. CWAAS*, new series, **8** (1908), which now needs revision. How, if at all, did the region's only other cloth, the 'Carptmeales' made around Cartmel in Furness referred to in 4 Jas. I c. 2 differ from Kendal cloths?

2 1 & 2 P. & M. c. 7; D. W. Woodward, 'The background to the Statute of Artificers: the genesis of labour policy, 1558–63', *EcHR*, 2nd series, **33** (1980), p. 35; J. Patten, 'Patterns of migration and movement of labour to three pre-industrial East Anglian towns', in J. Patten (ed.), *Pre-Industrial England* (1979), p. 146.

3 J. Thirsk, *Economic Policy and Projects* (1978), p. 108.

4 R. S. Ferguson (ed.), *The Boke off Recorde of Kirkbie Kendall* (CWAAS, extra series, **7** 1892), p. 305. Kirkland, a contiguous part of the built-up area, which contains Kendal's parish church, was not incorporated in 1575. Kendal corporation quickly developed an easy relationship with Kirkland, for example, ibid., p. 218. Hereafter all discussion and figures exclude Kirkland unless otherwise indicated.

5 F. Braudel, *Capitalism and Material Life 1400–1800* (1973), pp. 378–9.

6 Thirsk, *Economic Policy*, pp. 109, 117.

7 G. D. Ramsay, 'The report of the Royal Commission on the Clothing Industry, 1640', *EHR*, **57** (1942), p. 491.

8 P. J. Corfield, 'Urban development in England and Wales in the sixteenth and seventeenth centuries', in D. C. Coleman and A. H. John (eds.), *Trade, Government and Economy in Pre-Industrial England* (1976), p. 221.

9 The sources and methods detailed in Notes 28 and 30 below suggest that the population of Appleby town in 1675 was about 821; no figure can be calculated for 1563. See also E. Hughes (ed.), *Fleming – Senhouse Papers* (1961), pp. 17–19. Corfield does not discuss Carlisle but see D. and S. Lysons, *Magna Britannia* (1816), vol. 4 pp. xxxvii–xxxviii. For Whitehaven see Corfield, 'Urban development in England and Wales', p. 245.

10 Corfield, ibid., p. 224, suggests a population of near 5000 by 1700. For 1664 B. G. Blackwood calculated only 950 from the hearth tax (x 4.5), in *The Lancashire Gentry and the Great Rebellion 1640–60* (Chetham Soc., 3rd series, **25** 1978), p. 8.

11 For the market towns see above, pp. 121–2. For roads see B. P. Hindle, 'Medieval roads in the diocese of Carlisle', *Trans. CWAAS*, new series, **77** (1977), pp. 91–3.

12 L. T. Smith (ed.), *The Itinerary of John Leland*, vol. 5 (1964), p. 46.

13 *Letters and Papers of the Reign of Henry VIII*, vol. 5 pp. 445, 453; vol. 6, pp. 139, 144, 661; vol. 21, part 2, p. 269.

14 ibid., vol. 5 pp. 749, 750.

15   C. W. and P. Cunnington, *Handbook of English Costume in the Sixteenth Century* (1954), p. 199. Kendal cottons may often be included as 'Northern cottons' in port books.

16   William Camden, *Britain*, trans. by P. Holland (1610), p. 759; C. Fiennes, *Through England on a side saddle* (1885), p. 159.

17   Richard Braithwaite, *The English Gentleman* (1630), pp. 125–6.

18   How do we classify Sandes? For his career see C. B. Phillips, 'County committees and local government in Cumberland and Westmorland, 1642–1660', *Northern History*, **5** (1970), pp. 42, 56, 63 (where I mistakenly call him a mercer); Ferguson, *Boke off Recorde*, p. 72; PRO, SP 28/216; Cumbria Record Office, Carlisle (hereafter CRO, Carlisle), Leconfield MSS, D/Lec, Correspondence, 169/1654; Cumbria Record Office, Kendal (hereafter CROK), Dallam Tower MSS, He4/37; Lancs. RO, Kendal deanery wills, Thomas Sandes pr. 1681.

19   For this controversy see J. Patten, 'Urban occupations in pre-industrial England', *Trans. Institute of British Geographers*, new series, **2** (1977); J. Pound, 'The validity of the freemen's lists: some Norwich evidence', *EcHR*, 2nd series, **34** (1981).

20   CROK, Kendal Corporation MSS, WD/MBK, Book of Record, 1575. See the appendix for the occupational structure used.

21   Rowland Sheffield and William Overend: Ferguson, *Boke off Recorde*, p. 76; *Kendal Parish Register, II* (CWAAS Parish Register Section 1922), p. 123; CROK, WD/MBK, Chamberlains' Accounts 1583, fol. 13.

22   Ferguson, *Boke off Recorde*, p. 81; *Kendal Parish Register, II*, pp. 173, 209.

23   C. B. Phillips, 'The population of the borough of Kendal in 1576', *Trans. CWAAS*, new series, **81** (1981), p. 59.

24   CROK, Fleming of Rydal MSS, D/Ry, box 32. The census can be compared with WD/MBK, book of (apprenticeship) indentures enrolled; the Cordwainer's book; and WD/Ag, the Cordwainer's book.

25   Pound, 'The validity of freemen's list', p. 58.

26   Probate Records: Lancs. RO, Archdeaconry of Richmond (WRW), Deaneries of Kendal, Furness and Lonsdale, *passim*, hereafter cited by initial letter of deanery and year of probate; court cases: CROK, WD/MBK, court rolls, 1579–1670 (few after 1640) (hereafter referred to as KCR, with term and year); CROK, WD/Ry, box 32; J. Brownbill (ed.), *Marriage Bonds for the deaneries of Lonsdale, Kendal, Furness and Copeland* (Record Soc. Lancashire and Cheshire, **84** 1920).

27   *Urban History Yearbook: 1979* (1979), pp. 60–76. P. Clark and P. Slack (eds.), *Crisis and Order in English Towns, 1500–1700* (1972).

28   For the whole of Cumbria the 1563 figures are BL, Harl. MS 594, fols. 85–7, 104–6. (Printed in summary in A. B. Appleby, *Famine in Tudor and Stuart England* (1978), Appendix A, for Cumberland (less the

parish of Alston, which I have excluded) and Westmorland. I have followed Appleby's estimates for the six missing Cumberland parishes, and added 372 households to Kendal parish for the chapelries as enumerated in the MS, but which Appleby appears to omit. For Cumberland in 1688: Lysons, *Magna Britannia*, pp. xxxv–xliv (Denton's figures are multiples of five, and the number of households can thus be identified). I have used a multiple of 4.75 to convert households to people.

29   Appleby, *Famine in Tudor and Stuart England*, pp. 27, 30–32.

30   The 1675 survey for all of Westmorland except Kendal and Kirkland is in CROK, WD/Ry, box 28, MS R. For Kendal and Kirkland see CROK, WD/MBK, HMC A9. The 1675 Kendal exemption certificates include the names of people not in the survey, although most of those exempted were included in the survey. The 8 per cent correction made in Table 7 adds non-rate payers exempted to the Westmorland total at the level found for Kendal. This is almost certainly an undercorrection. For this point see Philip Styles' introduction, pp. lxxiii, lxxvi–lxxxiv, in M. Walker (ed.), *Warwick County Records. Hearth Tax Returns, I* (1957). The figures in Table 7 differ from those calculated by Dr Appleby from a combination of the 1669 assessment and 1673 exemptions, Appleby, *Famine in Tudor and Stuart England*, Appendix A.

31   PRO, E 179/250/11.

32   E. A. Wrigley and R. S. Schofield, *The Population History of England 1541–1871* (1981), pp. 208–9, shows that it is South Westmorland and Furness which are out of step with their national trend.

33   CROK, WD/Ry, box 32.

34   For the sixteenth century evidence see Phillips, 'Population'.

35   In the late seventeenth century the number of Quakers and Presbyterians in the town of Kendal, as opposed to the parish, was small. Study of their vital records is difficult because it is not always clear who lived in the town. Counting known Kendalians, and allowing for some Quaker events recorded in the parish register, total burials exceed baptisms in the 1680s, and are in rough balance in the 1690s (CROK, Kendal Meeting Records, Digests).

36   Ferguson, *Boke off Recorde*, p. 102; CROK, WD/MBK, HMC A8; WD/MBK, unlisted views of wards, 1658, 1660.

37   Ferguson, *Boke off Recorde*, pp. 77, 93, 137, 140; cf. ibid., p. 164.

38   CROK, WD/MBK, list of town bonds, 1670. They cover arrivals in the 1660s and perhaps earlier.

39   CROK, WD/MBK, HMC, A8.

40   CROK, WD/MBK, unlisted view of wards, 1660.

41   Ferguson, *Boke off Recorde*, pp. 1–17; Phillips, 'Population', p. 59.

42   CROK, WD/Ry, box 32.

43   Ferguson, *Boke off Recorde*, passim.

Right 11–13 High Street, Totnes, in *c*. 1884

Below 26 and 28 High Street, Totnes (third and fourth houses from the left)

Above The Assembly Rooms, York, *c*. 1732 The Great Assembly Room from the south-west.

Below *The Cockpit* by Hogarth, 1759

44 Lancs. RO, WRW/K, pr. 1591.

45 Richard Braithwaite, *Strappado for the Divell*, edited by J. W. Ebsworth, (Boston 1878), pp. 193–5.

46 KCR, Easter 1584.

47 Lancs. RO, Kendal Deanery Wills. Shearmen's probate records were detected by examining probates for names from the shearmen's gild list, and then by the presence of a trade name, or of finishing tools. This method may underrepresent shearmen who were not finishers.

48 Lancs. RO, WRW/K, pr. 1615.

49 Figure 7 is based on cases in KCR. The rural industry was not in general decline at this point in time, although Armitt (see Note 1) may be correct in pointing to a decline in Grasmere. Dr Thirsk at first accepted the fact of its decline, but never Armitt's explanations. J. Thirsk, 'Industries in the countryside', in F. J. Fisher (ed.), *Essays in the Economic and Social History of Tudor and Stuart England* (1961), p. 81; J. Thirsk (ed.), *Agrarian History of England and Wales: IV* (1965), p. 21.

50 Davies-Shiel, *Wool is my bread*, pp. 21–5; Armitt, 'Fullers and free-holders', pp. 138–59; Farrer, *Records . . . of Kendal*, vols. 1 and 2 *passim*. J. Somervell, *Water Power Mills of South Westmorland* (1930).

51 N. Penney (ed.), *The Household Account Book of Sarah Fell of Swarthmore* (1920), pp. 17, 123, 293, 423, 453, 471, 493, 497.

52 I will provide inquirers with detailed references to the probate records, law suits, port books and secondary authorities on which the comments on trade, and Figure 8, are based.

53 T. C. Mendenhall, *The Shrewsbury Drapers and the Welsh Wool Trade in the seventeenth century* (1952), pp. 24, 28, 48; N. Lowe, *The Lancashire Textile Industry in the sixteenth century* (Chetham Soc., 3rd series, **20** 1972), pp. 64–70, 99; A. P. Wadsworth and J. de L. Mann, *The Cotton Trade and Industrial Lancashire 1600–1780* (1931), pp. 1–23.

54 See above, p. 109; also CROK, WD/MBK Town Quarter Sessions records, 1614.

55 Ferguson, *Boke off Recorde*, pp. 49–81, 258–73.

56 ibid., pp. 79, 268.

57 Hughes, *Fleming*, p. 7; T. Machel, *An Antiquary on Horseback*, edited by J. M. Ewbank (CWAAS, extra series, **19** 1963), pp. 60–1; *Journal of the Commissioners for Trade and the Plantations 1708/9–1714/15*, pp. 154–5 (I owe this reference to Peter Large).

58 F. Dendy (ed.), *Extracts from the Records of the Merchant Adventurers of Newcastle-upon-Tyne: I* (Surtees Soc., **93** 1897), p. 137; KCR, Easter 1640. LRO, WRW/K, pr. 1676.

59 Machel, *An Antiquary on Horseback*, p. 61. Richard Blome, *Britannia* (1673) p. 235, suggests that all the Kendal innovations helped the poor. He notices worsted stocking knitting in Kendal and Kirkby Stephen (p. 237).

60   J. D. Marshall, 'Kendal in the late seventeenth and eighteenth centuries', *Trans. CWAAS*, new series, **75** (1975), pp. 210–11. cf. Thirsk, *Agrarian History*, p. 21. Sir Daniel Fleming (Hughes, *Fleming*, p. 17) writing in 1671 noted the industry in and around Kirkby Stephen in North Westmorland, but not in Kendal.

61   For bloomery forges see, C. B. Phillips, 'William Wright: Cumbrian ironmaster', *Trans. Lancashire and Cheshire Antiquarian Soc.*, **79** (1977), p. 37; for decayed mills see sources in Note 50 above.

62   CROK, WD/MBK, chamberlains' accounts. (This new toll may be associated with that on apples and hides asked for in 1684 with Charles II's charter – below, p. 118 – and which was also collected in these years. All Kendal's tolls were usually farmed to one person. Because some half dozen prominent tradesmen, rather than the one lessee, pay these tolls I wonder if the manufactures so taxed have been 'put-out' by them to country people, so that the toll payers are paying on their own goods? If so, this would mark another change in Kendal's relationship with its hinterland. More evidence is needed on this question.) *Commons Journals*, **13**, p. 747.

63   Lancs. RO, Kendal and Furness Deaneries, 2 per cent statistically random sample survey. See also J. D. Marshall, 'Agrarian wealth and social structure in pre-industrial Cumbria', *EcHR*, 2nd series, **33** (1980), p. 515; and J. D. Marshall, 'The domestic economy of the Lakeland yeoman, 1660–1749', *Trans. CWAAS*, new series, **73** (1973), pp. 195–6. My sample includes the weaver George Fell for whose activities see Penney, *The Household Account Book, passim*. For late sixteenth- and early seventeenth-century evidence of these products see, for example, Lancs. RO, WRW/F Christopher Nicholson, pr. 1577 and sources cited in Note 76 below.

64   Patten, 'Urban occupations', p. 153.

65   R. S. Ferguson, *A History of Westmorland* (1885), pp. 178–9.

66   Fiennes, *Through England on a side saddle*, p. 159.

67   Lancs. RO, WRW/K, pr. 1717.

68   For example, those who purchased bark from Coniston forge *c.* 1674–94, CROK, WD/Ry, Coniston forge book; Lancs. RO, WRW/F Wm. Fleming pr. 1697.

69   CROK, WD/Ry box 32; WD/Ry Sir Daniel Fleming's account books.

70   Lancs. RO, WRW/F, pr. 1681.

71   CROK, WD/MBK, HMC A16. Outside London and Worcester in the seventeenth century there was such 'putting-out', L. A. Clarkson, 'The organisation of the English leather industry in the late sixteenth and seventeenth centuries', *EcHR*, 2nd series, **13** (1960), pp. 251–2.

72   The hypothesis that light leather-work was more suited to the countryside finds a little support in the 1660 Poll Tax return for the Norwich Hundred of Cheshire. Light leather-workers were more in evidence in

the countryside than tanners, but there was a scattering of rural shoe-makers. Even so, the four market towns of the hundred contained four more light leather-workers than the rest of the hundred. In all 73 per cent of the hundred's leather-workers were in these towns. See G. O. Lawton (ed.), *Northwich Hundred Poll Tax and Hearth Tax of 1664* (Record Soc. Lancashire and Cheshire, **119** 1979), pp. 25–199.

73 For example, CRO Carlisle, Earl of Lonsdale's MSS, D/Lons/W, Sir Patricius Curwen's account book; PRO, E 112/47/1; KCR, Easter 1591, Easter 1601, Easter 1602.

74 Lancs. RO, WRW/K, pr. 1623.

75 Ferguson, *Boke off Recorde*, pp. 21, 72.

76 C. B. Phillips, 'The Cumbrian iron industry in the seventeenth century', in W. H. Chaloner and B. M. Ratcliffe (eds.), *Trade and Transport. Essays in Economic History in Honour of T. S. Willan* (1977), p. 3; Lancs. RO, Sandys MSS, DDSa 2/7.

77 H. R. Schubert, *History of the British Iron and Steel Industry* (1958), p. 191; CROK, WD/MBK, unlisted indenture *re* town mills, 1661.

78 Lancs. RO, WRW/K, Thomas Greenhud, pr. 1684; WRW/L Henry Washington pr. 1679, and William Canny pr. 1681; WRW/Copeland deanery, Christopher Peile pr. 1679.

79 J. Hatcher and T. C. Barker, *A History of British Pewter* (1974), p. 125; *HMC*, 12th Report, App. VII, p. 198. What follows is based on all the surviving probate records of Kendal pewterers, and upon court cases in KCR.

80 Ferguson, *Boke off Recorde*, pp. 20, 24, 25–6, 77, 80, 111; Lancs. RO, WRW/K, James Forth pr. 1648; Wm. Cookeson pr. 1683.

81 Ferguson, *Boke off Recorde*, p. 185.

82 B. C. Jones, 'Westmorland packhorse men in Southampton', *Trans. CWAAS*, new series, **59** (1960), pp. 73, 74, 78, 82.

83 Lancs. RO, WRW/K, pr. 1636; there are many cases in KCR relating to his trade.

84 T. S. Willan, *The Inland Trade* (1976), pp. 55–6, 77–8; Lancs. RO, WRW/K, Christopher Fisher pr. 1672.

85 1 & 2 P. & M. c. 7.

86 Ferguson, *Boke off Recorde*, p. 342. On this point see the discussion in Willan, *The Inland Trade*, pp. 54–5.

87 Ferguson, *Boke off Recorde*, pp. 35, 39; and see Note 83 above.

88 Ferguson, *Boke off Recorde*, pp. 18, 19, 60, Lancs. RO, WRW/K, pr. 1669. He was probably a victim of the cavalier purge of 1662.

89 PRO, C 5/619/7; Lancs. RO, WRW/F; Edward Braithwaite, pr. 1705.

90 CRO, Carlisle, D/Lons/W, letters: Sir John Lowther of Whitehaven to Thomas Tickle, 14 November 1670, 4 April 1672 (I owe these references to Dr Roger Hainsworth).

91 Lancs. RO, WRW/L; James Backhouse pr. 1578; PRO, C 6/89/64.

92 Smith, *Leland*, pp. 45, 54, 55; Blome, *Britannia*, pp. 73, 136, 234;

Fiennes, *Through England on a side saddle*, p. 166. Blome (*Britannia*, p. 234) acknowledges help from Sir Daniel Fleming, but his judgement of markets shows some independence from Fleming (Hughes, *Fleming*, pp. 3–64 *et passim*).

93 Above, p. 121; Blome, *Britannia*, p. 136.
94 *VCH*, Lancashire, **8**, p. 275; Hughes, *Fleming*, pp. 5, 9, 16, 28–9; Blome, *Britannia*, pp. 135, 234, 235, 237; CROK, WD/RY, box 32, census of Burton; Lancs. RO, WRW/K, Thomas Greenhud pr. 1684.
95 Smith, *Leland*, p. 54; Blome, *Britannia*, pp. 70, 71, 72; Hughes, *Fleming*, p. 46. See also R. Millward, 'The Cumbrian town between 1600 and 1800', in C. W. Chalklin and M. A. Havinden (eds.), *Rural Change and Urban Growth 1500–1800* (1974), *passim*.
96 A. J. and R. H. Tawney, 'An occupational census of the seventeenth century', *EcHR*, first series, **5** (1934–5), p. 38. See Wadsworth and Mann, *The Cotton Trade*, ch. 3.
97 PRO, E 124/7, fols. 277, 321, 329; E 124/8, fol. 190. The patentee did not execute the office in Westmorland.
98 See D. M. Woodward, 'A comparative study of the Irish and Scottish livestock trades in the seventeenth century', in L. M. Cullen and T. C. Smout (eds.), *Comparative Aspects of Scottish and Irish Economic and Social History, 1600–1900* (1977), esp. pp. 149–50.
99 Marshall, 'The domestic economy of Lakeland yeomen', pp. 210–11.
100 P. Clark and P. Slack, *English Towns in Transition* (1976), pp. 24–5, 32, 104–5.
101 A. D. Dyer in *Urban History Yearbook: 1979*, pp. 64–6.

4 Migrants and the population structure of later seventeenth-century provincial cities and market towns

David Souden

Of the very many who went to town in the later part of the seventeenth century few can have been put off by the experience as much as was Ned, a Somerset yokel visiting the metropolis:

> Than going on London city zdid view
> And when zdid zeet schor a ready to spew
> What with the neezz and what with the smoake
> Twas Death in my ears, and schor a ready to choake.
> But oh how the coaches did vly up and down
> Iz thought the whole world had a been in ye town.

Shocked at the food and prostitutes' charges, and spurned by those he met, Ned turned tail and fled.[1]

His experience was surely far from typical. For towns in early modern England – and towns of all sizes, not only London – could hardly achieve their growth without a continued inflow of people from outside. Until sustained natural increase within urban populations became more common, late in the eighteenth and in the nineteenth century, urban growth is largely an index of net migration.

Research on the migrant in the later sixteenth and early seventeenth century has often been both directed and challenging, investigating the way movement into towns acted both as one of the 'safety valves' helping take up the surplus rural population (showing the pauper characteristics of much urban immigration), and as a means of introducing young people, especially males, into productive work opportunities in craft and trade.[2] Again, considerable attention has been paid to migration and the mid Victorian city, largely through the medium of the decennial census.[3] The period in between has been less well served, with the significant exception of recent work by Peter Clark.[4] The enormous expansion of the urban sector within England over the early modern period stands as witness to the importance of the net flow from countryside to town. In 1600 the proportion of the English population living in settlements of more than 2500 was something in the order of 10 per cent – more than half of whom were living in London. By 1800 that proportion had trebled, and London itself accounted for more than 10 per cent of the English population although its share of the urban sector population had fallen considerably.[5] At the midpoint, around 1700, the 'urban' share of the nation's population stood at 17 to 18 per cent. The *numbers* living in towns more than doubled in the seventeenth century, and almost trebled in the eighteenth century. In terms of the changing *share* of the population the urban sector increased its share by just over 100 per cent in the seventeenth, and by almost two-thirds in the eighteenth century. Over each of these two centuries, the national population grew by 23 per cent and 71 per cent respectively.[6]

Whichever way we measure it, urban population growth in the early modern period was considerable. In the first two-thirds of the seventeenth century the capital was making much of the running. Thereafter other, lesser towns took the lead in growth, and with that the pace of growth quickened. While the period 1600–70 saw rapid population growth and even faster urban growth, the subsequent thirty years saw a slight fall in the national population and an increased pace of urban population growth.[7]

Thus, while urban population increase in the seventeenth and eighteenth centuries almost always exceeded that of the nation as a whole, in at least one period that increase bit deeply into the total population. Other contributions to this volume demonstrate the ways in which provincial towns' economies and social organization changed through these two centuries. On the face of it there is every reason to suppose that changes in urban populations and economies were intimately linked, and linked above all through the processes of migration. The net transfer of people into urban environments was especially significant, if only in terms of its impact upon the whole population, in the latter years of the seventeenth century. It is those processes and transfers that I shall investigate here.

I

The measurement of migration in a pre-census, pre-population register age has exercised the minds of many. A recurring difficulty has always been that although we may usually identify patterns of migration, in terms of the geographical origins of migrants or the proportions of incomers in a population, or measure flows of migration among particular sub-populations, this rarely provides answers to some of the more important questions about physical mobility. What was the size of the migration flows, both gross and net? How were those flows composed? To what extent was movement dominated by factors at the origin or the destination?[8] For the most part, many such problems are, and will undoubtedly remain, intractable. Material presented here provides direct and 'back-door' methods of tackling some of these issues. The rationale of this paper is to examine a range of migrants (and their non-migrant neighbours) living in a variety of English towns, placed within the context of some knowledge of the overall population structure of settlements. For the composition of many urban populations is striking, and demands explanation.

The best opportunity to examine directly patterns of movement, for some towns at least, during our period lies with the deposition records of ecclesiastical courts. Witnesses before those courts represent a large and variegated group providing information on their past life- (and hence migration-) histories. Apprenticeship records, which many have used as a means of gauging migration patterns for towns of the late sixteenth and early seventeenth centuries, are here of limited utility – apprenticeship more commonly involved native rather than immigrant young males, while formal apprenticeship was on the wane.[9] The Settlement Laws were not working with the degree of documentary sophistication which the eighteenth century was to see, and surviving archival material is often difficult to interpret.[10] The tide of vagrancy and impoverished movement earlier in the seventeenth century appears to have lessened considerably, so that fewer revealing testimonies of wanderers survive.[11]

The individual histories which are provided in church court depositions have the advantage of being available on a large scale, and of being readily comparable with results already calculated for an earlier period. The material provides a description, albeit in general terms, of patterns of movement. Using the information on individual characteristics of migrants and non-migrants, deposition data demonstrate place-to-place features of movement, age and occupational differentiation, and provide the basis for an analysis of the economic and geographical environment of places from which migrants came as well as places to which they moved. These data do present a number of difficulties: information on flows of migrants can only be inferential, while disaggregation even within a large data source produces increasingly small numbers upon which to base conclusions. There is not sufficient information to permit short-term analysis of movement on, say, an annual or even adequately on a decennial basis.

Although all spiritual jurisdictions suffered from the hiatus in their activity during the Interregnum, and some church courts never recovered, a number of courts continued to function well into the eighteenth century. This activity was rarely at the level which had previously obtained, and most courts had experienced a serious decline in business by 1700, but it is premature to write them off completely, especially in areas outside the immediate orbit of London.

For our present purposes, indeed, that decline in ecclesiastical business in some ways *favours* analysis centred upon towns. A higher proportion of female witnesses, a higher proportion of urban-resident witnesses, and a lower proportion of the socially magnificent, appeared before the courts in the later seventeenth century. This is partly, but by no means wholly, an outcome of the greatly increased proportional importance of actions for defamation coming before the courts.[12]

Witnesses were generally expected to provide a potted autobiography, establishing themselves and their relationship to the principals in a case, and were then expected to append their mark or signature to the transcript of the testimony. Such preambles commonly give the name, status or occupation, and age of the witness, his or her place of residence and place of birth, and how long he or she had lived at the current place of residence. In some cases, although in a distinct minority, information on intermediate places of residence (and periods of stay) is recorded.[13] These preambles give the historian considerable scope for inquiry. A proportion of the witnesses claimed to have lived in their current place of residence since their birth. Of the witnesses who did record movements, we may determine the age at which they had first arrived and the date at which they did so, how far they had come, and from what type of community they had come.

The first part of this essay will be taken up with an analysis of the depositions of witnesses appearing before the courts of six ecclesiastical jurisdictions within the province of Canterbury, during the last four decades of the seventeenth century. Moving from west to east, these are the dioceses of Exeter, Bath & Wells, Salisbury, and

Oxford, the archdeaconry of Leicester, and the diocese of Norwich. (The Exeter, Bath & Wells, Oxford and Norwich material include some archidiaconal as well as episcopal jurisdictions.)[14] These cover quite fully the counties of Devon, Somerset, Wiltshire, Oxfordshire, Leicestershire and Norfolk, and to a limited extent Suffolk and Cornwall.

A total of 2262 people living in towns and appearing as witnesses forms the basis of this body of data.[15] As Table 9 shows, a very large proportion come from the Exeter diocesan courts, which remained effective legal agencies up to the end of the century and beyond. The larger cities of Norwich, Exeter and Oxford dominate the material. Totnes, Crediton, Tiverton and Cullompton, Wells and Leicester are all represented by more than fifty witnesses, while towns like Salisbury, Glastonbury and Great Yarmouth fall just below that number. Although the coverage of the larger towns is thus by no means even, it seems a fair reflection of the spread and variety of urban settlements. The lower proportion of witnesses from Exeter itself suggests that people from other parts of that far-flung diocese were more ready to come to have their cases heard than was true elsewhere.[16] Overall, males appeared more frequently as witnesses than did females. This is shown by the sex ratios, the number of males per 100 females. Nevertheless, women from later seventeenth-century towns, and especially from the cities, appeared more regularly as witnesses before these courts than had their sisters before the English Revolution.[17]

Table 9   *Coverage of the deposition data 1661–1707*

Jurisdiction	Dates	Number	Sex ratio
Diocese of Exeter	1661–92	1064	204.0
Diocese of Bath & Wells	1661–1700	258	309.5
Diocese of Salisbury	1663–77	132	407.7
Diocese of Oxford	1665–94	251	248.6
Archdeaconry of Leicester	1661–1700	177	390.2
Diocese of Norwich	1663–1707	380	239.3
	Total	2262	240.7
including:			
City of Exeter		475	162.4
City of Oxford		139	215.9
City of Norwich		232	197.4

Almost every witness gave his or her age. With mean ages around 40, we are able to capture relatively recent movement, rather than the mis-remembered moves made many years previously by a population of nonagenarians. So approaching two-thirds of the deponents who had immigrated to the towns analysed here moved in after 1650. Comparing the age structure of witnesses with the estimates we have for the national population's age structure (discounting those under 15), the two distributions are remarkably similar.[18]

Overall, the largest proportion of the males who appeared were employed within the textile and clothing sectors – 26.4 per cent of all those who gave an occupation or their status (1527 out of 1598). The proportion was highest in the diocese of Exeter (31.2 per cent) and in the diocese of Norwich (32.9 per cent). One-eighth of the men described themselves as gentlemen.[19] Providers of urban services and of goods also feature prominently; so do men styling themselves 'yeoman' and 'husbandman'. Retailers of food and drink average some 11 per cent of the total, while yeomen and husbandmen together account for only 6 per cent in the Norwich material, but 21 per cent in Bath & Wells. Undoubtedly some of these did follow agricultural pursuits, especially on the rural fringes of towns. (Yeomen and husbandmen are considerably less prominent in the largest towns.) For others, an agricultural occupational title must have been a status ascription divorced from their current employment. For women it is rare for anything other than their marital status to be recorded: 'wife of so-and-so', widow, spinster, occasionally *famula domestica*. Overall, 19 per cent of the women were widowed, and 31 per cent were spinsters. The text of the testimony provides on occasion important additional information on the work that these women performed. Since a high proportion of female witnesses were unmarried, they are more likely to have been independent and economically active.

If women did participate to a marked extent in the labour force, they did not share as fully in the skills of literary, at least as measured by the ability to sign.[20] A third or less of men did not sign their name, as opposed to more than two-thirds of the women. But women in the biggest towns were more literate.

Although it is difficult to ascertain with much certainty the extent to which this witness population is generally representative of the population at large, the coverage here seems plausible. Although biased upwards socially to some extent by the large-scale presence

of gentlemen, this imbalance is less marked than it had been before
the Interregnum. The presence of the clergy as witnesses was considerably diminished in the post-Restoration courts. Exeter and
Norwich, cities both dominated by textile production, have large
numbers of witnesses from the cloth trades.

So, how many inhabitants of later seventeenth-century towns
were migrants? Taking the whole witness population, 42.2 per cent
of all males, and 46.2 per cent of all females, claimed to have lived
always in the town or city of their birth. There was considerable
local variation in the *proportions* who moved: our six jurisdictions
divide neatly into two groups, with the West Country jurisdictions
having higher percentages of immobile men and women than in
those towns covered by the Oxford, Leicester and Norwich courts.[21]
In the diocese of Salisbury, 57 per cent of males claimed that they
had always lived in their birthplace, while the proportion was 29 per
cent in the diocese of Oxford. In the diocese of Exeter 51 per cent of
women recorded no move, as opposed to 33 per cent in the diocese
of Norwich.[22]

So between a half and two-thirds of these urban residents were
migrant. Table 10 shows the extent to which larger towns usually
had lower proportions of people claiming never to have moved, but
even in the major cities there remain considerable differences
among the proportions permanently resident.[23]

Migration propensities vary with age. Taking all six jurisdictions
together, one finds that among males aged 25 and under, 56 per cent
were unlikely to be resident elsewhere than their birthplace, while
among those aged 20 to 60 and 60 and over, the comparable figures

Table 10   *Non-migrants*

Diocese	*Smaller towns* Male Number %		*Female* Number %		*Larger towns* Male Number %		*Female* Number %	
Exeter	91	50.3	30	49.2	252	47.9	146	51.2
Bath & Wells	61	44.9	23	51.1	20	42.6	5	35.7
Salisbury	38	54.3	7	43.8	17	63.0	2	40.0
Oxford	32	39.5	15	55.6	19	20.2	15	34.9
Leicester	24	43.6	5	29.4	20	28.2	9	42.9
Norwich	23	30.3	5	27.8	30	24.4	20	34.5
All	269	44.9	85	46.2	358	40.3	197	46.2

Witnesses recording no moves

were 44 per cent and 35 per cent. The decline with age is more marked in the case of women, 56 per cent of those aged up to 25, 44 per cent of those between 25 and 60, and 29 per cent of those over 60 had stayed in the same place. This rate of decline is found quite uniformly throughout the data.

The sample sizes are fairly small but we can reach some broad conclusions about occupation-specific propensities to move. Craftsmen and various textile and clothing workers often exhibited considerable levels of immobility, while those in the food and drink trades, especially in the smaller towns, were very commonly immigrants. This is likely to be an expression of a growing tertiary sector, with the newest growth taking place in smaller urban centres, and more established retailing and services carried on in the larger communities.[24] If one takes as an example towns within the diocese of Exeter, a higher proportion in most occupational groups were immigrants in the city of Exeter as opposed to other towns. This effect is especially marked for weavers, combers, tailors and their wives. Table 11 shows the varying tendencies for movement among men and through the hierarchy of towns.

Overall the analysis of the deposition material indicates significant variations in mover/stayer propensities, including regional differences with lower immigrant proportions in the West, and contrasts between occupational and status groups, with men and women of higher status more likely to be immigrant. Using literacy as a broad indicator of status, we find that some 41 per cent of both males and females who could sign were immobile, compared with 45 per cent of males, and 48 per cent of females, who made their mark.[25] Again there is a differential between those living in the largest towns and those living in other urban centres. We may also see variation over time. Compared with data covering the earlier part of the seventeenth century, proportions of residents who were immigrants were smaller.[26]

Evidence from a further large body of data would seem to confirm some of these features. Family reconstitution studies of parishes, using a technique that examines combinations of registered vital events for married couples and their families, provide an indication of patterns of lifetime mobility. The lengthy time span of the family reconstitution data facilitates comparison over time.[27] Banbury in Oxfordshire, and Gainsborough in Lincolnshire represent the middle rank market centres and their registers give particularly full occupational information. For the period under discussion one can

Table 11 *Male occupational differences in immobility*

Witnesses recording no moves

	Smaller towns		Larger towns	
	Number	Per cent	Number	Per cent
Agriculture	71	53.8	33	37.9
Textile/leather	85	51.2	163	48.2
Wood/building	28	62.2	19	30.6
Metalworking	12	48.0	14	42.4
Retail/distribution	29	33.7	48	41.0
Gentlemen/professionals	30	26.8	69	36.3

see that a growing proportion of the population was long-term or permanently resident, while mobility differentials between the various occupational groupings were preserved over time.

None the less, we should remember that these figures from church court archives (and from the family reconstitution material) represent *proportions* of those immobile and mobile: that is to say, we may identify the *shape* of the distribution of the mover population, but not the *level* without additional information – that is knowledge of the population at risk. In the city of Norwich, for example, the population stood at some 12,000 in the early seventeenth century, and at some 30,000 by the end of the century. If we estimate the proportion of non-movers from our deposition data to have been under 20 per cent in the first part of the century, and nearer 30 per cent in the later, that still means that the *volume* of migration to the city would have increased, and probably increased quite substantially. In the context of generally stable numbers in the national population during the post-Restoration period, populations which were growing, and growing rapidly, were doing so at the expense of other settlements. The economic and social blandishments of some towns were sufficient to overcome the more equitable local opportunities which demographic stagnation and higher real wages (and incomes) brought about. Lower residential mobility, at least of settled married adults, seems to have characterized the later seventeenth-century countryside, partly as a result of these circumstances.[28]

We can now turn to an examination of the characteristics of those who *were* migrants to our towns. Bearing in mind the fact that various social and occupational groups were not uniform in their liability to move, the deposition evidence provides details of the

provenance and characteristics of many migrants. Some two-thirds
of those male deponents and a little over a half of the females came
into town from villages: men were more often rural-born within the
dioceses of Exeter and of Bath & Wells than elsewhere(Table 12).
Comparing the three largest towns, a higher proportion of men in
Exeter had come from rural settlements than was the case elsewhere.

All groups were reasonably close in the age-specific composition
of their movement. Men moved into towns at fractionally lower
average ages than did women, but the differences are not significant. The modal age at immigration for all groups was 20, the
median 23 and the mean 25.[29] Since the various groups of witnesses
were reasonably consistent in their age-structure, these averages
are not contaminated by internal variation. To control for the
age-compositional effects in order to obtain an age-specific migration profile, we may conveniently examine recent migrants within
each age group. In Table 13, migrant deponents are divided into
five-year age bands, and the proportion calculated for each band of
those who had moved in within the previous five years. There is a
suggestion of a bimodal distribution. High proportions immigrated
in their later teens and early twenties, while movements are also
notable at much higher ages. About one-fifth of widowed women
aged over 50, for example, were recent immigrants: almost all of
them had moved to one of the three larger cities in the sample
(Table 13).

Where did these men and women come from? How far had they
moved before reaching the town of their choice? Men overall had
moved a mean 41.4 kilometres,[30] women 36.0 kilometres.[31] These

Table 12   *Origins of migrants*

Witnesses born in villages

Diocese	Males Number	Per cent	Females Number	Per cent
Exeter	229	65.6	90	54.5
Bath & Wells	14	70.0	3	50.0
Salisbury	16	50.0	7	77.8
Oxford	67	56.6	19	47.5
Leicester	47	58.8	17	73.9
Norwich	82	59.0	24	50.0
All	452	61.7	160	55.0

Table 13 *Age-specific migration profiles*

Migrant witnesses arriving within previous five years				
Age	*Male*		*Female*	
	Number	*Per cent*	*Number*	*Per cent*
16–20	35	81.4	36	85.7
21–5	69	47.0	56	76.7
26–30	58	46.8	38	46.3
31–5	33	22.1	15	31.9
36–40	34	20.1	13	31.0
41–5	6	6.7	7	28.0
46–50	7	4.2	5	8.5
51–5	6	8.3	3	12.0
56–60	9	9.7	3	7.0
61–5	1	2.2	0	—
66–70	3	8.3	2	15.4
70+	6	13.3	5	17.9
Total	265		188	

averages were skewed by some longer-distance migrants, since the median was 23 kilometres for both sexes. The averages also conceal considerable differences between places: men moving to the three largest towns moved 48.8 kilometres on average,[32] women 44.7 kilometres;[33] the median distance moved by these men was 30 kilometres, by the women 32 kilometres. Distances moved to smaller towns were significantly less. Differences between men and women in terms of distances moved were slight, if not nonexistent, and the considerable upward shift in distances moved by women to the larger cities is especially noteworthy.[34]

Again using the ability to sign as a shorthand social indicator, there was considerable selectivity in distances moved. Those who could sign their name always moved greater average distances than those who could only make a mark. For example, of migrants who arrived in their current place of residence in the decade 1661–70, men had moved a mean 49.6 kilometres, females 43.5 kilometres.[35] 'Literate' men had moved 55.9 kilometres, women 69.2 kilometres, while their 'illiterate' brothers and sisters had moved on average only 33.2 kilometres and 32.2 kilometres respectively.[36]

Breaking down the male population into broad occupational categories, as is done in Table 14, three groups of migrants emerge. First, building, wood and metal workers had relatively

Table 14   *Distances travelled by migrants*

Occupational group	Mean distance (kilometres)		Town size			Number
	Mean	Standard deviation		Mean	Standard deviation	
Agriculture	33.7	60.8	smaller	26.6	48.1	71
			larger	63.5	94.0	17
Textile and leather	37.9	49.8	smaller	29.7	41.6	109
			larger	47.2	56.4	96
Wood and building	29.4	37.1	smaller	23.6	39.3	25
			larger	36.3	34.0	21
Metal	28.0	26.9	smaller	20.0	11.8	11
			larger	34.4	33.7	14
Retail and distribution	50.8	63.8	smaller	52.5	70.7	68
			larger	46.1	40.0	25
Gent. and professional	53.5	63.6	smaller	49.4	68.0	89
			larger	59.3	56.9	63

circumscribed movements. They moved some 22 kilometres on average to the smaller towns, and some 35 kilometres to the largest. Textile and leather workers travelled further – 30 kilometres to smaller towns, 50 kilometres to larger. Professional men and retailers moved in an average 50–60 kilometre range. Looking at the city of Exeter, for which we have reasonable numbers of witnesses, this tripartite division is clearly distinguishable.

This feature can be amplified from other sources. During the 1660s Exeter proceeded against many 'strangers' who were being entertained within the city, particularly in the poorest parishes.[37] Of 139 individuals ordered out in the years 1660–8, only ten were women, all spinsters: textile workers were especially well-represented among the men – fifty-nine weavers and twenty-two combers. These expelled inmates had travelled a mean 51.2 kilometres to Exeter;[38] however, the weavers had usually come from closer at hand, on average only 21 kilometres,[39] principally from other towns in the vicinity, from Crediton, Tiverton and Cullompton. The pressures to exclude strangers were undoubtedly greater in these years of textile depression before the later Stuart boom.[40] The process by which these poorer craft migrants insinuated themselves into town is well illustrated from this source.

Weavers, widows, innkeepers and tailors were the most common receivers of immigrants. In forty-four cases we know the occupation of the householder and the incomer – and in twenty-seven cases both had the same occupation. Eighteen of those twenty-seven were weavers. As an example, in 1661 John Whaddon, William Lendon and John Quash, all weavers, were ordered to leave Nicholas Gloyne's house and the city. The previous year the poll tax had enumerated Nicholas Gloyne, weaver, and his wife, with John Quash (who was unable to pay) and one Anthony Wolland. This suggests the considerable turnover of inmates that is commonly found.[41]

Consistent relationships between distances moved and the urban size hierarchy emerge from the deposition data. Those coming to town from villages moved shorter distances than those coming from other towns, while the larger towns received migrants from further afield. This is not unusual in itself: what is especially noticeable here is the fact that the migration distances for men and women are very close to each other in terms of their means and standard deviations, and certainly closer than had been the case earlier in the seventeenth century.[42] The significance of this will emerge. Tables 15 and 16 present the data on migration distances according to whether witnesses were born in village or in town, whether or not they signed their name, and whether they moved into a larger or a smaller town. The progression of distances travelled stands out in these tables –

Table 15   *Distances from rural and urban birthplaces*

| Birthplace | Mean distance (kilometres) | | | | | |
	Mean	Standard deviation		Mean	Standard deviation	Number
Males						
Village-born	35.1	46.2	mark 25.1	32.3	132
			sign 39.0	50.1	339
Town-born	58.2	73.0	mark 40.0	55.0	49
			sign 65.3	78.0	125
Females						
Village-born	28.9	33.2	mark 25.9	26.2	142
			sign 39.9	50.1	39
Town-born	52.6	59.7	mark 38.6	37.6	57
			sign 90.6	87.8	21

Table 16   *Distances moved and the urban size hierarchy*

Birthplace	Town size	Mean distance (kilometres)		
		Mean	Standard deviation	Number
Males				
Village born	smaller	29.2	43.6	274
	larger	42.8	48.3	200
Town-born	smaller	53.3	73.9	117
	larger	68.1	70.0	58
Females				
Village-born	smaller	18.5	23.1	92
	larger	39.7	38.4	89
Town-born	smaller	49.6	60.4	35
	larger	55.0	59.8	43

the way in which those who could sign and who moved to smaller towns had the same average migration distance as those who did not sign and who moved to larger towns, and particularly the way in which the data in Table 16 are so neatly in step.

The patterns of movement from countryside to small town are strikingly uniform throughout the whole area studied within the larger towns, Oxford tended to receive immigrants from within a smaller range than the other cities – urban-born immigrants to Oxford came on average 37 kilometres, while those to Exeter came 61 kilometres, and those to Norwich 93 kilometres. Other Oxford evidence clearly supports this conclusion on the extent of its migration field.[43]

The larger cities thus attracted reasonable numbers of immigrants from some distance. Over a third of men and women had travelled more than 50 kilometres, twice as high a proportion as in the streams of movers to smaller towns. 9 per cent of men and 6.3 per cent of women had come further than 100 kilometres: here again the links between literacy skills and longer distances hold. 10.5 per cent of males who could sign, as opposed to 5.3 per cent of those who could not, came more than 100 kilometres; only 2.6 per cent of the women unable to sign their name came further than 100 kilometres, while 18.6 per cent of the women who could sign moved such long distances. Professional men, retailers and weavers were most commonly represented in this category of longer distance migrants: among men in the various retailing occupations 14.1 per cent of those able to sign, and 9.1 per cent of those unable to, came more than 100 kilometres.

Thus some distinctive occupational patterns emerge, rooted in the changing economic character of towns. Weavers, for example, were either very likely to have been born in the town in which they lived, or else to have come from significant distances. Norwich, Exeter and Leicester all saw considerable growth in the textile sectors of their economies in the later seventeenth century, and hence would prove attractive to migrants as well as providing little incentive to leave. Meanwhile there was a considerable influx of those in retailing and distributive occupations, many travelling significant distances, reflecting the expansion of marketing and shopkeeping.

Looking further at the origins of migrants, for every urban-born female living in one of our three largest cities, two had been born in villages – whereas for every town-born male there were over three who came from rural settlements. In the smaller towns the ratio for rural-born to urban-born immigrant males and females was broadly similar, at around 2.5 to 1. There is thus some suggestion of greater female movement between towns. These were also women who were still rather unusual in their possession, or acquisition, of sign literacy.

Having seen something of the characteristics of the longer-distance migrants, in terms of their status, origins, skills, and sex, what were the spatial configurations of movement? Historians of towns in the later sixteenth and earlier seventeenth centuries have consistently stressed the long-distance, frequently marginal character of much movement, movement within regions to towns, and from the poorer Northern and Western regions to the more affluent, and more urbanized, South and East.[44] Some of the examples of 'subsistence' migration in the South and East are more spectacular than we may find in other regions, but nevertheless that pattern is to be found quite generally in the earlier seventeenth century.[45] The general incidence of longer distance movement, measured through deposition records, diminished after the Restoration. In town and countryside there was a tendency in the areas under examination for the typical distances travelled by men to contract. In the countryside both mean and median distances moved by men diminished, whereas a higher proportion (of a smaller population) did not move. The migration profiles of rural women changed little over the century.[46]

However, for the towns mean distances travelled by both men and women increased somewhat between the first and second halves of the seventeenth century. Modal and median distances travelled by men had declined, demonstrating the existence of a group of longer-distance migrants together with contracting migration fields for other groups. We have seen that these two divisions reflect the differences between men in professional and service occupations, and those in crafts and trades. On the other hand, modal and median distances moved by women remained unaltered throughout the seventeenth century, suggesting that the forces for contraction in local migration evident among males were absent. Setting that alongside evidence for a group of women moving greater distances into towns, our findings indicate marked shifts over time between the relative movement patterns of men and women.[47]

The data confirm the impression that longer-range movement from the previously disadvantaged North and West was of diminished importance. Norwich still retained links with Northern counties, but these were of lesser significance.[48] The links which Oxford had seen at earlier dates with Northern and Western counties were much diminished, and apparently continued so.[49] Devon was distinctive, with quite considerable movement from Cornwall and Western Devon into the east of the county – to Exeter, but also to Crediton, Tiverton, and other towns there.[50] Higher proportions of migrants moved more than 50 kilometres (42 per cent of men and 37 per cent of women) than was the case for either Norwich or Oxford.

In addition to the main series of depositions which have been analysed here in detail, the court archives contain the testimony of a number of witnesses who had been born in towns or cities but now lived in villages within the jurisdictions studied. These number 218. Sixty-nine witnesses came from larger towns in our areas, thirty-seven from the three largest cities. The 122 men had moved on average 32.6 kilometres (standard deviation 65.9), the women 40.8 kilometres (standard deviation 66.1). Again, men and women who could sign their name moved further than those who could not. Those who had been born in the larger towns had not moved particularly far to villages within the area: the fifty-two men had moved a mean 11.8 kilometres (standard deviation 9.2), the seventeen women 13.4 kilometres (standard deviation 12.1).

Such examples as these can only suggest the extent of outward links from towns and cities to the countryside. Such evidence as there is on intermediate stays for these witnesses often provides examples of short-term residence in a town or a succession of towns (usually in service) before returning to village life. One servant girl, for example, returned to Wolvercote (Oxfordshire) six months before being called as a witness: she had spent three years in Oxford, and was aged 25; another, 21-year-old, servant had come home to Rockbeare (Devon) in 1674 after a five year spell in Exeter, and a 27-year-old servant girl in 1677 had spent only one month in Bradninch after periods of service in South Huish, Bishopsteignton, Exeter and Musbury, having been born in Exeter – the longest of the moves being over 50 kilometres. A Leicestershire spinster had been living in Bagworth for six months in 1670: she had lived there for a year in the early 1660s, and had been hired in the intervening period in Market Bosworth, Hinckley, Twycross and Osbaston; she had been born at Orton-on-the-Hill in 1645.[51]

Church court deposition evidence, especially in a period when the courts were undergoing a steady decline in their business and activity, can only cover a tiny minority of the inhabitants of towns during the later seventeenth century. Nevertheless, the data fit together consistently. Although a higher proportion of deponents claimed never to have moved than had been the case before the Civil War, this did not entail a diminution in the volume of migration: rather, the volume increased markedly. Regional patterns of immobility were preserved. Age structures of movement are consistent throughout, while a hierarchy of distances moved in terms of status, occupation, literacy, origin and destination, is apparent. The increased importance of women's movement emerges: distances travelled by females were greater than had been the case before, high proportions of females as opposed to males were migrants, and women were more commonly represented in the flows between towns than were men.

II

The findings from church court evidence demonstrate the process of migration; other material illuminates the structure resulting from that process, in terms of the composition of local populations. The survival of returns made under the Marriage Duty Act of 1695 allows us to investigate the populations of many towns and villages.[52] Possibly because of the greater difficulty of keeping track of the resident population in major centres, a number of towns made large-scale house-to-house enumerations of their populations, subsequently tying those names in with the (taxable) entries of vital events in the parish registers. These enumerations have been of considerable use to contemporary political arithmeticians[53] and to modern social historians alike.[54]

Although providing no direct indication of the origins of enumerated individuals, information on the size and structure of these populations gives important clues for some features of migration.[55] Table 17 presents summary data on various settlements for which returns (or calculations based upon them) survive.[56] For Norwich only Gregory King's manuscript notes are extant,[57] while a remarkably full set of multiple enumerations survives for Bristol.[58] Enumerations also survive for a miscellany of smaller towns and a number of villages. Some are especially useful, in that they ascribe

Table 17　*Sex ratios in towns and villages 1695–1705*

Year	Settlement	County	Total	Sex ratio	Servant total	Sex servant Ratio	Per cent	Lodger total
Large towns 1696–9			53 867	83.4	3 330	75.3		
1696	Bristol		20 212	80.2	2 049	79.7	10.1	401
1696	Norwich	Norfolk	28 546					
			*8 622	92.5				
1695	Ipswich	Suffolk	7 943	82.0				
1696	Gloucester	Glos.	4 756	81.0	473	69.5	9.9	194
1695	Bury St Edmunds	Suffolk	*3 170	85.7				
1696–9	Leicester	Leics.	*3 142	87.1	*259	85.0	11.6	*75
1696	Lichfield	Staffs.	3 038	81.4	239	67.1	7.9	
1696	Southampton	Hants.	2 984	82.4	310	56.1	10.4	20
Small towns 1696–1705			6 067	90.4	259	63.6		
1697	Buckfastleigh	Devon	1 111	99.8				
1697	Lyme Regis	Dorset	1 337	70.1	59	73.5	4.4	2
1697	Wootton Bassett	Wilts.	1 049	97.6	45	55.2	4.3	
1696	Sevenoaks	Kent	891	88.4	110	83.3	12.3	
1697	Rothwell	N'hants.	889	90.0	22	57.1	2.5	
1697	Swindon	Wilts.	790	96.5	23	53.3	2.9	
Villages 1696–1705 including								
1697	17 N'hants villages		3 598	98.5	161	75.0		
1701	5 Wilts. villages		2 450	100.5				
1705	11 East Kent villages		2 800	109.3	386	201.2		

* Partial enumeration only.

Note: Not all enumerations note servants and/or lodgers (N'hants villages, eight listings with servants; Wilts. villages four listings with servants; Kent villages, seven listings with servants).

occupations and ages to the inhabitants; others list names without indication of where households begin or end, or of the inhabitants' relationship to each other, and are, therefore, of limited use.

The most important feature to emerge from the table is the often extremely skewed pattern of the sex ratios in these populations, again measuring the sex ratio as the number of males per hundred females. Though the towns have sex ratios usually well below parity, the villages which fill the lower part of the table tend towards a surplus of males. The progression is obviously not a smooth one but the trend is unmistakably towards lower, more female-dominated sex ratios in towns. What produced this?

Almost universally, birth cohorts contain a slight excess of males over females, but higher male infant and child mortality levels rapidly tend to produce a slight female surplus. Greater female longevity (despite maternal mortality) produces often highly imbalanced sex ratios in old age, particularly when male populations may have been depleted by war or where working conditions may have been especially dangerous. The actions of differential mortality would thus have potentially powerful effects upon the age- and sex-structure of a single settlement's population.

At the same time, the sex ratio calculations in Table 17 may be distorted by errors in the original enumerations. In transcribing the population data available to him on Norwich, Gregory King estimated a 2 per cent omission rate in the enumerations.[59] If omissions were block ones, with whole houses or streets going uncounted, then the overall impact upon the sex ratios would undoubtedly be marginal. If, on the other hand, individuals were being omitted from their households, then we might expect children and women rather than men to be overlooked by enumerators. This if anything would reinforce the bias of the sex ratios. Since the lists were drawn up for fiscal purposes, they would undoubtedly be regarded as *de jure* censuses: even if householders were temporarily away, they should have been enumerated so that the tax upon them might be collected. Since bachelors over the age of 25, and childless widowers, were taxed at special rates, some misenumeration might result from these men disguising their true age or status: whether or not they could escape the assessor's eagle eye is open to question.

Another point needs to be considered. The sex ratios at death in England at the beginning of the eighteenth century were skewed – 98.2 males per hundred females were buried in 1700, and 101.1 per hundred in 1710, compared with sex ratios at baptism of 104.5 and

103.6.[60] This may well be because males had emigrated in the seventeenth century in substantially greater numbers than had females. Moreover, a larger proportion of emigrants came from towns rather than from villages.[61]

Despite the fact that the figures in Table 17 are affected by natural causes and external migration, one's impression is that the general information provided by these returns is trustworthy,[62] and we are left with the conclusion that a major determinant of these distinctive patterns was the action of differential migration. We have already seen the levels of urban growth in the later seventeenth century, and the processes of migration at that time, notably with men's and women's migration patterns starting to converge. This evidence on sex structures holds out the distinct possibility that migration flows to towns, and especially therefore *net* flows, were female-dominated.

Service was an important (and predominantly a life-cycle) phenomenon in early modern England. In agriculture, the servant population was dominated by men, although women were far from being unimportant in that role, particularly with the growth of pastoral agriculture in the period 1660–1740. Domestic servant groups were more commonly composed of females.[63] Domestic service was a characteristic feature of towns, and European towns in the early modern period often had a female surplus within their populations.[64] However, the figures in Table 17 show a remarkable predominance of women in English provincial towns, especially in view of the fact that servant populations in the enumerations are neither excessively large nor especially female-dominated.

In order to understand the causes of these skewed sex ratios, we need to examine some of the urban enumerations in closer detail. Tables 18 to 23 present information, in a similar format to that in Table 17, on individual parishes within Bristol, Gloucester, Southampton, Leicester, Norwich and Ipswich. In the previous table we saw the often important contribution made to a population by its servant component: in the following tables the parishes' sex ratios have also been calculated *without* the servants.

In Bristol, sex ratios in individual parishes ranged between 72.1 and 72.9 in the parishes of St Leonard and St Augustine respectively, and 97.1 in St Mary-le-Port. The wealthy innermost parishes of All Saints, St Ewen, and St Werburgh were densely populated: between 25 and 30 per cent of their populations were composed of servants, and five out of every eight of those servants were women.

Table 18   *Sex ratios in Bristol 1696*

Parish	Total	Sex ratio	Servant total	Sex ratio	Sex ratio without servants	Lodger total	Sex ratio
All Saints	278	75.9	83	59.6	84.0	—	
Castle	1376	75.7	185	83.2	74.6	77	120.0
Christchurch	710	75.7	n.a.	—		n.a.	
St Augustine	1610	72.9	212	71.0	73.1	35	34.6
St Ewen	155	82.4	40	73.9	85.5	—	
St James	2885	78.5	107	67.2	78.9	10	400.0
St John Baptist	906	82.3	109	84.7	82.0	35	84.2
St Leonard	315	72.1	57	103.6	66.5	18	50.0
St Mary-le-Port	404	97.1	56	115.4	94.4	13	33.3
St Mary Redcliffe*	1534	81.1	105	87.5	80.7	11	—
St Michael	984	78.9	111	46.1	74.5	7	40.0
St Nicholas	1256	85.0	217	72.2	87.9	48	71.4
St Peter	995	86.7	159	93.9	85.4	35	105.9
Ss Philip & Jacob*	1576	81.4	54	125.0	80.2	10	—
St Stephen	1800	80.0	189	81.3	79.8	65	54.8
St Thomas	1544	89.7	243	99.2	88.0	29	93.3
St Werburgh	291	91.8	80	60.0	81.9	8	166.7
Temple	1593	78.8	42	68.0	80.3	—	

* Lodgers in Ss Philip & Jacob and St Mary Redcliffe all males.
n.a. data not available.

Conversely, less than 4 per cent of the population of the suburban parishes of St James, Ss Philip & Jacob, and Temple, and 6.8 per cent of St Mary Redcliffe, were servants.[65] Nevertheless, these latter parishes had similar sex ratios to those holding in the city as a whole. Lodgers as such are found relatively infrequently (they formed just over 2 per cent of the total population), but particular concentrations are found in the newly-developed Castle area, and in the dockside parishes of St Nicholas and St Stephen.[66] The merchant-dominated portside parishes of St Leonard and St Mary-le-Port had significant numbers of male apprentices and servants. (The surplus of male servants in Ss Philip & Jacob parish is in part an expression of its residual agricultural character.) In a sea-faring city, a high level of widowhood might be expected, especially in parishes dominated by mariners, while many men may have been away at sea for extended periods.[67] The evidence of the enumerations suggests a large number of single persons living alone or in small groups, and considerable subdivision of the housing stock. The Bristol listings do not enumerate 'households', but in many parishes seem to mark off houses. So for instance, in the enumeration for St Thomas Street in St Mary Redcliffe, widow Howell and her daughter, George Browne and his wife, John Wilkins, his wife and six children, Ann Crooker and Jane Fowles, Morris Pearce and his wife, widow Robinson, widow Pope and her son, widow Price with her servant Mary Jones, Sarah Saunders, and John Wedmore, his wife and son, are bracketed together, all seemingly filling the same house or court.[68]

The skewed nature of the sex ratio was closely linked to urban growth. Considerable infilling took place in the course of the seventeenth century to house the rising – and predominantly incoming – population. We have both an enumeration of the population aged 16 and over in St James parish in 1633,[69] and the Marriage Duty Act enumerations for the parish 1695–9, all of which distinguish streets. Adding an appropriate value for the under-16s, the population in 1633 stood at something above 1300, and so more than doubled in the subsequent sixty years (while the city itself probably grew by some 50 per cent). Comparison of the enumerations by street between the two sets of lists shows the extent of the expansion and concentration of the built-up area.

For the city of Gloucester (Table 19), we only have the parochial totals, not the original enumerations. Again, as in Bristol, there was local variation around a strikingly similar general sex ratio, ranging between 56.8 in the College Precinct and 88.2 in St Michael's parish. Servant and lodger groups were more female-dominated than they had been in Bristol, and lodgers formed a larger proportion of the population (although were still a numerically insignificant group).

Southampton's population decline in the seventeenth century is

Table 19   *Sex ratios in Gloucester 1698*

Parish	Total	Sex ratio	Servant total	Sex ratio	Sex ratio without servants	Lodger total	Sex ratio
College Precinct	174	56.8	38	26.7	67.9	10	25.0
St Aldate	283	86.2	6	100.0	85.9	4	—
St Ewen	136	72.2	6	100.0	71.1	9	50.0
St John Baptist	634	81.7	54	107.7	79.6	41	70.8
St Katherine	422	85.1	2	—	84.2	26	73.3
St Mary Crypt	513	86.5	76	68.9	90.0	39	44.4
St Mary Grace	142	69.0	28	55.5	72.7	3	—
St Mary Lode	418	73.4	6	200.0	72.4	27	68.8
St Michael	504	88.2	79	71.7	91.4	10	11.1
St Nicholas	1090	81.7	127	69.3	83.4	22	37.5
Trinity	404	82.8	51	75.9	83.0	3	50.0

Table 20 *Sex ratios in Southampton 1696*

Parish	Total	Sex ratio	Servant total	Sex ratio	Sex ratio without servants	Lodger total	Sex ratio
All Saints							
without Bar	397	78.8	44	63.0	81.0	6	500.0
within Bar	378	79.1	33	65.0	80.6	1	—
Holy Rood	771	71.3	84	86.7	69.6	10	25.0
St John	216	75.6	11	37.8	78.3	11	175.0
St Lawrence	299	90.4	56	69.7	96.0	13	160.0
St Mary	178	81.6	26	160.0	72.7	0	
St Michael	670	97.6	48	71.4	100.0	29	—
Portswood	75	108.3	8	166.7	103.0	0	

well known: Celia Fiennes described the town as 'a very neat clean town and a good port . . . [but] now the trade has failed and the town almost forsooke and neglected'.[70] Hers was an over-hasty judgement. Although suffering from the withdrawal of most of its lucrative overseas commerce, the town's coastal trade was increasing, and Southampton continued to attract many immigrants.[71] The town was one of the few in this set suffering a marked decline in numbers over the seventeenth century, but it shared in the general experience of a surplus of females suggesting that it had structural features in common with expanding centres. St Michael and St John, the poorest parishes and those, together with Holy Rood, most closely connected with the port facilities, contained the lowest proportion of servants; St Michael had the most equitable sex ratio, and a high percentage of male lodgers. All twenty-nine lodgers in the parish were apparently resident in the same house – possibly therefore a late seventeenth-century seamen's hostel. The wealthy Holy Rood had a low sex ratio and a high proportion of servants. Outside the walls, the parishes of St Mary and Portswood were more agricultural in character, and thus had a male-dominated servant labour force.

Of the three parishes in Leicester (out of six) enumerated (Table 21), only St Martin and St Mary provide status designations. St Martin was wholly, and St Mary partially, within the old line of the town walls, and these, together with St Margaret, contained a clear majority of the town's population. St Martin was Leicester's wealthiest parish, reflected in the high proportion of servants, while St Margaret was rather more agricultural in character (taking in the town's East Field), and had a less predominant female element in its

Table 21   *Sex ratios in Leicester 1696–9*

Parish	Total	Sex ratio	Servant total	Sex ratio	Sex ratio without servants	Lodger total	Sex ratio
St Margaret	910	92.4	—			—	
St Martin	1537	85.9	191	73.3	87.7	56	80.6
St Mary	695	83.4	68	78.9	83.6	19	46.2

population. The fact that there were large numbers of males in the town, which was growing considerably at this time, is likely to be a reflection of the considerable expansion of hosiery.[72]

An exception to our general picture of female dominance is Norwich (Table 22). It is difficult to determine whether this represents the general picture for the city and its suburbs, since only for a minority of parishes does information on the constituent male/female populations survive. The sex ratios vary between 82.2 and 114.8 (excluding the two smallest parishes). The city parishes represented here are entirely within the southern half of Norwich, and were almost all among the poorest in terms of their inhabitants' ability to pay various mid and late seventeenth-century taxes.[73] Richer central parishes, of which St Peter Mancroft is the clearest

Table 22   *Sex ratios in Norwich 1696*

Parish	Total	Sex ratio
All Saints	425	99.5
Palace precincts	41	115.8
St Etheldreda	250	100.0
St Giles	812	114.8
St John de Sepulchre	780	93.1
St John Timberhill	667	107.1
St Julian	567	100.4
St Michael Thorne	856	94.5
St Peter Mancroft	1933	87.3
St Peter Permountergate	1381	85.4
St Peter Southgate	470	82.2
Bracondale	32	77.8
Earlham	48	100.0
Hellesdon	65	109.7
Thorpe hamlet	69	109.1
Trowse and Carrow hamlet	226	80.8

example, had low sex ratios, while some of the outer, agricultural parishes were male-dominated. Although many central parishes, where we might have expected more females, are omitted, it seems that Norwich's population would nevertheless have been less skewed than in other towns: as in Leicester, this may be at least in part a result of industrial growth, here of the worsted weaving industry.[74]

The general relationship between central location and lower sex ratios also holds for Ipswich (Table 23): outer parishes all have sex ratios lying above the mean, while all the central parishes with the exception of St Stephen come below the mean. The richest parish, St Lawrence, had the lowest ratio (apart from the anomalous St Mary Elm).[75]

These multi-parish urban areas permit us to penetrate a little further something of the towns' social geography. The more skewed sex ratios tend to be found in wealthier inner parishes, where demand for servants was greatest, while the quasi-rural fringes in some cases exhibited male domination. The general tendency even so remains for these larger towns to have more women, and often considerably more women, than men in their population. So, as a broad generalization, we may make a distinction between the cities and the more important towns, which tended to have

Table 23 *Sex ratios in Ipswich 1695*

Parish	Total	Sex ratio
St Clement	1146	81.3
St Helen	223	82.8
St Lawrence	361	68.7
St Margaret	1305	87.0
St Mary Elm	248	34.1
St Mary Key	605	74.9
St Mary Stoke	232	85.6
St Mary Tower	508	75.2
St Matthew	610	86.5
St Nicholas	612	79.5
St Peter	806	93.3
St Stephen	298	87.4
Bishop's hamlet	625	92.3
Brook's hamlet	117	91.8
Ufford hamlet	247	102.5

female-dominated populations, and smaller, especially rural agricultural, settlements which tended to be balanced or to be male-
dominated. With his usual perspicacity, Gregory King noted this
feature, but failed to recognize the degree of difference.[76]

III

Implicit in much of the preceding discussion has been an assumption
that the degree of numerical imbalance between the sexes which is
found in these returns under the Marriage Duty Act represented
some departure from preceding conditions. Although we have no
direct means of comparison, sex ratios at burial – especially of
adults – provide an indirect, if imperfect, measure. Many registers
employed the convention 'child of . . .', 'son of . . .', 'daughter
of . . .', 'infant', etc., and on the assumption that this almost always
referred to children, adults can often be separated out. Imperfec-
tions arise in part through the underregistration of vital events
(often acute during the Civil War and Interregnum), but principally
through the fact that mortality is not uniform throughout the age
structure, and that the very young and the elderly are likely to
predominate in any list of deaths. Moreover, random variation in
numbers from relatively small parishes is likely to produce extreme
volatility in the proportions of male to female burials. However, the
sex ratios of burials should provide some broad indication of
change. Table 24 shows data on sex ratios at burial combined for
five well-spread large urban parishes, displaying falling sex ratios
during the seventeenth century and into the eighteenth (and hence

Table 24   *Sex ratios at burial in five urban parishes 1600–1740**

	Number	Sex ratio	Adult Number	Adult Sex ratio
1601–20	5278	109.6	3245	103.1
1621–40	6254	99.3	3638	97.2
1641–60	5431	118.6	3146	105.9
1661–80	6594	101.2	3506	90.4
1681–1700	7075	97.2	4497	91.0
1701–20	5186	92.5	3118	78.1
1721–40	4424	95.4	2131	97.9

* Bristol St Augustine; Banbury, Oxfordshire; Bury St Edmunds St James, Suffolk;
Ludlow, Shropshire; Ottery St Mary, Devon.

increasing female proportions); the sex ratios before 1660 were usually markedly higher than those after. In general the highest sex ratios are found in the first two decades of the seventeenth century, and lowest in the last two decades of that century and the first two decades of the eighteenth.[77]

Conversely, despite the variation inherent in such series, a variety of registers for rural parishes show static or increasing sex ratios at burial during the seventeenth century. Not only does this evidence from burial registers appear to confirm the supposition that sex ratios in towns were falling in the seventeenth century, but also suggests (given the lag between age at migration and age at death) that the period concentrated upon in this paper often saw those sex ratios at their most skewed. How may we explain then the growing influx of women into towns? Employment in service – in domestic work in houses or in hostelries, and in retailing – was a significant element in producing this phenomenon. The returns made under the Marriage Duty Act show high female proportions among servants. In Boston (Lincolnshire), where we have direct evidence of the hiring of servant labour, one male was hired for every three females, and those females were relatively well-paid, comparing their contracts to those of the men.[78] Service can by no means account for the distinctiveness of these patterns in their entirety, however. The preceding tables reveal that, for the most part, sex ratios are little altered by the exclusion of servants from the totals, while the Bristol evidence cited earlier gave a number of single females living alone or in pairs, a circumstance also found in other towns.[79] The high proportion of girls as servants in central, wealthier parishes largely accounts for much of the female predominance there, but not in poorer or peripheral areas. Occasionally we have evidence of women owning and keeping shops – a phenomenon of growing importance with the blossoming of retailing – while the large numbers of alehouses and inns in such areas must have presented many opportunities for employment. On Bristol Back, Hannah Nicholas and Elinor Evans were recorded as victuallers, Dorothy Woodhouse was a vintner in Bristol High Street, Ann Alexander a milliner (with two maids) along the street, Charity Vaughan a victualler in Back Street, and Susanna Tayler a sempstress on St Nicholas Street.[80] The lack of occupational ascriptions in most of the listings makes such information difficult to acquire, but sufficient, if low-grade, employment opportunity was undoubtedly available – washing, sewing, spinning, charring, lodgings-keeping.[81] Expansion of the tertiary sector is very likely to produce widening scope for the employment of females.[82]

Although the evidence on sex ratios in towns at the end of the seventeenth century cannot provide an indication of both gross and net migration flows, something may be recovered by considering the general context of town economies. Since the urban sector was growing rapidly, and there is little direct evidence of outward movement from town to country, net rural–urban migration flows must have been a significant proportion of the gross flows. The decline of population in towns such as Southampton – for not all towns were growing – produced the same structural outcome as for towns that were growing fast. It seems unlikely that this was produced by an efflux of males leaving a residue of females. Rather, it reflected the continued (if significantly diminished) attractiveness of depressed towns to migrants with female movement predominant as elsewhere.

The data would suggest that while net streams of migrants to towns were disproportionately composed of females, a significantly high proportion of males was left in rural areas. This may have considerable demographic and economic implications.[83] The growth of towns in the later decades of the seventeenth century and the early decades of the eighteenth was, in part, the result of rising real incomes and the broadening of the basis of demand, the expansion of tertiary employment as well as of urban industry, and of rising agricultural productivity releasing many from the land.[84] We have seen some of the results of this in terms of female preponderance in urban populations (fuelled by large inflows of women migrants) and the large proportions of men in many village populations. This balance would undoubtedly result in diminished local marriage opportunities, especially if the migrations were permanent, with a surplus of unmarried males in many villages, of unmarried females in many towns, and relative economic opportunity continuing to keep them apart. We do find that celibacy was a marked feature of the seventeenth century, with high proportions of the population not marrying in mid and later seventeenth-century cohorts.[85] Combined with high marriage ages (and net overseas emigration), this was a powerful check to population growth, contributing to a national fall in numbers. Thus we may have a circular system in which female-selective urban immigration, low population growth, and high real incomes (arising from low rates of growth combined with high productivity in agriculture) produced female-selective movement into towns. The onset of sustained population growth in the eighteenth century, with the overwhelming expansion of large industrial centres, may have broken this particular system, although female-selective migration to many towns remained strong.

IV

The slowing of population growth in the latter part of the seventeenth century seems to have promoted two opposing migration effects. Whereas residential mobility within the countryside slowed, all the evidence points to continued large-scale movement into towns. Urban demographic increase bit deeply into the population of the countryside. Fortunate coincidence has produced the combination of sources used in this paper, covering a period which may turn out in many ways to have been crucial for the development of an early industrial urban society. Much analysis of the dimensions of migration into towns has usually taken place within a genderless framework, while discussion of particular groups of migrants has generally assumed the importance of men in an urban economy. After all, most sources concentrate on males, and little attention has been paid to the determination of populations at risk in towns, or the male/female divisions within them. As has often been said before, the fact that sources are silent on the employment opportunities of women did not mean that they had none.

Large-scale quantitative sources describing the movements of newcomers to towns in the eighteenth century are of a different character from those used here for the seventeenth. The position of marked female domination of town populations was not peculiar to the final decades of the seventeenth century, but persisted throughout the eighteenth century.[86] The continued growth of the urban population, despite greater natural increase within towns, was still largely a product of immigration.[87] During much of the seventeenth and eighteenth centuries those attributes of town life – carriages and servants, eating houses, shops and brothels – which frightened off our yokel Ned played a major part in the attraction of many others to town life.

Acknowledgements

For their helpful comments, I wish to thank Peter Clark and the other contributors to this book, Tony Wrigley, Roger Schofield, Richard Smith, Richard Wall and Ann Kussmaul.

Notes and references

1   Somerset RO, DD/SF 1343, MS poem *c*. 1690.
2   P. Clark, 'The migrant in Kentish towns 1580–1640', in P. Clark and P. Slack (eds.), *Crisis and Order in English Towns 1500–1700* (1972), pp. 117–63; J. Patten, *Rural–Urban Migration in Pre-Industrial England* (University of Oxford School of Geography research paper 1973); V. Brodsky Elliott, 'Marriage and mobility in pre-industrial England' (unpublished PhD thesis, University of Cambridge 1979).
3   M. Anderson, 'Urban migration in nineteenth century Lancashire: insights into two competing hypotheses', *Annales de démographie historique 1971*, pp. 13–26.
4   P. Clark, 'Migration in England during the late seventeenth and early eighteenth centuries', *P. and P.*, no. 83 (1979), pp. 57–90. D. C. Souden, 'Pre-industrial English local migration fields' (unpublished PhD thesis, University of Cambridge 1981), uses sources covering the seventeenth and eighteenth centuries, concentrating upon changing movement within the countryside and relating changes in the demographic environment to migration processes.
5   Estimates from P. Corfield, 'Urban development in England and Wales in the sixteenth and seventeenth centuries', in D. C. Coleman and A. H. John (eds.), *Trade, Government and Economy in Pre-Industrial England* (1976), pp. 214–47; P. Corfield, *The Impact of English Towns 1700–1800* (1982), pp. 8–11; E. A. Wrigley, 'Urban growth in early modern England', *Journal of Interdisciplinary History* (forthcoming 1984). I am grateful to Professor Wrigley for providing me with a copy of this paper.
6   Wrigley, 'Urban growth', Tables 2 and 3; E. A. Wrigley and R. S. Schofield, *The Population History of England 1541–1871* (1981), pp. 528–9.
7   Corfield, 'Urban development', pp. 229–30; Wrigley, 'Urban growth'.
8   Souden, 'Pre-industrial English local migration fields', pp. 1–24, considers some of these questions in greater detail. Patten, *Rural–Urban Migration*, examines the sources and the literature before that date.
9   J. Patten, 'Patterns of migration and movement of labour to three pre-industrial East Anglian towns', *Journal of Historical Geography*, 2 (1976), pp. 118–28; Brodsky Elliott, 'Marriage and mobility', parts 2 and 3; Clark, 'Migration in England', pp. 61–2.
10 P. Styles, 'The evolution of the Law of Settlement', in P. Styles, *Studies in Seventeenth Century West Midlands History* (1978), pp. 187–207; R. A. Pelham, 'The immigrant population of Birmingham 1686–1726',

Trans. Birmingham Archaeolog. Soc., **61** (1940), pp. 45–80; Clark, 'Migration in England', pp. 62–3, 83–8.

11 Clark, 'Migration in England', pp. 85–8; Souden, 'Pre-industrial English local migration fields', pp. 270–85.

12 Souden, 'Pre-industrial English local migration fields', pp. 45–59.

13 ibid., pp. 40–4, 59–63.

14 Devon RO, Chanter 864–80, 8297–99, Exeter Cathedral Lib., AE/III/1; Somerset RO, D/D/Cd 93, 95–7, 102, 106, 108, 155; Salisbury Diocesan RO (now at Wiltshire RO), B/DC 58–61; Bodl. MSS Oxf. Dioc. papers *c.* 28–30, Oxf. Archd. papers *c.* 119–20; Leicestershire RO, 1 D 41/4 xxix–xxxiii, xxxv–xxxvi, xxxix, xli, xlvi–xlviii; Norfolk and Norwich RO, DEP/46–54, ANW/7/9.

15 J. Adams, *Index Villaris* (1680), was used as a means of determining whether or not a place was a town at this time. This gazetteer is by no means ideal, for some places with market functions which are listed there were barely viable as any sort of settlement. Such small settlements, however, rarely produced any witnesses, and certainly produced none in any numbers, while the better-represented larger settlements would more readily be described as towns or as possessing some urban functions.

16 The data from Norwich represent a sampling of the deposition material there. See Souden, 'Pre-industrial English local migration fields', pp. 32–40 for a description of the sampling strategy and of the larger collection of seventeenth-century church court depositions of which those analysed here are a subset.

17 ibid., pp. 46–56. Whether this is a result of greater independence, social significance, or numerical predominance of women – or a result of the lowered prestige of the courts, and hence fewer social barriers to women's testimony – is an unresolved problem. Since defamation cases were of greater proportional significance in the courts' business, more women would have appeared simply as witnesses to the fact.

18

Age structure of witnesses			National age structure (excluding children under 15)	
			1661	1691
Age	N	Per cent	Per cent	Per cent
<25	458	20.2	26.5	24.5
25–59	1573	69.5	60.2	62.4
>59	231	10.2	13.3	13.1

The national population age structure is taken from Wrigley and Schofield, *Population History*, pp. 528–9, for 1661 and 1691.

19　Internal evidence suggests that a number of these were lawyers appearing before the courts and giving testimony.

20　For a full discussion of the utility of measuring sign-literacy, and of levels of literacy and sex/location differentials during this period, D. Cressy, *Literacy and the Social Order: Reading and Writing in Tudor and Stuart England* (1980).

21　For evidence on similar regional trends in rural populations, Souden, 'Pre-industrial English local migration fields', pp. 72–97.

22　Clark, 'Migration in England', pp. 65–7, also shows this pattern, although with slightly less variation between the constituent female populations than here.

23　The larger/smaller distinction used here is essentially a pragmatic one, based upon the main towns within each jurisdiction, especially those well-represented in the deposition material, and all other towns.

24　For recent expositions, see Corfield, *The Impact of English Towns* esp. pp. 82–98; P. Borsay, 'The English urban renaissance: the development of provincial urban culture c. 1680–1760', *Social History*, no. 5 (1977), pp. 581–603.

25　For the general correlation between sign-literacy and social status, Cressy, *Literacy and the Social Order*.

26　Souden, 'Pre-industrial English migration fields', pp. 72–8, 80–4, 87–97.

27　For a fuller description of the technique, ibid., pp. 154–8, and for the results mentioned here, ibid., pp. 234–48.

28　These themes are developed at greater length in Souden, ibid.

29　Ages at apprenticeship for boys undoubtedly account for much of the difference; the differences are somewhat smaller than was the case in the first half of the seventeenth century, an artefact possibly of the lesser significance in our period of the institution of craft apprenticeship in towns. ibid., pp. 98–101, 104–5, 107–20.

30　Standard deviation 55.5.

31　Standard deviation 44.2.

32　Standard deviation 54.9.

33　Standard deviation 46.8.

34　Distances between places are linear, measured 'as the crow flies', and are calculated using the National Grid co-ordinates of the Ordnance Survey, *Gazetteer of Great Britain* (1980).

35　Standard deviations 60.7 and 54.9 respectively.

36　Males, N = 148, N signing = 107, standard deviation 67.2 (literate), 34.7 (illiterate); females, N = 49, N signing = 15, standard deviation 82.0 (literate), 33.2 (illiterate).

37　Devon RO, ECA book 102, fols. 165–86.

38　Standard deviation 61.1.

39　Standard deviation 26.5.

40　W. B. Stephens, *Seventeenth-Century Exeter* (1958), pp. 85–102.

41 Devon RO, ECA book 102, fol. 166; W. G. Hoskins (ed.), *Exeter in the Seventeenth Century* (Devon and Cornwall Record Society, new series, **2** 1957).

42 Souden, 'Pre-industrial English migration fields', pp. 124–5.

43 *VCH*, Oxfordshire, **4**, pp. 115–18, 138–9.

44 Clark, 'Migrant in Kentish towns'; P. A. Slack, 'Vagrants and vagrancy in England 1598–1664', *EcHR*, 2nd series, **30** (1974), pp. 360–79.

45 Souden, 'Pre-industrial English migration fields', *passim*.

46 Clark, 'Migration in England', pp. 69–73.

47 Souden, 'Pre-industrial English migration fields', pp. 127–39.

48 cf. Patten, 'Patterns of migration'.

49 C. I. Hammer Jr, 'The mobility of skilled labour in late medieval England: some Oxford evidence', *Vierteljahrschrift für Sozial-und Wirtschaftsgeschichte*, **63** (1976), pp. 195–210; E. G. Thomas, 'The Poor Law migrant to Oxford 1700–1795', *Oxoniensia*, **45** (1980), pp. 300–5.

50 This pattern is also found for villages in South-East Devon: Souden, 'Pre-industrial English migration fields', Figs. 2.13–2.16.

51 Bodl. MS Oxf. Archd. papers c. 119; Devon RO, Chanter 875; Leicestershire RO, 1 D 41/4 xxxiii.

52 6 & 7 Wm & Mary, c. 6.

53 G. King, *Natural and Political Observations and Conclusions upon the State and Condition of England* (1696); cf. D. V. Glass, 'Two papers on Gregory King', in D. V. Glass and D. E. C. Eversley (eds.), *Population in History* (1965), pp. 159–220.

54 P. Laslett, 'Mean household size in England since the sixteenth century', in P. Laslett and R. Wall (eds.), *Household and Family in Past Time* (1972), pp. 125–58; R. Wall, 'Regional and temporal variation in English household structure since 1650', in J. Hobcraft and P. Rees (eds.), *Regional Demographic Development* (1979), pp. 89–116; D. Souden and G. Lasker, 'Biological interrelationships between parishes in East Kent: an analysis of the Marriage Duty Act returns for 1705', *Local Population Studies*, no. 21 (1978), pp. 30–9.

55 Some lists are annotated with inhabitants' movements in the years after the enumerations: Bilston, Staffordshire RO, D667/3/1; Gt. Parndon, Essex RO, D/P 34/1/2.

56 Bristol: E. Ralph and M. Williams (eds.), *The Inhabitants of Bristol in 1696* (Bristol Record Society, **25** 1968). Derbyshire: R. E. Chester Waters (ed.), *A Statutory List of the Inhabitants of Melbourne, Derbyshire in 1696* (1885). Devon: BL, Harl. MS 6832. Dorset: Lyme Regis, Dorset RO, B7/M1/2; Colway, Dorset RO, B7/H2. Essex: Essex RO, D/P 34/1/2. Gloucestershire: Gloucester, G. King, 'MS Journal', in P. Laslett (ed.), *The Earliest Classics: Graunt and King* (1973), p. 118; Stinchcombe, Gloucestershire RO, P312 MI3. Hampshire: Southampton RO, SC14/2/66A, 67A, 69–70, 70A, 71–2, 73A. Kent: New

Romney, Kent AO, NR/RTb2; Sevenoaks, Riverhead and Weald, King, 'MS Journal', pp. 90–1; rest, Kent AO, Q/CTz2. Leicestershire: King, 'MS Journal', p. 90. Middlesex: King, 'MS Journal', p. 90. Northamptonshire: Northamptonshire RO, C(TM)90/1–7, 9–12, 14–22. Norfolk: King, 'MS Journal', p. 118. Staffordshire: Bilston, Staffs. RO, D667/3/1; Lichfield, King, 'MS Journal', pp. 90–1. Suffolk: Bury St Edmunds, St James, Suffolk RO, Bury branch, 508/1; Ipswich, G. R. Clarke, *The History and Description of the Town and Borough of Ipswich* (1830), p. 69. Warwickshire: Coleshill, King, 'MS Journal', p. 90; Fenny Compton, P. Styles, 'A census of a Warwickshire village in 1698', in Styles, *Studies in Seventeenth Century West Midlands History*, pp. 90–107, esp. p. 94. Wiltshire: Wilts. RO, 212B/WG8.

57   King, 'MS Journal', p. 118. Very many returns survive for London: D. V. Glass (ed.), *London Inhabitants Within the Walls, 1695*, (London Record Society, **2** 1966).

58   Ralph and Williams, *The Inhabitants of Bristol*; Bristol RO, Rates and taxes, returns under 6 & 7 Wm & Mary, c. 6, 1695–1706, 84 enumerations.

59   King, 'MS Journal', p. 118.

60   Wrigley and Schofield, *Population History*, p. 225.

61   D. Souden, ' "Rogues, whores and vagabonds"? Indentured servant emigrants to North America, and the case of mid-seventeenth-century Bristol', *Social History*, no. 3 (1978), pp. 23–41; D. Souden, 'English indentured servants and the trans-Atlantic colonial economy', in S. Marks and P. Richardson (eds.), *Essays on International Labour Migration* (forthcoming); H. A. Gemery, 'Emigration from the British Isles to the New World, 1630–1700: inferences from colonial populations', *Research in Economic History*, **5** (1980), pp. 179–231.

62   The Norwich data are supported by an enumeration of 1693, returning totals for all parishes (as do King's notes): these match closely. *Gentlemen's Magazine*, **22** (1752), p. 347.

63   A. Kussmaul, *Servants in Husbandry in Early Modern England* (1981), pp. 12–13, 143–7.

64   R. Mols, *Introduction à la Démographie Historique des Villes d'Europe du XIVᵉ au XVIIIᵉ Siècle* (Louvain 1955) **2**, pp. 183–99. For an investigation of the structure of households within a town with even greater female preponderance, in wartime, see R. Wall, 'The composition of households in a population of six men to ten women: south-east Bruges in 1814', in R. Wall with J. Robin and P. Laslett (eds.), *Family Forms in Historic Europe* (1983), pp. 421–74.

65   The Bristol enumerations blur the distinctions between male servants and male apprentices, so the two categories are amalgamated here.

66   For mariners and merchants renting lodging in these areas, see, for example, Bristol RO, 04439(3), Depositions 1657–61, (unfol.) 17 May

1658, depositions of John Richardson, Richard Wall and Richard Gray, 18 February 1659, deposition of Abraham Plea.

67　This might also help explain the skewed nature of sex ratios in places such as Lyme Regis and Ipswich.

68　Ralph and Williams, *The Inhabitants of Bristol*, p. 115.

69　Bristol City Reference Lib., 4531 s. 165–9.

70　C. Morris (ed.), *The Journeys of Celia Fiennes* (1947), p. 54. The relative decline of Southampton *vis-à-vis* other Hampshire towns is tabulated in A. Rosen, 'Winchester in transition, 1580–1700', in P. Clark (ed.), *Country Towns in Pre-Industrial England* (1981), pp. 144–95, esp. p. 175.

71　A. T. Patterson, *A History of Southampton 1700–1914: I* (Southampton Records Series, **11** 1966), pp. 3–11; Southampton RO, SC/ AG6/1–3 Examinations books 1712–70, SC9/4 Sessions papers.

72　*VCH*, Leics., **4**, pp. 153–8, 350–69.

73　J. T. Evans, *Seventeenth Century Norwich* (1979), pp. 15–17.

74　P. Corfield, 'An English provincial capital in the later seventeenth century: the case of Norwich', in Clark and Slack, *Crisis and Order*, pp. 263–310, esp. pp. 278–87.

75　G. R. Clarke, *The History and Description of the Town and Borough of Ipswich* (1830), p. 69. Clarke double-counted females, in heading the column of parish totals 'males' (M. Reed, 'Economic structure and change in seventeenth-century Ipswich', in Clark, *Country Towns*, p. 137 n.) so the anomalous figures for St Mary Elm may be the result of a transcription error.

76　King, 'MS Journal', p. 39.

77　J. S. W. Gibson (ed.), *Baptism and Burial Register of Banbury, Oxfordshire, 1558–1723* (Banbury Hist. Soc. **7, 9** 1966–8); A. Sabin (ed.), *The Registers of the Church of St Augustine the Less, Bristol, 1577–1700* (Bristol and Gloucestershire Archaeol. Soc., Records Section, **3**, 1961); S. H. A. Hervey (ed.), *Bury St Edmunds St James Parish Registers: Burials 1562–1800* (Suffolk Green Books **17** 1916); *Ludlow Parish Register 1558–1812* (Shropshire Parish Registers [diocese of Hereford], **13–14** 1912–15); H. Tapley Soper (ed.), *The Register of Baptisms, Marriages and Burials of the Parish of Ottery St Mary, 1601–1837* (Devon and Cornwall Record Soc., **3** 1908–29). Bristol data are not available after 1700, Banbury data are not available after 1720.

78　Boston Borough Offices, 3/D/1.

79　Above, pp. 153–4.

80　Ralph and Williams, *Inhabitants of Bristol*, pp. 136–48. St Nicholas parish was the only enumeration giving occupational titles with any frequency.

81　Thus, contrary to the argument advanced in A. Clark, *The Working Life of Women in the Seventeenth Century* (1913), there may have been greater, rather than less, female participation in the active labour force by the later seventeenth century. She provides a wide-ranging description of women's productive work in early modern England.

82 Employment of women as sempstresses, shopkeepers, etc. in London earlier in the century is noted in V. Brodsky Elliott, 'Single women in the London marriage market: age, status and mobility, 1598–1619', in R. B. Outhwaite (ed.), *Marriage and Society: Essays in the Social History of Marriage* (1981), pp. 81–100, esp. pp. 91–2. Borsay, 'English urban renaissance', discusses the significance of that expansion only in terms of the widening of the base of men's occupations in towns.

83 The discussion in R. M. Smith, 'Fertility, economy and household formation in England over three centuries', *Population and Development Review,* **7** (1981), pp. 595–622, explores a number of such feedback mechanisms within early modern English society. That argument may usefully be extended to encompass the phenomena discussed here.

84 An elegant formulation of this is found in Wrigley, 'Urban growth'.

85 Wrigley and Schofield, *Population History*, pp. 257–65.

86 Corfield, *The Impact of English Towns*, p. 99.

87 Settlement papers and examinations, the principal source to be used for the direct study of eighteenth-century movement into towns, need as careful a scrutiny for their utility as depositions have received.

5 Urban growth and agricultural change in the West Midlands during the seventeenth and eighteenth centuries

Peter Large

One of the salient features of urban growth from the late seventeenth century was the emergence of provincial manufacturing towns. The cluster of West Midlands metalware towns was a major area of development, and Birmingham, the leading settlement in the region, grew from its market town origins in 1660 to become the fourth largest urban area in England by 1801 with a population of 69,000.[1]

The century from 1660 to 1760 was described by Professor Court as 'the great age of Midland industrial development' in which the labour intensive metalware trades developed in and around the South Staffordshire coal-field and the increasing population supported substantial urban growth.[2] The availability of coal and the accessibility of the region by road and river were important factors in this early industrial and urban growth, but the developments were also deeply rooted in the countryside and the rural society out of which they emerged.[3] The 'wood-pasture' characteristics of the region were a crucial factor in the nascent industrial growth of the sixteenth century and agricultural development continued to play an important role in determining the pace and shape of the urban and industrial advance through the seventeenth and eighteenth centuries.

I

Metalworking became increasingly important in the pastoral parishes of the region from the 1560s as the growth of the indigenous population and waves of immigration, during the 1580s and 1600s, stimulated the emerging metalware trades.[4] By the beginning of the seventeenth century, the area was producing a wide range of metalwares including nails, locks, buckles, spurs, stirrups, bridlebits, arrowheads and scythes. Although the manufacture of these goods was spread over the pastoral regions of South Staffordshire, West Warwickshire and North Worcestershire, it was centred on the South Staffordshire plateau. In early decades of the seven-teenth century, the commons of Sedgley and Smethwick were being overwhelmed by nail-makers' cottages and 'corn, grain and other victuals' were being drawn from beyond the hardware district to support the population.[5]

During the seventeenth century the metalware trades expanded upon the firm foundation already established by 1600. The pace of progress in the short term was dictated by the rhythms of the economy as a whole and the quality of the harvests. However, any setbacks seem to have been superficial rather than structural and the complaints of hardship voiced by branches of the English textile industry were rarely echoed by the West Midlands metalworkers. The hardware trades were primarily orientated towards the domestic market and supplied commodities in constant agricultural and domestic use to the regions of Midland, Southern and Western England. During the final quarter of the seventeenth century the growing export trade to the American and West Indian colonies and to Europe supplemented the domestic markets but did not supplant them.[6]

The growth of the home and export markets for metalware was accompanied by the increasing concentration of the trade on the South Staffordshire plateau and in the Birmingham region and the localization of particular skills. Willenhall, for example, became the centre of the lock-making industry, while saddlers' ironware was concentrated in Walsall. Nail-making was ubiquitous but spread most densely in Dudley, Rowley Regis and Sedgley. The growth of these labour intensive industries within the confines of South Staffordshire and the Birmingham region resulted in a significant increase of population. The population of the South Staffordshire plateau seems to have expanded by two and a half to three times between the 1560s and the 1660s.[7] In Sedgley, one of the rapidly growing centres of nail-making, the number of inhabitants rose from less than 600 in 1563 to more than 2300 in 1663 and cottages sprawled across the heathland to form the townships of Coseley and Ettingshall.[8] The parishes of Darlaston and Kingswinford also witnessed dramatic increases in population during the late sixteenth and early seventeenth centuries and their waste lands were slowly covered with cottages. Richard Baxter, the renowned clergyman, knew the Dudley area well in the mid years of the seventeenth century and noted 'the exceeding populousness of the Country, where the Woods and Commons are planted with Nailers, Scithe-

Smiths, and other Iron-Labourers, like a continued Village'.[9] The development of these labour intensive metalworking trades was reflected in urban growth. The old market towns emerged as the nerve centres of the growing iron trades. Ironmongers distributed rod and bar iron from their warehouses in Birmingham, Wolverhampton, Stourbridge and Walsall while the towns themselves became the centre for more sophisticated metalware manufacture and major markets for increasing volumes of foodstuffs.

The last quarter of the seventeenth century saw the beginning of the remarkable growth of Birmingham. The population of the town rose from under 6000 at the Restoration to about 7000 in 1700. This growth occurred within the confines of the old town and was based upon an expansion among the smiths and cutlers, the traditional ironware trades centred on Deritend.[10] In the 1690s Guy Miege observed that Birmingham 'drives a great Trade of Iron and Steel Wares, Saddles, and Bridles, which find good vent at London, Ireland, and other parts'.[11] In the eighteenth century development was more rapid; the population reached 11,400 in 1720 and 23,700 by 1750.[12] As the number of inhabitants multiplied, building activity increased. In 1660 the town was aligned along the main routes leading from the South Staffordshire plateau to the crossing of the River Rea at Deritend. From the 1690s new streets spread to the north across the well-drained hillside away from the Rea.[13]

The expansion of Birmingham resulted from the emergence of the town as an industrial, commercial and service centre. Until the end of the seventeenth century the population of the town specialized in the manufacture of nails, saddlers' ironmongery and edge tools. From the 1690s, however, smiths and cutlers were superseded by the growth in the manufacture of guns, buckles, buttons and steel toys. These new trades advanced rapidly during the first half of the eighteenth century and their ascendancy was reflected in the building of the New Hall estate which was inhabited largely by the small masters of the buckle, gun and toy trades.[14]

Birmingham was also the hub of the commercial life of the metalware region. The roads from Wolverhampton, Wednesbury, Dudley and Halesowen converged on Birmingham and the town was well placed between the South Staffordshire coal-field and the markets of Southern and Eastern England. In 1726 the London to Shrewsbury road between Birmingham and Wolverhampton had 'great number of Carriages constantly employed on carrying of Iron and Iron Goods'. The road from Dudley was used 'in carrying

Iron-wares, coals and Lime to Birmingham; and so into the Counties of Warwick, Northampton and other counties'.[15] Birmingham ironmongers controlled the organization of the South Staffordshire iron trade and the marketing of its products and they were the most important purchasers from the Foley and Knight Ironworks.[16] An ironmonger, John Pemberton, was responsible for building the elegant Old Square. By 1719 this square comprised sixteen imposing properties of which nine were occupied by leading ironmongers.[17]

As the town developed industrially and commercially, it also evolved as a service centre. Attorneys and physicians dwelt in Temple Row, while retail shops spread down the High Street, New Street and Bull Street, and booksellers and printers settled around High Town.[18] However, Birmingham shared its position as a social centre with Stourbridge. The latter had always attracted the gentry and in the early eighteenth century it held the most prestigious race meeting in the district.[19] As in Birmingham, the more affluent ironmongers built elegant streets including Holloway which was considered to be 'like Cheapside' and 'the glory of the town'.[20]

If Stourbridge was placed second to Birmingham as a social centre, Wolverhampton was similarly placed as a commercial and industrial town. The population of Wolverhampton grew from about 5600 in 1665 to 7450 in 1750.[21] The town supported a small professional class and an elaborate retail network, but it was primarily important for the distribution of rod and bar iron and as the centre of lock-making. Walsall served the same functions as Wolverhampton on the east of the coal-field. It was dominant in the production of saddlers' ironmongery and became increasingly involved in buckle-making during the eighteenth century. The town's population increased from 4260 in 1665 to 6100 in 1695.[22]

Urban growth in the West Midlands was accompanied by the spread of the metalware trades which depended less on the availability of raw materials than on the application of skill. Birmingham in common with other towns on the edge of the coal-field, turned to the new manufacture. But the basic trades continued to be the principal focus of growth, and the nail-making villages of the coal-field continued to expand during the eighteenth century as the whole region emerged as an industrial district comprising a network of ironworking villages and market towns. Increasing population density was a steady process and in 1776 Arthur Young echoed Richard Baxter, the mid seventeenth-century observer, when he referred to 'one continued village of nailers' between West Bromwich and Birmingham.[23] In this setting the vital function of the towns was to distribute raw materials, finished metalware and food-stuffs. As the population grew the demand for foodstuffs increased. This steady expansion involved adjustments in the agricultural balance of the West Midlands which were in themselves important in shaping the urban and industrial development of the region.

II

The farmers of the light soils on the periphery of the South Stafford-shire plateau were ideally situated to supply the increasing demands for grain from the industrializing towns and villages. In the six-teenth century, however, in this peripheral area at the foot of the Clent and Lickey Hills, a pastoral and industrial rural economy had evolved. In the late sixteenth century textile production and nail-making were springing up in the more remote pastoral hamlets of Bromsgrove while Chaddesley Corbett and Belbroughton were the heart of the West Midlands scythe-making industry. In the latter, stock rearing was the primary agricultural activity during most of the sixteenth century and scythe-making was more important than sheep grazing before the 1580s.[24] During the first quarter of the seventeenth century, however, grain production and sheep grazing became increasingly prominent. This shift towards mixed farming and the concomitant increase in the use of the common wastes stifled the spread of metalworking.

From the late sixteenth century arable farming was growing in importance in this area. In the opening years of the seventeenth century the traditional crop rotation of rye, barley and fallow was beginning to undergo modification. Oats and pulse were introduced into the spring crops and wheat was sown in the winter crops alongside rye.[25] In the spring of 1603, for example, John Norisse of Winterfold had about 50 acres in arable. Of this, 26 acres were sown with rye and the remainder was divided between barley, oats and pulse. During the previous year he had experimented with wheat, and still had some of the grain in his barn.[26] By the 1620s wheat was fully established as an integral part of the arable rotation and in 1621, another Winterford farmer John Heath sowed six acres of wheat and ten acres of rye as his winter crops and twelve acres of barley and nine acres of pulse in the spring rotation.[27] The smaller farms were also fully involved in the improvement of arable farm-ing. In 1627, for instance, John Backe of Yieldingtree was growing

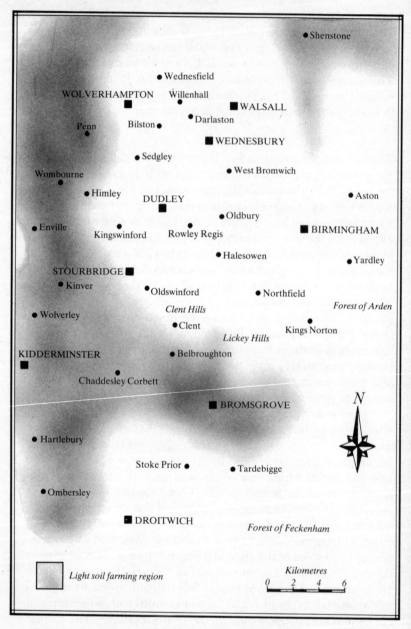

Figure 9   *The West Midlands metalworking region and agricultural periphery*

4 acres of wheat and rye, half an acre of oats, 2.5 acres of pulse and 3.75 acres of barley.[28]

The improvement in arable farming was based upon the more intensive use of the common wastes to which all the tenants had access. The application of manure from sheep grazed on the waste lands was fundamental to the success of more intensive arable farming and as the variety of crops increased so did the number of sheep grazed on the commons. In both Belbroughton and Chaddesley Corbett, the common waste limits were eighty and 120 sheep respectively and observance of the manorial stinting regulations ensured common pasturage for all the tenants.[29]

Tighter control of the common wastes had profound implications for the metalworking trades. As the commons were progressively absorbed in sheep grazing, Belbroughton and Chaddesley Corbett were less able to offer prospective immigrants the attractions of redundant land. While Bromsgrove, Tardebigge and Stoke Prior were subject to immigration following the disafforestation of Feckenham before and during the Interregnum, Belbroughton and Chaddesley Corbett were untouched. Thus, the body of surplus labour associated with many of the more basic metalware trades was absent. In contrast to South Staffordshire and the Sheffield region, where scythe-making was part of a larger assemblage of metalware trades, in Chaddesley Corbett and Belbroughton the scythesmiths and grinders stood alone.[30]

Although in many areas scythe-making was found in proximity to the more basic metalware trades, almost everywhere there was a social distinction between the scythesmiths and the less skilled metalworkers. Edge tool-makers were the élite of the rural metalworkers; their manufacturing processes were more complex than those of the mass trades and they tended to operate independently of the ironmongers and factors.[31] In most areas scythesmiths were more deeply involved in agricultural activities than the less prosperous nailers. Farming, particularly stock rearing on a commercial scale, provided working capital for scythesmiths and enabled them to hold stocks of raw materials and finished scythes and to sell on credit. Richard Smith of Drayton in Chaddesley Corbett was typical in the extent to which he tied up capital in the manufacture and marketing of scythes. In late January 1608, at the beginning of his scythe-making campaign, he had three tons of bar iron worth £37.9.0d and steel valued at £25. He was also owed £9 for scythes sold during the previous spring and summer to various people as far away as Nottingham.[32] In May 1605, at the end of the scythe-making season, Richard Prynn of Belbroughton was similarly laden with stock, but largely in the form of 'sithes redye wroughte' valued at £100 and 'yron and Steele unwrought' worth just £9.[33]

Scythe-making in North Worcestershire was a seasonal business which took place between January and April each year. Iron and steel were purchased in late autumn and manufacture reached its climax in March and April when the fast-flowing streams of the area made the blade mills most effective for grinding. The newly wrought blades were sold in the spring and summer to meet the mid year agricultural demand for scythes and sickles.[34] By concentrating production in the first quarter of the year, the scythesmiths minimized the period over which they were financing large stocks of materials and blades. Moreover, this routine suited the work rhythms of rearing and winter corn production, which left the early months of the year quite free.

However, as the opportunities for sheep and corn husbandry became more evident in the early seventeenth century, the equilibrium of pastoral farming and scythe-making was disrupted. The essence of the improvement in arable farming was the adoption of a greater variety of spring crops, especially pulses, and more intense manuring by sheep. The growth in the acreage of spring tillage naturally involved more ploughing in the early months of the year, but above all, the rise of sheep breeding created entirely new work. Lambing took place between the beginning of January and the end of March, at the time when scythe-making was at its height.[35] During the first half of the seventeenth century scythe-makers in Chaddesley Corbett and Belbroughton became increasingly committed to arable farming and sheep breeding. In 1608, Christian Sykes, a scythe-maker, of Drayton had thirteen 'day worke' of rye and 22 acres of lent grain as well as a flock of seventy-three sheep and a small herd of five cows.[36] Involvement in mixed farming on this scale tended to overshadow scythe-making and by the 1620s those who were engaged in the trade were beginning to consider themselves primarily as farmers. John Smith of Drayton, for example, made 1200 scythes in the early months of 1620, but entitled himself 'yeoman' in contrast to his father, who in 1608 described himself as a 'sithsmith'. In 1608 Richard Smith had shown particular concern in his will for the disposition of his scythe-making tools and had instructed John to teach his younger brother the trade. By 1620, John Smith was far more concerned about disposing of his agricultural land and in his will made detailed reference to 'all such corne as is now tilled and growing on the said landes and to be tilled this present season with barley, pease, otes or any other greaine'.[37]

Thus, between the 1580s and the 1640s Chaddesley Corbett and Belbroughton were transformed from early centres of the metal-ware trades into important grain producing parishes in which even the long-established scythe-making industry was beginning to recede. This change was made possible by the commercial oppor-tunities for corn growing offered by the expanding population of South Staffordshire and the Birmingham region. As we have seen, the rise in cereal production was underpinned by the regulated grazing of the common wastes and the cultivation of pulse crops which together facilitated an increase in the number of sheep and thereby improved the supply of manure. Sheep fold sustained and enhanced arable productivity and, in particular, supported more intensive barley cultivation. The introduction of convertible husbandry throughout the region was an additional prop to arable productivity because it helped to *restore* fertility after tillage. Ley farming however did little to *improve* fertility since livestock grazed on natural grass leys tended to take out as much as they put in.[38] Only by feeding sheep on the wastes and folding them on the arable, or by growing leguminous crops like pulses as animal food, could fertility be transferred to the arable land.

In the second half of the seventeenth century, however, these sources of fertility were supplemented by the introduction of the 'artificial' grasses in the form of various clovers and rye grass. These grasses were legumes which fixed nitrogen directly in the soil through their roots, but their major contribution was as fodder crops. The new grasses improved leys dramatically, and by increas-ing the supply of fodder they allowed more sheep to be kept and better fed, thus producing more dung. Heavier applications of manure improved the yields of fodder crop as well as cereals and facilitated a further increase in livestock. The new grasses were particularly suited to light soils which were dry enough for sheep to be kept on the land during winter to feed off the fodder crops, thus returning manure for a following cereal crop.[39]

The diffusion of the artificial grasses, particularly clover, occurred in the light soil region of North Worcestershire during the third quarter of the seventeenth century. the introduction of clover was of primary importance in increasing the supply of grain for the expanding centres of the metalware trades in South Staffordshire and around Birmingham. Andrew Yarranton, one of the early advocates of clover, knew this area intimately and emphasized, above all, the increase in tillage which the use of clover made possible. Writing in 1663 he referred specifically to the light soils of North Worcestershire and claimed that he wished 'to give my countrymen a remedy for this gravelly, dry, sandy or rye land which is worn out with tillage and liming'.[40] By the 1670s the success of clover was such that the value of clover hay had become a major cause of strife between tithe owners and farmers in Belbroughton, Bromsgrove and Chaddesley Corbett.[41]

As a result of the introduction of clover both livestock numbers and crop yields increased and a wider range of cereal crops was adopted. During the second half of the seventeenth century, barley rather than oats and rye dominated in more complex crop combinations which included wheat and particularly pulse crops. The probate inventories for Belbroughton, Bromsgrove and Chaddesley Corbett clearly reveal the increase in the number of livestock and the range of crops.

Table 25   *Mean livestock numbers and crop acreages in Belbroughton, Bromsgrove and Chaddesley Corbett*[42]

	Livestock			Crop acreage				
	Cows*	Sheep	Horses	Wheat	Rye	Bar.	Oats	Pulse
1600–40	5.8	68	2	2	12	8	6	3
1670–1700	9.1	95	4.5	5	7	14	2	6

* Including heifers.

Stimulated by the heightened demand for foodstuffs from the metalware region to the north, the local trade in grain began to accelerate from the 1660s. During that decade the 'markett way' to Stourbridge from Chaddesley Corbett began to deteriorate under the burden of an increased traffic of grain wagons and from the 1680s the farmers were dealing in quantity with the corn factors of Kidderminster and Dudley.[43] These commercial forces prompted further improvements in husbandry.

The diffusion of clover was accompanied by other developments intended to release more land for arable by increasing hay and manure production from the existing cultivated area. Most important was the floating of meadows. Some systems of floating were elaborate and expensive, like the provision for 450 acres made by Edward Broad on his Dunclent estate, where in 1665 'All the meadows and pasture grounds' were floated with a constant current of water 'at pleasure either Wynter or Somer and may be mowed of grased'.[44] From the 1670s, Thomas Foley continued these improvements and during 1674 he was censured by the manorial court for leaving trenches unfenced along the side of Barnets Hill common in Chaddesley Corbett. During the 1690s at a cost of over £500, he had completed an extensive system of irrigation drawing on the streams that ran through Chaddesley Corbett. By this system almost 400 acres of 'very poor arable land' and sandy cony-warren worth 5 shillings per acre were transformed into verdant meadows worth over 30 shillings per acre.[45] At the same time, however, many new watermeadows were more modest investments, often undertaken by tenant farmers at their own expense. Some were independent ventures like the watercourse cut by a copyholder from Bournheath, Bromsgrove, in Sandy Lane meadow for the 'floating and improving' of the meadow.[46] Others were communal ventures like the 'great watercourse' in Chaddesley Corbett from which water was drawn along cuttings dug by the copyholders.[47] Extensions like these could be made all too easily and during the 1660s farmers in Bromsgrove with land near Catshill Brook found 'new ways to water more land' at the expense of Thomas Dewce who had privately financed a system of irrigation from which water was freely drawn.[48]

Throughout the light soil region a concerted effort was being made to improve meadow ground to support more livestock. More generally, farmers were attempting to cultivate all land as intensively as possible. By the 1680s in Belbroughton pressure was mounting to convert marginal land into tillage and the common wastes were being put under unprecedented stress by the need to provide feeding grounds for the increasing population of sheep. In 1679, George Robinson of Belbroughton took some of his land of 'a rough, scrubby, barren nature of meagre value and unfit for tillage' and sowed 17 acres with oats, 11.5 acres with wheat and rye and four acres with pease.[49] By the late 1680s, as a consequence of the rise in sheep numbers, the division of Bell Heath between the tenants of the two small manors of Moore Hall Bell and Brian's Bell became impossible. Stinting arrangements were ignored and the scramble for sheep pasturage led to chronic overstocking.[50]

The response of farmers in North Worcestershire to the market opportunities open to them, clearly indicates that increased production, despite improved yields, absorbed more land. By the late seventeenth century an intensive demand for waste land had been generated within North Worcestershire. While Yarranton suggested enclosing the commons for coppices, farmers were stocking the wastes with sheep, or converting them to tillage. The attraction of good local markets for grain among the urban and industrial population stimulated similar agriculture improvements in the lowlands to the west of the South Staffordshire plateau. Arable production, particularly barley and oats, became increasingly important in the lowlands during the late seventeenth century as part of a more sophisticated cattle-corn husbandry.[51] The growth in arable production was accompanied by enclosure of open fields in Enville, Himley, Penn and Wombourne, on the western edge of the plateau from the 1680s, and in Shenstone to the north, between 1717 and 1723.[52] Metalworking had not developed in these areas before the 1660s, and the intensification of the existing agricultural economy formed a barrier to its growth. Lock-making, for example, radiated from Wolverhampton into Bilston, Sedgley, Wednesfield and Willenhall, but did not spread into the adjacent parish of Penn. The agrarian cordon strengthened as initial differences in social structure were reinforced and by 1716 most of the land in Penn was occupied by just eight tenant farmers.[53]

In North Worcestershire, where metalworking had been fostered in the pastoral economy of the sixteenth and early seventeenth centuries, the consequences of agricultural change were more decisive. Metalworking declined as the growing attraction of arable farming altered the economic prospects for those who combined farming and industry in the light soil belt, and as intensive agriculture absorbed the remaining commons. In both Chaddesley Corbett and Belbroughton, where scythe-making had flourished in the sixteenth century, the impact of agricultural innovation was profound. During the early seventeenth century the advance of spring tillage and sheep breeding disturbed the seasonal pattern of scythe-making and the industry began to take second place to farming. The adoption of clover compounded these problems because it involved additional work in the spring.

As agricultural productivity rose the attractions of devoting everything to farming must have increased, particularly when the rewards of intensive agriculture were clearly visible. In 1673, for instance, one of the leading farmers in Chaddesley Corbett, John Oldnoll of Hillpool, was already exploiting the opportunities afforded by an improved supply of fodder. He maintained a dairy herd of seven cows, two heifers and four calves as well as a flock of twenty couples and 110 dry sheep on his holding. He had clover hay worth £4 in his barn and manure valued at £3 in his foldyard. On his arable lands he was growing 12 acres of wheat and rye, 17 acres of barley and 13 acres of pease and oats.[54] He must have been a good example to his scythe-making neighbours of the advantages of mixed farming.

By the 1680s many of the scythe-makers of Chaddesley Corbett had followed Oldnoll's example and turned exclusively to farming.[55] The proximity of an expanding market led many to prefer selling grain at Dudley or Stourbridge for cash as a profitable alternative to selling scythes on credit, in distant markets like Nottingham and Stow-on-the-Wold, as their ancestors had done.[56] Moreover, as the comparative advantage shifted towards agriculture, the momentum of industrial decline was reinforced. The more complex mixed farming demanded constant labour, and as the labyrinth of watermeadows spread, water was drawn from the streams which had previously supplied the blade mills. Provisions concerning the distribution of water to meadows during the early eighteenth century were indicative of the overall shortage of water which proved an additional constraint upon scythe-making.[57] A similar process was responsible for the decline of scythe- and lock-making in Clent. Even in Belbroughton, where the mills hidden in the narrow valley of Barnets Brook continued to produce scythes, industrial growth was attenuated. By the early eighteenth century, the centre of the scythe-making industry had shifted northwards into Halesowen, Kingswinford, Oldswinford and Sedgley.

The rural economy of North Worcestershire was transformed from one dependent upon the combination of pastoral farming and metalworking, to one in which mixed farming dominated. As we have seen, this involved the absorption of waste land for pasture and tillage. Consequently, as cottages were engulfed by the advance of agriculture, the growth of metalworking upon the commons was suppressed. Men like John Whittaker, a workman scythesmith, and Andrew Hill, a nailer, who had built cottages and enclosed gardens upon Belheath in Belbroughton were the first to suffer from a more intensive land use.[58] By the end of the seventeenth century the parishes of North Worcestershire were no longer attracting metalworkers to their wastes.[59]

In Belbroughton and Chaddesley Corbett, the advance of

intensive mixed farming gradually displaced scythe-making during the course of the seventeenth century and it also discouraged the spread of other labour intensive rural industry. In Bromsgrove, by contrast, the first phase of agricultural improvement, before the 1650s, was accompanied by an increase in immigration and the emergence of rural industry. The influx of population was particularly marked during the 1630s in the wake of the disafforestation of Feckenham and again in the 1650s and was followed by the emergence of nail-making in the industrial hamlets of Catshill and Sidemore during the 1660s.[60]

In Bromsgrove, as elsewhere on the light soils, arable farming became more sophisticated during the first half of the seventeenth century and sheep grazing on the commons increased. But in Bromsgrove the common wastes were sufficiently abundant to serve both the farming community and meet the various demands of the cottagers, weavers and glovers of the industrial townships. However, as the second phase of agricultural expansion gained momentum, the extensive common wastes of Bromsgrove, like those elsewhere in the area, were controlled more carefully for the benefit of the farming population. By the 1670s a number of farmers considered their common rights on the Lickey to be worth up to one-third of the yearly value of their holdings, and understandably they supported the vigilant 'drives' of the commons that protected this valuable asset from enclosure and encroachment.[61] John Carpenter of Bournheath, for example, made abundant use of clover and dug his own watercourse to float Sandy Lane meadow, but was also heavily dependent on common pasturage on the wastes. Throughout the year he kept between 200 and 300 sheep on the Lickey during the day and brought them into the sheep cote at night. In the lambing season and when snow was on the ground the sheep were put in the enclosures, but otherwise they remained on the waste. At spring time, while the enclosed grounds 'got a head of grass', cows were also grazed on the Lickey as were young beasts, mares and colts between May Day and harvest. Carpenter, who was one of the most enterprising and progressive of the Bromsgrove farmers, considered common rights on the Lickey to be worth at least 25 per cent of the value of his holding.[62]

The emergence of nail-making in the 1660s coincided with the more intensive agricultural use of the common wastes and appears to have slowly filled the economic vacuum left in the lives of the numerous Bromsgrove cottagers by the gradual loss of pasturage on the common. In the 1660s, some nailers had modest agricultural interests; Thomas Hall, for example, kept three cows and fourteen sheep on the common in Chadwick in 1670.[63] But as nail-making was pushed increasingly into the industrial hamlets of Catshill and Sidemore and into the township of Bromsgrove, agricultural involvement among the nailers diminished, and wage labour became the sole source of income. By the 1690s at least one nail factor was beginning to bring nailers together in small workshops alongside poor flax-dressers, preparing flax for the spinners and weavers of nearby Stoke Prior. In 1696, John Hunniat had a 'Flax Shop' in which he employed five flax-dressers and a 'back shop' for three nailers.[64] Thus, the descendants of cottagers who left Feckenham in the 1630s and those who came in search of new opportunities on the commons in the 1650s were disappointed as agricultural change removed the major prop of their livelihood. By the mid 1670s the population of the parish of Bromsgrove had risen to almost 3740 inhabitants. The town was clearly an important focus for industrializing activities, although its economy was also boosted by more traditional agricultural processing industries like tanning and brewing which served a local market.

The town of Bromsgrove was the exception as an industrializing community and elsewhere in the light soil area of North Worcestershire and the lowlands of West Staffordshire industrial growth was checked. The metalworking area was no longer restricted mainly by the limits within which coal and iron could be profitably distributed. Agricultural developments confined metalworking to a smaller area in which land and labour were not employed by intensive farming. Agriculture took precedence over industry in what was to become the periphery of the Black Country. Agrarian change helped to concentrate industry in that part of South Staffordshire where it was to develop further during the late eighteenth and nineteenth centuries. The abrupt division between urban and rural landscapes, so apparent today when viewed from the Clent Hills, was partly the result of the response of agriculture to the demands of industrial growth.

III

From the late seventeenth century, agriculture effectively circumscribed the area within which the metalworking industries could continue to develop. This relationship between agriculture and industrial location had its origins primarily in the demands for foodstuffs, which increased almost in proportion to the output of manufactures. Although craft specialization led to an improvement in productivity in buckle-making and lock-making, the enlargement of the labour force remained the major component of industrial growth in the area. Population expansion began to transform South Staffordshire during the early eighteenth century. In Sedgley, cottages sprawled across the heathland, to form the townships of Coseley and Ettingshall.[65] Between 1701 and 1768, the number of cottages on the wastes in Dudley, Kingswinford and Rowley Regis, increased fourfold. Pensnett Chase was dismembered as industrial settlements like Brierley Hill emerged, and as mining honey-combed the land with abandoned coal pits.[66] By 1700 industrial concentration was already making inroads into the agricultural potential of the South Staffordshire plateau, and as population density rose, agricultural activity among metalworkers declined.

Between 1601 and 1640 over half the metalworkers in this area leaving inventories owned a herd of at least three cattle; between 1681 and 1720, 45 per cent had no cattle and the remainder only one or two. Pig keeping did not replace cattle rearing, and after 1680, 70 per cent of the metalworkers had no swine. Horse ownership also waned and by the early eighteenth century, less than a third of the metalworkers owned a horse.[67] As their agricultural interests declined dependence on wage labour increased. A greater proportion of metalworkers joined the ranks of cottagers, competing for a rapidly diminishing quantity of waste land out of which to supplement their wages.

The consequences of industrial dependence were evident when trade slumped. Dr Wilkes was concerned for the lock-makers of Willenhall, knowing that dire poverty would be imminent 'if trade were in any way to cease or the people were to live out of the land'. In 1728–9, at a time of both high prices and trade depression the lock-makers had to rely on poor relief because they had no agricultural holdings and their wages were insufficient to provide savings.[68] Similarly, in 1738 the fall in demand for nails threw families of nailers on to the parish for support, and the workmen were 'ready to starve'.[69] In these circumstances employment on any terms had to be sought, and ironmongers did not hesitate to exploit those whose bargaining strength had been eroded by a total dependence on wage labour.

Industrial concentration and declining agricultural activity among metalworkers coincided with an intensification of attempts to reduce wages by truck payments. During the 1690s nailers with 'no other dependence but their trade to live upon' complained about ironmongers in Dudley, Wednesbury and Walsall who gave 'Truck as Cheese, Tobacco, Herrings and such like'. These iron-mongers had recently achieved a general reduction in wages because 'Honest Dealers' were forced to reduce their rates to compete.[70] Abuses like truck were endemic in nailing because the low levels of skill, the minimal investment and the ease of entry were conducive to poverty. But attempts to reduce wages were more effective when the vast majority had no permanent supple-mentary source of income.

In this context it is not surprising that the metalworkers played an important part in agitating for truck legislation during the 1700s.[71] Between the 1680s and 1720s the balance of industrial bargaining power altered profoundly and wage rates could no longer be pro-tected. The decline in agricultural activity and the reduction in wage rates had catastrophic consequences for family income; nailing, lock-making and buckle-making took on the characteristics of sweated trades. William Hutton was shocked by the sight of women nailers 'thundering at the anvil' on his first visit from the East Midlands in 1741, but by then the employment of women was commonplace.[72] Where dual occupation survived and nail-making still ceased during the harvest as in South Yorkshire, wage rates were more easily maintained. In the 1730s and 1740s it was well known, that 'Staffordshire people work at about 11 shillings per Ton under the Yorkshire'.[73] Furthermore, the greater bargaining strength and status of South Yorkshire nailers was reflected in the tenor of wage negotiations. While the nailers in South Staffordshire demonstrated against wage reduction in the streets of Walsall, the South Yorkshire nailers were able to engage in discussion with the ironmongers directly.[74]

By the mid eighteenth century the metalworkers of the West Midlands were essentially dependent on industrial employment and the vast majority on wage labour. The virtual severence of rural involvement in the industrial villages was a further spur to urban growth. As the industrial hamlets thickened and the pastoral origins of industrial growth faded away, the towns expanded as centres of distribution.

By 1750, the metalware region was heavily dependent on the import of agricultural commodities from the surrounding agricul-tural districts, while the communities of metalworkers gathered in the industrial villages had become increasingly reliant upon the iron-mongers, and therefore the towns, for their livelihood. The lock-makers of Willenhall looked to Wolverhampton for raw materials and foodstuffs; the nailers of Lye relied upon Stourbridge; and the metalworkers of West Bromwich upon Birmingham. The densely populated industrial villages had no urban identity themselves but they were an eighteenth-century equivalent of the east ends of nine-teenth century industrial towns. Wednesbury alone developed from an industrial village into an independent town with a well-known market for dairy produce, and a centre for rod iron distribution.

Agriculture both facilitated and accentuated the remarkable urban growth and industrial concentration of the region, within the general framework provided by the availability of coal and iron. Agriculture responded with alacrity to the demands of industrial growth and thereby accelerated general changes in the economy and society of the West Midlands. Before the combination of coal and steam power created the Black Country, the area had taken on the physical form which it was to retain, and the old market towns were already emerging as the nerve centres of the metalware trades upon which the population of the industrial villages increasingly relied for their livelihood.

Acknowledgements

I am particularly grateful to Dr Joan Thirsk under whose guidance my research was conducted and whose understanding was a major inspiration; and to Professor E. L. Jones for valuable comments on an earlier draft of this paper.

Notes and references

1 P. J. Corfièld, *The Impact of English Towns 1700–1800* (1982), pp. 7–10, 15–16, 22–31.
2 W. H. B. Court, *The Rise of the Midland Industries, 1600–1838* (1938), pp. 161.
3 J. Thirsk 'Industries in the countryside', in F. J. Fisher (ed.), *Essays in the Economic and Social History of Tudor and Stuart England* (1961); Court, *Midland Industries*, pp. 1–148; M. B. Rowlands, *Masters and Men in the West Midland Metalware Trades before the Industrial Revolution* (1975), pp. 1–53.
4 P. M. Frost, 'The growth and localisation of rural industry in South Staffordshire, 1500–1720' (unpublished PhD thesis, University of Birmingham 1973), pp. 278–350.

5   Rowlands, *Masters and Men*, pp. 6–7. J. Thirsk and J. P. Cooper (eds.), *Seventeenth Century Economic Documents*(1972), p. 209.

6   Court, *Midland Industries*, pp. 132, 148; Rowlands, *Masters and Men*, pp. 99–106.

7   Frost, 'The growth and localisation of rural industry', pp. 283–5. Comparative figures for 1563 and 1663 have survived for ten parishes.

8   ibid., pp. 283, 376.

9   M. Sylvester (ed.) *Reliquiae Baxterianae* (1696), p. 14.

10   C. Gill, *History of Birmingham: I*, (1952), pp. 56–7; *VCH*, Warwickshire, **8**, pp. 6–7.

11   G. Miege, *The New State of England* (1691), p. 235.

12   C. M. Law, 'Some notes on the urban population of England and Wales in the eighteenth century', *Local Historian*, **10** (1972), p. 26; *VCH*, Warwicks., **7**, pp. 6–7.

13   M. J. Wise (ed.), *Birmingham and its Regional Setting: A Scientific Survey* (British Association 1950), pp. 156–7, 174–8; M. J. Wise, 'Birmingham and its trade relations in the early eighteenth century', *University of Birmingham Historical Journal*, **2** (1949), pp. 55–7.

14   Wise, *Birmingham*, pp. 177–8.

15   *Commons Journals*, **20**, pp. 741, 746.

16   Rowlands, *Masters and Men*, pp. 59, 70.

17   ibid., p. 116.

18   Wise, Birmingham and its Trade Relations', pp. 71–3; J. Hill, *The Bookmakers of Old Birmingham* (1907) p. 19.

19   Worcestershire RO (hereafter Worcs. RO), Foley Scrap Book IV, p. 179.

20   Herefordshire RO, Foley Correspondence, F/IV/AD, 9, 17.

21   Law, 'Some notes on the urban population', p. 25; J. F. Ede, *History of Wednesbury* (1962), p. 99.

22   Ede, *History of Wednesbury*, p. 99; E. J. Homeshaw, *The Corporation of the Borough and Foreign of Walsall* (1960) pp. 4–6.

23   Court, *Midland Industries*, p. 195.

24   J. S. Roper, *Early North Worcestershire Scythesmiths* (1967), pp. 1–5.

25   Worcs. RO, BA 3585, 1601/47; 1602/70; 1600/138; 1606/133; 1614/226; 1620/152; 1627/25.

26   Worcs. RO, BA 3583, 1603/138.

27   Worcs. RO, BA 3585, 1621/145.

28   Worcs. RO, BA 3585, 1627/25.

29   Three farmers in the two parishes are recorded as having kept the full complement of sheep; Worcs. RO, BA 3585, 1603/138; 1611/31; 1618/165.

30   Rowlands, *Masters and Men*, pp. 18–26; D. Hey, *The Rural Metalworkers of the Sheffield Region* (1972).

31   Hey, *Rural Metalworkers*, pp. 20–6; Rowlands, *Masters and Men*, pp. 30–2.

32   Worcs. RO, BA 3585, 1608/113.

33   Worcs. RO, BA 3585, 1605/39.

34   Probate inventories portray the seasonality of scythe-making very clearly. January inventories reveal substantial stocks of iron and steel. In April and May scythe-makers' inventories record large quantities of scythes but few raw materials. Summer and autumn inventories record only small quantities of raw materials and finished blades. Worcs RO, BA 3585, 1608/13; 1614/226; 1620/152; 1643/15; 1647/145.

35   J. Thirsk, 'Farming techniques', in J. Thirsk (ed.), *The Agrarian History of England and Wales: IV* (1967) p. 187.

36   Worcs. RO, BA 3585, 1608/51.

37   Worcs. RO, BA 3585, 1608/113; 1620/152.

38   Dr Kerridge saw convertible husbandry as one of the most important aspects of agricultural improvement, responsible for a doubling of productivity: E. Kerridge, *The Agricultural Revolution* (1967), pp. 39, 207-9. This claim has been conclusively refuted by Professor Jones: E. L. Jones, 'Agriculture and economic growth in England, 1660–1750: agricultural change', *Journal of Economic History*, **25** (1965), pp. 4–5.

39   Jones, 'Agriculture and economic growth', pp. 3–5, 10–11; E. L. Jones, 'English and European agricultural development, 1650–1750', in R. M. Hartwell (ed.), *The Industrial Revolution* (1970), pp. 60–1, 72–3: C. Lane, 'The development of pastures and meadows during the sixteenth and seventeenth centuries', *Agric. Hist. Rev.*, **28** (1980).

40   A. Yarranton, '*The Improvement Improved by a second Edition of the Great Improvement of land by Clover* (1663), pp. 32. Andrew Yarranton was a Worcestershire landowner. He lived in Astley, just across the River Severn from Ombersley, and farmed light land similar to that of the light soil region. There appears to be no first edition of his book on clover and it is possible that the published work is a revision of a manuscript guide to clover husbandry.

41   Shakespeare Birthplace Trust Library (hereafter SBL), DR 5/3149, 3168; PRO, E134/5 William and Mary/Easter 25.

42   Worcs. RO, BA 3585. This table is based on a selection of thirty-one inventories which comprises all the summer inventories for farms with recorded arable of between 15 and 60 acres.

43   SBL, DR5/3149; court rolls. PRO, E134/7 William and Mary/Easter 22; E112/706/50.

44   Worcs. RO, Estate Particulars, BA 484: Survey of the Dunclent Estate, 1665.

45   SBL, DR5/3149: court rolls; T. Nash, *Collections for the History of Worcestershire* (1781), vol. 2, p. 38; W. Pitt, *General View of the Agriculture of the County of Worcester* (1813), pp. 207–8.

46   Worcs. RO, BA 3585, 1699/351.

47   SBL, Coughton Hall MSS 1485: leases.

48   Kidderminster Public Library, 6/6582: lawsuit papers.

49 PRO, E112/540/184.

50 PRO, E112/760/36; E134/5 William and Mary/Easter 24.

51 P. M. Frost, 'The growth and localisation of rural industry', pp. 206, 252; P. M. Frost, 'Yeomen and Metalsmiths: Livestock in the dual economy in South Staffordshire 1560–1720', *Agric. Hist. Rev.*, **29** (1981), pp. 32–4.

52 Frost, 'The growth and localisation of rural industry', pp. 269–70; William Salt Library, Stafford (hereafter WSL) Pearson 744, M. 389.

53 Staffordshire RO, D593/J/2/1.

54 Worcs. RO, BA 3585, 1672/271.

55 An examination of all the probate inventories for Chaddesley Corbett between 1670 and 1700 did not reveal any active scythe-makers after 1680.

56 In 1709, Richard Smith of Drayton, whose ancestors had been among the most prominent scythesmiths, was involved exclusively in agriculture. He kept a dairy herd of seven cows and three heifers and considerable arable lands. He had ten tons of clover hay worth £8.15.0d in his barn. Worcs. RO, BA 3585, 1709/385.

57 SBL, Coughton Hall MSS 1506: leases.

58 Worcs. RO, Settlement Papers BA 4247/4, 5.

59 PRO, C22/644/65.

60 PRO, C22/644/65.

61 PRO, C22/644/65.

62 PRO, C8/207/87; C22/644/65; Worcs. RO, BA 3585, 1697/351. Carpenter had clover hay valued at £18 when he died in 1696.

63 Worcs. RO, BA 3585, 1670/265.

64 Worcs. RO, BA 3585, 1696/348.

65 Dudley Public Library (hereafter DPL), Dudley Archives, DA7/10; DA 23/5.

66 C. H. Bayley (ed.), *The Rent Rolls of Lord Dudley and Ward in 1701* . . . (1882), p. 7; DPL, DA/we/5; D. R. Guttery, *The Story of Pensnett Chase* (1950), pp. 11, 31.

67 Frost, 'The growth and localisation of rural industry', pp. 220–2, 228–9, 234–5. Frost, 'Yeomen and metalsmiths', pp. 36–41.

68 WSL Salt MSS 467, p. 56.

69 *Commons Journals*, **23**, pp. 109, 111.

70 PRO, C9/486/30.

71 G. W. Hilton, *The Truck System* (1962), p. 71, *Commons Journals*, **14**, p. 145; **16**, p. 519.

72 *The Life of William Hutton* (1817), p. 110; M. W. Flinn, *Men of Iron: The Crowleys in the Early Iron Industry* (1962), pp. 237–8; *Commons Journals*, **23**, p. 110.

73 Hey, *Rural Metalworkers*, pp. 34–5, 46.

74 ibid., pp. 47–9; Rowlands, *Masters and Men*, p. 82; *VCH*, Staffordshire, **2**, p. 241.

6 A dynamic society: social relations in Newcastle-upon-Tyne 1660–1760

Joyce Ellis

> Methought a City to my Eyes appear'd,
> Where Towers and Temples high their summits rear'd.
> Where honest Industry bore up her Head,
> And Arts and Sciences, around her spread;
> Where decent Chearfulness stood forth confess'd,
> Where social Harmony warm'd every Breast,
> And sober Plenty shew'd that every House was bless'd.

This vision of Newcastle-upon-Tyne in 1741, contained in an anonymous work obligingly entitled *Is This The Truth? A Poem*, could well be said to represent the traditional ideal of urban life.[1] It portrays the town as a single community, enjoying the economic and cultural benefits that flow from the hard work of all its members in their due station and accepting without question both the established order and the set of social values which it embodied. The partial eye of civic pride would no doubt lead contented citizens to believe that material blessings were heaped upon their own particular town that were denied to the country at large. However, there is little evidence that urban society in general was perceived as being significantly different from that existing outside the town. The conventional view applied to town and country alike: society was harmonious, 'that gracious institution of God, wherein by his appointment both rich and poor meet together', as the Bishop of Durham expressed it, and within which 'All Men (as Men) have a Right of Common . . . [being] justly Entitled to the common Offices of Humanity.'[2]

Belief in social harmony and in the divine origin of the social order was obviously appealing to contemporaries who had to enforce an authority based essentially upon subordination rather than representation. Yet such models of early modern society seem also to appeal to an increasingly influential school of modern commentators who reject interpretations that emphasize crisis, conflict

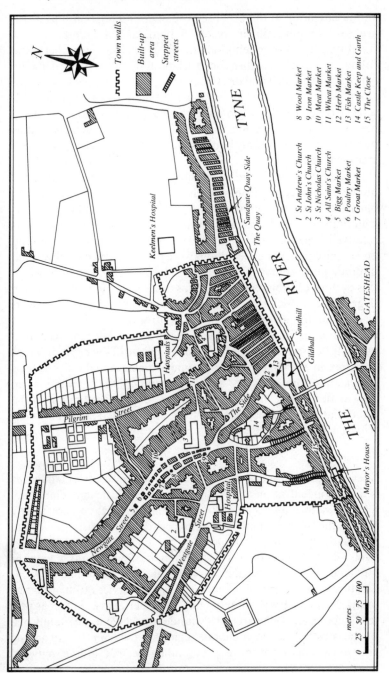

Figure 10 *Newcastle-upon-Tyne in the 1730s*

and polarization at the expense of the ties and relationships which are said to have given society a fundamental orderliness and stability. These proponents of harmony as opposed to conflict as the ruling principle of English social relations do not actually deny the existence of conflict and division but they argue that the low level of violence and rancour that accompanied these divisions indicates a society based on the acceptance of subordination and submissiveness.[3] The debate on the nature of early modern society is thus presented as a dichotomy between harmony and discord, or indeed crisis and order.

Against this, it seems to be more generally accepted that the quickening pace of economic change in the eighteenth century, particularly in the great commercial and manufacturing towns, eventually tipped the balance towards discord and confrontation, as relative inequalities of income and status became more pronounced and rising consumer expectations were frustrated by the uneven and unpredictable course of 'progress'.[4] However, the extent to which this pattern of urban social relations differed in kind rather than in degree from those prevailing in other communities remains unclear, as does the timing of the supposed transformation. What is clear is that the nature and development of the social order in this period can only be assessed by thorough investigation of the many different societies in which English men and women actually lived. This paper therefore presents an examination of social relations in Newcastle-upon-Tyne in the century after the Restoration in the hope that the evidence derived from this detailed study may contribute to the wider debate.

I

Social relationships are subject to an immense variety of influences but the concentration of population within a particular community and the nature and scale of its economic organization are clearly among the most formative. By these criteria, Newcastle was in the vanguard of urban development in the period between 1660 and 1760. By the year 1700 it was about the fourth largest town in England, with a thriving agricultural hinterland and a well-established role as a supplier of goods and services to that hinterland: 'the great Emporium of all the Northern Parts' in fact as well as in reputation.[5] The area of Tyneside as a whole was certainly one of the most advanced economic regions in the country and among the most important of the expanding sectors in the national economy. It might, therefore, be reasonable to expect that developments in Newcastle society had much in common with the emerging industrial towns.

This expectation is reinforced by the fact that the predominance of large units of heavy industry and the scale of the trade involved meant that the workforce on Tyneside had the character of an embryonic organized proletariat. Since the sixteenth century the basis of Tyneside's, and thus Newcastle's, prosperity had been the coal trade and the revenues that it generated. The town was renowned as the place where 'the perfection of coalery' was to be found, and visitors marvelled at the thousands of workmen employed in the collieries that surrounded it and the shipping that crowded the harbour during the summer trading season. It was estimated in the 1720s that the coal trade earned £250,000 a year for Newcastle and thus financed not only a vast return trade in food-stuffs and commercial goods but also the circulation of capital and credit that supported local industry. Contemporaries were in fact well aware that a long-term decline in coal exports would have such a disastrous effect on employment, land values, shipping and local industries dependent on the coal trade that 'there is not a Cobler that will not suffer greatly'.[6]

The dependence of several sectors of Newcastle's industry on coal was obvious and direct; for example, the increased volume of the trade during the seventeenth and early eighteenth centuries stimulated the growth of shipbuilding and repairing and related trades, such as rope-making. Moreover, the availability of cheap fuel and river transport encouraged the development of salt and glass works. Glass-making in particular expanded as the period progressed, benefiting from supplies of sand brought in as ballast in exchange for bulky cargoes of coal and salt. Meanwhile, the coal, salt and shipping industries demanded increasing quantities of assorted ironwork, encouraging the growth of a metalworking industry using both local and imported iron. It was therefore to be expected that the growth of these heavy and predominantly mineral-based activities would cause a relative decline in Newcastle's more traditional industries like textiles and leather-working; however, both these industries continued to play a modest part in the town's export trade as well as in the vital task of supplying the swelling ranks of its local consumers.[7]

The result of this clustering of industrial activity in and around the valleys of the Tyne and its tributaries was a significant concentration of population in the area, where it spread out along the waterside as well as crowding into Newcastle itself. This dispersal of the industrial work force at least mitigated demographic pressure within the town without apparently holding back its expansion, because in the century after 1660 Newcastle's urban population growth seems to have kept pace with that of the Tyneside region as a whole. Although the figures should be treated with caution, the best available estimates of the population of Newcastle and its Gateshead suburb suggest that the town almost doubled in size in this period, increasing from about 16,000 in the 1660s to around 29,000 in the mid eighteenth century. It also seems that the most rapid phase of growth coincided with a notable expansion in the volume of the coal trade, confirming that the town was successfully tapping the prosperity of the hinterland in this period.[8]

Newcastle was not, however, predominantly an industrial town. Like most major urban centres, it achieved its status by combining several functions and the male occupational structure revealed by the parish registers is more notable for breadth and variety than for specialization in anything but the widest sense (see Table 26 and Appendix). The customs house, cellars, warehouses, coffee houses and Exchange building encouraged the merchants and fitters or coal factors who controlled the major export trades to operate from Newcastle, as did the ferocious and exclusive privileges which

Table 26   *Male occupational groups (percentages) in Newcastle-upon-Tyne 1660–1729: baptismal register samples*

	1660s	*1700s*	*1710s*	*1720s*	*Total*
Professional	5.0	6.1	8.8	7.5	6.8
Service	0.3	0.3	0.4	0.6	0.4
Commercial	29.3	27.2	23.1	20.6	25.1
Agricultural	1.0	2.2	0.8	1.2	1.3
Industrial:	50.9	53.4	54.6	60.7	54.9
Construction	12.5	12.1	11.6	13.3	12.4
Textiles	9.7	11.0	9.0	11.1	10.3
Food and drink	7.1	9.6	8.7	9.3	8.7
Animal products	10.7	10.2	9.9	8.7	9.8
Minerals	11.0	10.5	15.4	18.3	13.7
Miscellaneous	13.5	10.7	12.3	9.4	11.4

Source: See Appendix, p. 217–20.

retarded the gradual shift in the port's centre of gravity downstream to Tynemouth. A great port that lay 16 or 19 kilometres upstream could not be described as ideally placed, especially when the long, winding passage up the perilously shallow Tyne was often made impossible by high winds and stormy weather. As the ships involved in the coal trade grew larger, the danger that an alternative commercial centre would develop at the mouth of the river increased: even in the 1670s it had been argued that only Newcastle's privileges were keeping the town from sharing the fate of other inland ports. As the declining numbers of seamen and shipwrights living in the town between the 1660s and 1720s perhaps demonstrate, this traditional bulwark against local competition was becoming less effective as the period wore on, but it certainly helped to maintain the size of the commercial sector in general, and in particular the numbers of watermen operating along the river and living predominantly in Newcastle.[9]

However, occupations connected directly with the port seem to have been outnumbered by those created by the so-called maintenance industries whose link with Newcastle's commerce was indirect. The expansion of the local industrial and commercial work force required the services of an efficient and sophisticated market which could obtain supplies from a wide area and channel them into the shops, public houses and specialized street markets that so impressed contemporary visitors. The Saturday Flesh Market attracted particular attention, 'not only as it supplies the Town in great Measure, but as it also furnishes the Country for several Miles round', as well as supplying provisions for the coal fleets that gathered in Tynemouth haven. Moreover, the growing demand from Newcastle's consumers for the basic necessities of life provided a market for the products of the town's manufacturing sector, in which clothing, shoemaking and construction were prominent. In fact Defoe's comments about the importance of popular purchasing power seem particularly appropriate to Newcastle's economy:

These are the People that carry off the Gross of your Consumption; tis for these your Markets are kept open on Saturday nights; . . . in a Word, these are the Life of our whole Commerce, and all by their Multitude.[10]

The very size of this popular market, however, constituted a considerable handicap to any development of more sophisticated crafts and services to supply the wealthier sections of regional society. Newcastle was undoubtedly too heavily involved in trade and industry to become a centre of fashionable resort: a visitor wrote in the 1770s that 'the whole has a most forbidding appearance, especially to those who have lived in towns where there is not such a dependence on commerce'.[11] On the other hand, it was not a particularly unpleasant place in which to live permanently if you avoided the jostling lower town beside the Tyne and chose instead the pleasantly 'retired' areas amid meadows and gardens which survived into the nineteenth century in the northern parishes of St Andrew's and St John's. The presence in the town of a reasonable number of luxury crafts, retail outlets and professional services seems to indicate that Newcastle was large and wealthy enough in its own right to generate a market for leisure and luxury as well as to exert some social 'pull' within its extensive hinterland. Newcastle's summer season, for example, seems to have been well-established by the early eighteenth century, when the period between its main race meeting and Assize week was enlivened by balls, assemblies, raffles, plays and concerts.[12]

However, despite this evidence of the infiltration of the arts and sciences of leisure, Newcastle remained an irredeemably 'busy' town, permeated by the 'honest Industry' of its own citizens and of its hinterland. Its economy was in fact a paradigm of Defoe's seaport towns 'where Navigation, Manufacturing, and Merchandize seem to assist one another'; its occupational structure was therefore not dominated by just one major sector of employment, as Norwich was by the textile industry, but reflected this more broadly-based dependence on the activities summarized by contemporaries as 'trade'.[13] As a result, social relations in Newcastle were conditioned by two very important factors. First, the town was the focus of a large and highly independent local population of coalworkers. The mayor was undoubtedly being alarmist when he complained in 1740 of 'a numerous People in our Neighbourhood, too ready, on any Occasion, to join in an Insurrection', but, as Bristol found with the Kingswood colliers, assertive coalworkers were a force to be reckoned with. Moreover, the mayor of Newcastle could not rely on guarding the approaches to the town: despite the fact that the nature of the coal industry favoured a dispersed pattern of settlement, a worrying number of pitmen were actually living inside his jurisdiction, forming one of the largest single occupational groups after the keel or watermen.[14]

Second, the nature of Newcastle's economy seems to have encouraged an unusually uneven distribution of wealth and status within the town itself. In this period, such disparities were not, of course, peculiar to Newcastle and it cannot be automatically assumed that they fostered social discord and division. However, at the very least it can be said that the disparities found in Newcastle seem sharper than those found in many other English towns. The distribution of wealth deduced from the Hearth Tax returns of 1665 reveals a smaller group of rich or even prosperous households than could be found in, for example, contemporary Exeter. The dangers of taking Hearth Tax evidence as a simple indicator of social structure are considerable, since the deceptively straightforward correlation between wealth and number of hearths ignores the complexities introduced by occupational variation and the life cycle, while changing local assessment practices make comparisons between towns, or even over time, of doubtful value. Nevertheless, it is at least possible that the apparently narrower concentration of wealth in Newcastle accentuated social differentiation between an unusually restricted élite and the vast, quasi-proletarian multitude of the poor. In the 1660s the latter made up around 76 per cent of Newcastle's population, crowding into the business area in the lower part of the town, along and below the high bank down which the castle was linked to the river-front and bridgehead by steep, narrow lanes. In the riverside ward of Sandgate as many as 79 per cent of the population were exempt from the Hearth Tax; taking the town as a whole 43 per cent were exempt, a figure comparable with that of Exeter and perhaps even below that of Norwich, but higher than those of Warwick, Leicester and York.[15]

It is unfortunate that no later sources comparable to the Hearth Tax returns seem to survive for Newcastle and that the extant records of parish relief are neither complete nor conclusive enough to illuminate the inroads made into the problem of poverty by the town's increasing prosperity over this period. The most that can be said is that it retained a reputation for the 'prodigious number' of its poor as well as for the liberality of its poor relief. Given the fluctuating nature of the trade on which so much of the town's employment was based, periods of depression in the coal trade or of hard weather had to be dealt with promptly by the distribution of food and fuel to the poor and the provision of public works. These crises did not, however, obscure the less dramatic but more insidious effects of endemic seasonal unemployment, which made it difficult for casual labourers, in particular, to maintain their precarious hold on solvency. It was accepted that 'when the Coal Trade is brisk, that all other Business is so too, and when it is otherwise . . . that there is a certain Deadness in all Trafick'.[16] It was, therefore, also accepted that private or public relief had to be available not only for paupers but for those at the mercy of the local economy. Local clergymen combined a firm belief in the wickedness of the generality of Newcastle's poor with a recognition that those more fortunate had an obligation to exercise their generosity. The corporation itself supplemented parish relief out of its own income and was reported in 1709 to be spending over £800 a year on various charitable schemes, but these were probably outweighed by the contributions of private benefactors. In this respect the traditional source of bequests, most notably that of Sir William Blackett who left a fund of £1000 for the poor of St Andrew's parish in 1706, seem to have been overtaken by public subscriptions and door-to-door collections, one of which raised upwards of £1000 in 1757.[17]

It seems, therefore, that a high proportion of Newcastle's population remained vulnerable to the shocks administered by its unstable economy and that the problem of poverty, if not pauperism, continued to occupy the town's establishment. Another enduring feature was that the concentration of the poorest sections of the population into the strip of land that stretched eastwards from the castle and the main market area continued throughout the eighteenth century. The parish registers suggest that the eastern parish of All Saints held around half of Newcastle's total population in the mid eighteenth century, just as it had done in the 1660s, and that may well be an underestimate since the parish was a dissenting stronghold even before the arrival of John Wesley. It was said to be one of the largest cures in the kingdom, with estimates of its size ranging from 16,000 souls to simply 'vastly populous', and despite changes taking place in the absolute levels of poverty it retained its character as 'the poorest and most contemptible part of the town'.[18] Meanwhile, there is some evidence that social segregation in residential terms was increasing as prosperous inhabitants moved out of the lower town. This was remarked upon several times in the 1730s and comments on one street in particular, the Close, suggest that many of Newcastle's principal residents had forsaken the lower town within memory and moved uphill to the more socially desirable districts of Westgate and Pilgrim Street. In the 1660s the riverside area had remained relatively wealthy and select but by the early eighteenth century there is a tone of surprise in descriptions of good quality, modern houses in the old town.[19] Perhaps even more telling is a petition about poor rate assessments in 1749 which strongly suggests that shopkeepers in the central commercial district around St Nicholas's church were living in other parts of the town and thus being assessed for poor relief in the less burdensome parishes of St Andrew's and St John's.[20]

However, social zoning still had a long way to go before it could replace the complex residential pattern revealed by Langton, based on occupational districts that were in some cases reinforced by 'class zoning' but in others undermined by it.[21] The parish registers of the first decade of the eighteenth century reveal that, for instance, Butcher Bank and the Flesh Market were still dominated by butchers, Castle Garth by tailors and Sandgate by watermen; while Henry Bourne pointed out in the 1730s that the Keyside 'is chiefly inhabited by such as have their Living by Shipping', which included merchants, fitters and brewers as well as many in humbler employments.[22]

Occupational concentration was not necessarily a recipe for social peace; in fact, this sort of concentration could make it much more easy for informal protests to arise in times of hardship if it was combined with the active street life associated with an economy based on open markets and workshops.[23] However, living in the same neighbourhood as your employer might have strengthened feelings of economic interdependence, if not community of interests, and certainly reduced the anonymity that could be associated with urban life. William Scott, a fitter who actually lived on the Keyside, instigated a successful challenge to a strike in 1738 by using this sort of pressure on the pickets. This strike, the latest in a long succession of disputes between the keelmen and their employers, the fitters, on the issue of wages and working conditions, was prompted by the long-term effects upon employment and income of coal-owners' cartel which had been operating since 1732. Events seem to have been brought to a head by the opening of a parliamentary inquiry into the coal trade, which made both coal-owners and fitters extremely sensitive to complaints arising from their illegal activities and was thus thought likely to reduce their resistance to a strike. The fitters counter-attacked by calling individual skippers before the majesty of the corporation, where many of them agreed to return to work. One hardy spirit, however, refused to go back 'except upon Terms', and in any case the first attempt to break the strike was defeated by a line of picket boats below the bridge. A few days later though another attempt was made, in front of over a thousand interested spectators on the Keyside, and it was then that Scott made his decisive intervention, calling

> several of the Keelmen that were prepared to Board the working Keels, some by their Names. . . . Threatening them at the same time, which was seconded by the Rest of the Fitters, whilst some of the working Keels got by.

The keelmen were taken by surprise by the abrupt crumbling of resistance and so in fact were their employers, one of whom commented that 'Perhaps there never was so great a Body of Men, after the Magistrates had used their utmost endeavours, and to no purpose, brought to their Duty by so lucky a turn'.[24]

Another force serving to strengthen the bonds of society may have been the public celebration of both private and public events that frequently punctuated the working life of the town. Social differentiation in the form of what might be called 'clubability' was certainly visible in Newcastle by the early eighteenth century, as advertisements for the meetings of increasing numbers of élite and artisan societies demonstrate. Charitable societies, like the Sons of the Clergy, which had been established in 1710, were soon joined by other groups representing the varied interests of wealthy local residents, from the Freemasons to the Florists, while there was, by the 1720s, a flourishing gentlemen's club on the London model. Artisan and trade societies were slower to advertise their activities, but it is clear that the friendly societies, like the Keelmen's Hospital, owed a great deal of their popularity to their clubrooms and regular feasts.[25] However, the phenomenon had not yet become so exclusive as to deny the populace all participation in the rituals and amusements of their fellow citizens, even if only in the role of onlookers to the apparently obligatory grand procession. Although Henry Bourne in his *History of Newcastle* gives the impression that civic pageantry had declined by the 1730s, the corporation too continued to celebrate important events with public rejoicing of an expansive kind, with bonfires, pealing bells, gunfire, processions and the vital element of generous quantities of free drink. The show put on for the Coronation in 1727 was exceptional but more modest celebrations occurred on a regular basis: in 1734, for example, they marked such occasions as a royal wedding, the safe arrival home from London of a local MP, a ceremonial visit from Lord Scarborough and both council and parliamentary elections.[26] These corporate rituals served to consolidate the power of the civic élite as well as to attract neighbouring gentry into the town but they may also have reinforced Newcastle's sense of identity and its almost tangible local pride. The citizens of Newcastle lived surrounded by what Defoe termed 'abundant business for an antiquary' and felt perfectly equal to the comparison. One local coalowner compared his waggonways, modestly, to the Via Appia, and Bourne continued the allusion in his *History of Newcastle*, claiming that 'these Waggon-ways, a small part of the whole Coal Works, may Vie with some of the great Works of the Roman Empire'.[27] Indeed, it may not be too fanciful to see Bourne's *History* as evidence of the early flourishing of urban self-confidence and self-esteem in Newcastle, drawing as it does on Gray's *Chorographia* of 1649 and on the manuscript collections of several local residents.[28]

Aside from civic rituals and local pride, another factor which might have strengthened community of interest was the participation of many adult male citizens in town affairs and in political life more generally through membership of trade and craft gilds. Many of the main Newcastle gilds seem to have attained a peak in membership in the first decades of the eighteenth century and although their appeal subsequently diminished the pace of the decline was neither rapid nor uniform.[29] The numbers recorded as taking up their civic freedom fell sharply in the early years of the new century, probably as a result of political manipulation, but then expanded rapidly once more. There were around 2000 freemen in the 1660s and 3000 in the 1740s, so that numbers roughly kept pace with population growth.[30] Given that in Newcastle, as in other towns, freedom was not necessarily dependent upon residence, it would be unwise to rely too heavily on the evidence of the freemen's register. However, there is little sign that Newcastle suffered unduly from absentee freemen and one can make the tentative suggestion that over 50 per cent of adult male householders shared in the privileges of the town to some extent, which compares very favourably with figures available for other major towns.[31] One of the local poets illustrates this formal corporate solidarity in painstaking detail by listing the guests at a mayoral dinner; descending from noble peer, fat merchant, noted painter, famous viewer and rich hostman to rough sailor, prick-louse tailor and poor hatter, all being entertained by the town's orchestra at the foot of the hall. The verse is if anything worse than that of the anonymous writer who prefaced this paper but the assumption that civic harmony transcended social and economic divisions is precisely the same.

II

How far this formal unity prevailed in practice, however, may be another matter, and there is considerable evidence that there were occasions when

> . . . lo! the pleasing Prospect vanish'd quite;
> As beauteous Forms are lost in Shades of Night.
> Loud Uproar strait ensu'd, and lawless Will,
> And decent Language, chang'd to Clamour shrill.[32]

On the other hand, the mere existence of conflict does not in itself disprove the fundamentally harmonious basis of social relations in Newcastle, any more than the existence of unhappy families, for example, disproves the ubiquity of the family. Conflict can take many forms, from clashes of personality in the market-place and power struggles within the political élite to disputes over work and wages and other wider confrontations. Understanding their precise significance depends on the careful analysis of the context of dissension, particularly when the evidence is ambiguous or apparently contradictory.

In political terms, for instance, the relatively large proportion of freemen within the population implies a degree of corporate unity that is belied by occasional glimpses of a powerful groundswell of resentment among the main body of freemen against the narrow élite which actually ran the town. Although the literary evidence portrays poor mechanics and 'laborious husbands' as taking an active part in civic affairs, not all freemen were equal in constitutional terms; some were decidedly more powerful as well as more wealthy. Basically, successive charters had contributed to placing complete control over the trade and even the shoreline of the Tyne in the hands of an oligarchy drawn from the Merchants' company. As Table 27 demonstrates, this élite safeguarded their economic position by a virtual monopoly of places on the aldermanic bench, guaranteed by an electoral process that conceded an illusory representation to the twelve principal gilds while maintaining in practice a system of co-option.[33]

The élite owed this unassailable position to a royal decree of 1515, which brought to an end a succession of assaults on the

Table 27 *Gild affiliations of eighty-three aldermen elected in the period 1660–1759*

Gild	1660–79	1680–99	1700–19	1720–39	1740–59	Total
Merchant:						
Boothman	12	9	9	6	6	42
Mercer	8	6	6	2	1	23
Draper	2	3	1	—	—	6
Merchant	—	1	—	—	—	1
Hostman	—	1	—	—	3	4
Personal	—	2	—	1	—	3
Untraced	—	3	—	1	—	4
Total	22	25	16	10	10	83

Sources: Tyne and Wear Archives Department 589/6: Common Council Book 1656–1722; 589/7: Common Council Book, 1722–82; M. H. Dodds (ed.), *The Register of Freemen of Newcastle upon Tyne* (Newcastle Records Series, **3** and **6** 1923, 1926); F. W. Dendy (ed.), *Extracts from the Records of the Merchant Adventurers of Newcastle upon Tyne* (Surtees Soc., **101** 1899).

Merchants' company by the craft gilds stretching back to the four-teenth century and left the craftsmen still disgruntled, but impotent. However, as the wealth generated by the coal trade increased and appeared to flow in greater abundance into the pockets of the élite than into those of the lesser merchants, the latters' attempts to share the authority and the spoils more widely provided a new forum for the expression of discontent. In this context the chartering of the Hostmen's company in 1601 represented a further attempt by the élite to entrench their position, but discontent and agitation swelled again in the unsettled atmosphere of the early seventeenth century and culminated in the 1640s in the unseating of the now-royalist élite by the now-parliamentary opposition. The 'new men' who took over the town in the Interregnum were predominantly drawn from the second rank of merchants, a revolution that was no less real for being apparently limited.[34] Moreover, the restoration of the élite in 1661 did nothing to remove the underlying grievances: once again the issues of national politics were coloured, to say the least, by local disputes that had taken on an extra edge as a result of the political and religious tensions generated by the war. Although the town's two parliamentary seats went more often than not to Tory candidates, in general the large freeman electorate and the high political temperature made for vigorous and polemical campaigns and much 'intestin division' even within the enclosed corporation. The 1710 election was particularly hotly contested, with the ritualized battles of the hustings spilling over into accusations of abuse and actual assault among the participants.[35]

The continuing local power struggle can be detected in occasional outbursts of resentment against the élite whose power, embodied in the corporation and Merchants' company, had, in effect, reduced the freemen to second-class citizens in their own town, forced to pay tolls and prosecuted if they dared to trade in what were known as 'Merchants' Goods'. Apart from general and perhaps predictable expressions of disrespect to the mayor and magistrates from individual freemen, there is evidence of more formal opposition. On several occasions craft representatives disrupted elections, as in 1684 when they 'willfully absented [themselves] and obstinately refused to come or make the Election'.[36] There were also attempts to challenge the magistrates' vigorous enforcement of the merchants' privileges, which developed on occasions into attacks on the privileges themselves and on the charter that embodied them. For example, petitions which have survived from 1714 complain that 'the Magistrates have made such affinity by marriages that they are linked in Interest and become formidable . . . and now there is no balance of power between the Merchants of Newcastle and the other trades'. The petitions emphasize that the corporation was well worth controlling: the extent of its powers meant that immunities from the restrictions that it could enforce were very marketable commodities, while its income of around £10,000 a year from rents, dues and tolls gave it considerable political strength, allegedly leading to the discouragement and impoverishment of all but the magistrates and their supporters. It was claimed, for instance, that the concentration of economic and social power within the town had led to a contraction in the number of merchants engaged in overseas trade as well, so that there were only four or five merchants left conducting an extensive foreign trade.[37] Certainly the group dominating Newcastle's overseas trade in the early eighteenth century was noticeably smaller than that in Hull, amounting to no more than seven or eight members of élite families; however, this might well be explained by the greater emphasis placed on the coastal trade in coal in Newcastle rather than by the machinations of the corporation. Recruitment to the Merchants' company does appear to fall off faster than that of other gilds and the number of merchants picked up in parish register samples declines dramatically between the 1660s and 1720s, but this evidence is inconclusive.[38]

The members of Newcastle's wealthy and restricted élite could usually be relied on to unite in defence of their privileges, but there is evidence of dissension even within this charmed circle. Indeed, power struggles within the corporation provide some of the clearest indications that social divisions within the freeman body had created an electoral interest which repaid cultivation. In the 1720s and for several decades thereafter attacks on the town's élite concentrated on the Ridley family in particular, while the freeman's cause was traditionally championed by the Blacketts. Thus one of the election poems composed in 1741 to defend Walter Blackett's claims to his family's parliamentary seat against the candidacy of Matthew Ridley made political capital out of attacking Ridley's powerful father:

> Thus Felix reign'd the Terror of the Town
> And sole Disposer of the Scarlet Gown:
> Her Places, Profits, he had all to give;
> None but his Tools he'd suffer for to live.[39]

It is probably significant that the author, Edward Chicken, was a former pupil of one of Newcastle's charity schools and an official of the Weavers' company. It is certainly significant that Blackett came top of the poll, 'the majority of the freemen striving to excell each other in wreathing laurels to decorate his brow'; the celebrations in fact almost equalled those held in 1734 when Blackett was first elected to the corporation.[40] Indeed, the continuing populist nature of the Blackett family's support is made clear by a complaint that Matthew Ridley would be succeeded as mayor in 1746 by 'a man of no education, a mere tradesman, attached to Mr. Blacker's [*sic*] party in opposition to Mr. Ridley's'.[41]

It is doubtful whether the lot of the poor freemen from the craft gilds actually improved as a result of the Blacketts' championship of their grievances, although competition for their electoral favours may have produced some material benefits.[42] It is true that the élite's old power base in the Hostmen's company was undermined in the 1690s when Sir William Blackett led a campaign to throw it open in fact as well as in theory to all members of the twelve principal trades.[43] However, this did not usher in an era of freer trade or a wider distribution of power; the élite consolidated behind their control of the most influential sectors of the Merchants' company, leading to complaints from members of the least favoured sector, the drapers, that even they were being squeezed out.[44] There seems to have been very little widening of the élite in the later seventeenth and early eighteenth centuries. In general, potential aldermen continued to be drawn from a relatively small pool, and more often than not from a group of families established in the town for several generations and united by business and family ties. Indeed the Blackett, Carr, Fenwick, Johnson and Ridley families provided Newcastle's mayor in fourteen of the thirty-three years from 1695 to 1727 and 25 per cent of new aldermen in the century as a whole. In fact, there were signs that the already narrow access into the élite was becoming more rather than less restricted over this period and that trading merchants generally were increasingly excluded from the magistracy. The mayor castigated in 1746 as 'a mere tradesman', Cuthbert Smith, was actually a member of the same section of the Merchants' company as Matthew Ridley, besides being the son of a gentleman and the former apprentice of a magistrate: his shortcomings seem to have lain solely in the fact that he earned his living from trade rather than from coal and landownership or the law. During the same period the number of new recruits to the corporation declined, while in the 1730s and 1740s, in particular, the number of well-connected young men who achieved promotion within a few years of obtaining their freedom increased.[45] The Newcastle élite were never entirely closed to wealth, and well-connected outsiders but this recruitment left the thousands of lesser citizens untouched and unmollified.

The extent to which dissension between the lesser freemen and an increasingly entrenched magistracy contributed to the development of social polarization in a wider sense is one of the most fundamental problems raised by the evidence. Given the numbers involved and the apparent maldistribution of wealth within the town, it might seem likely that many of the poorer freemen would have more in common with the unenfranchised labourers and members of incorporated crafts, such as the porters and keelmen, than with the merchant princes of the coal trade. People in the building and metalworking trades, for example, appear from the 1665 Hearth Tax returns to have had on average less than two hearths in their houses and the large proportion of Newcastle households which were not taxed at all undoubtedly included some of the poorer freemen.[46] This information has to be evaluated with caution: for instance, the problem of exemptions granted to industrial hearths needs to be taken into account. However, there is also fragmentary but unmistakable evidence from gild records and depositions that many of the craftsmen were wage-earners rather than independent artisans, although it is not possible to estimate what proportion of the freemen were involved in the labour market in this way.[47] Disputes within craft gilds can often be traced to the conflict of interests that naturally arose between employers and the employed, and in fact the Newcastle gilds seem to have been quite active in ways that could perhaps be seen as shading over into primitive unionism. The shoemakers, for example, formed their own friendly society in 1719 although the earlier case of the Keelmen's Hospital is better known.[48] Nor were the keelmen and coalworkers the only ones to go on strike: in 1705 the shipwrights, for instance, were presented for refusing to work for their 'ancient wages' and in 1733 the masons expelled several brethren who apparently refused to join a strike.[49]

However, none of this evidence is conclusive. Disparities of wealth and status do not necessarily lead those at the bottom of the social spectrum to identify with the rest of the poor and humble in a common cause against the more fortunate. In fact, it is possible to interpret many of the instances of gild activity or of the formation of artisan societies as signs of increasing differentiation among the lower orders of Newcastle society rather than as signs of polarization. The records of these bodies certainly contain graphic examples of friction between different trades as well as between employers and the employed; in 1740, for example, the Keelmen's Hospital Society condemned a joiner for

a proud haughty fancy reflection against this Company and a lessening of the Company and exalting the freemen as if the Hospital's Company were not fit to take place or [be] compared with freemen and that because they are freemen.[50]

Moreover, a good case can be made for the assertion that rising prosperity was leading to the growth of such differentials as the period progressed. It has recently been suggested that commercial advances in the later seventeenth and early eighteenth centuries were instrumental in producing a major increase in the literacy levels of Newcastle's trade and craftsmen, so much so that by 1700 they were comparable with the levels of London. The timing of this advance, moreover, seems to coincide with a great increase in the disposable incomes and consumption of these same social groups, as inventories are progressively overwhelmed in a tide of pewter, silver and fine linen. It is possible to find instances where these advances are shared by the groups at the bottom of Newcastle's social hierarchy. But in general it could be argued that the increasing levels of literacy and wealth had the effect of reinforcing a widening social gulf between artisans and manual labourers.[51]

Against this, Dr Houston's recent work on Newcastle's social hierarchy in the period between 1640 and 1760 does not reveal a clear-cut division between members of the craft gilds and those in labouring occupations. Rather he shows that coalworkers in particular were not as isolated from the main community as is often assumed. Indeed, both pitmen and watermen seemed to be fairly well integrated into the main low-status grouping of trades and crafts. Some crafts, like weavers, shipwrights and tanners, actually ranked below them in social status and tended towards keelmen, labourers and common sailors at the very bottom of the hierarchy. These findings are all the more striking when it is realized that the distinction between watermen and keelmen assumed by Houston in his analysis is debatable since the term 'keelman' is in fact very rarely used in Newcastle parish registers and hardly appears at all in those of All Saints' Parish.[52] This would suggest that the poorer members of Newcastle society may sometimes have recognized that they had some common interests or even some sense of common identity. This is not to deny the evidence of differentiation and friction, still less to suggest that the actions and attitudes of the town's craftsmen and labourers were consistently determined by this sort of basic labour consciousness. At the same time it is important to recognize that differentiation and identification are not exclusive concepts; most individuals probably developed an ambivalent view of society and tended to adopt attitudes or express views according to the context.[53] In other words, friction between joiners and keelmen over the order of precedence at civic functions does not necessarily imply that they would not act together in different circumstances.

Given that social attitudes reflect the influence of both work and community, it is not surprising to find that the least deferential sections of Newcastle's population were to be found in the crowded and industrious parish of All Saints and particularly in what Henry Bourne called 'the busy hot-headed Genius of Sandgate', which the authorities viewed with the liveliest apprehension. Its inhabitants inspired fear in the first place through sheer weight of numbers: as Bourne pointed out, Sandgate

has in it a vast Number of narrow Lanes on each Side of it, which are crowded with Houses. . . . The Number of Souls in this street and the Lanes belonging to it, is computed to several Thousands. . . .

The eruption of even a small proportion of its underprivileged residents could pose insurmountable difficulties for the raw and undisciplined town guard.[54] The one good thing about this concentration from the magistrates' point of view was that Sandgate lay outside the walls and in an emergency the gates could be shut to prevent a tide of humanity sweeping in from its densely-packed tenements. As the benefactor of St John's charity school remarked, it was 'near great towns rather than within them [that] the poorer sort generally inhabit'. On the other hand, there was always a possibility that the gates could be held against the forces of authority. In 1701, for example, a striking keelman was presented for buying gunpowder 'to keep a guard in Sandgate'.[55]

In the case of All Saints, the effects of purely geographical concentration and the predominance of low status occupations may have been reinforced by cultural factors breeding a sense of community and of independence from establishment values. The parish had a substantial minority of 'Scotch Presbyterians': the curate of All Saints estimated in 1736 that about a third of its population were dissenters, who buried their own dead and refused to pay fees to the established church. This probably paved the way for the warm welcome given to Wesley when he arrived in 1742, while his own success might account for the rising proportion of dissent in the parish in the later eighteenth century.[56] In fact, it seems likely that the religious character of All Saints was heavily influenced by the Scottish origins of a substantial part of its workforce. This link was most often remarked upon and most fully documented in the case of the keelmen: a sample of about 250 taken from a survey made in 1740 shows that nearly 70 per cent were born outside Newcastle and the adjacent riverside areas and that around 55 per cent came from Scotland, principally from Fife, Stirling and the Lothians.[57] Here migration may have created a sense of group identity mediated through the influence of the kirk or chapel.

There were also other forces at work in the specific case of the keelmen or watermen, who formed a sizeable minority of the population of All Saints and dominated Sandgate itself, which was said to be 'like the Wapping of London' in character. The conventional estimate was that there were between 1500 and 1600 men employed on the keels in the early eighteenth century and this was probably not too wide of the mark.[58] They were therefore the largest single occupational group in the town, but it was more significant in this particular context that their pattern of work made the keelmen ideal material for organized militant action. They worked for relatively big employers, few fitters employing less than twenty-four men and some employing seventy to eighty or more; and yet they worked in small, independent units, three men in a boat, plying up and down a 19 kilometre stretch of river in a rhythm determined by the tides rather than by the clock. In fact the whole riverside economy from ale and lodging houses upwards was geared to this tidal rhythm.[59] The keelmen's work was, moreover, both hard and dangerous since it involved loading from the coal-staiths upriver, negotiating the shoals, flat calms and currents, and then manhandling the cargo up over the sides of ocean-going colliers at Tynemouth. The nature of the employment, together with the high proportion who were migrants, suggests this was an age-specific occupation rather than a hereditary one, which is borne out by the ages recorded in the 1740 survey and the scarcity of family groups working the keels.[60] How far their hazardous and arduous labour was adequately rewarded is, unfortunately, very difficult to judge. In the early eighteenth century the agreed rates of payment included a basic wage of 5s. 6d for the skipper of a keel and just under 4s. for each of his crew for a round-trip to Shields, but this was supplemented or in some cases modified by a bewildering variety of payments in cash and kind that were subject to underhand manipulation by the employers. Contemporary comment combines an insistence on their dire poverty with an equal insistence on their reckless spending, but it is perhaps significant that the keelmen could not only sustain protracted strike-action but also in a few individual cases build up a modest amount of real and personal property.[61] Clearly their problem was not so much one of chronically low wages as of the irregular rewards that went with employment in a fluctuating trade. Thus, their working conditions readily explain their industrial militancy. Moreover, their demanding job was responsible for the fact that they were sufficiently intimidating both in appearance and in reality to give even the redoubtable Wesley pause. They had also developed a uniform: a blue bonnet at all times and a distinctive costume for Sundays.[62]

The keelmen's sense of group loyalty, together with a fierce independence and unbiddable sharpness, was proverbial. They were said to live on credit during the winter months when trade was slack but it would be an unwise trader who refused credit and risked being blacklisted. Lord Harley reported their reaction to

an affront given to them by a person who kept a public house on the north side of the Tyne. The keelman that was injured went and spit upon a stone near the house, and renounced any further communication with it, and the rest that were of his mind performed the same ceremony, and they have kept so religiously to their view that the people are obliged to quit their house for want of business.[63]

The most tangible sign of their independence was their determination to provide for their own poor, which led them to finance the building and maintenance of what was termed 'a very Capacious, Beautiful, and Useful Hospital' capable of housing at least 160 people, at a total cost of around £360 a year.[64] Although this initiative was sponsored by Sir William Blackett and generally welcomed by the local clergy, the corporation regarded it with some suspicion and control over the charity was wrested from the keelmen as soon as its potential as a strike fund was realized. Their vigorous rearguard action lasted for several decades and was aided by Defoe's press campaign in the *Review*, which highlighted the inequity of handing over effective control of the funds to the Newcastle magistrates and the fitters.[65] It was perhaps predictable, therefore, that the authorities' final victory in 1723 was marked by a precipitous decline in contributions to the hospital. This was attributed officially to the keelmen's feckless, free-spending habits, but no doubt owed something to popular resentment.[66]

As the dispute over the hospital demonstrated, the keelmen were far from being the anarchic mob of 'Brutes' suggested by many contemporary and some modern authorities. They certainly swore a great deal, as did the entire population of Newcastle according to Wesley, but they enjoyed as much of the patronage of the Blacketts as the lesser freemen did and there is really little evidence that they were not fully integrated into the community, albeit the under-privileged riverside community, into which they or their children eventually merged.[67] What really alarmed the authorities was that they were ready to take direct and highly disciplined industrial action against their employers rather than erupting into more 'instinctive' protests. Keelmen serving individual fitters were quite capable of refusing to work for collieries whose coal was not in demand and of appealing against deteriorating working conditions to the coal-owners themselves, who often had a keen personal interest in supervising their fitters' activities.[68]

Few decades of the early eighteenth century passed without a major strike on the Tyne, which invariably involved successful picketing, sometimes holding up trade on the river for weeks at a time. The seven-week strike of 1750 was perhaps the longest in this period, but somewhat shorter disturbances in 1701, 1708, 1710, 1719 and 1738 all caused grave disruption to Newcastle's coal-based economy and demonstrated the keelmen's collective strength.[69] Their organization seems to have been fluid and spontaneous, like that of many later strike committees, arising out of meetings on the Keyside or in public houses, but it was none the less effective. In 1719, for example, a delegation of ten Newcastle keelmen met their Sunderland counterparts at Great Usworth to sign a joint declaration prepared by a Wearside schoolmaster on their wage demands. They were also well aware of the benefits to be gained from effective publicity. In 1710, 1719 and 1738 they petitioned local coal-owners and members of Newcastle corporation as possible mediators, setting out their case in terms most likely to arouse a sympathetic response to the hardships suffered by their starving wives and families.[70] Indeed, in 1710 they petitioned the Privy Council and in this case, as in 1738, they seem to have consciously enhanced their bargaining power by drawing public attention to restrictive practices in the coal industry. By 1750 they were reported to be displaying printed bills in public places setting out their grievances, indicating a development in tactics as well as the 'advanced' nature of these industrial disputes.[71]

It was this evidence of organization and control that was most disturbing to the authorities, partly because it threatened comfortable contemporary assumptions that all members of the lower orders were 'a sort of Unthinking people', and partly because of the authorities' relative impotence in the face of a simple, orderly, refusal to work. Although the mayor appealed for help from the government in the face of such 'mutinies', expressing fears of violent disorder, even some contemporaries suspected that the fitters would have welcomed the occasional simple riot so that they could resort to equally simple coercion. In 1750, for instance, a local coal-owner reported that the fitters had contrived to have twenty to thirty of the supposed ringleaders arrested in order to tempt 'the Rable part' of the keelmen to violence

so as millatary force might have been Turnd upon them and obligd them to work . . . but instead of that they are allowed to go with the utmost civillity whatever before some Hundreds of the Keelmen who offered to go them selves to jail if required and Did and has since the Stop behaved very civilly.[72]

The constantly-repeated claim that the keelmen were espousing Jacobitism may also be traced to this desire to translate the strikes into something that fitted into the accepted framework of the social order. In fact the Scots Presbyterian keelmen seem to have been fairly safely anti-Jacobite ever since the Sandgate crowd assisted in the demolition of James II's statue on the Sandhill in 1688, and in 1719 they achieved official recognition as 'the only well affected Mob in England'.[73] However, they were impatient of authority and could be found using a variety of provocative slogans in what seems to have been a conscious challenge to the establishment. In 1746, for example, the two men guarding the Sandgate gate alleged that a group of keelmen had threatened 'that in two days they would make a second Sheriffmuir of it . . . that the mayor might go to hell and that they would shake his house about his ears'.[74] Most of the accusations of sedition seem to have amounted to no more than this sort of graphic demonstration of disrespect, but the disrespect was sometimes expressed in worrying forms. In 1738, for instance, some strikers drew up a petition complaining that they were treated with 'a Barbarity abhorred by Jews, Turks and Infidals' and demanding that employers as well as employees should enter into a yearly bond specifying conditions of service. Their spokesman defended these radical demands by asking 'What need you be afraid of [using] such Expressions to the Magistrates. . . . When the like have been delivered to the King and Parliament.'[75]

It is not surprising then that in the later eighteenth century the keelmen were included among those who were strongly impressed with 'the new doctrine of equality'. Moreover, their early and successful demonstrations of solidarity seem to have sparked off a reaction in the rest of the local community that went beyond simple labour consciousness. During the major riot of 1740 a barber appealed to the crowd to stand true to one another, and neighbouring collieries went on strike while awaiting the outcome of subsequent legal action against the rioters. There is much to support Morris's contention that the origins of nineteenth-century class society are to be found on Tyneside rather than in the Lancashire cotton industry.[76]

III

Even if the Sandgate crowd had stood alone, their vociferous and highly independent existence might have been enough to invalidate any attempt to portray Newcastle as a unified or harmonious society in the period 1660–1760. And, as the evidence presented in this paper suggests, they did not stand alone in their opposition to the wealthy élite, but merely represented the opposite pole in Newcastle's individual 'field-of-force' around which the remainder of the population aligned themselves as changing circumstances dictated.[77] Between Sandgate on the one hand and the Guildhall on the other there was an immense gulf, so immense that Henry Bourne felt obliged to record the customs of his flock for the benefit of the educated public in the manner of a missionary facing an alien culture. In fact, Bourne was probably one of the few men in Newcastle who could appreciate the extent to which the town was occupied not by one community but by several: he was himself the son of a poor tailor and had actually been apprenticed to a glazier before the corporation decided to sponsor his education. As his case demonstrates, it was possible to move between the different communities but the opportunities for doing so were limited and may have become more so as the period progressed.[78]

Given the increasing rewards for success and the increasing penalties for failure, it would not be surprising if Newcastle society displayed the tensions and open discontent associated with competition and raised levels of expectation. This is certainly the impression which Newcastle gave to contemporaries. Bourne's *History* suffered from the prejudices generated by social mobility and the long-running power struggle within the town, which led to suspicions

that it might be of dangerous Consequence to shew ancient Writings, that He was but a Curate that undertook the Work, [and] that his Abilities therefore of Pocket and Mind must be vastly unequal to such a Task.

Wesley, for his part, noted that the members of his society there were unusually prone to internal recriminations, 'this being the sin which, of all others, most easily besets the people of Newcastle'. Against this, there were relatively few occasions when the discontents and aggressions of the Newcastle population were expressed in open, physical protest in the streets. Wesley's rather ill-judged attempt to persuade the inhabitants of All Saints to abandon their habitual Sunday promenade on the Sandhill was defeated in a peaceful but determined fashion, and he commented in some surprise that

the very mob of Newcastle, in the height of their rudeness, have commonly some humanity left. I scarce observed that they threw anything at all; neither did I receive the least personal hurt.[79]

In fact, stone-throwing was rather more common than Wesley allowed but it is true that there was only one real outbreak of popular violence in the whole period, the occasion in 1740 when a militia detachment drawn from the Merchants' company shot some demonstrators on the Sandhill who were agitating about the price of grain: they had the interior of the Guildhall comprehensively smashed for their pains. And not only was this solitary food riot the product of an unlikely chain of circumstances, it was also remarkably restrained in that the rioters smashed objects rather than people and on capturing the city armoury threw the weapons into the Tyne. Civic action against the offenders was also restrained and no one was sentenced to death.[80]

In view of the wide economic and cultural divisions that undoubtedly existed within the densely populated town, it would be tempting to suggest that this relative absence from the records of open and violent confrontation is a sign of an unusual degree of social harmony and acceptance.[81] This would, however, be misinterpreting the evidence and would be presenting a view of Newcastle society just as biased as one that took into account only the outbreaks of popular violence. The natural human desire to avoid disrupting everyday life and the pursuit of happiness was reinforced by the lack of any practical alternative to the existing social order at this time: however deep their grievances were, ordinary townspeople had to express them within the established framework of social organization. In these circumstances, the lack of violent dissent is clearly not conclusive proof of the essentially harmonious nature of society.

A more satisfactory interpretation may be one that points to the underlying tensions in urban society, tensions that are emphasized by the extent of the measures taken to mitigate them. For instance, the town's well-deserved reputation for liberality to the poor may have owed as much to prudential calculation as it did to Christian charity. The vulnerability of so great a part of the workforce to frequent and often unpredictable periods of unemployment imposed clear obligations on the corporation and on the wealthier residents of Newcastle to provide some sort of charitable safety-net, obligations of which the riots in 1740 were a sharp reminder. And there is no doubt that the practical value of such munificence was very well appreciated: the founder of St John's charity school commented that 'your corporation's eminent charities no doubt have been a means of its long prosperity and preservation against the attempts of its enemies'.[82] It is also clear that the keelmen, in particular, were handled with the utmost care in order to avoid trouble whenever possible; and that there was of necessity a practical, conciliatory attitude to the grievances of the workforce. The first step in any strike was for the magistrates to begin negotiations to settle the dispute as soon as possible, and even when arrest and coercion were used to force the men back to work the final settlement usually conceded many of their demands and was accompanied by a release of most of the prisoners.[83] It is probably significant that when the corporation wanted to check Sandgate for 'inmates' and Sunday tipplers they employed keelmen to do it. It was a polarized society in which the authorities had a healthy respect for the limits of their effective jurisdiction and where the 'reciprocity of gentry-crowd relations' emphasized by E. P. Thompson was a matter of hard bargaining.[84]

In some important respects this recognition and the avoidance of confrontation that went with it were just as much a product of Newcastle's complex and autonomous municipal institutions as of the keelmen's muscle. Strikes and disputes were defused by the intervention of town officials who mediated between workers and employers; and the mutual familiarity of officials, workers, employers and the town guard meant that conflicts were likely to be less violent and more easily compromised. The ritualization of divisions and discord through both official and unofficial spectacles may also have helped to defuse tensions. In addition, the fact that important sections of the workforce had shifted the focus of their discontent towards wages and working conditions and tended to institutionalize their protests had a considerable impact on the nature of social relationships. The gilds and less formal organizations like that of the keelmen were clearly instrumental in directing conflict away from spontaneous and violent eruptions in the market-place and towards forms of industrial action that were less destructive and easier to settle by mediation.[85]

In sum, the avoidance of violence is not necessarily a sign of harmony; it can also be a sign that social conflict had proceeded far enough to encourage the first stirrings of class consciousness and the development of workers' organizations to bargain with those of the élite. In fact, the conventional dichotomy between harmony and discord is profoundly misleading because it ignores the essential ambivalence of English social relations in the late seventeenth and eighteenth centuries: certainly in the particular case of Newcastle an approach that stresses the flexibility and ambiguity of society seems to offer a more adequate means of conceptualizing the problem. From the Newcastle evidence urban society could be described as broadly consensual, though consent was certainly not merely acceptance of subordination and deference. It was consent 'upon Terms', as the intrepid keelmen pointed out in 1738, and the terms were hammered out, adjusted and sometimes restated through forms of conflict. Newcastle was sufficiently idiosyncratic in its development to rule out any claims for its 'typicality' as a model of social relations. However, this close study of how the social rate of exchange was adjusted in one particular community underlines the need to move away from the current rather polarized debate towards a more sophisticated view of social relationships in the early modern period. Newcastle's society in the period 1660–1760 was both ambivalent and dynamic, impelled and constrained by economic change and by the many frictions that were generated in the process. Its apparent stillness was in fact a product of vigorous motion: like a spinning top, it had 'the ease of intense well-balanced activity' and kept its balance through the interaction of opposing forces.[86]

Appendix Occupations of male residents of Newcastle-upon-Tyne, 1660–1729*

Occupations	1660s	1700s	1710s	1720s	Total
Professions					
Customs, tax officials	1	8	12	12	33
Town officials	7	0	8	9	24

Occupations	1660s	1700s	1710s	1720s	Total
Armed forces	1	3	19	4	27
Clergy, ministers	3	9	6	8	26
Lawyers	1	10	6	6	23
Goldsmiths, scriveners	5	2	4	1	12
Physicians, surgeons**	23	25	21	25	94
Apothecaries	4	2	0	0	6
Musicians	3	6	4	3	16
Teachers	4	5	6	13	28
Total	52	70	86	81	289
Services					
Inn, alehousekeepers	0	0	1	4	5
Domestic servants	2	2	2	3	9
Services	1	2	1	0	4
Total	3	4	4	7	18
Commerce and transport					
Merchants	75	32	26	23	156
Hostmen, fitters	7	12	8	10	37
Chapmen	5	7	2	0	14
Mariners, seamen	76	65	43	50	234
Watermen	131	184	138	130	583
Cartmen, porters	13	11	8	11	43
Total	307	311	225	224	1067
Agriculture					
Farmer, husbandmen	1	3	0	1	5
Bailiffs, surveyors	0	3	0	1	4
Gardeners	10	19	8	11	48
Total	11	25	8	13	57
Construction					
Printers, instruments	2	5	8	3	18
Wrights, toolmakers	0	7	5	4	16
Shipbuilders	41	24	23	23	111
Carpenters, joiners	41	39	37	50	167
Masons	12	15	14	20	61
Other builders	23	32	16	26	97
Painters, glaziers	12	16	10	18	56
Total	131	138	113	144	526

Textiles and clothing

Weavers	15	25	18	24	82
Fullers and dyers	3	11	4	10	28
Other textile workers	5	2	7	19	33
Clothiers, drapers	4	2	3	1	10
Tailors	71	60	34	53	218
Wigmakers	1	7	2	1	11
Hatters	1	2	4	1	8
Others	1	5	9	3	18
Ropemakers	1	12	7	9	29
Total	102	126	88	121	437

Food and drink

Butchers	29	33	41	48	151
Victuallers×	2	4	6	5	17
Bakers	4	5	1	7	17
Millers, mealmakers	11	28	14	7	60
Brewers†	28	40	23	34	125
Total	74	110	85	101	370

Animal and vegetable products

Leather workers	53	53	43	37	186
Shoemakers	56	61	52	54	223
Gluemakers, tallow	0	1	1	1	3
Basketmakers	3	2	1	2	8
Total	112	117	97	94	420

Minerals

Pitmen, coal-workers	65	63	65	105	298
Clay, earthenware	6	5	5	4	20
Glassmakers	3	5	12	18	38
Metalworkers	5	5	12	11	33
Smiths	36	42	56	61	195
Total	115	120	150	199	584

Miscellaneous

Baronets, esquires	10	5	6	2	23
Gentlemen	21	2	1	2	26
Yeomen††	60	24	87	43	214
Labourers	51	90	26	55	222
Beggars	0	1	0	0	1
Total	142	122	120	102	486
Total	1049	1143	976	1086	4254

Occupations	1660s	1700s	1710s	1720s	Total
Total baptisms in samples	1649	1296	1264	1414	5623
Per cent occupations recorded		63.6	88.2	77.2	76.8	75.7

Source: Northumberland County Record Office, Baptismal registers of All Saints', St Andrew's, St John's and St Nicholas's parishes, 1660–1760

Notes

* It should be emphasized that these samples exclude women, children, apprentices and most servants, who constituted a sizeable part of the workforce, particularly in the service sector and victualling trades. Moreover, samples taken from baptismal registers may overstate the proportion of industrial workers: see J. Langton and P. Laxton, 'Parish registers and urban structure: the example of late eighteenth-century Liverpool', in *Urban History Yearbook 1978* (1978), pp. 78, 80. The registers of St John's do not record occupations consistently enough to permit samples to be taken for other decades.

** Surgeons include barber-surgeons and barbers, since their functions are not clearly differentiated.

× Victuallers include chandlers, cheesemongers, confectioners, grocers and tobacconists.

† Brewers include coopers, distillers, maltsters, vintners and wine-coopers, as well as a number of bakers and brewers.

†† 'Yeoman' seems to have been used as a status rather than as an occupational description in the North-East.

Acknowledgements

I am grateful to the British Academy Small Grants Fund for supporting part of the research on which this paper is based and to Dr P. J. Corfield and Dr K. Wrightson for their help in reading earlier drafts.

Notes and references

1   Anon, *Is This The Truth? A Poem* (1741?), p. 4.

2   E. Chandler, *A Charge Delivered to the Grand-Jury at the Quarter-Sessions held at Durham, on Wednesday, the 16th of July, 1740* (1740), pp. 6–7; N. Ellison, *The Obligations and Opportunities of doing Good to the Poor* (1710), pp. 7, 13.

3   For example, see V. Pearl, 'Change and stability in seventeenth-century London', *London Journal*, **5** (1979), pp. 3–34.

4   P. J. Corfield, *The Impact of English Towns 1700–1800* (1982), pp. 125, 137–8, 165–7.

5   P. J. Corfield *et al.*, *The Traditional Community Under Stress* (1977), p. 42; T. Cox, *Magna Britania et Hibernia* (1724), vol. 3, p. 608. For useful brief accounts of Newcastle, see C. Morris, (ed.), *The Journeys of Celia*

Fiennes (1947), pp. 109–12 and D. Defoe, *A Tour Thro' the Whole Island of Great Britain* (1727), vol. 3, pp. 156–9.

6   E. Birley, 'Sir John Clerk's visit to the north of England in 1724' *Trans. Archit. and Archaeolog. Soc. of Durham and Northumb.*, **11** (1958–65), p. 223; J. Macky, *A Journey Through England* (1722), vol. 2, p. 217; *HMC*, Portland MSS., **6**, pp. 105–6; Northumberland County Record Office (NCRO), Carr-Ellison MSS ZCE 10/6: Cotesworth to Sanderson, 15 April 1722.

7   For a fuller account of Newcastle's trade, see J. M. Ellis, *A Study of the Business Fortunes of William Cotesworth, c. 1668–1726* (New York, 1981), pp. 10–18.

9   P. W. Brassley, 'The agricultural economy of Northumberland and Durham in the period 1640–1750' (unpublished BLitt thesis, University of Oxford 1974), pp. 16–34; W. G. Hoskins, *Local History in England* (1972), p. 239; C. M. Law, 'Some notes on the urban population of England and Wales in the eighteenth century', *Local Historian*, **10** (1972–3), p. 25. Information about coal exports derived from North of England Institute of Mining and Mechanical Engineers (NEIMME), Buddle Collection, **14**, pp. 205–6.

9   R. North, *The Lives of the Norths* (1826), vol. 1, p. 249; J. Brome, *Travels over England, Scotland and Wales* (1700), pp. 173–4; Gateshead Public Library (GPL), Cotesworth MSS CK/5/1: minutes of evidence, 1722, p. 48.

10   Morris, *The Journeys of Celia Fiennes*, p. 211; H. Bourne, *A History of Newcastle upon Tyne* (1736), p. 54; D. Defoe, *A Plan of the English Commerce* (1728), p. 102.

11   N. Spencer, *The Complete English Traveller* (1771), p. 571; Macky, *A Journey Through England*, p. 217.

12   Bourne, *History of Newcastle upon Tyne* pp. 22, 81, 146–7, 150; E. MacKenzie, *A Discriptive and Historical Account of Newcastle* (1827), vol. 1, pp. 320, 351–2, 369–71; *Newcastle Courant*, 11 July 1724; 18 May, 1 and 16 June, 27 July 1734.

13   Defoe, *Plan of English Commerce* p. 85; P. Corfield, 'A provincial capital in the late seventeenth century: the case of Norwich', in P. Clark and P. Slack (eds.), *Crisis and Order in English Towns 1500–1700* (1972), pp. 276–87.

14   Tyne and Wear Archives Department (TWAD), Keelmen's Papers, 394/11: mayor to duke of Newcastle, 19 July 1740; C. R. Dobson, *Masters and Journeymen* (1980), pp. 34–6. However, watching the gates did have its uses; see above, pp. 213–14.

15   R. Howell, *Newcastle upon Tyne and the Puritan Revolution* (1967), pp. 12–13; J. Langton, 'Residential patterns in pre-industrial cities', *Trans. Inst. of British Geographers*, **65** (1975), pp. 8–23. Exemption rates elsewhere were 61.7 per cent in Norwich, just over 40 per cent in Exeter, 27.4 per cent in Leicester, 20.4 per cent in York: Corfield, 'A

provincial capital', pp. 266, 302n; 31 per cent in Warwick in 1663 and 39 per cent in 1670: figures supplied by Peter Borsay. In Warwick's poorest wards the exemption rates were 54 per cent in 1663 and 66 per cent in 1670.

16 Defoe, *Tour*, vol. 3, p. 159; *Newcastle Courant*, 5 January 1734; 19 and 26 January, 2 February 1740; GPL CK/5/9: affidavit, 1 September 1722.

17 J. Ellison, *Our Obligations to do Good, and the Manner of Doing It* (1750?), pp. 26–7; Ellison, *Obligations and Opportunities*, pp. 10, 19, 25, 28–30; J. Straker, *Memoirs of the Public Life of Sir Walter Blackett* (1819), pp. xxi–xxii.

18 NCRO, Newcastle parish registers; Bourne, *History of Newcastle upon Tyne*, pp. 107, 154; Newcastle City Library, L 253/21245: Bishop Chandler's visitation, 1736; University of Durham, Department of Palaeography and Diplomatic, Auckland Castle Records: Clergy visitation book, 1774; N. Curnock (ed.), *The Journal of the Rev. John Wesley* (1938), vol. 3, p. 14.

19 J. Loveday, *Diary of a Tour in 1732* (1890), pp. 168–9; Bourne, *History of Newcastle upon Tyne*, pp. 126–7, 133.

20 TWAD, 540/16: Quarter Sessions Order Book 1744–77, Midsummer sessions 1749. There was also a tendency for wealthy residents to own country houses: see Loveday, *Diary of a Tour*, p. 172; Bourne, *History of Newcastle upon Tyne*, p. 16n.

21 Langton, 'Residential patterns', esp. pp. 18–21.

22 NCRO, Newcastle parish registers; Bourne, *History of Newcastle upon Tyne*, p. 133.

23 See L. H. Lees, 'The study of social conflict in English industrial towns', in *Urban History Yearbook: 1980* (1980), pp. 36–7.

24 *Newcastle Courant*, 12 January 1734; BL Additional MSS 40748: Bowes Papers, fols. 81–2; GPL, Ellison MSS, A 31/12: from Sir Henry Liddell, 18 May 1738; TWAD, 394/9: Keelmen's strike papers, 1738. Fitters were trading members of the Hostmen's company, employed by coal-owners to manage the shipment of their coal downriver and themselves employers of the keelmen.

25 J. Smith, *A Sermon Preached to the Sons of the Clergy* (1711?), pp. a–b; *Newcastle Courant*, 1 June 1734; [C. Ellison], *A Most Pleasant Description of Benwel Village, in the County of Northumberland* (1726), p. 152; *Newcastle Journal*, 15 August 1747; GPL A 47/4: from Airey, 11 February 1729; TWAD 1160/2: Keelmen's Sick Book 1739–69.

26 Bourne, *History of Newcastle upon Tyne*, p. 125; *Newcastle Courant*, 13 October 1727; 16 March, 6 April, 11 May, 3 August, 26 October 1734; *HMC*, Portland MSS, **16**, pp. 104–6.

27 Defoe, *Tour*, vol. 3, pp. 159–60; BL, Additional MSS 40747, fols. 184–5: to Jurin, 22 April 1721; Bourne, *History of Newcastle upon Tyne*, p. 159.

28 W. Gray, *Chorographia: or a Description of Newcastle upon Tyne* (1649). See also, J. Horsley, 'Materials for the history of Northumberland, 1729–30', in J. Hodgson Hinde (ed.), *Inedited Contributions to the History of Northumberland* (1869); J. Brand, *The History and Antiquities of Newcastle upon Tyne* (2 vols. 1789). Bourne was also one of the first English writers to develop an interest in popular culture: see *Antiquitates Vulgares: or, the Antiquities of the Common People* (1725).

29 This assertion is based on work still in progress on the records of several Newcastle gilds to be found in the Tyne and Wear Archives Department or in the publications of the Surtees Society.

30 These estimates are arrived at using average decennial enrolment figures with a multiplier based on the life expectancy of citizens, assuming this to be about twenty-seven years before 1700 and about thirty-three years thereafter: M. H. Dodds (ed.), *The Register of Freemen of Newcastle upon Tyne* (Newcastle Records Series, **3** and **6** 1923, 1926); E. A. Wrigley, 'Mortality in pre-industrial England: the example of Colyton, Devon, over three centuries', *Daedalus*, **97** (1968), p. 560.

31 The ratio of freemen to non-freemen elsewhere has been estimated to be 75 per cent for seventeenth-century London, Pearl, 'Change and stability', pp. 13–14; 75 per cent for York, 50 per cent for Bristol and a substantial minority for Exeter in the early part of the century, and 30 per cent for Norwich in the 1690s; J. T. Evans, *Seventeenth Century Norwich* (1979), pp. 12–13. If Newcastle is taken in this context to exclude the population of Gateshead, the ratio rises to around 60 per cent.

32 [Ellison], *Pleasant Description*, pp. 190–2; Anon, *Is This the Truth?*, p. 4.

33 It should be noted that a high proportion of the Common Council were also members of the Merchant's company, with only token representation of the craft gilds; see TWAD, 589/6: Common Council Book, 1656–1722; 589/7: Common Council Book, 1722–82; Dodds, *The Register of Freemen passim*.

34 F. W. Dendy (ed.), *Extracts from the records of the Merchant Adventurers of Newcastle upon Tyne* (Surtees Soc., **93** and **101** 1894, 1899); J. U. Nef, *The Rise of the British Coal Industry* (1932) vol 2, pp. 125–8; Howell, *Newcastle upon Tyne, passim*.

35 C. H. Hunter Blair, 'Members of Parliament for Northumberland and Newcastle upon Tyne, 1559–1831', *Archaeologia Aeliana*, 4th series, **23** (1945); R. R. Sedgwick, *The House of Commons, 1715–54* (1970), vol. 1 p. 298; BL, Loan 29/321: Dyer's Newsletter, 7 November 1710; GPL, A 35/9: Liddell to Cotesworth, 10 November 1710; Anon, *The Whigs Defeated* (1710); TWAD, 540/3: Quarter Sessions Order Book 1700-19, Christmas 1710; NCRO, 33/11: Quarter Sessions Papers, Christmas 1710.

36 TWAD, 540/3: index of defaulters, 1690–1706.

37   GPL, CG/5/84: The case of the freemen of Newcastle upon Tyne (1714); CG/5/81: Heads for a petition, November 1714; J. Taylor, *A Journey to Edenborough* (1903), pp. 86–7.

38   PRO, E 190/211/3 (1705–6); 235/5 (1730–1); G. Jackson, *Hull in the Eighteenth Century* (1972), p. 96.

39   E. Chicken, *No: This is the Truth* (1741?), pp. 4–5; Anon, *The Town of Newcastle's Attempt to make a Monopoly of the Coal-Trade in the River Tyne* (1722?); BL, Additional MS 27420, fol. 59.

40   Mackenzie, *Discriptive and Historical Account*, pp. 351–2; Straker, *Memoirs*, p. iv; *Newcastle Courant*, 11 May and 26 October 1734; *Newcastle Journal*, 23 May 1741.

41   I owe this reference to Prof. W. A. Speck; Culloden Papers, fols. 211–2: Wightman to Lord President, 26 September 1746.

42   Anon, *Is This The Truth?*, pp. 6–8; Chicken, *No: This is the Truth*, pp. 9–11; Anon, *No; That's a Mistake* (1741?).

43   F. W. Dendy (ed.), *Extracts from the Records of the Company of Hostmen of Newcastle upon Tyne*, (Surtees Soc., **105** 1901), pp. xl–xli, 155; Newcastle University Library (NUL), Montagu Papers, 85: to Baker, 14 August 1697.

44   As Table 27 demonstrates, only six drapers became aldermen between 1660 and 1760 and two of these were intruded by James II; GPL, CG/5/44: copy of M. Bell's affidavit, *c.* 1722.

45   Dendy, *Merchant Adventurers*, p. 101; GPL, A 17/27, 28: from R. Ellison, 6 and 9 October 1741. Matthew Ridley himself was the most notorious case, gaining his freedom in October 1731, a place on the bench in February 1732 and the mayoralty in October 1732, a month before his twenty-second birthday, making him the youngest man to have held that office; see Sedgwick, *House of Commons*, vol. 2, pp. 29, 283; Dodds, *The Register of Freemen*, vol. 6, p. 173.

46   Langton, 'Residential patterns', p. 15.

47   TWAD, 395/51: Hutchinson's examination, I July 1740; 597/16: petition to Common Council, 1733/4; NCRO 3/3: Easter sessions, 1685.

48   TWAD, 597/16: petition 1733/4, makes the distinction between 'meeting' and 'free' brothers of the mason's company; 597/64–8: petitions, May 1734; 401/2: Minute book of the Cordwainer's company, 1716; 540/3: Michaelmas sessions, 1716 and Christmas, 1718.

49   TWAD, 540/3: Easter sessions, 1705; 597/16: petition, 1733/4.

50   TWAD, 1160/1: Minute book of the Keelmen's Hospital Society, 1739–1842, p. 7; 394/52: English's examination, 1740. See also, E. P. Thompson, *The Making of the English Working Class* (1968), p. 458.

51   R. A. Houston, 'The development of literacy: northern England, 1640–1750', *EcHR*, 2nd series, **35** (1982); pp. 206–15. Information on consumer expenditure is derived from work still in progress on Newcastle probate records (Durham PD Department) and from Lorna Weatherill.

52 R. A. Houston, 'Aspects of society in Scotland and north-east England, *c.* 1550–*c.* 1750: social structure, literacy and geographical mobility' (unpublished PhD thesis, University of Cambridge 1981), pp. 87–94. Because occupational terms conceal wide variations in income and status, it is possible that these conclusions apply to only a minority of pit and watermen but there seems little reason why other trades should not also be affected by this distortion.

53 See H. Newby, *The Deferential Worker* (1977), p. 366 *et seq.*, which explores many of the same issues with reference to the attitudes of modern agricultural workers.

54 Bourne, *History of Newcastle upon Tyne*, pp. 124, 154; PRO, SP34/12/102: from Ridley, 23 June 1710; 36/51/127: from Fenwick, 20 June 1740; *HMC*, Portland MSS, **6,** p. 105.

55 For example, see TWAD, 394/11: memoranda, 10 July 1740; NCRO, Ridley MSS, ZRI 27/8: account of 1740 demonstrations; PRO, SP 36/70/110: from General Huske, 4 October 1745; 36/83/145: affidavit, August 1746; TWAD, 540/3: Quarter sessions, 1701.

56 NCL, 253/21245: Chandler visitation, 1736; MacKenzie, *Discriptive and Historical Account*, pp. 369 *et seq.*; Curnock, *Wesley's Journal*, vol. 3, pp. 14–15, 51 *et seq.*; Durham PD Department: Clergy visitation book, 1774; T. Dockwray, *The Operations of the Holy Spirit Imperceptible* (1743?), pp. 5, 14–15, 21.

57 PRO, SP 34/12/120: from mayor, 6 July 1710; TWAD, 394/11: lists of keelmen employed by Armorer, Atkinson, Johnson, Simpsons, Vonholte and Watson, 1740. Houston, 'Aspects of society', p. 93, found just over 60 per cent of a somewhat smaller sample to have been migrants.

58 Anon, *The Case of the Poor Skippers and Keelmen of Newcastle* (1712?); [D. Defoe], *A Review of the State of the the British Nation*, vol. 8 no. 139 (1712), p. 560; NCRO All Saints' parish registers, 1660–1760. See also J. M. Fewster, 'The keelmen of Tyneside in the eighteenth century', *Durham University Journal*, **50** (1957–8), pp. 24–33, 66–75, 111–23.

59 TWAD, 394/11: lists of keelmen employed, 1740; 394/51, 52: examinations and informations, 1740. Bourne, *Antiquitates Vulgares*, p. 38, implicitly contrasts the later hours kept in towns with rural early rising but must have been aware of the more fluid pattern of his own curacy; see E. P. Thompson, 'Time, work-discipline and industrial capitalism', *P. and P.*, no. 38 (1967), pp. 59–60.

60 GPL, CG/5/9, 30: affidavits, August–September 1722; TWAD, 394/11: lists of keelmen employed, 1740.

61 TWAD, 589/12: Common Council minutes, 27 March 1705; 394/9: Keelmen's strike papers, 1738; [Defoe], *A Review*, vol 8, no. 139, p. 560; Anon, *Case of the Poor Skippers*; GPL, A 32/21: from Liddell, 14 January 1729; Durham PD Department: wills of P. Hall and R. Hinckster, 1707; of W. Armorer, 1746.

62   NUL, 85/2: to Baker, 2 January 1697; Curnock, *Wesley's Journal*, vol. 3, pp. 14, 60, 80–1; BL, Additional MSS 40748/ 81–2: from Gomeldon, 12 May 1738. Note that the earliest manuscript of *The Keel Row* dates from 1752.

63   GPL, A 32/21: from Liddell, 14 January 1729; *HMC*, Portland MSS, **6,** p. 105.

64   Ellison, *Obligations and Opportunities*, pp. 19–20, 28; Bourne, *History of Newcastle upon Tyne*, pp. 153–4; TWAD, 1160/1: Keelmen's Hospital society minutes, preface. The building was criticized in the nineteenth century for being over-elaborate. Wesley often preached in its courtyard on his visits to Newcastle; Curnock, *Wesley's Journal*, vol. 3, pp. 51, 60.

65   Anon, *Case of the Poor Skippers*; Dendy, *Hostmen's Records*, pp. 157–8, 171–2, 177–80; Anon, *The Case of the Poor Skippers and Keelmen of Newcastle, Truly Stated* (1712?); *A Review*, **8** nos. 139–42 (1712); TWAD, 394/2, 4–5; Keelmen's charity papers, 1708–22.

66   Dendy, *Hostmen's Records*, pp. 188–9; Bourne, *History of Newcastle upon Tyne*, p. 154. It was replaced in 1730 by a more general friendly society which had a somewhat chequered career; TWAD, 1160/1: Keelmen's Hospital society minutes, 1740–1842.

67   [Ellison], *Pleasant Description*, pp. 309–10; Curnock, *Wesley's Journal*, vol. 3, p. 13; NUL, Jacobite Letters, 30/12: from Liddell, 10 October 1715.

68   NUL Clavering Letters, 10/173: to Liddell, 9 May 1713; 10/202: to Liddell, 5 January 1714; Ellis, *Business Fortunes*, pp. 95–102.

69   TWAD, 540/3: Quarter sessions, 1701 and 1708; 394/1, 3, 7, 9, 21–7, 29–30: Keelmen's strike papers, 1659–1770. For the circumstances and resolution of the 1738 strike, see above pp. 199–200.

70   TWAD, 394/51, 52: examinations and informations, 1740; Durham PD Department, Shafto Papers, 494: Makepeace to Spearman, Whit 1719; PRO, SP 44/281/44: affidavit, 13 May 1719.

71   GPL, CJ/3/6: minutes of grievances, 1710; CJ/3/10: petition, 1719; TWAD, 394/9: keelmen's demands, 3 May 1738; GPL, A 35/4: Liddell to Cotesworth, 29 July 1710; PRO, SP 44/109: to mayor, 1 August 1710; SP 44/281/60: to magistrates, 16 June 1719; NEIMME, Brown Letter Book, 16/1: to Spedding, 30 April 1750.

72   GPL, A 32/21: from Liddell, 14 January 1729; A 35/9: Liddell to Cotesworth, 21 November 1710; PRO, SP 34/12/101: from mayor, 23 June 1710; SP 34/12/126: from mayor, 11 July 1710; NCRO, ZCE 10/4: Cotesworth to Sanderson, 17 May 1719; NEIMME, 16/1: Brown to Spedding, 30 April 1750.

73   NUL, 30/19: from Liddell, 27 October 1715; PRO, SP 36/70/110: from General Huske, 4 October 1745; Bourne, *History of Newcastle upon Tyne*, pp. 89, 126; NCRO, ZCE 10/4: Cotesworth to Banks, 19 June 1719. It seems appropriate that the statue was recast to provide new bells for All Saints.

74 *Newcastle Courant*, April 1750; PRO, SP 36/83/145: affidavit, August 1746. Compare N. Rogers, 'Popular protest in early Hanoverian London', *P. and P.*, no. 79 (1978), pp. 83–100.

75 TWAD, 394/9: petition, 9 May 1738.

76 TWAD, 394/52: Reaves's information, 1740; NCRO, ZCE 10/13: Carr to Burnett, 8 August 1740; R. J. Morris, *Class and Class Consciousness in the Industrial Revolution, 1780–1850* (1979), pp. 17–18.

77 E. P. Thompson, 'Eighteenth-century English society: class struggle without class', *Social History*, no. 3 (1978), p. 150 *et seq*.

78 Bourne, *Antiquitates Vulgares*, pp. ix–x; MacKenzie, *Discriptive and Historical Account*, p. 320n; Charles Hutton (b. 1737), the son of a Newcastle pitman, rose still further to become Professor of Mathematics at the Royal Military Academy of Woolwich: J. Bruce, *A Memoir of Charles Hutton* (1823), pp. 2–14.

79 Bourne, *History of Newcastle upon Tyne*, pp. v–vi; Curnock, *Wesley's Journal*, vol. 3, pp. 165, 80–1.

80 J. Ellis, 'Urban conflict and popular violence: the Guildhall riots of 1740 in Newcastle upon Tyne', *International Review of Social History*, **25** (1980), pp. 332–49.

81 Pearl, 'Change and stability', p. 18, suggests this in the case of seventeenth-century London.

82 Ellis, 'Urban conflict' pp. 337–8, 348; TWAD, 589/12: Common Council minutes, 1699–1718, fols. 118–20.

83 NUL, 85: Montagu to Baker, 7 July 1696; GPL, A 47/14: from Airey, 1 May 1729; TWAD, 394/1 *et seq.*: Keelmen's papers.

84 TWAD, 589/12, fol. 40; Thompson, 'Eighteenth-century English society', p. 158.

85 Lees, 'The study of social conflict', pp. 37–41.

86 Quotation taken from *Oxford English Dictionary* (1926 edn), 10.i.147.

7 'All the town's a stage': urban ritual and ceremony 1660–1800

Peter Borsay

Every year at Whitsuntide the city of Lichfield was transformed by a ceremony known as 'the Green Bower Feast' or 'Whitsun Bower'. Descriptions of the event vary a little, but that published by the Reverend Stebbing Shaw in 1798 is among the most detailed. Early on Whit Monday morning a party of civic officials, entertainers and 'ten men, armed with fire-locks, and adorned by ribbons', met at the Guildhall and then processed to 'the bower on Green-Hill, an eminence at the south-east extremity of the town'. After a 'Court of Array, or View of Men, and Arms' was proclaimed, the company marched to every ward in the city and summoned 'the dozener (a petty constable) of that ward to attend. He immediately comes forth, bearing a pageant on a pole [and] joins the cavalcade', which visited each house in the ward. The procession then returned to the bower where the name of every inhabitant was called, and those who attended were regaled with a feast. 'Late in the evening', after all the twenty-one wards had been treated, the morning procession reassembled, accompanied this time by the dozeners and their pageants, and moved on to the market-place. There the formalities were completed with a patriotic oration delivered by the town clerk, after which 'the dozeners deposit their pageants in the belfry' of St Mary's.

The Whitsun Bower was a peculiar mixture of two medieval customs, a court of array to inspect the standards of civil defence in the town, and the Whitsuntide gild celebrations. Remnants of the latter can be seen in the dozener's 'pageant', the processional nature of the event, and more positively in Celia Fiennes description of 1698, of 'the ceremony of dressing up baby's [presumably an effigy] with garlands of flowers and green and carrying it in procession through the streets'. However, by the late seventeenth and eighteenth centuries the original purposes of the ceremony must have held little significance. By then the 'Bower' was part of a Whitsun holiday that spread across several days; and its most appealing features were those that corresponded with Whitsun-Ale festivities, such as the splendid feast available in the bower ('with cold hanged beef, stewed prunes, cakes, wine, and ale'), the 'morris dancers, and fool fantastically dressed, and drums and fife' in the procession, and the sheer spectacle of the occasion.[1]

The continued existence of events like the Whitsun Bower raises important questions for the urban historian of post-Restoration England. How widespread were such spectacles, to what extent had and were they being modified, and what role did public ritual and ceremony play in the culture of the town? A central problem is defining what is meant by 'ritual' and 'ceremony'. Anthropologists differ considerably in their understanding of these terms and of the circumstances in which they would apply them.[2] For the working purposes of this study a broad interpretation is adopted, which stresses the standardized or repetitive nature of the actions; their essentially constructed or 'artificial' form; the richness of the language employed in their operation; and, above all, their expressive and symbolic quality. Most human behaviour contains some of these characteristics. The crucial point is the *degree* to which they are present, and concentrated together, in any set of actions. To narrow further the types of occasions investigated, attention will focus on the public and secular fields. Such an approach allows a distinctive body of events to be isolated and examined. None the less, it is also broad enough to encompass activities as diverse as recreations and patriotic celebrations, and therefore to place ritual and ceremony in their wider cultural context.

The most striking feature of the Lichfield Whitsun Bower was its theatricality, with its use of music, entertainers, costumes, props, human movement and the pseudo-stage of the bower. In this it was characteristic of much of post-Restoration urban ritual and ceremony. Though the Reformation had undermined the formal drama of the gild pageant and miracle play and may have temporarily created a vacuum in this area of urban culture, by the late seventeenth century spectacle and display (though of a different kind) were again a flourishing part of town life. The theme of ritual as theatre will be a central aspect of this essay. But the Whitsun Bower raises more specific issues, which will form the five areas to be examined: the types of rituals and ceremonies to be found in the town; their language; their social and political uses; their psychological role; and finally, their changing nature and context during the years to 1800.

I

The formidable variety of public rituals and ceremonies that operated in the English town in the late seventeenth and eighteenth
centuries can be divided into three rough categories; civic, élite and
popular. Though these categories overlap, they provide a simple yet
meaningful framework in which to arrange the evidence. Civic
rituals were largely associated with urban government. Understandably, the most sophisticated and best documented examples
come from corporate towns. The centre-piece of their institutional
ritual was the election of the mayor. In early eighteenth-century
York this was particularly elaborate. In late January the full corporation assembled at the Guildhall. The common council chose three
aldermen. Their names were then submitted to the mayor, remaining aldermen and sheriffs, who retreated into an inner room and
made the final selection. The procedure was largely a ceremonial
charade, since strong conventions, especially of seniority, pre-
determined the result. About a week later, on St Blaise's Day (3
February), the new mayor was inaugurated. The ceremony began at
the council chamber on Ouse Bridge, where the mayor elect was
presented with various seals of office, civic regalia, and the splendid
mayoral kitchen ware and dining service. The inner corporation
then moved to the Guildhall (later this was the scene of both
ceremonies), where the common council was assembled. Here the
retiring mayor made a speech and his successor 'was sworn to the
new oaths, and . . . took his place and made his speech, and
delivered his bonds'. After those present had sworn fidelity to the
new mayor, they processed to his house for a feast. On route were
provided 'three gallons of wine . . . to be drunk at the Pavement's
Cross in the procession', which was probably accompanied by the
sound of church bells. Following dinner the retiring mayor customarily invited the company back to his house for further entertainment.[3]

Similar inaugural ceremonies were found in other towns. A feast
was almost compulsory; that at Leicester in 1685 was on an extrava-
gant scale, including brawn, 'venison pasty', 'grand sallett', roast
geese, 'tongues and udders', wild fowl, lobsters, sturgeon, rabbits,
tarts, custards and mince pies.[4] Often the church was used during
inauguration; at Preston 'the old mayor delivered him [the new
mayor] the staff in church', at Colchester there was a special
sermon, and at Norwich a procession to the cathedral.[5] In the latter

city during the 1690s the ceremonies were especially lavish. Celia
Fiennes observed how the citizens 'new wash and plaster their
houses. . .; all the street in which the mayor elect's house is, [is]
very exact in beautifying themselves and hanging up flags the colour
of their companies, and dress up pageants, and there are plays and
all sorts of shows that day'.[6]

Alongside these institutional rituals ran a further group designed
to affirm the areas of civic jurisdiction. Many towns and urban
parishes mounted an annual procession round their boundaries of
civic officers (and sometimes town companies), clergymen and local
youth, often sustained by alcoholic beverages and a subsequent
feast.[7] Less common were 'aqua-perambulations', which sought to
confirm river rights. On Ascension Day at Newcastle-upon-Tyne
the corporation made 'an annual procession by water in their
barges, visiting the bounds of their jurisdiction on the river [Tyne],
to prevent encroachments, &c. – Cheerful libations are offered on
the occasion to the genius of our wealthy flood'. A similar jamboree
graced the Ouse at York, fortunately for the health of the city's
patricians, only septennially. In 1768 the refreshments stowed on
board the city barge included 208 pounds of meat, eight gallons of
spirit, six dozen bottles of wine, and twenty-six gallons of ale and
beer.[8] One of a town's most jealously guarded privileges was to hold
markets and fairs, and the occasions were often marked by a proclamation ceremony, and perhaps followed by a treat. At Walsall
there was (until about 1789) an 'annual procession on the 9th of July
(the eve of the great fair) of men in antique armour, preceded by
musicians playing the Fair-tune, and followed by the stewards of the
deanery manor, the peace-officers, and many of the principal
inhabitants'.[9]

In addition to institutional and jurisdictional rituals, there were
ceremonies of a circumstantial type, in which the town responded to
past and present events. These constituted a remarkably rich set of
practices, often of a highly politicized or patriotic nature. One
group sought to commemorate or mark particular events. The
anniversaries and successes of public figures were celebrated,
especially those of the royal family. The monarch's proclamation,
coronation, birthday, restoration, safety and death stimulated a
stream of loyal demonstrations, with bell-ringing, bonfires, ale-
drinking, feasts, processions and church services.[10] Local patrons,
politicians, military commanders and artists could be similarly
treated. Preston celebrated Lord Derby becoming Lord Lieutenant

of Lancashire in 1688; Birmingham, the Tory election victory of 1710 and William Bromley's choice as Speaker; 'London, and many other cities', the birthday of Admiral Vernon (victor of Porto Bello) in 1740; and Stratford and Gloucester the jubilees of Shakespeare and Handel in 1769 and 1789 (the latter inexactly calculated).[11] Also widely marked were political successes, diplomatic treaties and military victories, all richly supplied in the early eighteenth century. For example, the fifth of November, the 'delivery from popery' (1688), raising the siege of Derry (1689), victories in Brabant and at Ramillies (1706), the Treaty of Union (1707), Sacheverell's trial (1710), the Treaty of Utrecht (1713), victory over the rebels (1746), and the treaty of Aix-la-Chapelle (1747), all provided cause for widespread civic festivity.[12] Commemorative points in the seasonal and Christian calendar further engaged corporate participation. Easter, Whitsun and Midsummer saw some of the most colourful urban ceremonies; the Easter Hare Hunt at Leicester, the Whitsun Bower at Lichfield (earlier described), the Corby Pole Fair also at Whitsun, and the Midsummer Pageant at Chester.[13] Many institutional and jurisdictional rituals were also tied to the Christian calendar. Michaelmas was a favourite time for mayoral elections.[14]

Civic involvement in cyclical commemorative events was probably declining; the present proved more interesting that the past. This was evident in a second type of circumstantial rituals, those that accompanied the visits of dignitaries and celebrities. The royal family, nobility, bishops, political figures and the judiciary expected and often received lavish treatment, sometimes on a triumphal scale. When in 1684 the Duke of Beaufort merely passed through Worcester on his way to making a 'visitation of his commands in . . . Wales', he was met at Pershore by the county gentry, 'and not far from thence by the Mayor, Sheriff, Dean and many of the most eminent citizens of Worcester'. After lodging in the Bishop's palace, the duke was escorted next day by the corporation to a service in the cathedral, and then processed 'with drums, trumpets and city waits, hautboys, flutes, and other wind music, together with harps, Welsh and Irish, viols, violins and other stringed instruments, to the town-hall'. There his second son was presented with the city's freedom, and before leaving Beaufort was 'entertained with a very great and noble collation'.[15]

The years after the Restoration witnessed the forging of increasingly strong links between town and gentry, as a powerful relationship emerged based on mutual economic, social and political benefits. This became the life-blood of many towns, reshaping their cultural life and guaranteeing them renewed prosperity. These changes were reflected in the development of new types of élite urban ritual, especially in the areas of recreation and politics. From the late seventeenth century there was a remarkable expansion in fashionable urban leisure, with the growth of theatre, music, assemblies, walks, sports, and the development of leisure resorts.[16] All of these contained elements of ritual. Assemblies were often organized according to precise conventions. At Tunbridge Wells,

everything here is conducted with the utmost regularity. The ball is always opened with a minuet by two persons of the highest distinction: when this is concluded the lady returns to her seat, and the master of ceremonies brings the gentleman a new partner. The same order is observed by every suc-ceeding couple, each gentleman being obliged to dance with two ladies'.[17]

But what ceremonialized these occasions was not only points of behaviour, but also the sumptuous clothes and make-up people wore, the splendid architecture and lighting, and the intoxicating mixture of music, dancing, food and drink. As Drake wrote of the York race balls in the 1730s, a real tribal assembly for the county gentry,

here it is that York shines indeed, when, by the light of several elegant lustres, a concourse of four or five hundred of both sexes . . . are met together. In short, the politeness of the gentlemen, the richness of the dress, and remarkable beauty of the ladies . . . and the magnificence of the rooms they meet in, cannot be equalled, throughout, in any part of Europe.[18]

In the larger resorts individual recreations were welded together into a grand ceremonial cycle by 'the daily routine'. This controlled the actions of visitors at any point in the day, whether it was drinking the waters in the morning, parading on the walks after dinner, or dancing in the evening. So powerful was this routine that life became like clockwork, creating an almost magical world sealed from the outside. As a contributor to the English Magazine wrote in 1737, 'you cannot well be a free agent, where the whole turn is to do as other people do; it is a sort of Fairy Circle; if you do not run round in it, you cannot run at all, or are in every body's way'.[19]

During the seventeenth century the spotlight of political activity, and therefore of gentry interest, was increasingly turning towards the town, in its capacity either as parliamentary borough or the forum for county elections. Behind this development lay the intensified struggle for control of the House of Commons, the growth of the electorate, the emergence of party politics and the high frequency of elections and contests. Consequently towns became the focal point of a good deal of political ritual during election time. The streets would be filled with the razzamataz of meetings and processions, adorned by banners, effigies and political badges, to rally the faithful and sway the undecided.[20] Moreover, victory brought with it unrestrained celebrations. After the Warwickshire election in 1710, Sir John Mordaunt received a bill for payments to 'five drummers and two trumpeters', the bell-ringers at Warwick's two parish churches, and his 'tenants who carried him from the Shire Hall to the Swan'.[21] The chairing of the member, vividly portrayed in Hogarth's Election Series of 1754, was an unashamedly ritual salute of triumph. A victory salute of a different kind followed the Warwick borough election of 1734. The original result was overturned when '150 of mushroom votes were struck off (. . . understood to be people that had no right to vote) . . . there were great rejoicings on the occasion and a bonfire in Smith Street . . . something in the form of a mushroom was burnt in the bonfire'.[22]

Ordinary townspeople often participated, albeit in a supporting role, in civic and élite rituals. However, the cultural gap between plebeian society and that of their leaders was growing, as an increasingly distinctive body of plebeian customs emerged.[23] Four categories of these can be distinguished; recreational, subversive, calendrical and 'legal'. Bull, badger and bear baiting, bull running, cock fighting and throwing were, as Malcolmson has written of pre-industrial football, 'frequently soaked in ritual'.[24] The bull running at Tutbury in Staffordshire was a case in point. It was associated with the annual court of minstrels held in the town. After the latter's proceedings had finished and the minstrels had eaten 'a plentiful dinner', they went to the gate of the town's priory. There a bull (donated by the owner of the Priory) was released among them, 'as soon as his horns are cut off, his ears cropt, his tail cut by the stumple, all his body smeared over with soap, and his nose full blown of beaten pepper'. If the beast escaped over the river into Derbyshire, then he was returned to his benefactor. However, if one of the minstrels could 'cut off but some small matter of' the bull's 'hair and bring the same to the market cross', then the animal was captured and baited in the bull-ring in High Street, 'the first course allotted for the king, the second for the honour of the town, and the third for the king of the minstrels'. By the 1680s the minstrels had been quite unofficially joined in their sports 'by the promiscuous multitude, that flock thither in great number', and before its abolition in the late eighteenth century, the running had become 'a serious matter of contention between the mob of the two counties' of Staffordshire and Derbyshire.[25] Cock fighting was similarly ritualized and aggressive, with its elaborate preparation of the birds and rules governing the event, the bond between man and animal, the violence of the fight, the comic abasement of those who failed to pay their gambling debts, and above all, the intense passions raised – 'the people, gentle and simple . . . act like madmen'.[26]

Recreations were often seen as socially disruptive, and they overlap with a second category of popular rituals of a potentially (if not necessarily actually) subversive nature. Though England had nothing on the grand scale of the European carnival,[27] with its theme of social inversion, the Twelve Days of Christmas were still celebrated, which among 'the generality of the vulgar' continued 'till Candlemas' (2 February).[28] Moreover, there was Shrove Tuesday, the nearest English equivalent to the European custom. As Brand wrote in 1777, 'at Newcastle upon Tyne, the great bell of St. Nicholas' Church is tolled at twelve o'clock at noon on this day; shops are immediately shut up, offices closed, and all kind of business ceases; a sort of little carnival ensuing for the remaining part of the day'.[29] Violent sports such as cock throwing and football were a feature of the occasion, the latter disrupting town life and creating a *mardis gras* atmosphere.[30]

An inversion of normal behaviour occurred in other customs, such as Easter Liftings and Hocktide, when women extorted money from men by lifting or binding them, or the Kellums ceremony in Kidderminster, where a period of disorder was permitted between the retirement of the old town bailiff and the installation of the new.[31] The chimney-sweeps' May Day celebrations in London were an extraordinary piece of social parody. In 1763 they danced 'before Lord Bute's door . . . beating time, as usual, with their shovels and brushes. This motley band was decked with all their May-Day finery; heads covered with enormous periwigs, clothes laced with paper, and faces marked with chalk'.[32] Bute's political career was at this moment on the slide, after his resignation as Prime Minister in April, and this must have added considerable piquancy to the sweeps' 'serenade'. Such behaviour bordered on the disorderly, and sometimes popular customs spilled over into riots, as during the Shrove Tuesday celebrations in York in 1673.[33] Indeed, the wealth of research into pre-industrial disturbances suggests riots themselves were heavily ritualized, with their use of processions, clothing, music and effigies, their ritual targets, their threatened rather than actual use of violence, and their moral underpinning.[34]

Like civic rituals, popular ones often followed a calendrical cycle. The Easter period was widely marked. At Newcastle carlings or peas fried in butter were 'given away, and eaten as a kind of entertainment' on the Sunday before Palm Sunday, and at Easter itself the children were given 'eggs, stained with various colours in boiling, and sometimes covered with leaf-gold', known as paste-eggs.[35] In the case of May Day Aubrey noted that at Woodstock in Oxfordshire, 'they every May-eve go in the park, and fetch away a number of hawthorn trees, which they set before their doors', and at Oxford, 'the boys do blow cow horns and hollow caxes all night'.[36] Citizens of Newcastle were awakened on May Day itself 'by the noise of a song, which a woman sung about the streets, who had garlands in her hand, and which . . . she sold to any superstitious enough to buy them'.[37] In eighteenth-century Horncastle there was a procession in the morning, followed by a bonfire in the evening, and in London the milkmaids and chimney-sweeps staged splendid dances and parades.[38] Similarly celebrated were Whitsun, wakes days and Midsummer's Eve. Bourne gives a striking account of the latter:

> it is usual in the most of country places, and also here and there in towns and cities, for both old and young to meet together and be merry over a large fire, which is made in the open street. Over this they frequently leap and play at various games, such as running, wrestling, dancing, &c. But this is generally the exercise of the younger sort; for the old ones, for the most part, sit by as spectators, and enjoy themselves and their bottle. And thus they spend the time till mid-night, and some-times till cock crow.[39]

A final group of popular rituals sought to enforce customary law. The highly ritualistic charivari or skimmington made a scathing use of street theatre to uphold the moral standards of the community.[40] Less frightening, was the practice of wife-selling, in which divorce and re-marriage were sanctioned by the ritual sale in the town market-place of a woman, adorned with a symbolic halter, to her new husband.[41]

II

All rituals and ceremonies were a piece of theatre in which the participants conjured a drama around themselves. Critical to the performance, and our interpretation of it, was the complex language and dramatic devices employed, which exploited not only words, but the full range of human sensations, appealing to the eye, the ear, the mouth and the body. Among the most important stage-props were visual ones. Clothing played a key part, whether in the assembly rooms or the town hall. It was reported from Bath in 1764 that 'the rooms were prodigiously crowded with very uncouth figures most wonderfully dressed; those whom nature designed to be homely, art rendered hideous, and many, who education made awkward, mantua-makers, tailors, friseurs and milleners made monstrous'.[42] Corporations frequently reminded their less diligent brethren of the need to wear their gowns at meetings and on public occasions. At Preston these exhortations were backed up by stiff fines, though the regulations were softened a little by permitting councillors 'to provide and furnish themselves with such light and decent gowns for the summer time as to them shall seem convenient'.[43] Less personal were the wide range of movable artefacts available. Processions might contain banners, floats, giants and monsters, sometimes of an elaborate nature. The dragon constructed in the 1730s at Norwich for the inaugural procession of the mayor, was made of basketwork, covered with painted cloth, and could flap its wings and distend its head.[44] In popular and political rituals effigies were an essential prop, though often a transitory one, since many would be consigned to a bonfire. Corporations possessed a fine array of civic regalia to be displayed on ceremonial occasions; maces, swords, seals, chains, dining ware and special barges and coaches.

As important as artefacts was architecture. Splendid new assembly rooms and town halls, like a stage and scenery, were an inseparable part of the drama they housed. Civic church pews, tiered according to the ranks of the council, were carefully maintained and jealously guarded. Churches, civic buildings, streets and gates were adorned with coats of arms, statues and paintings of town, nobility and royalty. As events on the political stage shifted, so these pieces of scenery were changed. At Newcastle in 1651 the statues and arms of James I and Charles I over the Magazine Gate were replaced by those of the Commonwealth. After the Restoration Charles II duly displaced his usurpers on the gate, while later a statue of James II, 'in a Roman habit, on a capering horse', was erected on Sandhill. This was unceremoniously dumped in the Tyne in 1688, and during the disturbances of 1740 the portraits of Charles and James in the Exchange were badly damaged.[45] Clearly, idolatry and iconoclasm outlived the Reformation. Among the most striking visual aids were those using light: inside, chandeliers and window lamps (as a mark of allegiance), outside, street illuminations, 'emblematical transparencies', fireworks, and the ubiquitous bonfire.[46]

Not only the eyes were exercised in ritual. The sound of cannons, guns, drums, trumpets, horns, pipes, 'rough music' and especially church bells, was used to seduce or jostle the senses. Visitors to Bath perhaps experienced both sensations, when they were welcomed 'to the city, first by a peal of the Abbey bells; and, in the next place, by the voice and music of the city waits'.[47] The rousing salute given to a visiting dignitary occasionally backfired. In 1702 Bristol Corporation heard a petition from Elizabeth Scott, whose son 'was maimed the day the Queen was here in town by firing of a gun on board the ship Diligence'.[48] Oral stimulants also played their part in rituals, with sumptuous feasts and plentiful supplies of alcohol. In 1773 the parish boundaries of Oundle were beaten in particularly festive mood, with 'almost all the Peramblers charmingly drunk'. At Newcastle the coronation celebrations for George II included 'a fountain' in the market-place 'which ran wine; where the magistrates, common-council, clergy and gentry, drank the healths of the King, Queen and royal issue, with many other loyal healths, in presence of many thousand spectators . . . the conduit running wine all the time for the populace'.[49] Finally, we must recognize the impact of movement and dance. Processions accompanied many urban rituals. These elevated the occasion, whether a coronation or a charivari, by the use of a potent type of corporate human movement. Sometimes dancers formed part of the procession, such as the morris men in the Whitsun Bower ceremony at Lichfield, or the 'four couple of morris dancers with their prancing horse, in holland shirts with laced hats ribboned, and cross swashes and garters with bell', in the coronation procession at Bath in 1702.[50]

The props and stimulants used in rituals not only massaged the senses, but also engaged the mind, since they often carried coded messages.[51] Edward Thompson has reminded us of popular politics, that 'as we move back from 1760 we enter a world of theatrical symbolism which is the more difficult to interpret'.[52] This was a world of visual language, in which a piece of wool, a ribbon, an oak branch, a coat of arms or a statue could unequivocally declare one's political loyalties. Sometimes the imagery was extraordinarily rich. On 29 May 1750, the anniversary of Charles II's entry into London at the Restoration, an effigy of George II was hung in Walsall market-place.

His head was a barber's block, with an old wig upon it, and there was fixed to a hinder part of it a horse tail . . . he had upon his hands white gloves and upon his legs white stockings . . . in one hand was an orange, and in the other a bunch of turnips . . . upon [the] gibbet they hung by the neck . . . the figure . . . with a pair of horns set upon his head . . . and after . . . frequent . . . huzzaings . . . they next had the impudence . . . to fire shots at the body . . . and after they burned the body.[53]

The date of the occasion, the comic symbols of Hanoverian rule, the props of the charivari, and the parody of fashionable clothes, royal regalia and loyal greetings created a highly expressive ritual, a drama needing no recourse to words.

III

The wide variety of public rituals and ceremonies to be found in the later Stuart and Hanoverian town played a major part in the way politics and society operated, both locally and nationally. This role derived from ritual's special capacity, much of it a product of its emotive language, to mobilize deep-seated feelings of authority, consensus and conflict. Much civic ritual sought to establish the innate power of corporate institutions and officers. Council members, acting as a body, regularly attended church on Sundays and days of public festivity, so confirming at a supernatural level their secular authority. The church was also often used during the inauguration of a new mayor. The transference of the mayoralty was the most sensitive point in the corporate institutional structure, since the town was left momentarily leaderless, and with a pressing need to invest the new civic head with the full powers of his office. Ceremonial rites of passage, such as those discussed earlier for York, helped to secure and exploit this liminal phase of authority.[54]

The pseudo-democratic element often found in the election of a mayor, by which the common council nominated the candidates for selection, sought to ritually mobilize the approval of the citizenry as a whole. The toing and froing between inner and outer rooms in the town hall, and processions between civic and religious buildings, topographically reinforced the movement of office, and confirmed the position of its new occupant. But paradoxically, and more important in the long term, was the impression created that the office and the man were separated. In this way the corporation acquired an immutable identity and authority, impervious to the changing fortunes of those who occupied its offices. A further example of this process was the role played by civic regalia, since these artefacts physically symbolized the separation of office and individual. Sometimes they were seen to be almost magically imbued with corporate authority. In 1711 the Tories at Coventry sought to frustrate the inauguration of a Whig mayor by attempting to hijack the city sword and mace, thereby nullifying the ceremony. Though frustrated on this occasion, they later made 'several attempts . . . to obtain the sword and mace, but all without effect; upon one occasion it seems, to avoid danger, they were privately conveyed in a basket of wool to Canley'.[55]

A major use of ritual was to reinforce social ties. Nowhere was the need for this more compelling in the years after the Restoration than among the ruling élite. The bitterness of the political and religious divisions exposed during the Great Rebellion, and for two generations afterwards, hung like a cloud over the nation's leaders. Not only did it sour their own internal relations, but it left the whole structure of authority vulnerable. The growth of fashionable urban leisure, with its various rituals, was to play a subtle and important part in healing the dangerous wounds, and contributing to long-term political stability.[56] Among those who visited the spas and resorts, the centres of the new leisured life, there developed an enforced sense of community, as they were drawn into what contemporaries knew as 'the company'. Membership required participation in the daily routine, that threw the visitors together in an orgy of public intercourse. For those who foolishly imagined that they could slip into town unobserved, and enjoy the waters in private, there were the sounds of church bells and city waits to announce their arrival. Heading 'the company' in several resorts was a master of ceremonies. At Bath and Tunbridge Wells the office was occupied by the flamboyant Beau Nash. He believed that it was his duty to encourage maximum contact between the visitors, and developed 'rules', such as those governing the conduct of balls, to promote social mixing. Moreover, he was willing and able to criticize, often using biting satire in the manner of a court fool, those who failed to observe the conventions. He thereby managed to mitigate the potential hostility of visitors of differing status and opinions, or as his eighteenth-century biographer eulogized, 'he was the first who diffused a desire of society, and an easiness of address among a whole people . . . thus the whole kingdom by degrees became more refined'.[57] If the rituals of a fashionable culture helped to weld together a divided élite, so did the content of that culture. Music, dancing, recreations, literature and learning represented an alternative framework of thought and feeling, that bridged political and religious differences, and poured balm into the wounds of the ruling class. As Burr wrote of Tunbridge Wells:

The coffee-house, and the bookseller's shop, are places where the social virtues reign triumphant over prejudices and prepossessions. The easy freedom, and cheerful gaiety, arising from the nature of a public place, extends its influence over them, and every species of party spirit is entirely stripped of those malignant qualities which render it so destructive of the peace of mankind.[58]

In 1662, Preston Gild drafted detailed and highly stylized conventions to govern the conduct of council meetings, to prevent the 'great animosities and much distractions among councillors' that 'tendeth much to the great prejudice and disquiet of the weale public', and 'for the prevention of all such mischiefs and evils in the future'.[59] Not only was this a reaction to the bitter years of the Civil War, but it also acknowledged the general need of the corporation to act like a community. These expectations were reinforced by the frequent practice of eating, drinking and praying together. Two particularly sensitive areas were those of clothing and seating. At Preston it was felt that the failure of councillors to wear their gown of office, 'tends to infringe and lessen that decency and good order . . . kept up and preserved very much for the honour and credit of the community', and the use of the civic pew was thought 'to manifest much concord within . . . an incorporated community'.[60] So important was the latter that access to it was carefully protected. At Hereford a porter attended the door of the pew 'to keep all the people out but the common council men's wives and children', and the door at Preston was locked for a similar purpose, 'until Mr Mayor comes into the Church'.[61]

Towns used rituals not only to bolster their own corporate identity, but also to establish their relationship with the wider local and national society. This relationship was fundamental, for on it could depend a town's political and economic survival. Moreover, it was one of growing importance and volatility in the late seventeenth century, as crown and gentry took an increasing interest in the town. Thus citizens went to extraordinary lengths to curry favour with county society and national government, through the exchange of gifts, commemoration days, patriotic ceremonies and lavish treats for visiting dignitaries. The operation of these rituals was governed by a strict etiquette, whose procedures had to be perfectly executed if they were to convey the proper message. Any failure, however minor and accidental, could lead to embarrassed confusion, potentially backfiring and upsetting the relationship that the ritual was intended to foster. One poignant example occurred during a royal visit to Norwich in 1671. In accordance with custom it was essential that the King and Queen were met at the city confines, and given a ceremonial passage across its boundaries. Therefore, about one o'clock on 28 September, 'Mr Mayor, attended by his brethren in scarlet, sword, cap of maintenance, maces, &c. and 100 young citizens, went on horseback' to wait for the King on the Yarmouth Road. All would have been well, were it not that the Queen was arriving separately, though some time later, on the London Road. As the minutes ticked away, and no Charles appeared, the welcoming party were faced with the awful prospect of being unable to cross the city, and receive the Queen in the required fashion. In desperation, Lord Howard's sons and the town clerk were dispatched across town, to make 'the city's excuse and compliment . . . her Majesty'.[62]

Not all rituals promoted, or sought to express, social consensus.[63] Many popular rituals, and even some élite ones, revelled in the display of conflict. It is argued that such conflict, especially in the form of inverse behaviour (as displayed during Liftings, Hocktide, Kellums or Carnival) merely reinforced the established order. Thus Gluckman has written that 'to act the conflicts, whether directly or by inversion or in other symbolic forms, emphasises the social cohesion within which the conflicts exist'.[64] Though valuable in some contexts, the explanation is unconvincing for rituals where conflict was at an altogether more open level. No amount of anthropological casuistry can explain away the sheer level of aggression displayed during bull running, cock fights, football matches, electioneering and popular disturbances. In such cases we are forced to reject the argument that all rituals reinforce a single set of values, and more broadly, the holistic view of society on which it is based. Instead, society must be seen as inherently divided, with individuals and groups holding irreconcilable beliefs and attitudes. This approach makes more sense of the rapidly changing, individualized, and politically divided world of post-Restoration England, than do the consensual models often associated with primitive tribes. If our interpretation is correct, then it was essential to the long-term stability of society that safe but effective means were found to express the differences and tensions that existed. Ritual, with its capacity (derived from its symbolic nature) to *threaten* but *not to enact*, was to prove the key method for achieving a measure of equilibrium. So there developed a series of ritual theatres, many located in the town, in which men and women, competing individuals, neighbouring parishes and counties, Whigs and Tories, gentry and popular society, paraded their differences before each other. Through them there emerged what Edward Thompson has called 'some reciprocity in the relationships between rich and poor . . . some mutuality of relationship', or Victor Turner a 'tensed unity', in which contradictions could be openly exhibited and tolerated, and which might lead to a real exchange of power, without recourse to considerable violence.[65] So the expression of conflict, through the mediating offices of ritual, contributed to the stability of a divided society.

IV

The richness of the language employed in the operation of ritual and ceremony points to their fundamentally theatrical character. This could be exploited for the political and social functions suggested above. However, a quite different use, predominantly psychological in nature, was the pure dramatization of life. Much of the pleasure and excitement of a drunken perambulation round the parish boundaries or a chaotic bull running, derived from the experience of the performance itself, and the way in which it threw into temporary dramatic relief some underlying theme in people's lives. As Geertz has written of the Balinese cock fight, 'it makes nothing happen. . . . Its function, if you want to call it that, is interpretative; it is a Balinese experience, a story they tell themselves about themselves'.[66] This is not to imply that this 'function' is in anyway a lesser one. The creation of drama and the performance of roles is central to the human condition. For through theatre and its manipulation of the senses, rich and poor can feel the exhilaration of success and power, and the bare facts of existence can be transformed into a creative experience.

Of the latter, the most important text was provided by the human life cycle. Rites of passage marked each point of transition in the cycle, culminating in the final scene of death itself. A pre-funeral wake helped to dramatize the occasion. At York the corporation made several attempts to curtail 'the usage of causing those that were invited, to sit and stay long, before the corpse was carried to church', perhaps because of the unbecoming fesitivity of the occasion. As Bourne wrote in 1725, 'how unlike to' the 'decent manner of watching, is that of the vulgar, which is a scene of sport and drinking and lewdness', and Brand confirmed half a century later, 'they still continue too much the ancient Bacchanalian orgies'.[67] Not that the great passed uncelebrated. At Newcastle in 1728, Sir William Blackett lay in state for several days before being interred with great pomp.[68] The death of George II transformed the whole atmosphere in London.

Twas astonishing to see the amazing consternation, hustle and confusion . . . [the death] was published about twelve, when instantly the streets were in buzz, the black cloth carrying about, and in half an hour every shop was hung with appendages of mourning. . . . Tuesday, November 10th, the great bell of St Paul's and every other church in London, tolled from 6 to 11, and minute guns fired; all which formed the most melancholy sound tis possible to imagine.[69]

Awful as death might seem, the rituals applied to it briefly transformed the dull routine of those still living, and in the longer term invested the neutral facts of the human life cycle with a sense of profound importance. The natural world was treated in a similar way, with the seasons celebrated by events such as carnival (with its ritual reversal of time, as the year cavorted backwards to begin again), May Day and Midsummer's Eve. The significance of the natural cycle derived not only from the importance of seasonal changes to the economy, but also because their movement paralleled that of human development.[70] Thus a complex drama of echoes and reverberations developed, in which the human and natural cycles were intertwined. The church bells in eighteenth-century Newcastle tolled not only at the funeral of a citizen, but also at the commencement of 'carnival', at six every morning and eight in the evening, and on 30 January [sic], when they were muffled – 'the sound on that occasion is peculiarly plaintive'.[71] Mediating between these two cycles was Christianity, its calendar often interlinked with seasonal changes, and its ceremonies replaying the most extraordinary of human dramas, between Christmas and Easter each year.

If the immutable facts of birth, growth and decay, provided one text for the dramatization of life, the contingent world of contemporary affairs offered another. For kings, politicians and mayors, enjoyment of power went way beyond the mere exercise of it. The clothes they wore, the processions they starred in, and the way they were greeted and treated, allowed them to bask in the *feeling* of power. In this way, ritual helped to dramatize the social structure. But such feelings were not confined to the great. All those who participated in coronation festivities, celebrations for military victories, or the campaign of a political party, could enjoy the vicarious pleasures of pride and success. Popular disturbances had a similar effect, in the heat of the riot momentarily inverting the flow of power, and allowing the humblest man to become a hero. In a society where the real fruits of power were so narrowly distributed, the importance of this cannot be overestimated. But perhaps more central to the process were recreations. Around the meanest of props, such as an inflated bladder or some terrified animal, the grandest of dramas was constructed, often stimulating a frightening onrush of psychic energy among the participants. Cock fighting and bull running were good examples. To unsympathetic observers the passions generated seemed diabolical, yet to those involved it was a vital experience. Through the safe medium of ritual, the struggle dramatized the inherent personal and social tensions in any community, creating intense excitement as success and failure hung in the balance. In the cock fight this was all summed up in the anthropomorphic manner in which the combatants were viewed. Macky wrote of how 'wonderful' it was 'to see the courage of these little creatures, who always hold fighting on till one of them drops'.[72] The attribution of human qualities helped forge a surprisingly affectionate bond between man and, his surrogate, the bird. As Brand observed when visiting a sick Northumbrian collier, who was to die within a few days:

to my great astonishment I was interrupted by the crowing of a game cock, hung in the bag over his head; to this exultation an immediate answer was given by another cock, concealed in a closet, to whom the first replied, and instantly the last rejoined . . . it had been, it should seem, industriously hung there for the sake of company – He had thus an opportunity of casting, at an object he dearly loved in the days of his health and strength.[73]

V

Though by their nature rituals and ceremonies draw heavily upon tradition, they can also be highly sensitive to change. Those to be found in the post-Restoration town were therefore a complex amalgam of old and new. For example, cyclical seasonal ceremonies appeared to be declining. The Midsummer Watch in London had been abandoned by the late sixteenth century, while John Aubrey wrote of the fires lit throughout the country on St John's Eve (at midsummer), that 'the Civil Wars coming on have put these rites, or customs quite out of fashion'. Yet the main features of the Watch were transferred to the Lord Mayor's show in October, and bonfires continued to be widely employed in the patriotic and political rituals that filled the streets of eighteenth-century towns. Though in London the very end of the century saw the decay of the Lord Mayor's show and the prohibition of bonfires, May Day celebrations flourished. Sustained by the milkmaids and later the chimney-sweeps, the festivities were continually modified and updated, not least in the years between 1770 and 1790, with the introduction of the almost paganesque Jack in the Green.[74] Old ceremonies therefore survived more tenaciously, and new ones emerged more deviously, than might be imagined. But the impact of change was not substantially blunted by tradition. In the years after 1660 urban ritual and ceremony were subtly transformed, especially by the changing cultural context in which they operated, so that by 1800 they had already assumed something of their modern character.

One of the central features of this transformation was the break-down and reconstitution of what may be called traditional culture. The latter was a corpus of beliefs, customs, recreations and festivals, concerned with local rather than national affairs, rooted in magic rather than reason, employing oral and visual rather than literary forms of expression, located in public rather than private space, and intimately tied to the seasonal and Christian calendars. Because it was shared by a broad range of social groups, though often on an unequal basis, it contributed a good deal to social cohesion.[75] This traditional culture came under pressure as many among the middling and upper ranks in society began to withdraw from it. The modernity and extent of the process should not be exaggerated. Its origins can be traced back to the Reformation,[76] while the resurgence of traditionalism at the Restoration may even have briefly reversed the trend.[77] Moreover, the more conservative citizens and gentry continued to support popular recreations and ally with plebeian society in defence of traditional political and religious values throughout the eighteenth century. But such qualifications should not mask the powerful undercurrent of cultural alienation that continued, now more decisively, to draw polite society away from traditional practices.

At its most straightforward withdrawal meant a refusal to participate in or patronize such practices. Brand wrote in the 1770s of the Easter celebrations in Newcastle, that 'the younger people of the town . . . are no longer countenanced in their innocent festivity by the presence of their governors', and expressed fears about the survival of Pancake Tuesday rituals 'if the present fashionable contempt of old customs continues'.[78] Such 'contempt' was probably responsible for the end of the Midsummer Show at Chester in 1678, and at Walsall of Rogation Week processioning in about 1765, and 'walking the fair' two decades later.[79] In his study of popular recreations, published in 1801, Strutt claimed that 'bull and bear baiting is not encouraged by persons of rank and opulence in the present day; and . . . is only attended by the lowest and most despicable part of the people . . . this barbarous pastime was highly relished by the nobility in former times'. In the early eighteenth century bull baiting and running still enjoyed quite widespread civic patronage, though this was being increasingly withdrawn. In Chester, where it was usual to mark the end of the presiding mayor's term of office by a baiting at the High Cross, the custom was discontinued in 1754 when the corporation removed its support. As early as 1726 Preston council had ordered 'that hereafter there shall be no bull bought or baited at the charge of the corporation', because 'the power and authority of the magistrates or other civil superiors hath not been sufficient upon these occasions to restrain the turbulent and unruly passions of the common people'.[80] Such fears suggested more positive forms of withdrawal. Throughout the period urban authorities attempted to suppress a wide range of traditional rituals and ceremonies, largely because of the apparent danger they posed to public order. These included Shrove Tuesday celebrations, barring out ceremonies, wakes, Easter Liftings, bonfires, street football and bull baiting and running.[81] It was a measure of the urban élite's profound disengagement from traditional culture that activities once shared and supported were now perceived as threatening.

Critical to this process of withdrawal were changes in the intellectual and cultural milieu of better-off townsmen. The continuing impact of the expansion of learning and literacy, and its concentration among these social groups, tended to divide society into the educated and uneducated, the former displaying less sympathy for 'ignorant' and 'superstitious' customs. The growth of scepticism and rationalism after the Restoration had a similar effect, since magical beliefs were an important feature of traditional rituals.[82] These intellectual realignments were strengthened in the late seventeenth century by the rapid development of a commercialized, fashionable culture, much of it based on the town, that was the antipathy of its traditional counterpart (though, as has been argued, it was no less ritualistic; 'polite' customs merely replaced 'barbaric' ones). Together these changes created an alternative cultural framework that made withdrawal both desirable and feasible. In the years after 1660 they assured the demise of traditional culture among those with aspirations for status, by associating it not only with ungodliness (as previously) but also with social inferiority.

The natural consequence of the withdrawal of the middling and upper social groups from traditional customs was their evolution into a genuinely popular culture. Writing in 1725 'of that vast number of ceremonies and opinions, which are held by the common people', Henry Bourne commented that 'tho some of them have been of national and others perhaps of universal observance, yet at present they would have little or no being, if not observed among the vulgar'.[83] Popular society therefore became the reliquary of traditional ritual and ceremony. But it was much more than a passive receptacle. Attempts to suppress customs could be tenaciously resisted. In 1673 the Dean of York's efforts to prevent the use of the Minster during Shrove Tuesday celebrations led 'the youth of the town' to force 'open the church doors . . . during Divine Service', and later to attack the Dean's house 'with such violence that they broke all the windows, pulled down their frames, plucked up and broke 57 yards of pales, &c., to the damage of about £50'. When in the late eighteenth century the trustees of the Moseley Dole in Walsall tried to abolish 'the very odd custom of giving a penny loaf yearly on the twelfth eve to every person belonging to the town, and out-hamlet of the parish, that will come to fetch it . . . the populace by their clamorous and riotous disposition forced the continuance of it'.[84] Moves to curtail traditional sports could provoke the most vigorous reaction; at Stamford this delayed the abolition of the annual bull running for over fifty years (1788–1840).[85] Resistance to the erosion of customary practices and values as a whole, was therefore an inherent part of the translation of traditional into popular culture, and was reflected in the growing importance of the rituals of riot. In this process two further factors must be considered. The strength in plebeian society of the organs of customary law, such as the charivari and wife-selling; and the emergence of a plethora of clubs and trade associations[86] (with their elaborate rituals of affiliation and organization), offering an alternative framework of allegiance to the more socially integrated but decaying institutions (such as parish and gild) of traditional urban society.

The polarization of polite and popular culture was also reflected in the changing spatial and temporal context of ritual and ceremony. High society's disengagement from traditional culture was paralleled by the élite's withdrawal from public to privately controlled space, such as that provided by walks, gardens, assembly rooms, theatres and coffee-houses. Any threat of intrusion was treated seriously. In 1732 the directors of the new Assembly Rooms in York instructed that a shed abutting the Rooms be demolished because it was 'a great nuisance by reason of people's getting upon it, and looking in and lifting up the sashes'. Despite such precautions the threat from plebeian voyeurs and intruders continued, and in 1736 it was further 'ordered that four iron pins be made for the windows in the Weekly Assembly Rooms to hinder people on the outside from lifting up the sashes'.[87] One difficult area was that of horse-racing, where courses remained open until the late nineteenth century. The construction of splendid new grandstands in the 1750s and 1760s probably reflected a desire to introduce a more effective method of segregation, especially since there may have been a popular invasion of the major urban courses at this time.[88] Reinforcing this process was the increasing social zoning to be found in some towns, with new classical squares and streets forming ghettoes of gentility, and the emergence of resorts catering for markedly different social clienteles.[89]

Hand in hand with these changes went mounting pressure on the spaces that had been used to accommodate traditional recreations.[90] This partly reflected urban expansion and enclosure. When in 1727 Ralph Allen added a grand Palladian extension to his home in the heart of Bath, 'a third part of the Bowling Green having been granted to his house, smock racing and pig racing, playing at foot-ball and running with feet in bags in that Green . . . thereby received their final end'. Similarly, the enclosure of Shields Field in Newcastle in 1738 destroyed an area of public leisure, though here there was considerable resistance when 'the hedges thereof' were 'broken down by several persons presuming to trespass on the same'.[91] The spread of polite culture itself could directly threaten the availability of traditional recreational space, such as when the Forth at Newcastle was converted into a fashionable bowling green in the mid to late seventeenth century.[92] Moreover, it had long been clear that the church and churchyard, the medieval centres of traditional culture, were no longer acceptable areas for recreational activity (as was evident in the Shrove Tuesday riots in York in 1673). The cumulative effect of these pressures led to a marked differentiation in the spatial presentation of ritual and ceremony, concentrating popular activities in the street and its annexe, the alehouse.[93] By the late eighteenth century even the former was under pressure, with improvement commissioners and other urban authorities attempting to clear the thoroughfares of the more disorderly sports.

Just as polite and popular culture operated in different spatial contexts so also their rituals reflected different attitudes to time. The cyclical calendar of the seasons and Christian liturgy retained its appeal far longer in plebeian society, where Shrove Tuesday, Easter, May Day and Midsummer's Eve remained important festivals. This reflected the traditional arrangement of the year, characterized by its division into 'ritualistic' and 'secular' halves, the former occupying the period between late December (Christmas) and late June (Midsummer). However, upper-class society developed a recreational calendar that ran roughshod over the traditional one. For example, the regular York assemblies were largely contained in the months October to April, and the national horse racing season in the period April/May to October. In addition, while popular festivals (especially fairs and wakes) seem to have been deliberately timed to mesh with the agricultural calendar, this had little impact on the organization of polite leisure.[94]

The growing attractiveness of town society to the gentry, and the rising level of wealth to be found among the urban bourgeoisie and skilled workers, stimulated the commercialization of urban leisure. This in turn was to prove a further engine of cultural polarization. The effect of commercialization was felt earliest in the lucrative market of fashionable recreations, where performers, entrepreneurs, self-interested corporations and innkeepers promoted such facilities as assemblies, walks, theatrical performances and race meetings.[95] The victualling trade also encouraged the growth of plebeian entertainments. Mid eighteenth-century Birmingham saw the establishment of two new popular festivals in the town, Chapel Wake and Bell Wake. Though the introduction of both was superficially associated with improvements in church facilities, it was argued that Chapel Wake was 'hatched and fostered by the publicans for the benefit of the spiggot . . . Bell Wake . . . originating from the same cause'.[96] By the very late eighteenth century, and probably earlier in London, victuallers were joined in their support of popular recreations by a growing body of impresarios and professional performers, in fields such as prize fighting, theatre and circus, all seeking to exploit the market potential of the rapidly expanding towns.[97] The impact of these commercial developments was threefold. First, they provided the financial and organizational support for a variety of rituals and ceremonies associated with recreational activity, thereby guaranteeing their continuing vitality. The lack of such support had caused the demise of traditional civic ritual in the early sixteenth century.[98] Commercialization was particularly important in the context of popular leisure, which was increasingly starved of élite patronage, and needed the professional skills and risk capital of entrepreneurs to marshal the financial resources of the mass market. Second, it helped to weaken the association between tradition and culture and make the latter more sensitive to social change. Entrepreneurs and professional performers were far more likely to innovate, in anticipation of capturing or sustaining a share of the market, than 'amateur' custodians of culture. Third, as a consequence of its economic support and encouragement for the development of polite and popular recreations, and its responsiveness to social change, commercialization unconsciously promoted the widening cultural rift to be found in society.

The changes outlined above suggest the growth of two autonomous though associated cultures, employing separate bodies of ritual and ceremony. In these circumstances it is tempting to see ritual being modified by, and contributing to, an emerging class society. But such an approach must be treated with caution. Many an apprentice and servant was attracted by the fashionable life-style of their superiors, and some leading townsmen continued to patronize 'popular' recreations. Moreover, England was culturally a pluralist society. 'Godly people' resisted equally the excesses of popular culture and high society. Most important, a national political culture developed that was built on patriotism and party conflict. The ceremony and spectacle that was so much a feature of this continued to make considerable use of public space (church, street and market-place), and frequently bridged the divide between polite and popular society. It may be that the heavy corporate investment of the period in patriotic ritual, some of which flowed to the populace, was an attempt to compensate for the declining cohesive powers of traditional civic ritual. Significantly, however, the tone of this common ceremonial was changing, with plebeian society playing more of a spectator role, and the important junkettings retreating into select indoor forums.

VI

Spectacle, ritual and ceremony were important features of urban culture in the years 1660 to 1800. This was so not only because of their prevalence and variety, but also because of the major role they played in the political and social life of town and country. Such a role derived from their innate powers to mobilize sentiments of authority, consensus and conflict. In this capacity ritual and ceremony were highly responsive to the forces of change. Thus their character, and the context in which they operated, were transformed during the period, with the development of polite culture, the mutation of traditional into popular culture, and the growth of a national political culture. These developments both exacerbated and released tensions in society. For example, the rise of fashionable urban culture helped to heal the political and social divisions among the nation's rulers, at the same time as polarizing relations between themselves and popular society. Underpinning the operation of ritual and ceremony was their theatrical nature, reflected in the language they deployed. This permitted a good deal of political and social conflict to be transacted at one remove from 'reality', and therefore diminished the chances of it spilling over into serious disturbances. Their theatrical character also invested ritual and ceremony with a psychological role, since by dramatizing facets of society, and features of the human and natural life cycles, they heightened, moulded and enriched personal feeling. In these contexts the town became a sort of stage. This was evident in the Lichfield Whitsun Bower ceremony, where, as we have seen, the whole city was transformed into dramatic space, with sub-sets at the Guildhall, the bower and the market-place. Such events, repeated in different forms elsewhere, must have left a lasting impression that endowed towns with a distinctive image and cultural function, that of a theatre for all society. As Defoe wrote of the leisured routine at Bath:

In the afternoon there is generally a play, tho the decorations are mean, and the performances accordingly; but it answers, for the company here (not the actors) make the play, to say no more.[99]

Acknowledgements

I am grateful to the Pantyfedwen Fund at Saint David's University College, Lampeter for financial assistance in researching this paper, and for the helpful comments I have received from Robert Malcolmson, Keith Thomas, Jonathan Barry, Anne Borsay, those who attended my session at the Social History Society Conference in December 1981 (at which an earlier version of this paper was read), and my fellow contributors to this volume.

Notes and references

1 S. Shaw, *The History and Antiquities of Staffordshire* (1798), vol. 1, pp. 316–18; C. Morris (ed.), *The Journeys of Celia Fiennes* (1947), pp. 164–5. See also T. Harwood, *The History and Antiquities of the Church and City of Lichfield* (1806), pp. 352–4; A. F. Wright, *British Calendar Customs. England I: Movable Feasts*, edited by T. E. Lones (1936), pp. 166–7; C. Hole, *A Dictionary of British Folklore* (1978), pp. 118–19, 326–8; R. W. Malcolmson, *Popular Recreations in English Society 1700–1850* (1973), pp. 31–3.
2 D. L. Sills (ed.), *International Encyclopedia of the Social Sciences* (1968), vol. 13, pp. 520–6; G. D. Mitchell (ed.), *A Dictionary of Sociology* (1968), pp. 146–8; J. Goody, 'Religion and ritual: the definitional problem', *British Journal of Sociology*, 12 (1961), pp. 142–64; R. Bocock, *Ritual in Industrial Society* (1974), pp. 37–40; E. Muir, *Civic Ritual in Renaissance Venice* (1981), pp. 57–8.

3   York City Archives (YCA), House Book, 15 January 1700–1, 3 February 1700–1, 3 February 1707–8, 3 February 1710–11, 3 February 1730–1; *VCH*, York, pp. 175–8, 238.

4   J. Nicholls, *The History and Antiquities of the County of Leicester* (1815), vol. 1 part 2, pp. 436–7.

5   A. Hewitson (ed.), *Diary of Thomas Bellingham* (1908), p. 21; P. Morant, *The History and Antiquities of the County of Essex* (1768), vol. 1, pp. 113–14; E. C. Cawte, *Ritual Animal Disguise* (1978), p. 37.

6   Morris, *Journeys of Celia Fiennes*, p. 149.

7   YCA, House Book, 14 September 1733; S. McIntyre, 'Towns as health and pleasure resorts: Bath, Scarborough and Weymouth, 1700–1815' (unpublished D.Phil thesis, University of Oxford 1973), p. 68; Hole, *Dictionary*, p. 269; J. Brand, *Observations on Popular Antiquities* (1777), pp. 269–70; Hewitson, *Diary*, p. 72; J. L. Cartwright, 'Oundle in the eighteenth century through the eyes of John Clifton', *Northamptonshire P. and P.*, **5** part 4 (1976), p. 343.

8   Brand, *Observations*, p. 270; *VCH*, York, p. 238.

9   Shaw, *Staffordshire*, vol. 2, p. 165. See also T. Kemp, *History of Warwick and its People* (1905), p. 57; Hewitson, *Diary*, pp. 24, 79; Hereford Corporation Manuscripts, Common Council Proceedings, October 1706; J. A. Picton (ed.), *City of Liverpool Municipal Archives and Records* (1886), p. 126.

10   See, for example, Hereford Corporation Manuscripts, Common Council Proceedings, April 1702, March 1704–5; Nicholls, *Leicester*, vol. 1, part 2, p. 444; *The Lancashire Journal*, 6 November 1738; *The Bath Advertizer*, 15 November 1755.

11   Hewitson, *Diary*, p. 23; Warwickshire RO, CR 1368/3/61; *Gentleman's Magazine*, **10** (1740), p. 569; C. Deelman, *The Great Shakespeare Jubilee* (1964); W. Shaw, *The Three Choirs Festival* (1954), p. 13.

12   Hewitson, *Diary*, pp. 26, 51, 78; Nicholls, *Leicester*, vol. 1, part 2, pp. 440–1; YCA, House Book, 14 April 1707; G. S. Holmes, *The Trial of Doctor Sacheverell* (1973), p. 234; Warwicks. RO, CR. 1618, W.13/5, 1710/11; Shaw, *Three Choirs*, p. 2; J. Brand, *History and Antiquities of the Town and County of Newcastle upon Tyne* (1789), vol. 2, pp. 530–3.

13   Hole, *Dictionary*, pp. 78–9, 96–7; Shaw, *Staffordshire*, vol. 2, p. 165.

14   H. Bourne, *Antiquitates Vulgares; or, the Antiquities of the Common People* (1725), pp. 219–20; Morant, *Essex*, vol. 2, pp. 113–14.

15   T. Nash, *Collections for the History of Worcestershire* (1781–2), supplement, pp. 87–8, quoting a contemporary manuscript.

16   P. Borsay, 'The English urban renaissance; landscape and leisure in the provincial town, c. 1660–1770' (unpublished PhD thesis, University of Lancaster 1981), chs. 8–11.

17   T. B. Burr, *The History of Tunbridge Wells* (1766), p. 122.

18   F. Drake, *Eboracum: or, the History and Antiquities of the City of York* (reprinted 1978), p. 241.

19 Quoted in A. Barbeau, *Life and Letters at Bath in the Eighteenth Century* (1904), pp. 49–50. See also J. Wood, *A Description of Bath* (reprinted 1969), pp. 437–44; Burr, *Tunbridge Wells*, pp. 115–23.

20 W. Speck, *Tory and Whig. The Struggle in the Constituencies 1701–1715* (1970), pp. 42–3.

21 Warwicks. RO, CR. 1368/3/100.

22 Warwicks. RO, CR. 15/96, Deputations on the 1734 election.

23 See below, section V.

24 Malcolmson, *Popular Recreations*, p. 35.

25 S. Pegge, 'The bull running, at Tutbury in Staffordshire, considered', *Archaeologia*, **2** (2nd edn.) (1809), pp. 86–91 (this includes Plott's description published in 1686); Shaw, *Staffordshire*, vol. 1, pp. 52–5.

26 Malcolmson, *Popular Recreations*, pp. 47–50; Brand, *Observations*, pp. 377–9; F. Siltzer, *Newmarket* (1923), pp. 124–5.

27 E. Le Roy Ladurie, *Carnival in Romans* (1981), ch. 12; Muir, *Venice*, pp. 156–81; P. Burke, *Popular Culture in Early Modern Europe* (1978), ch. 7.

28 Bourne, *Antiquitates*, pp. 151–7.

29 Brand, *Observations*, p. 331.

30 Bourne, *Antiquitates*, p. 181; Malcolmson, *Popular Recreations*, pp. 36–48; Hole, *Dictionary*, pp. 272–5, 325; J. Strutt, *The Sports and Pastimes of the People of England* (2nd edn) (1810), pp. 250–1; F. P. Magoun, 'Shrove Tuesday football', *Harvard Studies and Notes in Philology and Literature*, **13** (1931), pp. 9–46.

31 Hole, *Dictionary*, pp. 99–101, 141–8, 172; F. H. Crossley, *Cheshire* (1949), p. 45.

32 *Whitehall Evening Post*, 26 May 1763, quoted in R. Judge, *Jack in the Green* (1979), p. 10.

33 *CSPD*, 1672–3, pp. 546–7; 1673, p. 367.

34 E. P. Thompson, 'Patrician society, plebeian culture', *Journal of Social History*, **7** no. 4 (1974), esp. pp. 400–2; J. Ellis, 'Urban conflict and popular violence. The Guildhall riots of 1740 in Newcastle upon Tyne', *International Review of Social History*, **25** part 3 (1980), pp. 341–2; J. Stevenson, *Popular Disturbances in England 1700–1870* (1979).

35 Brand, *Observations*, pp. 310, 325.

36 J. Aubrey, *Remaines of Gentilisme and Judaisme*, edited by J. Britten (1881), pp. 18, 119.

37 Brand, *Observations*, p. 262.

38 Hole, *Dictionary*, pp. 195–6; Strutt, *Sports and Pastimes*, pp. 315–16; Judge, *Jack in the Green*, pp. 3–20.

39 Bourne, *Antiquitates*, p. 210.

40 E. P. Thompson, ' "Rough Music": le charivari anglais', *Annales E-S-C*, **27** (1972), pp. 285–312; V. Alford, 'Rough Music or charivari', *Folklore*, **70** (1959); R. W. Malcolmson, *Life and Labour in England 1700–1780* (1981), pp. 105–6; Brand, *Observations*, p. 409.

41   S. P. Menefee, *Wives for Sale* (1981); Malcolmson, *Life and Labour*, pp. 103–4; J. Simpson, *The Folklore of the Welsh Border* (1976), pp. 118–19.
42   *HMC*, Bath MSS, **1**, p. 334.
43   Preston Corporation Manuscripts (PCM), Guild Rolls, 1682, pp. 226–7. See also YCA, House Book, 2 December 1702, 25 March and 21 December 1705.
44   Cawte, *Ritual Animal Disguise*, p. 37.
45   Brand, *Newcastle*, vol. 2, pp. 29–31; H. Bourne, *The History of Newcastle upon Tyne* (1736), p. 126.
46   See for example, Strutt, *Sports and Pastimes*, pp. 329–33; Burr, *Tunbridge Wells*, pp. 63–4.
47   Wood, *Bath*, p. 417.
48   Bristol RO, Common Council Proceedings, 23 September 1702.
49   Cartwright, 'Oundle in the eighteenth century', p. 343; *Newcastle Courant*, quoted in Brand, *Newcastle* vol. 2, p. 516.
50   Shaw, *Staffordshire*, vol. 1, p. 317; Morris, *The Journeys of Celia Fiennes*, p. 22.
51   V. Turner, *The Ritual Process* (Chicago 1969), pp. 15, 18–42, 52; Ladurie, *Carnival in Romans*, ch. 12.
52   Thompson, 'Patrician society'; p. 400.
53   *Gentleman's Magazine*, **20** (1750), quoted in Stevenson, *Popular Disturbances*, pp. 26–7.
54   M. Fortes, 'Ritual and office in tribal societies', in M. Gluckman (ed.), *Essays on the Ritual of Social Relations* (1962), esp. p. 86.
55   Anon., *The History and Antiquities of Coventry* (1810), pp. 89–90.
56   See J. Cannon (ed.), *The Whig Ascendancy* (1981), esp. the thought-provoking essay by Geoffrey Holmes.
57   O. Goldsmith, *Collected Works of Oliver Goldsmith*, edited by A. Friedman (1966), vol. 3, pp. 288–9. See also Turner, *The Ritual Process*, pp. 116–17.
58   Burr, *Tunbridge Wells*, pp. 126–7.
59   PCM, Guild Rolls, 1662, p. 121.
60   PCM, Council Minutes, 15 February 1719–20.
61   Hereford Corporation Manuscripts, Common Council Minutes, 9 November 1694; PCM, Council Minutes, 11 June 1732.
62   R. H. Hill (ed.), *The Correspondence of Thomas Corrie* (Norfolk Record Soc., **27** 1956), pp. 32–3.
63   See E. Hammerton and D. Cannadine, 'Conflict and consensus on a ceremonial occasion: the Diamond Jubilee in Cambridge in 1897', *Historical Journal*, **24** (1981), pp. 111–46; Ladurie, *Carnival in Romans*, pp. 282, 290–7; N. Z. Davis, *Society and Culture in Early Modern France* (1975), pp. 102–3, 117–23.
64   M. Gluckman, *Custom and Conflict in Africa* (1955), p. 125. See also C. Phythian-Adams, 'Ceremony and the citizen: the communal year at

Coventry', in P. Clark and P. Slack (eds.), *Crisis and Order in English Towns* (1972), pp. 67–9.

65   Thompson, 'Patrician society', p. 395; Turner, *The Ritual Process*, p. 83.

66   C. Geertz, *The Interpretation of Cultures* (1975), pp. 443, 448.

67   YCA, House Book, 23 May 1718; Bourne, *Antiquitates*, p. 16; Brand, *Observations*, p. 27.

68   Brand, *Newcastle*, vol. 2, pp. 516–17.

69   P. L. Powys, *Passages from the Diaries of Mrs Philip Lybbe Powys*, edited by E. J. Climenson (1889), p. 58.

70   A. van Gennep, *The Rites of Passage* (1977), pp. 178–83.

71   Brand, *Observations*, pp. 17–18.

72   J. Macky, *A Journey Through England* (1723), vol. 1, p. 129.

73   Brand, *Observations*, p. 379.

74   Cawte, *Ritual Animal Disguise*, pp. 24–6; Aubrey, *Remaines of Gentilisme and Judaisme*, p. 26; D. M. Bergeron, *English Civic Pageantry 1558–1642* (1971), p. 123; Strutt, *Sports and Pastimes*, pp. xxiii, 316, 330; Judge, *Jack in the Green*, p. 19.

75   See C. Phythian-Adams, *Local History and Folklore* (1975), pp. 12–30; Phythian-Adams, 'Ceremony' pp. 57–85.

76   Burke, *Popular Culture*, ch. 8, and pp. 23–9, 270–81; K. Wrightson, *English Society 1580–1680* (1982), ch. 7.

77   Phythian-Adams, *Folklore*, pp. 10–11; Thompson, 'Patrician society', p. 391; Hole, *Dictionary*, p. 206; Strutt, *Sports and Pastimes*, pp. xxvi–xxvii.

78   Brand, *Observations*, pp. 252–3, 333.

79   Crossley, *Cheshire*, p. 65; Cawte, *Ritual Animal Disguise*, p. 29; Shaw, *Staffordshire*, vol. 2, p. 165.

80   Strutt, *Sports and Pastimes*, pp. 227–8; Malcolmson, *Popular Recreations*, pp. 66–7; Crossley, *Cheshire*, p. 73; PCM, White Book, 11 November 1726.

81   Hole, *Dictionary*, pp. 100, 231; *CSPD*, 1672–3, pp. 546–7; K. Thomas, *Rule and Misrule in the Schools of Early Modern England* (1976), pp. 26–9; PCM, White Book, 19 September 1698; Strutt, *Sports and Pastimes*, p. 330; Magoun, 'Shrove Tuesday football', pp. 11–21; Shaw, *Staffordshire*, vol. 1, p. 55; Malcolmson, *Popular Recreations*, ch. 7; D. Reid, 'Interpreting the festival calendar: wakes and fairs as carnivals', in R. D. Storch (ed.), *Popular Culture and Custom in Nineteenth-Century England* (1982), p. 130.

82   Wrightson, *English Society*, pp. 184–99; K. Thomas, *Religion and the Decline of Magic* (1973), pp. 767–74, 794–800.

83   Bourne, *Antiquitates*, p. ix.

84   *CSPD*, 1672–3, p. 547; Shaw, *Staffordshire*, vol. 2, p. 73.

85   Malcolmson, *Popular Recreations*, pp. 126–35.

86   See, for example, J. Money, *Experience and Identity. Birmingham and the West Midlands 1760–1800* (1977), chs. 5–6.

87   YCA, M. 23/1, Assembly Rooms. Directors' Minute Book, 23 August 1732, 29 November 1736.
88   Borsay, 'Urban renaissance', p. 398.
89   D. Defoe, *A Tour through the Whole Island of Great Britain*, edited by G. D. H. Cole and D. C. Browning (1962), vol. 1, p. 157.
90   For slightly later developments in this direction see H. Cunningham, *Leisure in the Industrial Revolution* (1980), pp. 76–86.
91   Wood, *Bath*, p. 244; Brand, *Newcastle*, vol. 1, pp. 441–2.
92   Brand, *Newcastle*, vol. 1, pp. 418–19.
93   P. Clark, 'The alehouse and the alternative society', in D. Pennington and K. Thomas (eds.), *Puritans and Revolutionaries* (1978), pp. 61–4; Phythian-Adams, *Folklore*, pp. 17–21.
94   Phythian-Adams, 'Ceremony', pp. 70–5; Phythian-Adams, *Folklore*, pp. 21–5; Borsay, 'Urban renaissance', pp. 282, 398–400; Malcolmson, *Popular Recreations*, pp. 18–19, 24–5.
95   Borsay, 'Urban renaissance', pp. 321–3; J. H. Plumb, *The Commercialisation of Leisure in Eighteenth-Century England* (1973).
96   W. Hutton, *An History of Birmingham* (reprinted 1976), p. 134. See also D. Reid, 'Festival calendar', p. 127. I am grateful to Peter Clark for bringing this reference to my notice.
97   Cunningham, *Leisure in the Industrial Revolution*, pp. 23–35; Strutt, *Sports and Pastimes*, pp. 103–252.
98   C. Phythian-Adams, 'Urban Decay in late Medieval England', in P. Abrams and E. A. Wrigley (eds.), *Towns in Societies* (1978), pp. 176–8.
99   Defoe, *A Tour*, vol. 2, p. 35.

8 The development of urban retailing 1700–1815

Ian Mitchell

I

'There is a very great complaint in most of the market towns in this kingdom, of the *Great Decay of Trade*, both by many working, and especially by all ancient shopkeeping tradesmen, as the woollen draper, the linen draper, the mercer, the grocer, and others.'[1] These complaints from the 1680s, aimed mainly against those who had entered the retail trades without proper apprenticeship (and perhaps especially directed at hawkers), are echoed at frequent intervals throughout the eighteenth century. But by the 1780s there were also complaints of the excessive wealth of shopkeepers, particularly those in London: 'Do not . . . a considerable portion of them live in a style of opulence and even of splendour? . . . Do they not, in general, enjoy a much greater share of the conveniences and superfluities of life, than landholders of far superior property?'[2] Comments of this sort must be treated with scepticism but they do suggest that important changes were occurring in the retail trade during the eighteenth century. This is not surprising. It was a period in which much was happening to towns and their economies. Retailing needed to respond both to accelerating population growth and to increasing specialization in the provision and exchange of goods and services.

Retailing in Hanoverian England is therefore an important topic for our understanding both of urban development and of the behaviour of the tertiary sector during the onset of rapid industrialization. It has, however, been largely neglected by historians.[3] A major reason for this neglect is the paucity of the evidence. There is, for example, very little material on shop numbers before the 1780s and early trade directories, from which rough estimates of numbers can be derived, have to be treated with considerable caution. Retail traders have rarely left records, beyond perhaps an advertisement in a newspaper or a bill surviving among the household accounts of some landed family, and where more comprehensive records survive it is always hard to judge how typical they are. Legal and similar records are more likely to record exceptional events – or relatively trivial disputes – than to provide a picture of the norm. However, by using the full range of available sources and recognizing their limitations it is possible to build up a fairly full picture of the changing pattern of retailing at the local level. Here I have examined the urban economy in Cheshire, first to chart the development of the retail sector and changes in the relative importance of different types of retailing; and second to shed light on the advent of modern retailing by looking in some detail at fixed shops. To set this in context it may be useful to consider the nature of Cheshire's towns and their marketing zones.

II

Cheshire in 1700 was a county of about 100,000 people,[4] with one city and a dozen or so market towns. As far as contemporaries were concerned it was primarily noted for its cheese although some industries were beginning to grow in the east. In the Macclesfield area, button-making had been important since at least the late sixteenth century with Macclesfield merchants controlling numbers of outworkers and having trade links with London. In the early eighteenth century Macclesfield was perhaps the second largest town in the county with a population of 4000 to 4500. Nantwich, in the salt area, may have been a little smaller, while in the east Stockport and Congleton were beginning to show signs of developing as textile towns with populations in the 2000 to 3000 range. The other towns, generally with fewer than 2000 inhabitants, were of little more than local importance: they had their weekly market, two or three annual fairs and, no doubt, a few shops, professional men and perhaps one or two urban gentry. Chester, the county town, was clearly different. It had around 10,000 inhabitants in the early eighteenth century, was still important as a port, had inland trade links with much of North Wales and would, as the century progressed, develop as a centre for cultural and leisured activities.[5]

By 1800 there had been some striking changes. The East Cheshire towns, particularly Macclesfield and Stockport, were becoming important centres of the textile industry. In Macclesfield, silk-throwing became significant from the 1740s, and by the 1760s Macclesfield silk manufacturers were said to be employing around 3500 people[6] (including, presumably, numerous outworkers in the surrounding area). Silk weaving was introduced in about 1790 and the number of persons employed grew rapidly in the early nineteenth century.[7] Macclesfield's population roughly doubled between 1720 and 1800, and had doubled again by 1821. In Stockport, hat manufacturing become important from about the 1770s with Stockport hatters involved in making up hats for London firms. There was some silk manufacture in the town, but the dramatic development was the growth of the cotton industry from about the 1780s.[8] Around 100 cotton manufacturers are listed in Barfoot and Wilkes's directory for Stockport in the early 1790s.[9] Population growth at this period was rapid: the number of inhabitants in Stockport roughly trebled between 1780 and 1800.

These changes naturally had implications for the tertiary sector in Macclesfield and Stockport and necessitated some growth in retailing facilities. But this growth was probably primarily directed at meeting the needs of their own inhabitants rather than at serving a wide hinterland. Macclesfield and Stockport were, at least until the early nineteenth century, still ordinary market towns so far as their market area and range of service functions were concerned. Neither, for example, had its own newspaper in the eighteenth century and Stockport did not acquire one until 1822.[10] Chester, by contrast, although only very slightly larger than Stockport in 1801,[11] was virtually a provincial capital. During the eighteenth century the range of services it offered (including specialist shops, professional services, a racecourse and various cultural activities) increased and their quality improved. Thus its role as the primary service centre for West Cheshire, the Marches and North Wales was strengthened. At the other end of the spectrum the smaller market towns remained of local significance: some, such as Knutsford, may however have been developing some social and cultural life and were acquiring a reputation for prosperity.[12]

There is little to suggest that the market areas of the various Cheshire towns changed much in the course of the century, although Chester asserted its growing dominance in the west of the county. Chester probably had more than one marketing region, the largest being the distribution area of its newspapers. By the 1780s the proprietors of both Chester newspapers were sending newsmen to deliver their journals (and carry parcels) over virtually all Cheshire, North Shropshire, North-East Wales, South Lancashire (including Liverpool, Wigan and Manchester) and North Staffordshire. The *Chester Courant* employed nine newsmen in 1783 and the

Chester Chronicle seven, with regular weekly routes and each newspaper covered approximately the same area in its distribution.[13] As a shopping centre, Chester did not have quite such a large market area although the city was important in supplying goods and services to North Wales and much of Cheshire. Many Welsh landed families would purchase goods (other than basic foodstuffs) there, as is indicated by the household accounts of the Davies family at Gwysaney in Flintshire[14] or Simon Yorke at Erddig near Wrexham who bought cloth, stockings, hats, wine, groceries and hops in Chester in the late eighteenth and early nineteenth centuries.[15] Other towns offering some competition to Chester in this area were Wrexham, Mold, Denbigh and Shrewsbury.

There is, similarly, evidence for individual shopkeepers having customers scattered over a wide area and of some Chester shopkeepers recognizing the value of having Welsh-speaking employees.[16] Probate inventories provide information on customer distribution. For example, Abner Scholes, an upholsterer, whose estate was appraised at £1675 in October 1736 had money owing to him in North Cheshire and especially in several towns in North-East Wales such as Wrexham, Denbigh and Ruthin.[17] William Earle, a staymaker, whose inventory was drawn up in 1780 had debts due to him in the major Welsh towns, in a number of villages around Chester and in several of the more important Cheshire towns, even as far afield as Macclesfield and Knutsford.[18] A similar customer distribution is found for George Lowe, a silversmith, who in 1810 was in regular contact with customers living in most of Cheshire and North Wales, as far distant as Anglesey. Many of these customers were probably local gentry but a few were retailers. In Macclesfield, William Royston, ironmonger and jeweller, was buying from Lowe as was the town clerk, John Clulow.[19] Men like this were no doubt exceptional and the average Chester trader must have drawn his customers from a much smaller area, but the potential importance of Chester is well illustrated.

As suggested above, the shops and markets of the East Cheshire towns provided primarily for the needs of a rapidly growing urban population. Even so, the Leghs of Lyme on the Derbyshire border were buying corn, grocery, ironmongery, cloth, shoes and paper in Stockport, and paper, oil, soap, candles, stocking and shoes in Macclesfield in the 1720s and 1730s. More specialized goods, including wine and books, tended to come from Manchester or even London.[20] The Ardernes, much nearer to Stockport, shopped there regularly in the 1730s and 1740s although cloth was often bought in Manchester and plate in London. In the 1790s they dealt with Stockport food dealers, drapers, tailors, upholsterers and druggists, but also with a Manchester grocer and Manchester cloth dealers.[21] The Stanleys at Alderley and the Finneys at Wilmslow both made use of Macclesfield retailers although both families also had goods sent from Manchester.[22] In Macclesfield itself, the trader John Swanwick bought bread, flour, meat, groceries, beer, shoes, drugs, hats and paper from his fellow shopkeepers in the town and only rarely bought elsewhere. Crockery on at least one occasion came from Ollivant and Sons in Manchester and in 1798 he bought two tubs of butter direct from a supplier in Shrewsbury.[23]

These towns could by 1800 meet most of the shopping needs of their own inhabitants and had some local importance as shopping centres, although Manchester's market area must have extended well into East Cheshire. Such evidence as there is of customer distribution for Macclesfield and Stockport shopkeepers not un-expectedly shows a predominance of local customers. For example, out of forty-two affidavits sworn by Macclesfield shopkeepers con-cerning money owed them for goods sold between 1764 and 1782, thirty-eight gave the residence of the debtor as Macclesfield and only four elsewhere, all in the Macclesfield area.[24] Lists of debts drawn up by insolvent debtors show a similar pattern. Two Stockport provisions dealers (Thomas Shawcross, flour dealer and John Jackson, shopkeeper) who drew up inventories in 1801 had four-fifths or more of their customers in their home town and almost all the remainder coming from under 7 kilometres away. Even a more substantial trader such as Peter Lowe of Macclesfield, a woollen draper who had 209 debts owed to him in 1814, was mainly serving the town and its immediate neighbourhood. Only one customer in eight came from more than 7 kilometres away, although these included people in Ashton-under-Lyne, Lancashire, Stockport and Congleton in Cheshire, and Chapel-en-le-Frith in Derbyshire.[25] Shopkeepers in the smaller towns and villages probably served a yet more local area, although one or two of the mid Cheshire towns such as Nantwich and Knutsford may have had some attractions for the local gentry. In any case, the markets of such towns were no doubt important for local farmers (up to 7 or 16 kilometres away) and such limited evidence as survives on other markets suggests that village craftsmen travelled similar distances.[26]

III

Thus marketing zones and the relative importance of the various market towns as service centres did not change dramatically in eighteenth-century Cheshire. But the structure and organization of retailing certainly changed in response to general social and economic developments. The most important of these were population growth, particularly after 1750, growing consumer demand, and the rising prosperity of farmers and, more erratically, industrial workers. In an emergent consumer society traditional forms of retailing (market, fair and craftsmen–retailer) were no longer likely to be adequate. It is tempting to envisage a long-term progression from the traditional market, where stall-holders were primarily producer–retailers, through itinerant full-time retailing, to the 'modern' fixed shop, and to see the triumph of the fixed shop as a consequence of industrialization and urbanization. This may be true to some extent, but each type could and did coexist with the others. Not only has the fixed shop a long history prior to the eighteenth century, but the more traditional types had an important role to play in an era of rapid industrial expansion. This was probably due to the ease of entry to non-fixed shop retailing and the inherent flexibility of those types of retailing for which little capital or training was required.

At first sight, there may seem to be relatively few developments affecting markets in the eighteenth century. The number of market towns in Cheshire grew a little after having fallen sharply between the Middle Ages and the mid seventeenth century. Saturday, always the best day for a market, became slightly more popular as markets became primarily places for the urban poor to buy provisions.[27] There were, however, some important changes in the character of the public markets during the eighteenth century. Sale of corn by sample, possibly taking place in an inn rather than in the open market-place, was well known in market towns near London even in Defoe's time,[28] and by the end of the eighteenth century it was probably universal. There were complaints in the 1750s that corn was being sold in public and private houses on market-days in Macclesfield[29] and by 1817 Macclesfield had largely ceased to function as an open grain market.[30] In Chester in the 1760s it was said to be

Notorious that the Principal Farmers Constantly Sell in Gross All their Corn without bringing more (if any to Market) than a Sample to an Inn, at least 3d per Measure under the open Market, or pedling Price (as they call it).[31]

What saved the markets was their continued, and probably growing, involvement in retail provision particularly of necessities, although even here markets in some places lost out because of higglers retailing poultry, butter, eggs and similiar produce.[32] In general, however, markets and shops complemented each other in the food trade. Markets were characterized by low prices, perhaps low quality perishable goods and a few household items. Shop goods included not only durables, luxuries and most groceries but also bacon, oatmeal, flour and bread. At least some of the items chiefly handled in markets were goods that in rural society could be produced by most families or bought from local farmers and which only needed to pass through a marketing system when population was increasingly concentrated in towns. Tables of tolls from Macclesfield and Stockport show the types of goods expected in the markets, and in mid eighteenth-century Macclesfield meat, bread, fruit, roots, seeds, lard, honey and bacon are listed,[33] while at Stockport the tolls laid down in 1752 mentioned butchers, ginger-bread sellers, gardeners, tobacconists, bread and salt sellers.[34] By the end of the century fruit and vegetables were regarded as major items and included apples, peas, potatoes, turnips, carrots and nuts, while butter, geese and fowls also appear on the list.[35] Although cooked meats and cheese were not absent from the markets, hucksters' shops were probably slowly taking over the trade in such items and bread seems to have been disappearing from the markets by the early nineteenth century. Country bakers were selling at the Chester markets for much of the eighteenth century and in 1775 thirty or more loaves, deficient in weight, were seized from them;[36] but in 1807 a petition from corn dealers referred to the desertion of the market by rural bakers.[37]

The eighteenth-century market also retained a secondary import-ance in the distribution of clothing and household goods although many of these were also now traded in fixed shops. Market tolls at Macclesfield, probably for the 1740s, included charges on breeches-makers, glovers, shoemakers, glass dealers, hatters, cloggers, linen sellers and sellers of maps and pictures.[38] Stockport market was probably similar. Disputes over the payment of tolls occasionally provide a glimpse of the activity of such traders in markets. For example, in 1759 Mark Furnall, a breeches-maker, was in dispute with Macclesfield corporation over goods he was offering for sale in the market-place,[39] while at Stockport in 1738 tolls were regularly being collected from shoemakers.[40] Some of these traders had probably come to the market from other towns or villages but others, including Furnall, also had shops in the town and were additionally using stalls in the market. This may have been a growing trend. Clothing was still being purchased in Macclesfield market in the 1830s when there were complaints of excessive tolls,[41] and Chester had a mug market in the early nineteenth century where rough Staffordshire pottery was sold.[42]

As the eighteenth century progressed two particular problems affecting markets became more acute. The first concerned the siting of the market. Traditionally markets were held near the centre of the town and usually took up space in the streets obstructing traffic and, particularly if items like meat or livestock were sold, causing a considerable nuisance. As town populations grew the nuisance became worse and, at least in those places which had pretensions as shopping and cultural centres, the smell, filth and chaos were intolerable. Moves to tidy up the market and ease congestion were a major aspect of eighteenth-century town improvement. For example, the Macclesfield authorities tried in the 1760s and 1770s to restrict the location of stalls and some property was pulled down in 1776 and 1778 to enlarge the market-place.[43] In the early nineteenth century the butchers were provided with eighty new stalls and in the 1820s a new Town Hall included space for sellers of flour, meal, cheese and butter.[44] Attempts to improve Stockport market-place in the 1770s and 1780s were less successful, although the problem of a cramped and inconvenient site was well recognized; it was not until the 1820s that the market-place was repaved and levelled and a new corn exhange and meal mart built.[45] Chester also obtained a new market hall in the 1820s, following earlier attempts to relocate markets in order to avoid congestion and general nuisance in the increasingly well-appointed, main shopping streets.[46]

The second problem concerned attempts by traders to avoid operating through the market. The gradual abandonment of the public markets from the sixteenth century by wholesale grain and produce dealers wishing to escape market tolls and regulations is well known. But there were also similar developments on the retail side. For example, it was alleged in mid eighteenth-century Macclesfield that

Several Inhabitants living in and near the Market Place have Annexed Sheds and Pentices to their houses and buildings and on Fair and Market Days Erect Stalls or Standings under them of which They make a profit by setting them to Huxters and others to the detriment of the Lessee of the Tolls.[47]

This all looks rather like private enterprise competition for the profits to be derived from markets and in Chester there was even a short-lived attempt to set up a rival market at Gloverstone, a street near the Castle and technically outside the city.[48] It was also, however, a sign of growing demand for retailing facilities.

IV

Some of this demand, so far as the retailing of goods was concerned, was met by traders operating outside the public markets but not as fixed shop retailers. Traditionally many came at fair time and in Chester especially, the fairs offered greatly increased opportunities for consumers in the city. Traders came from many parts of Northern England and from London and displayed their goods in rooms in the main streets. Eastgate Street seems to have been the principal street frequented by retailers at the fairs and Eastgate Row was called the Manchester Row in the 1740s, since it was 'Where Manchester Tradesmen usually take Shops for exposing their Wares and Merchandizes to sale at the time of the Fairs'.[49] One example of such a trade arrangement is the leasing by William Huntington of Chester, whitesmith, of two shops in Eastgate Row to Benjamin Blinkhorn of Pendleton, Lancashire, dealer in Manchester wares. Blinkhorn was to hold the property at fair time for a period of seven years at a rent of £2 15s. per fair; before he took up occupation at Michaelmas 1747 Huntington was to convert the shops into one and fit counters and shelves to display goods.[50].

Retailers attending fairs frequently advertised their presence and in 1751 William Lloyd of London announced that he sold linen drapery and haberdashery, while one Alcock, also a London linen draper, gave notice that he would open a shop in Eastgate Street. Thomas Minshull advertised that:

He Will be at Mr Maddox's Cork Cutters Shop . . . in the Eastgate Street, Chester during the time of the Fair, with great Choice of China Ware, of the best and newest fashions, viz . . . Dishes . . . Plates . . . Bowls . . . Teapots . . . Sugar Dishes . . . Cups . . . Glasses etc.

Minshull was clearly a regular at the fairs and announced that this would be the last one he intended to keep and that therefore he was selling cheaply and was willing to consider exchanges for old clothes, old gold or old silver.[51] If London dealers seem to have been particularly well represented, Zephaniah Kinsley, a Bristol linen draper, was renting a shop under the Eastgate for fairs in the 1760s.[52] Trading of this nature was still continuing in the 1780s, although newspaper advertisements suggest that the number of London drapers at fair time may have declined.

By then some degree of disillusionment with traders at the fairs can be detected. Thus in 1775 Mrs Read of Chester wrote to Miss Kitty Bolland at Nercwys Hall, Flintshire to advise her on the choice of material for a new dress, and added, 'But there is no occasion to be in a violent hurry for there is always great variety of choice in the Shops and full as cheap as what the people bring to the fair'.[53] In the next century Thomas Hughes expressed similar sentiments with regard to the decline of trade in the Commercial and Union Halls, 'Even the Cestrians have discovered that one of the worst things they can buy is "a pig in a poke"; and that their own tradesmen sell articles every whit as cheap and as good as did those itinerant pedlars'.[54]

The 'itinerant pedlars' contemptuously referred to by Hughes did not appear just at fairs and certainly did not operate exclusively from purpose-built accommodation. Inns were unquestionably one favourite haunt of travelling retailers, although in Chester the existence of halls built specially for use at fair time may have meant that they were less used than elsewhere. Nevertheless, a Mr Ell announced in December 1765 that he would be at the Wolf's Head in Watergate Street, Chester selling foreign china which he had just brought from London,[55] and Peter Billet advised the citizenry in 1784 that he was selling seeds and flower roots at the George in Chester.[56] In the following year a bankrupt's stock of men's clothes was advertised for sale at the Talbot Inn.[57] Some of Chester's inns seem to have been used regularly at fair time, such as the Red Lion in Bridge Street where Stafford Pryse, a Shrewsbury bookseller offered a stock of Welsh and English books, mostly religious works.[58] Other inns provided permanent accommodation for craftsmen–retailers: for example, a thread-maker operated from the Golden Ball in Chester and a handkerchief-maker from a warehouse behind the Green Dragon in Eastgate Street.[59] More generally, the inns served as important meeting places for those involved in marketing agricultural produce in Cheshire and elsewhere. They were also the venue for special auctions arranged by travelling retailers. Shop retailers frequently resented competition of this sort and a pamphlet of 1720 describing the practice of persons taking rooms in inns and selling cheap goods for cash claimed that one such trader could rob the shopkeepers of six towns of much of their trade.[60] A Macclesfield example of such a travelling retailer is Samuel Reddish, a dealer in upholstery goods who arrived in the town in 1738, hired a room at the Angel Inn and proceded to sell his carpets and coverlets, having first circulated bills announcing his presence. Reddish returned to the town in 1739 and 1740 and eventually became involved in a dispute with the corporation which wanted to exact stallage from him. So far as the authorities were concerned men like Reddish were hawkers; in Macclesfield at least toll collectors had clear guidelines about collecting dues from Scotchmen, hawkers and pedlars who sold goods from door to door, and in private and public houses.[61]

Hawkers were petitioned against by the shopkeepers of Chester in February 1730 on account of 'Great Decays in their Trades, occasioned by the clandestine Trade and Dealings carried on by Hawkers, Pedlars and petty Chapmen'.[62] The term hawker covered a multitude of types of trader, ranging from men with extensive wholesale links, to itinerant retailers operating at fairs and in inns, down to street traders.[63] The natural progression for the more substantial hawkers was probably to become fixed shop retailers.[64] Street traders by contrast sought their custom among the very poor and might deal in poor quality food or food that had lost its freshness and could no longer be sold by shopkeepers. There is virtually no information about their numbers although these must have been growing by 1800. Subsequent licence figures (probably mainly reflecting numbers of hawkers travelling between towns rather than those operating within one town) suggest a rapid increase over the next decades.[65] Street traders were found especially in the new industrial towns. Their main appeal to the poor was their apparent cheapness and their willingness to break bulk and thus supply people who had to buy very frequently in small quantities.[66] They were thus perhaps filling a similar function to the 'huxters' and 'shopkeepers' listed in early trade directories. They may also have provided an essential link in rapidly growing areas between the first housing development and the appearance of fixed shops.

Not unnaturally there is very little direct evidence of the activities of street traders and costermongers and when they appear in the records it is usually because a complaint has been made against them. A possible early example is the baker John Chapman who in 1740 was accused of using hucksters to sell bread for him in parts of the city away from his bakehouse. It is not entirely clear that these hucksters sold from door to door rather than from small fixed shops, but their customers were said to include poor labouring people living in Handbridge, just across the Dee from Chester.[67] In general, however, complaints about street traders are more common in the expanding towns of the early nineteenth century. Thus in 1822 a letter to Stockport's newspaper objected to hawkers exposing various kinds of goods for sale almost daily at private houses,[68] and in the same year Chester butchers complained of meat being hawked from door to door by country butchers.[69] Attempts to bring such traders to heel by subjecting them to the rules and regulations of public markets were usually doomed to failure and it was only when the provision of fixed shops improved that their numbers began to diminish.

V

Fixed shops had, of course, been found in market towns, and probably in some smaller places, for a considerable time, but there are significant developments in the second half of the eighteenth century. It was then that a provincial city like Chester became recognizably a shopping centre, that towns like Stockport or Macclesfield required a substantial number of provision and similar shops, and that the widespread existence of shops can clearly be demonstrated. The shop tax, introduced in 1785 and abandoned four years later provides useful information on the broad extent of retail provision in the county.[70] The amount of tax collected from each township does not precisely reflect the value of the shops in the community, but the tax does give an indication of the relative value of shops in different places and thus indirectly of the relative size of the retail trade. The method of assessment – a sliding scale based on rental value – tends to overemphasize shops of high value but, when compared with directories which merely show numbers of shops and encourage the user to equate the fashionable emporium and the corner shop, this is not entirely a disadvantage.

The shop tax data for Cheshire indicates that shops were to be found in about sixty places with about half having just one shop and a further quarter just two (see Table 28). This was the pattern in

Table 28   *1788 shop tax returns for Cheshire*

	Townships	
Tax per township	Number	Per cent
Paying £50 or more	1	2
Paying £10–£50	2	3
Paying £1–£10	10	16
Paying under £1	48	79
Total	61	—
Townships with one shop	27	44
Townships with two shops	13	21

Source: Public Record Office, Exchequer Tax Accounts, Land and Assessed Taxes, Subsidiary Documents 1785–8 (E 182/96 Cheshire).

small villages, and since the tax did not cover bakers or shops valued at under £5 it seems likely that there was a basic provision of shopping facilities right across the county. The next level comprised smaller market towns and the more substantial villages (for example, Frodsham, Malpas, Chelford or Wilmslow) having several small shops and perhaps one or two substantial ones. The more important market towns had assessments of around £10 (Congleton), around £15 (Macclesfield) and just over £30 (Stockport). Stockport's assessment increased by £5 between 1786 and 1787 (to £33 pounds); this may simply indicate a better coverage in the later year but it could conceivably indicate just how quickly Stockport was growing at the end of the eighteenth century, with a corresponding need for an increase in shop provision. The most striking feature of the Cheshire assessments, however, is the dominance of Chester. Shops in the county town paid £170 in 1786 and £150 in 1788, around 65 per cent of the county total, and the charge on Eastgate Ward alone was almost as much as that on Stockport, Macclesfield and Congleton together. These figures reflect not only the fact that Chester had many more shops than the other towns but, perhaps most importantly, that its shops were much more valuable and probably larger.[71]

The shop tax data for Cheshire raises important questions about retail provision towards the end of the eighteenth century in Chester and the newly industrialized towns of Macclesfield and Stockport. As noted earlier, population growth in the latter towns was very rapid: Macclesfield's population nearly doubled in the second half of the century while Stockport's increased fivefold. Chester, by contrast, grew more slowly to 15,000 in 1801.[72] Moreover, the character of Macclesfield and Stockport probably changed with much of the increased population representing a factory proletariat, dependent on the market for their needs and not themselves involved in supplying goods or services directly to final consumers. Chester remained a city of small producers, craftsmen and members of the distributive trades, together with growing numbers of professional men and urban gentry providing relatively up-market demand for consumer goods.

How effective was retailing in responding to changes, particularly in the new industrial towns? Detailed evidence for the 1790s is provided by trade directories.[73] As the figures in Table 29 indicate, a wide range of shops was to be found in each of the towns, covering not only basic needs but also catering for growing consumer

Table 29   *Shop provision in three Cheshire towns in the 1790s*

| | Numbers | | | Shops per 5000 inhabitants | | |
	Macclesfield	Stockport	Chester	Macclesfield	Stockport	Chester
Food and drink						
Provisions dealers and bakers	21	69	67	13	31	23
Grocery trades	41	27	47	26	12	16
Butchers	8	7	19	5	3	6
Wine and spirit dealers	3	4	18	2	2	6
Cloth and clothing						
Mercers and drapers	8	16	23	5	7	8
Tailors	10	15	27	6	7	9
Other clothes trades	22	18	58	14	8	20
Shoe trades	18	24	26	11	11	9
Others						
Glass and china dealers	3	4	3	2	2	1
Furniture trades	5	4	14	3	2	5
Watch and clock makers	6	6	11	4	3	4
Druggists	3	2	8	2	1	3
Booksellers and stationers	2	1	8	1	½	3

Sources: P. Barfoot and J. Wilkes, *The Universal British Directory*, 5 vols, (no date); 1801 census.

demand for non-essentials. In real terms (i.e., when adjusted for population) there was little to choose between Macclesfield and Stockport on the one hand, and Chester on the other, in respect of shopping for necessities. The figures, however, suggest something of a contrast at the 'luxury' end of the market. Chester's distinctive nature as a shopping centre is revealed by the number of wine and spirit merchants, mercers and drapers, clothes-makers and dealers, furniture traders and booksellers and stationers in the city.

Comparative data for earlier periods is difficult to come by. However, it seems likely that significant changes were concentrated in the last quarter of the eighteenth century. This is particularly the case with regard to increases in the number of shopkeepers catering for working-class demand, for instance, food shops and butchers in Macclesfield and Stockport. It is possible that after some improvement in shop provision at the end of the eighteenth century there may have been a real deterioration in the early years of the nineteenth.[74] In Chester, by comparison, the overall picture was more stable with change mainly taking the form of increased specialization and concentration on luxury trades.

Some of the general trends can be illustrated by looking in more detail at particular trades. Bakers were a traditional part of any town's community, although their role was often as much baking for others as selling their own bread. This indeed seems to have been the traditional role of the Chester bakers,[75] while in early nineteenth-century Manchester it was said that nearly half the bread consumed in the town was prepared at home and baked in public ovens.[76] Other dealers in perishables (for example butchers, fishmongers and poulterers) may slowly have become more shop-, rather than market-oriented.[77] But the most significant developments in the food trades are probably to be found among the provision dealers, variously referred to in directories as shopkeepers, hucksters, cheesemongers and flour dealers. Shops of this type are not easy to identify from directories, being precisely those most likely to be omitted, but the twenty-eight hucksters listed in Stockport in the *Universal British Directory* were almost certainly general provisions dealers. Similar shops must have existed earlier. In the 1750s, Sarah Brown kept a shop at Stockport selling cheese, butter, bacon, wheat, flour, oatmeal, potatoes, eggs, mugs, soap, candles, sugar and other goods. She was purchasing from corn dealers and other traders in Cheshire and in 1759 had £100 worth of goods in her shop.[78] A huckster, Stephen Pearson, had butter stolen from his shop in Stockport in 1799,[79] and in 1802 Samuel Maddocks, a Chester huckster, was robbed of bacon by a man who had bought some eggs from him and asked to buy some hung beef, an article Maddocks did not stock.[80] In Manchester, James Bentley was selling flour, bread, salt, potatoes, eggs, butter, cheese, tea, sugar and coffee and similar goods in the 1800s, together with some household items like candles and paper. He bought from a large number of wholesalers in small amounts at frequent intervals and most of the time sold in small quantities.[81]

There must have been little, back-street shops dealing in cheap clothes and various household goods, but again few of them have left much mark in the records. There are occasional indications of the existence of second-hand clothes shops in the later eighteenth century. For example, after a theft of some cloth from a stallholder at the 1765 Chester fair it was alleged that the stolen goods had found their way to Mrs Moreton who sold old clothes in Northgate Street, and two other second-hand clothes dealers.[82] One of the etchings of Chester streets prepared in the 1810s by George Batenham shows a Bridge Street shop with the sign 'Old Clothes bought and sold by Mr Evan',[83] and in Macclesfield a clothes warehouse with a stock of new and second-hand clothes was advertised for sale in 1811.[84] There was probably a ready market for second-hand clothes among the poor but it is unlikely that respectable shops were doing much off-the-peg business until the mid nineteenth century. In the furniture and household goods sector, lower-class shops occasionally surface. There was certainly a range of establishments dealing in earthenware, china and glass, including some which may have stocked cheaper goods. Among the retailers of ready-made furniture were those whose emphasis was on cheapness rather than fashion, such as Hugh Lomas of Macclesfield who advertised his cheap chair shop in 1812.[85] There were also one or two dealers in old furniture in Chester by the 1790s.

Since few records survive regarding shopkeepers of this sort, it is not possible to offer any statistical evidence about the economics of small-scale retailing – initial capital, value of stock, annual turnover. But it is reasonable to assume that all these must have been small. Early eighteenth-century inventories suggest that bakers, butchers, provisions dealers, tailors and the like were not generally men of great wealth (over £200 was unusual) and, if probate valuations are any guide, this had changed little by 1800. Shop prices may, however, have been relatively high. Selling goods on extended credit was almost certainly the norm and even if competition meant that shops were not able to exploit their customers as much as village shops were said to do,[86] there was likely to have been some effect on prices. Widespread credit also entailed significant risks. For example, a Stockport provisions dealer was reportedly in difficulties in 1756 because, having sold cheese, butter, bacon, flour, potatoes and eggs on credit, she had to pay her suppliers before she could collect the money owed to her.[87] Credit, coupled with erratic consumer demand, meant that business failures were common. One indication of this is the rapid turnover of names in trade directories. For example, around two-thirds of the traders dealing in basic goods in Chester in 1783 had disappeared by 1797; and been replaced by new hopefuls.[88]

We know much more about 'luxury' shops, catering especially in Chester for the increasing wants of the rich and of the affluent middle layers of urban society. These were the shopkeepers who regularly advertised their return from London with a large and fashionable assortment of cloths, shoes, soft furnishings, furniture and any other product for which a market existed or could be created. They wanted the best town sites and by about 1800 there was a grouping of fashionable shops of various kinds on the south side of Eastgate Street and the east side of Bridge Street. Here, for example, were to be found Brown's, the silk mercers and milliners, and Lowe's, the silversmiths.[89] Both shops were to become Chester institutions and remain so to this day. Shopkeepers of this class were naturally concerned about how they displayed their goods and there are examples from the 1760s of Chester traders seeking leave to extend and lighten their shops to make them more attractive.[90] Credit was universal, although by 1800 or soon after one or two shopkeepers were exploring the possibility of fixed price, ready money trading. In general it was these shopkeepers (mercers and drapers and some of the grocers, furniture dealers and luxury traders) who were in the forefront of innovations in retailing.

The leading retailers in any town, in terms of wealth, status and size of business, were generally the mercers and drapers. They sold a bewildering variety of types of cloth, various small items such as ribbons, buttons, handkerchieves, gloves and stockings and occasionally a ready-made cloak or coat.[91] They were primarily pure retailers although some woollen drapers combined the sale of cloth with a tailoring service. For example, Richard Orme of Chester announced in 1806 that he had received a consignment of fashionable cloth from London and added, 'Orders executed as usual, whether the articles are purchased of him or not'.[92] London was naturally a major centre for purchases by mercers and drapers, although some dealt directly with local textile manufacturers. Customers came from a wider area than was common for most retailers and the Chester mercers and drapers, in particular, did substantial business among the Welsh gentry. What mattered above all when selling goods of this type was fashion and price, with traders regularly advertising that they had just received the latest fashions and sometimes linking this with a mention of their low prices.[93] Probably more than any other retailers, mercers and drapers had to be aware of the latest fashions and be responsive to changes in consumer demand. No doubt they also encouraged such changes and were fashion makers.

Similar features can be found in other retail trades. Fashionable paper hangings and carpets were sometimes offered for sale by cabinet-makers and upholsterers, and in 1806 Samuel Nickson of Chester announced his return from London with, 'An entirely new and superb assemblage of printed Furnitures, Moreens, unwatered, with Egyptian Etruscan Borders printed on in the present fashion . . . Carpets and Hearth-rugs, of the most approved patterns; Dining and Drawingroom Chairs . . .' and similar items including tables and beds.[94] The same style of advertisement was used by fancy goods dealers, glass and china traders and similar retailers. Indeed, as early as 1750, George French, a Chester toyman, was advertising his shop, 'Where all Persons may be served with Goods of any Kind whatsoever in the Toyshop Business, intirely new, from London'.[95] Toys in this context means a whole range of trinkets and miscellaneous metal items.

Booksellers and stationers were not immune from fashion fever although generally they might be counted among the more sober retailers. Chester, in particular, was well supplied with representatives of the book trades, including printers, bookbinders, booksellers and stationers, and individuals combining any two or more of these trades. The booksellers themselves probably dealt mainly in second-hand books although they were willing and able to order new books from London publishers. Peter Broster seems to have been the leading bookseller in Chester from about 1780 until about 1815. He was author and publisher of a series of Chester guides in the 1780s and 1790s, was mayor of the city in 1791, and in the 1800s corresponded with other antiquaries supplying them with information about Chester. He traded from a shop in the Exchange, Chester's Town Hall, and counted Chester Cathedral among his customers. A catalogue issued by Broster in 1783 listed 2000 or so works that he had acquired from valuable libraries and were to be sold (at fixed prices and for ready money) from 15 September onwards.[96] In 1806 Broster and Son advertised a new stock of modern publications and announced that they transmitted orders to London every Wednesday and Saturday; some years later Peter Broster referred to the fact that he had goods from Longmans every week.[97] Other eighteenth-century Chester booksellers also had large and wide-ranging stocks. For example, Thomas Ledsham was offering over 1000 titles in 1757, including works by Swift, Dryden and Pope,[98] and in 1792 John Poole issued a catalogue listing over 5000 titles in such categories as histories, poetry, plays, novels, philosophy, mathematics, trade, law books, divinity, sermons, classics, French and Italian books and music.[99] Stockport and Macclesfield had booksellers but little is known of them and it is unlikely that they were in the same league as those in Chester.

Given the great variety of shopkeeping trades, generalizations are clearly difficult. But some contrasts can be made. On the one hand there were those trades, typified by mercers and drapers but also including some grocers and house furnishers, who required substantial initial capital (at least £500), held considerable stocks (£1000 or more), needed wide trade contacts, and had to be thought credit-worthy by London wholesalers. In addition they offered a range of fashionable and elegant goods backed up by conscientious service, to the urban middle classes and country gentry and more prosperous farmers. At the other extreme were those small general shopkeepers, and some of the producer–retailers in the clothing and household goods trades, who valued their stocks in tens rather then hundreds of pounds, who bought locally (often from larger traders in the same line of business) and did not expect customers to come from more than 2 or 3 kilometres away. But there were some common features. Each end of the spectrum included men and women who simply bought and sold rather than made and sold and whose skills were commercial rather than handicraft. Of course, there were also numerous producer–retailers and craft skills long remained important, but by the start of the nineteenth century even members of traditional craft trades like shoemakers and furniture makers can be found buying ready-made goods for resale. The separation of production and retailing functions became even more significant later. Second, retailers throughout the spectrum had to provide credit to customers. This could involve substantial risks, as much for the corner shopkeeper in years of trade depression as for the smart mercer whose gentry customers found settling bills uncouth. The concept of selling for ready money only, and of setting prices, seems to have been coming in by the end of the eighteenth century, introduced by some of the larger and more fashionable shops. Changes in retail practices took place only slowly, but there were innovators especially among the higher-class traders.

VI

The outward appearance of a small provincial shopping centre in 1800 may not have been vastly different from its appearance in 1700. There would be more shops and perhaps more market stalls, in some cases very many more; general provisions rather than corn would dominate the public market; and the shops might be larger and more visually attractive. The changes had been evolutionary rather than revolutionary. It would, however, be a mistake to assume that nothing important had happened, particularly in those towns which had experienced rapid population growth and the development of new industries or the expansion of old ones. For if nothing had in fact happened then the inhabitants of such towns would have been in dire straits when it came to satisfying their basic needs for food, clothing and essential furnishings. The development of urban retailing was arguably as crucial for the growth of the new industrial centres as was technological innovation. In general retail provision seems to have coped (just) with the increased demands placed on the distribution system and the number of outlets more or less kept pace with population growth. The retail system coped, moreover, in a very flexible and informal way, particularly small huckster's shops and street traders, making few demands on scarce resources of capital or skill. At the same time the late eighteenth century saw the advent of recognizably modern forms of retailing – the sophisticated, specialist shop which was the precursor of departmental and multiple stores. In a city like Chester, shops were by 1800 a vital element in a flourishing urban culture.

Notes and references

1   *The Trade of England Revived* (1681), in J. Thirsk and J. P. Cooper (eds.), *Seventeenth Century Economic Documents* (1972).

2   *A Vindication of the Shop Tax* (1789), p. 42.

3   Some exceptions are D. Davis, *A History of Shopping* (1966); T. S. Willan, *The Inland Trade* (1976); D. Alexander, *Retailing in England During the Industrial Revolution* (1970); D. Hey, *Packmen, Carriers and Packhorse Roads. Trade and Communications in North Derbyshire and South Yorkshire* (1980); R. Scola, 'Food markets and shops in Manchester, 1770–1870', *Journal of Historical Geography*, **1** (1975), pp. 153–68; S. I. Mitchell, 'Retailing in eighteenth- and early nineteenth-century Cheshire', *Trans. Historic. Soc. of Lancashire and Cheshire*, **130** (1981), pp. 37–60.

4   P. Deane and W. A. Cole, *British Economic Growth, 1688–1959* (1967), p. 103.

5   For the roles of towns see, S. I. Mitchell, 'Urban markets and retail distribution 1730–1815 with particular reference to Macclesfield, Stockport and Chester' (unpublished DPhil thesis, University of Oxford 1974), ch. 2; population estimates derived from Francis Gastrell *Notitia Cestriensis: I*, edited by F. R. Raines (Chetham Soc., 1st series, **8** 1845).

6   *Commons Journals*, **30**, pp. 216–19.

7   C. S. Davies, *A History of Macclesfield* (1961), esp. pp. 122–32.

8   On Stockport see W. Astle (ed.), *History of Stockport* (1922); and G. Unwin, *Samuel Oldknow and the Arkwrights* (2nd edn) (1968).

9   *The Universal British Directory*, (1790–8).

10   *The Stockport Advertiser*.

11   Chester's population was 15,052 in 1801 and Stockport's 14,830. By 1811 Stockport was the largest town in Cheshire.

12   C. R. Bennett, *The Story of Knutsford* (1976), pp. 12–16.

13   P. Broster, *The Chester Guide* (with Directory for 1783) (1782), pp. 66–8.

14   Flintshire RO, Gwysanny Rentals, Accounts and Disbursements.

15   Flintshire RO, Erddig Estate Papers, Cash Books 1797–1811.

16   For example, advertisement by Mr Wynn, ironmonger and grocer for an apprentice. *Chester Chronicle*, 14 August 1775.

17   Cheshire RO, Inventory of Abner Scholes upholsterer, 1736, WS series.

18   Cheshire RO, Inventory of William Earle, staymaker, 1780, WC series.

19   Lowe and Son, Silversmiths, Day Book 1810–11. Held by the firm.

20   Stockport Reference Library, Lyme Hall Steward's Overseers Accounts, 1728–38, Deed Box 21A.

21   Cheshire RO, Arderne Collection, Vouchers for Expenditure, DAR/A/81–94.

22   John Rylands Library, Manchester, Sir J. T. Stanley, Housekeeping Book, 1784, Eng. MS 1096; Cheshire RO, Finney of Fulshaw Collection, Letters 1765–7, DFF 28/1–13.

23   John Swanwick of Macclesfield, draper, Household Vouchers. In private hands.

24   PRO, Special Collections, Macclesfield Court Papers, Borough Affidavits, 1764–91, SC2/324/2.

25   PRO, Palatinate of Chester, Exchequer, Papers in Causes, Bankruptcy, 1730–1820, Chester 10/1.

26   For example, a 1672 list of stallholders at Macclesfield market shows most came from the surrounding villages, although a few came from neighbouring market towns. Birkenhead Reference Library, Macclesfield (John Stafford) Collection, MAB/II/10.

27   Information on markets and market days from R. Blome, *Britannia* (1673); and W. Owen, *Owen's New Book of Fairs* (various editions).

28   D. Defoe, *The Complete English Tradesman* (1727), vol. 2, pp. 43–5.

29   Birkenhead Reference Library, MA/B/II/18.

30   J. Corry, *The History of Macclesfield* (1817), p. 50.

31   House of Lords RO, Committee Papers (HL), Papers of the Committee on the Dearness of Provisions, 19 March 1765, Letter from Thomas Brock of Chester.

32   One example is Faversham on which see E. Jacob, *The History of the Town and Port of Faversham in the County of Kent* (1774), p. 63.

33   Macclesfield Town Hall, Council Minute Book, 1734–68.

34   J. Thorp, 'A history of local goverment in Stockport between 1760 and 1820' (unpublished MA thesis, University of Manchester 1940), pp. 160–1.

35   Manchester Public Library, Alfred Burton, 'History of Stockport', Burton MSS, **9,** pp. 43–4.

36   *Chester Chronicle*, 31 July 1775.

37   Chester City RO, Assembly Files, 1805–11, AF 59.

38   Chester City RO, Earwaker Collection, CR 63/2/341.

39   ibid.

40   Stockport Museum. Warren Papers, Document D.

41   *PP* (1837–8), **35.** *Municipal Corporations Commission, Reports on Certain Boroughs by T. J. Hogg*, p. 223.

42   Chester City RO, Treasurers Account Book 1798–1822, TAB 9.

43   Macclesfield Town Hall, Council Minute book, 1769–1824.

44   *The History and Directory of Macclesfield and its Vicinity* (1825), pp. 11–12.

45   P. M. Giles, 'The economic and social development of Stockport 1815–36' (unpublished MA thesis, University of Manchester 1950), pp. 454–5.

46   Chester City RO, Assembly Committee Minute Book 1805–35, AC/1, fols. 28, 61 and 91–2.

47   Birkenhead Reference Library, MA/B/II/18.

48   Chester City RO, Corporation Lawsuits C/LP/118a.

49 PRO, Palatinate of Chester, Exchequer, Paper Pleadings, Chester 16/133.
50 ibid.
51 *Adam's Weekly Courant*, 24 September.
52 Chester City RO, Quarter Sessions Examinations 1766, QSE 15/62 and 102.
53 Flintshire RO, Nercwys Hall MSS, Letters of Bagot Read to Kitty Bolland 1766–75, Letter of 14 October 1775, D/NH/1070.
54 T. Hughes, *The Stranger's Handbook to Chester* (1865), p. 107.
55 *Adam's Weekly Courant*, 3 December 1765.
56 ibid., 13 April 1784.
57 ibid., 5 July 1785.
58 E. M. Willshaw, 'The inns of Chester, 1775–1832' (unpublished MA dissertation, University of Leicester 1979), p. 23.
59 ibid., p. 31.
60 *The Case of the Fair Trader* (c. 1720), p. 2.
61 Chester City RO, Earwaker Collection, CR 63/2/341.
62 *Commons Journals*, **21**, p. 448.
63 Over 2500 hawkers and pedlars were licensed under an Act of 1696–7, including nearly 100 from Cheshire (PRO, Register of Hawkers Licences 1697–8, AO 3/370).
64 M. Spufford, *Small Books and Pleasant Histories* (1981), p. 123, cites an example of a Lincoln linen draper, William Johnson, who progressed from pedlar to shopkeeper.
65 *PP*, 1844, **32**. *Report of the Number of Hawkers Licensed in England, Scotland and Ireland in each of the Years 1800, 1810, 1820, 1830, 1840, and 1843*, p. 377.
66 On street traders generally see Alexander, *Retailing in England*, ch. 3.
67 PRO, Palatinate of Chester, Exchequer Paper Pleadings 1743, Chester 16/130.
68 *Stockport Advertiser*, 29 March 1822.
69 City of Chester, Butchers' Company, Company Book 1656–1812. Held by Company Steward.
70 For a description of the tax see, I. Mitchell, 'Pitt's shop tax in the history of retailing', *Local Historian*, **14** (1981), pp. 348–51.
71 Very roughly Chester had twice as many shops as Stockport and two-and-a-half times as many as Macclesfield but paid four-and-a-half and nine times as much shop tax respectively.
72 Sources for population estimates: Gastrell, *Notitia Cestriensis*, vol. 1; Bodleian Lib., Watson MSS, Collections towards a History of Cheshire, MS Top. Cheshire b.1. (for Stockport); 1801 Census Return. Macclesfield had a population of 8743 in 1801, Stockport 14,830 and Chester 15,052.
73 This data must be treated with caution: eighteenth-century trade directories are notoriously inadequate and although the *Universal British*

Directory looks better than most, it must omit a number of shops, perhaps especially those which would have served a growing working-class population.

74   This may be especially true in Stockport and particularly of trades in the clothing and household goods rather than food sectors. Nevertheless, an approximate comparison with the figures for population per shop outlet in 1822 and some later years in Alexander, *Retailing in England*, appendix 2, suggests that the Cheshire towns in the 1790s and after were not deficient in shop provision.

75   Chester City RO, Assembly Files 1732–40, AF 52.

76   *PP*, 1814–15, **5**, *Report from the Committee of Laws relating to the Manufacture, Sale and Assize of Bread*, p. 1341, appendix 8, p. 147.

77   See, for example, advertisements in the *Macclesfield Courier* by William Wrigg, 9 November 1811, and A. Johnson, 19 November 1814.

78   PRO, E 112/1089/117.

79   Cheshire RO, Sessions File, Chester, January 1799, QJF 227/1/109.

80   Chester City RO, Quarter Sessions Examinations, 1802, QSE 17/24.

81   Manchester Public Library Archives Department, Day Book of James Bentley, 1798–1828, Misc. 258/1.

82   Chester City RO, Quarter Sessions Examinations, 1766, QSE 15/106.

83   T. Hughes (ed.), *Ancient Chester: A Series of Illustrations of this Old City . . . Drawn and Etched by George and William Batenham and John Musgrove* (1880).

84   *Macclesfield Courier*, 21 September 1811.

85   ibid., 22 February 1812.

86   See, for example, *Annals of Agriculture*, **29** (1797), pp. 30–7, on Oxfordshire village shops.

87   PRO, E 112/1089/117.

88   Broster, *Chester Guide*, editions for 1783 and 1797.

89   Shop locations determined from: Chester City RO, Earwaker Collection, Plan of Eastgate Street, *c.* 1754, CR/63/2/133; Broster, *The Chester Guide* (editions for 1781, 1787, and 1797); Hughes, *Ancient Chester*.

90   Chester City RO, Chester Assembly Minutes Calendar, 1725–85 fols. 200v, 259v (AB/4).

91   Inventories of, for example, Simon Johnson of Chester, 1755, Chester City RO, Sheriffs' Files 1755–6, SF 187; and William Bracegirdle of Stockport, 1751, Cheshire RO, WC series.

92   *Chester Chronicle*, 5 September 1806.

93   A series of advertisements by Thomas Steele in *Adam's Chester Courant* in 1785 did this and provoked a counter-attack from his competitors.

94   *Chester Chronicle*, 28 March 1806.

95   *Adam's Chester Courant*, 17 April 1750.

96   *A Catalogue of Scarce and Valuable Books . . . offered . . . by P. Broster* (178).
97   *Chester Chronicle*, 18 April 1806; other information on Broster from Chester City RO, Earwaker Collection, CR 63/2/133.
98   Chester City RO, Earwaker Collection, CR 63/1/14.
99   *Poole's Catalogue for 1792* (1792).

9   The financing of church building in the provincial towns of eighteenth-century England

C. W. Chalklin

There was very little church building in the sixteenth and seventeenth centuries, apart from the special case of the churches in the City of London rebuilt after the Great Fire of 1666. A few instances of medieval parish churches rebuilt and of the erection of new churches may be cited for the seventeenth century, such as the new building of St Johns, Leeds, finished in 1634, or the reconstruction after a fire of All Saints, Northampton in 1676–80.[1] Yet the number was trifling compared with that for succeeding centuries. It was partly the consequence of the ample inheritance of church buildings from the Middle Ages. There was also little concern for the fabric of church buildings as a result of changing attitudes to religious worship after the Reformation. New churches were not built in the towns (except for London) in part because population growth was not sufficiently rapid to make the existing church accommodation hopelessly inadequate. Nonconformist chapels before 1689 were small and relatively few compared with the following period because, apart from a few years of acceptance in the 1650s, the Protestant sects were only briefly granted religious toleration.

More generally, there was very little interest in non-residential building. Some large schools, colleges and almshouses were erected, particularly in the South and the Midlands, but the new market buildings and crosses, town halls and prisons were generally small and cramped structures. With the limited interest in street improvement (such as paving, cleansing and lighting) it reflected an absence of concern for the urban environment outside the bounds of a person's own property. Building investment was almost entirely a matter of expenditure on private housing, either for letting or self-occupation.

During the eighteenth century the amount of non-residential building greatly increased. It included Anglican and Nonconformist churches and chapels, which are the subject of this paper. By the 1710s and 1720s a modest revival of Anglican church building is noticeable. In terms of the number of new churches the eighteenth century hardly ranks with the great and long era of construction during much of the following century, yet the period saw a succession of new churches appearing all over England. In the provincial towns alone some fifty Anglican churches were built or substantially reconstructed between 1700 and 1750, and about eighty between 1750 and 1800. Many more were built in country parishes outside the towns. There was also considerable church building in London; some of the largest churches erected in England in the early eighteenth century were built in the capital under the 1711 Act for building fifty new churches.[2]

In the early eighteenth century the majority of undertakings in provincial towns involved the complete rebuilding or partial reconstruction of medieval parish churches; the rest were new buildings in towns with rapidly growing populations. The number of both rebuildings and of new churches increased in the later eighteenth century. New churches were either chapels of ease in existing parishes, churches to serve newly created parishes, or chapels owned by one or more people ('proprietary churches'). Most of the new churches were erected in about a dozen towns which were fast expanding on account of their commercial or industrial importance. For example, in Whitehaven, a burgeoning port in the early eighteenth century, churches were built in 1715 and 1753, in addition to the first church erected in 1693 which replaced a tiny chapel. In the manufacturing town of Birmingham, where the population grew from about 6000 in 1700 to over 100,000 in 1820, new churches were raised in 1715, 1735, 1747, two in the 1770s and another between 1803 and 1813. The rebuilding of medieval churches took place all over England in towns of very varying size, including market towns such as Whitchurch, Shropshire (1712–13), Helston, Cornwall (1756–62), and East Grinstead, Sussex (1790–2). Sometimes the church was partly rebuilt, as at Warminster, Wiltshire (1724), or in Bury, Lancashire, where St Mary was rebuilt except for the steeple (1773). While most medieval churches survived into the nineteenth century without rebuilding or important alterations, in a few towns, such as Lincoln and Worcester, the majority of churches were rebuilt in the course of the century.

There were many more chapels erected in provincial towns to serve Presbyterians, Unitarians, Congregationalists, Baptists, Quakers and Methodists, though these were on a much smaller scale. The Toleration Act of 1689, which allowed religious worship in registered buildings, led to the appearance in the next two decades of hundreds of meeting-houses, either purpose-built or converted from tenements or barns. In the early eighteenth century their numbers varied from area to area; the largest towns usually had several. According to Defoe's *Tour*, Cornwall had only three chapels, but Devon had seventy, including 'many large and fine'; Bristol had seven meeting houses.[3] During the course of the eighteenth century the volume of chapel building fluctuated according to the state of Nonconformity. Between the 1710s and 1750s fewer new chapels were built as the number of Nonconformists declined. Building increased again towards the end of the century, and particularly from about 1790, with the growth of the General and Particular Baptists and the Congregationalists, and the rapid spread of Methodism. To use a medium-sized town as an example, in Macclesfield (population 8743 in 1801) in the later eighteenth century the Friends used a chapel built in 1705; the Methodists erected chapels in 1764 and 1779 (after previously using a stable and a rented cottage); the Independents constructed a meeting-house in 1787–8, and the Baptists used a converted building in the 1790s.[4] In the largest towns, such as Birmingham and Liverpool, chapels were built, enlarged and rebuilt, sometimes on new sites, in the course of the century, and as many as twenty or thirty building undertakings were involved.

I

Eighteenth-century church building has been the subject of considerable interest to scholars. Two modern monographs have dealt with Anglican churches. M. Whiffen, *Stuart and Georgian Churches* (1947–8), considers the architectural dimension, and B. F. L. Clarke, *The Building of the Eighteenth-Century Church* (1963), deals with various aspects of church building in London, the provincial towns and the countryside with careful accounts of particular examples. For Nonconformist buildings, Friends' chapels have been recently studied on a regional basis by D. M. Butler, *Quaker Meeting Houses of the Lake Counties* (1978). This essay concentrates on the financial aspects of building, a theme only partly explored by Clarke in his book on Anglican churches. Town, parish church and chapel histories with information about building are numerous, and have served as an important source for this study. In addition, research was carried out on manuscript church and chapel records held in county record offices throughout England and also into diocesan faculty papers. Much more material remains to be explored, however, and the present essay must be taken only as an introductory survey of a fascinating and important subject.

In financial terms most Anglican churches in the towns were substantial undertakings costing at least £2000 or £3000, though churches built for as little as £500 or £1000 were not uncommon. Some of the smallest replaced medieval churches in towns where the population was distributed among two or more parishes. Lincoln had been a sizeable medieval city with fifty-two churches; several tiny churches appear to have been rebuilt in the eighteenth century for a few hundred pounds or less.[5] One of the medieval parish churches of Southampton, St Mary, which had been destroyed in the sixteenth century, was rebuilt in 1711, with a new nave, for £920.[6] Churches costing £2000 or £3000 were also common among those rebuilt in towns with several parishes. St Martin, Worcester was rebuilt in 1768–72 for £2215, the building being a typical rectangular Georgian church measuring 19 metres by 14 metres with a 22 metre tower.[7] But such a figure was relatively small, and numerous medieval churches serving populations of 2000 or 3000 (and in some cases as much as 5000 or 6000) were rebuilt at a cost of between about £4000 and £8000. Gainsborough church, serving a whole town of about 3000 people, 'besides Dissenters' was built in 1736–48 for £5230.[8] In Bristol, one of the largest provincial towns, most of whose parish churches were rebuilt in the course of the century, St Nicholas (1763–9) cost over £7500; this was for a spacious rectangular building with interior dimensions of 30 metres by 14 metres.[9] A few provincial town churches erected in the 1790s were even more expensive. This was partly the result of the rising cost of materials (particularly timber) in this decade (with prices increasing by some 25 per cent), but it also reflected the great surge of business prosperity of the later 1780s and beginning of the 1790s, which encouraged vestries to levy higher rates and to make substantial borrowings. St Chad, Shrewsbury, an ambitious architectural project with portico, circular hall, anteroom, nave or rotunda (with gallery) and chancel, cost £17,752.[10]

New churches had a similarly wide range of sizes and hence building costs. The small church erected at Maryport, Cumberland in 1759–60 for only £765 reflected the tiny numbers of the original settlement begun in 1749: probably there were only 150 or 200 families there at the time.[11] Most of the new churches were built in rapidly expanding towns to serve populations of several thousand,

and their cost was therefore usually much greater. The building of St Peter, Liverpool, the first church in the town of Liverpool, a substantial large rectangular building, cost £3500 in 1701–4 when the population (previously served by a parish church some distance away) was between 5000 and 6000.[12] The third church erected in Leeds as a chapel of ease in 1721–7 (Holy Trinity), when the town's population was about 8000, involved the expenditure of £4563.[13] Among the most expensive town churches were St John, Wakefield, a spacious building of four bays built after 1791 for £10,000, and the proprietary church of Christ Church, Hunter Street, Liverpool, costing £15,000 in 1797–8, though again account must be taken of the rising cost of building materials during the 1790s.[14] Possibly the largest provincial church erected in the eighteenth century was All Saints, Newcastle, rebuilt in 1786–96 at a cost of about £27,000.[15]

The motives for building new churches were various. Many of the well-to-do saw it as a Christian duty to provide for the religious needs of all classes of townspeople; church attendance was regarded as a means of inculcating sobriety and self-discipline among the labouring and artisan classes. However, in practice the spiritual needs of the poorer classes was usually not the principal concern. An exceptional case was the building of Christ Church, Montpelier Row, Bath, in the 1790s to provide a free place of worship for the poor, and it reflected the comparative neglect of these people in the other churches built in the town in the eighteenth century.[16] Specific pressure for a new church in established towns tended to come from prosperous tradespeople living in the newly built up areas who wanted more pew accommodation. Sometimes the initiative came from a group of these residents. In Bristol in the later 1780s the creation of a new suburb around Brunswick Square aroused agitation in St James parish for a new church, and St Paul was built.[17] The ownership or renting of a pew was normal practice among more substantial townspeople, partly because it was considered to be a mark of standing in the community; a large pew in a prominent position was a symbol of social leadership for the wealthiest tradesmen in the town. Further, listening to sermons was a popular and fashionable practice among the better educated.

In some cases urban estate owners and developers of building land provided a site and a financial contribution towards the building of a new church. One reason for this was to enhance the value of the building plots in the vicinity, as the purchasers or their tenants would be able to obtain a pew in a church in the immediate neighbourhood, though piety may also have been important. When, in 1772, the Weaman Estate in Birmingham gave a site for a church, the neighbouring Lench Trust agreed both to an exchange of adjoining lands and to the opening of a new street, 'being desirous to assist in promoting so pious a design and apprehending that the building of a church upon the land of the said Dorothy Weaman and Mary Weaman will increase the value of such of their lands as lye adjacent to the said intended church'.[18]

Proprietary churches were established so that the owners could appoint ministers whose preaching would be to their liking. There was also a financial motive in that pew rents yielded a return on the capital invested in the construction. These churches were only built in a few of the bigger provincial towns with a large number of wealthy inhabitants. At Bath, the leading inland spa with a growing number of leisured residents, proprietary chapels were being built from the 1730s. Twelve shareholders subscribed £2000 for the building of St Mary's Chapel in Queen Square in 1732–4, including the developer of the square, John Wood.[19] Several were also erected in Manchester and Liverpool at the end of the eighteenth century and in the early decades of the nineteenth. In Liverpool at the beginning of the nineteenth century the wealthy merchant John Gladstone built St Andrew's Church and school for £10,600 and St Thomas, Seaforth, outside Liverpool (with a parsonage), for £4000, and credited his profit and loss account annually with 5 per cent interest on the outlay. In its first two years St Andrew earned £2100 in pew rents.[20]

II

There were several possible reasons for the rebuilding of medieval churches. A few were rebuilt because of destruction by fire, such as at Blandford Forum, Dorset in the 1730s. Others were reconstructed because they collapsed or were in a dangerous condition. In 1727, Helston church in Cornwall was struck by lightning or a thunderstorm and was insufficiently repaired; in an application to the Bishop to allow rebuilding in 1754 it was said that 'our chapel tower and steeple belonging to the said chapel is in (such) a defective and ruinous condition in roof, walls and coverings that it is even hazardous and dangerous in times of Divine Service to meet and assemble'.[21] Some churches had fallen into a dangerous state because the fabric had been neglected in the preceding period.

The poor condition of a church was sometimes the main motive for rebuilding, but the opportunity might be taken to satisfy the need for more accommodation, and occasionally the wish of a prosperous vestry for a more spacious and fashionable building. In 1734, the committee asked to consider the state of Gainsborough church reported that 'the nave or middle part of the church, and also the isles, both on the north and south sides thereof, are so generally decayed and shaken, and the several parts thereof so declined and gone from their several positions, that the whole building is in a very ruinous and dangerous condition, and in imminent danger of falling down'. They wished to build a larger church more suitable for contemporary needs and tastes: 'and having observed the present form of the said building, and the many irregularitys and inconveniencys therein, they are of opinion the same ought to be rebuilt in a different manner'; they also stated that the church 'has been long thought too small to contain the inhabitants of the parish'.[22] This may have been the case at Worcester, where five out of the ten churches were rebuilt or altered between the 1730s and 1770s.

The need for more accommodation was a prime motive in church rebuilding. Room for more parishioners was an often-felt need by eighteenth-century vestries, though enlargement of the building was frequently avoided by the erection of galleries. This occurred often in country towns where population growth was modest. At St Mary, Wareham, the vestry agreed to the building of two new galleries in 1761, and in 1791 and 1811 faculties for a further gallery were obtained.[23] Nevertheless, particularly in the more rapidly expanding towns, there was strong pressure to rebuild to provide for the growing number of parishioners. In 1729 the vestry of St Michael, Bristol had a plan made for a new aisle for its increased population; in 1758 further estimates were obtained to enlarge the church 'by rebuilding, and adding a new Isle on the north side', and subscriptions were received; finally in 1774 when the church was said to hold only 550 out of a parish population of 2000 it was condemned as 'ruinous' and a new church built.[24]

The specific problem in the old churches was that of providing more pews for substantial townspeople. In the growing towns the greater prosperity increased the number of people who wished to rent or own pew accommodation. The use of pews had been spreading during the seventeenth century and they had become a regular part of the furniture of the church by the beginning of the eighteenth century. This frequently led to a 'promiscuous medley of square and ill-shaped pews' which took up a great deal of space. Poorer people were squeezed into the corners of the church and there was soon no room for more pews for substantial townsfolk.[25] The importance of more pews is clearly illustrated in surviving evidence about the obtaining of designs and estimates for the rebuilding of All Saints, Southampton in 1790. The ostensible reason for the decision to rebuild was its ruinous and dangerous condition which would have cost a considerable sum to repair. More crucially, the well-to-do parishioners wanted more space for pews, and the growing population of the previous two or three decades had probably increased this need. The church had seventy-four pews, and it was calculated that about 190 were needed. Eight men submitted designs and estimates accompanied by calculations about the number of pews in the body of the church and the gallery, and the number of people they would hold. Thus William Taylor of Newport, Isle of Wight calculated in terms of thirty-two double pews and ninety-two single pews in the nave and the aisles, and eighty in the gallery, holding 1030 people.[26] Vestries are unlikely to have been greatly influenced in their decision to rebuild by the need for more room for artisan and labouring people who could not afford private pews. Most of the pews in the new buildings were appropriated. Thus when Tetbury church was rebuilt in 1777–81 only thirty-two out of 110 pews were left free.[27]

The desire for an imposing or fashionable building sometimes added to the cost of the new structure. After the disastrous fire in 1694 which burnt much of the centre of Warwick, the rebuilding of St Mary became a matter of local pride. Most of the money collected nationally by brief (£11,000), largely for the townspeople who had sustained losses, was in fact spent on rebuilding the church, and the tower in particular was larger and more ambitious than it need have been.[28] At Shrewsbury, St Chad partly collapsed in 1788; instead of building up on ancient foundations and using the portions still standing (including the chancel), the parish committee decided on a new building on a fresh site and borrowed £16,000 to pay for it, which was not finally discharged out of the rates until 1870.[29] When Banbury church was planned in 1790 a portico was included in the scheme, but this had to be shelved for a while when financial problems overtook the parish.[30] As has been mentioned, the later 1780s and the beginning of the 1790s were years of exceptional national prosperity, when the prevailing spirit of optimism and easy credit encouraged extensive building of all kinds. It is clear that the availability of money or the ready ability to borrow it sometimes encouraged building committees to spend more lavishly than necessary. But a decayed or ruinous structure or the need for a bigger building were the basic reasons for the reconstruction of a medieval parish church.

III

Anglican churches were paid for in several ways; two or three methods were often used in combination. Occasionally one wealthy person paid for the construction, reimbursing himself partly or wholly by the sale or letting of pews. The church building work of John Gladstone in Liverpool has already been cited. In Macclesfield the entrepreneur Charles Roe built Christ Church in 1774–5, selling off some of the pews and graves and vaults in the churchyard.[31] More often a sizeable number of people subscribed to a building, with a wealthy person, sometimes the local landowner who provided the site, making the largest contribution. St Anne, Manchester, built in 1709–12, and the first new church erected in the town, was paid for by subscription, with a local landowner, Lady Ann Bland, giving the largest amount.[32] In the case of country towns and the smaller regional centres substantial contributions from local gentry were common. When the church of St Mary, Monmouth was rebuilt in the 1730s subscriptions were received from no less than 168 people, totalling £987, but £600 was the gift of the leading local magnate, the Duke of Beaufort and his family. Such people often subscribed to public buildings such as town halls or hospitals almost as a matter of course. They were the wealthiest people in the area, drawing a handsome income from rents, and their contribution was an accepted social duty. In 1744 the Duke of Beaufort gave £100 towards the repair of Monmouth market house following an appeal by the corporation.[33] Local Members of Parliament sometimes made a donation as a means of maintaining local electoral support and possibly from a sense of obligation. If the corporation was relatively wealthy, as at Bristol, it paid part of the cost, or less often, all of it. The bishop of the diocese might make a gift, but its size tended to be modest: the Church assumed as a matter of course that the parish and the local people were financially responsible for building work.

While outright gifts were welcome, subscriptions were often made to purchase pews. Such subscribers were the more substantial local residents. When Banbury church was rebuilt in the 1790s, of the 114 private subscribers for pews (at prices between £10 and

£100) at least seventy were tradesmen, master craftsmen, manufacturers or professional men.[34] All or most of the pews were
acquired for self-occupation. The trust deed for the construction of
the third church at Whitehaven (St James, 1753) arranged for four
classes of pews, selling for £50, £30, £20 and £10 'according to their
largeness and commodiousness of their respective situation'. The
deed lists the contributors to the church and, apart from the local
landowner, Lowther, who paid £500, twenty-three people paid £50,
one person subscribed £40, nineteen paid £30, twenty-one paid £20
and thirty-three paid £10, or a total of £3190. All the subscribers
(with the possible obvious exception of Lowther and also the £40
contributor who obtained at least two pews) took just one pew.[35]
Out of the 114 private subscribers for pews in Banbury church, only
twenty-two took more than one, including a bookseller and a grocer
who each acquired eight mostly cheaper pews, which would have
been let. In general subscription for pews spread the burden of the
cost of building among the parishioners and the locality.

Briefs were commonly used to raise money for church rebuilding,
permission being obtained from county quarter sessions for a
petition to the Lord Chancellor. This meant that money for a single
new church was raised all over England. When St Mary at the Walls,
Colchester was rebuilt in 1713–14, briefs collected £1555; money
was received from London and every English county, and there was
a small collection of just over £12 in Wales. Presumably individuals
who contributed paid no more than a few pence, or a few shillings at
the very most. The disadvantage of the brief was the heavy cost of
collection, which absorbed a substantial part of the takings. Thus, in
the case of St Mary at the Walls the expenses were 'the charges of
obtaining the brief, etc., from the Lord Chancellor, etc.' £144 4s.
4d, and 'the collectors, for collecting 10,671 briefs at 8d a piece, and
245 in London at 1s. 6d each', £374 1s. 6d.[36] In some cases the sale of
church property made another, usually small contribution to building expenses. Again a few churches, such as the chapel of ease at
Yarmouth erected in 1713–21 at a contract price of £3800, were built
by duties on coals landed at the harbour.[37] This followed the
example of London, where the erection of new churches under the
1711 Act was financed by a tax on coal.

Nevertheless, despite these varied sources, church rates
remained the basic means of financing church building, particularly
in the case of rebuildings. For this purpose it was the practice to
raise special rates to pay for all the cost, or, more usually, for part of

it, in combination with one or more of the methods already outlined. The rebuilding of Penrith (Cumberland) parish church (1720–2) cost £2252 16s. 9d. Apart from the brief money (£944 6s. 9d less £600 5s. 4d on expenses) and some gifts, £1423 17s. 9d was raised in four rates of 2s. in the pound in 1721–2.[38] Rates were normally paid by the occupiers of houses, other buildings and land in the parish; they were, of course, paid by Nonconformists as well as Anglicans. When special powers were obtained under an Act of Parliament, the burden of payment was shared between landlord and tenant. All Saints, Newcastle (1786–96) was mainly built by means of an annual rate of 2s. in the pound, paid equally by landlords and tenants.[39] The raising of money by rates spread the cost of building widely, as did the sale of pews. Depending on the size of the population of the parish, the charge could be borne by fifty or sixty or as many as several hundred people. When a rate was levied in connection with the partial rebuilding of West Malling church in 1780–2, the assessment comprised 138 people.[40] The cost to the individual ratepayer was no more than a few pounds a year, at most. Some paid no more than a few shillings.

In the numerous cases where several thousand pounds had to be raised by rates, it was usual to borrow all or part of the money in the first instance, so that the rate burden might be spread over one or more decades. When East Grinstead church was rebuilt at the beginning of the 1790s for over £6000, a brief totalled £568 15s. 5¼d and there were donations of over £1200, but the remainder was laid on the rates; £4000 was borrowed in the form of a £2000 annuity and two mortgages of £1000 each.[41]

Legislation for the building of a church sometimes stipulated the terms on which money might be borrowed. The Gainsborough Act (1735) provided that the cost of rebuilding (up to £2500) might be met by the assignment of the rates for twenty-five years as security for mortgages to raise this sum. To repay the mortgages (and interest) an annual rate of £210 was allowed, two-thirds being payable by landlords and one-third by tenants. Two years later the act for the rebuilding of All Saints, Worcester, permitted borrowing in a different way. The trustees were allowed to sell annuities for thirty-two years or for life, with maximum rates of return. The annuities were secured by an annual rate of up to 1s. 3d in the pound.[42]

In the later eighteenth century the principal source of loans were townspeople, notably parishioners and trustees under a building act. Bristol people predominated among those who lent money on mortgage towards the building of St Paul between 1788 and 1798.[43]

Table 30 *Expenditure on Anglican church building in provincial towns*

Church	Date	Amount spent
Deal	1707–16	£2171 12s.[44]
Whitchurch, Salop	1712–13	£4287 4s. 2d[45]
Whitehaven, Holy Trinity	1715	c. £1900[46]
Lincoln, St Peter at Arches	1722–4	£3373 14s. 4d[47]
Derby, All Saints	1723–5	£4588 8s. 8d[48]
Guildford, Holy Trinity	1749–63	c. £3400[49]
Helston	1756–62	£6000[50]
Devonport, St Aubyn	1771	£7000[51]
Bury, St Mary (except steeple)	1773	c. £3500[52]
Harrington, Liverpool, St James	1774	c. £3000[53]
Buckingham	1777–81	c. £7000[54]
Warwick, St Nicholas (except tower)	1779–81	c. £1500[55]
Leeds, St Paul	c. 1790–3	c. £10,000[56]
Liverpool, Trinity Church	1792	£7000[57]
Bridgenorth	1792	£6827 11s. 9d[58]

There is no evidence that in normal circumstances loans were difficult to obtain. This is understandable in view of the public security offered in the form of local rates. Only in the years between 1795 and 1798 is it noticeable that funds were generally scarce, on account of the war: both in the case of All Saints, Southampton, and of Banbury church craftsmen accepted bonds in lieu of cash payments because of the difficulty of borrowing locally.

IV

Most of the innumerable dissenting chapels erected or converted from other uses between 1690 and the mid eighteenth century were relatively small buildings accommodating 200–300 people and costing no more than £100 or £200. The congregation with an unbroken history through the period sometimes rehoused itself, or at least altered the existing chapel, several times. For example, in 1699 the Friends at Penrith bought a farmhouse on the edge of the town for £80. It was used for worship virtually as it was and occupied as a house until 1718, when £27 was spent on internal alterations to make it more suitable as a meeting-house. Seats were added in 1738 'at considerable expense' when it held about 250 people. In 1757 it was proposed to double its size, but nothing was done until 1803 when a new wing was built for £251 so that the meeting-house could seat up to 500.[59] The larger Nonconformist chapels built at the end of the seventeenth century and in the first decades of the eighteenth and costing between £400 and £1000 were mostly situated in the larger towns. The Presbyterian chapel in James Street, Exeter, was erected in 1687 for £443, while the Quaker meeting-house at York cost £562 in 1718. The Exeter building with galleries round three sides held about 600 people.[60]

Later in the eighteenth century more larger chapels were built and existing meeting-houses were extended where congregations were prosperous or numbers expanded as a result of a rapid spurt in conversions. In Bristol, the Broadmead Baptist church was enlarged at a cost of £1087 in 1764.[61] But many smaller chapels continued to be built. Some were erected by relatively new congregations of Methodists and Strict Baptists, such as the Independent Methodist chapel built in Chester in 1794–5 as a result of a split among the local Methodists, for the sum of £872.[62] Others were raised by older congregations in the smaller towns, like the Friends' meeting-house, Guildford, a building 12 metres by 8 metres which cost £1127 with the land in 1805–6.[63] Both these figures were inflated by the rising price of materials from the early 1790s. A few chapels were built in the largest provincial towns which were comparable in size to many Anglican churches, such as the new Old Meeting built in Birmingham in 1791–2 for about £5000.[64]

The most usual reason for building a new chapel was when an increase in the number of converts and hearers meant that the existing building or room in a house had become too small. The Clapham, Surrey, Congregational church was rebuilt on a new site in 1761 to house the enlarged congregation attracted by its minister.[65] Another frequent motive for a new building was the unsuitability of the existing accommodation for the hearing of sermons. Again, the growing prosperity of some of the members or a substantial legacy might lead to pressure for a larger and more spacious chapel. Sometimes the disrepair of the existing meeting-house was cited to justify a new building, or its inconvenient or unsuitable situation in the town. All these reasons were rehearsed when it was decided to rebuild the Bridport, Dorset, Unitarian chapel in 1791: 'the present meeting house is extreamly mean in its appearance – unbecoming the respectability and opulence of the

Society – incommodious both to the Speakers and the Hearers – insufficient for the accommodation of all those who wish to attend Divine Service there (several families being now without seats, and unable to get any in it), and is also in a very decayed and even ruinous condition'.[66]

A minority of the dissenting chapels (though none of the Quaker meeting-houses) were erected as a gift to the congregation by an individual, sometimes the officiating minister but more often a layman. At Faversham, Kent:

Mr John Simmons, of this town, in his lifetime, accommodated some dissenters from the Established Church, with a room at the rear of his dwelling for Public Prayer or Meetings. About two years before his death he erected, at his sole expense, the Chapel in Preston Lane, which was opened on 28th July 1789, by the . . . Chaplain to the Countess of Huntingdon.[67]

In this case Simmons was clearly a member of the congregation. Some wealthy people in the later eighteenth century paid for chapels for a number of congregations in different towns, to encourage the spread of their faith.

More often chapels were built with the support of a large number of subscribers. In the early eighteenth century, gifts of £10 or £20 or even £50 by the relatively affluent made a substantial contribution. In 1699–1700 £491 10s. was raised for a new meeting-house in Chester: 233 individuals subscribed and many donations were only a few shillings, but £151 10s. was given by twelve people.[68] In the later eighteenth century, congregations with wealthy members might receive as much as £50 or £100 towards a new building. The Octagon chapel built in Norwich in 1754 for £5254 attracted almost £4000 in subscriptions and at least ten people gave £100 or more.[69]

The well-to-do subscribers were usually leading local tradesmen or professional people. A new Wakefield Presbyterian church built in 1751–2 for £1288 was financed mainly by subscription. The congregation was headed by a group of wealthy cloth merchants, chiefly members of the Milnes family, at least two of whom had large houses in the immediate neighbourhood of the chapel. The sixty people contributing £547 11s. to the first subscription list in December 1750 included ten members of the Milnes family; the largest donation was £100 from Richard Milnes.[70] At Bridport, Dorset, in the 1790s, *The Universal British Directory* recorded that 'the trade of the town is principally in the twine and hat manufactories; also, in the sail-cloth manufactory'. The largest subscribers towards the new Unitarian chapel were three or four twine merchants and a woolstapler.[71]

Many chapels without wealthy supporters depended on collections from congregations of the same persuasion elsewhere. Wealthy chapels and individuals in London were a particularly important source of donations. Personal appeals by the minister to opulent congregations there were often very fruitful. This may be illustrated by the case of the Wareham Congregational church erected in 1789. A small building 14 metres by 10 metres with a vestry, it cost £459. By October 1790 only about £40 was owing. In the words of the trustees 'upwards of £150 has been raised in London by Rev. Thomas Reader, and £77 has been raised by Mr Ashburner's congregation in Poole . . . which sums together with various collections at Wareham, Taunton, Newport, Coventry, Blandford and other places amount to nearly £420'. The rest was collected in small sums in several Hampshire towns; at Romsey ten people subscribed £5 18s., while another £5 15s. was raised from a small group of people at Southampton; in Portsea there was a collection 'at Rev. Horsey's meeting' which subscribed £5; at Gosport eleven people subscribed £6 3s. and at Lymington eight paid £2 6s. 6d.[72]

Quakers obtained funds for building by collections in their own particular meeting, in their monthly meeting, and at other monthly meetings in the same region. The Friends' meeting-house at Carlisle, erected in 1776, appears to have been paid for largely by two subscriptions at the five particular meetings within Carlisle monthly meeting in 1776–7 totalling £374 14s. 6d (of which the Carlisle meeting contributed £191 18s.). But smaller collections were also made early in 1777 at the meetings in Holm monthly meeting.[73]

It was common to allocate the pews among the subscribers when members of the congregation contributed all or most of the money. The pews were valued and allotted in relation to the amount of the contributions and the bigger contributors might receive several pews (which could be let). At the time of the building of Benn's Garden chapel in Liverpool in 1727 the 114 pews were allocated to seventy-seven people who had subscribed to the building: Thomas Summers received pews valued at £18 15s., £18 2s. 6d, £16 5s. and £1 17s. 6d (a total of £55); and James Kennan £6 17s. 6d, £18 15s. and £1 17s. 6d (£27 10s.).[74] Alternatively the pews might be sold separately. Kendal Unitarian church, built in 1720, was paid for by collections in the town totalling £166 17s. 6d, 'assistance received from brethren abroad' (that is, in other parts of the country) £132 14s. 4d, and the sale of seats for £94 10s.[75] Catacombs were occasionally sold as a small additional source of money.

However, subscriptions and collections were often insufficient to cover building costs and money had to be borrowed. Sometimes part or all the debt was paid off within a few years. In 1776–7 the Friar Lane Baptist chapel in Nottingham which had been bought by the congregation for £100 in 1724, was enlarged for £175 8s. £95 8s. was raised by subscriptions, and £80 was borrowed at 4.5 per cent from two members of the congregation. One of the creditors (£30) was paid off in instalments out of subscriptions by February 1784, the other debt was cleared in 1787 out of a collection made by the minister in London.[76] In other cases debts remained unpaid for two or three decades. Their size naturally varied, but when the amount was relatively small interest payments were modest and the burden for the congregation inconsiderable. The Meadrow, Godalming meeting-house built in 1785–6 for just over £295 was paid for by subscriptions and a £100 loan.[77] The debt was still unpaid when it was decided to enlarge the meeting-house in 1812. In other cases loans paid for most of the cost of the building and the debt was a substantial long-term charge on the congregation. Walsingham chapel, Norfolk was erected in 1793–4 for about £870. The bulk of this was borrowed at the time of building; during the following years the debt was only slowly reduced and still stood at £490 in 1816.[78] The lenders were usually people connected with the congregation. The loan for the Godalming meeting-house was provided by a woman who was probably married to an elder of the congregation.

V

The way in which church building was undertaken remains to be considered. In the minority of cases where churches or chapels were built at the expense of an individual, his dominant role is obvious. In the more normal situation in which a vestry or group of trustees was responsible, the original initiative and direction of a single person was sometimes crucial, although the formal decisions were taken by the wider body. After the idea of building had been mooted the decision to go ahead was often the subject of considerable debate and delay, perhaps on account of the cost, or if the minister took a different view from the congregation, or the members of the vestry or trustees differed among themselves. When the rebuilding of a decayed church was considered it was often argued that repairs would be sufficient. The repair of All Saints, Derby was considered for many years before the appointment of a new incumbent, Michael Hutchinson, in 1719 precipitated the question of a new church. The same year he asked the architect and builder, Francis Smith, for a design and then an estimate. In 1722 a plan was again produced; many parishioners, and especially the corporation, were opposed to the wholesale destruction of the church, and meetings were held at which widely differing views were expressed, with Hutchinson pressing the scheme. In October a committee was appointed and the project went ahead early the next year, again under pressure from the incumbent.[79] The coming of a new minister was also the occasion for the building of a new Congregational church in Weymouth in 1802. 'After the settlement of Rev. B. Cracknell the subject of building a new place of worship became the topick of serious conversation; some thought it so improbable, arising of the great expence of such an erection, that they laughed when the plan was proposed. Others thought it desirable, and though not very probable, yet that an attempt should be made.' Cracknell forced a decision in favour of building by a sermon preached on 28 March.[80] Naturally the report of the surveyor or architect sometimes brought about the decision to rebuild, or was used to support the wishes of a majority of the vestry or trustees. Before the Above Bar Congregational church at Southampton was rebuilt in 1727 the trustees obtained a report on the existing building from several master carpenters and masons. They said that the roof was in a very weak condition, that the walls were unable to bear its weight and that of the galleries, and that the building was in danger of collapse.[81]

Once the decision to build had been taken, the vestry, trustees, or building committee appointed by them proceeded with the help of an architect or surveyor. He provided plans or a wooden model and (usually) estimates. He sometimes also contracted to erect the new church, particularly in the earlier eighteenth century. Mr Colvin has shown that Edward and Thomas Woodward, master masons of Chipping Campden contracted to rebuild Alcester church in 1730 (having probably supplied the design) and two years later they both designed and built the church of St John the Baptist at Gloucester.[82] Later it became more customary for the designer to act merely in a supervisory capacity. The architect was often not a local man and was chosen on the basis of an advertised competition for plans or because of his reputation. The committee responsible for the new church of St Chad at Shrewsbury in 1788 first applied to James Wyatt, the celebrated architect, and he promised early attendance on them at Shrewsbury; 'but this great architect frequently breaking his appointments, the committee became at length offended, and addressed themselves to Mr George Steuart, who had recently built houses at Attingham and Lythwood'.[83] Both Wyatt and Steuart were based in London. When the architect lived at some distance it was usual to employ a clerk of the works to supervise the contractor or craftsmen.

The vestry, trustees, or building committee continued to take decisions during the course of construction. The design was sometimes modified, decisions had to be made about getting subscriptions or levying rates, money had to be borrowed, and the seating was always the subject of careful consideration.

Building might be organized in several ways. One common practice was for the churchwardens or trustees to buy the materials themselves and to employ the various craftsmen separately on their particular tasks. This was the method used for the rebuilding of St Pancras, Chichester in 1749–50, which cost about £804. There were three suppliers of bricks (at a total cost of almost £60), and nearly all the brickwork was done by one bricklayer for £71 18s. Most of the stone probably came from one supplier outside Sussex, and the workmen included a stonemason, two carpenters, and a joiner; the ironwork and glass were supplied separately by local people.[84] Payment of the craftsmen (with their journeymen and labourers) was usually on a measure basis (for example, at a fixed price per rod of brickwork) in the case of the principal structural tasks, but labourers and sometimes craftsmen might be paid by the day for less skilled work.

Alternatively the principal craftsmen were paid for both materials and work. St Werburgh, Bristol (finished in 1761), and the alterations and new building of the Broadmead meeting-house for the Baptist congregation in Bristol in 1798 were handled in this way. For Broadmead chapel, out of a total expenditure of £2420, the carpenter received £1071, the tiler £590, the mason £423 and the plumber £190.[85]

Single contracts for the whole work with one or two undertakers were also used. The new chapel of ease at Yarmouth was built in 1715 under contract with John Price of Richmond (and John Price his son) for £3800, according to a detailed specification, which required 'all aisles of the church to be paved with good Swedish marble squared and polished laid crossways and the roof of the aisles to be coved like St Clement Danes'.[86] The Guildford Friends' meeting-house built in 1805–6 was erected by contract with two craftsmen, a carpenter and a bricklayer.[87] Yet another variant was the contract with a single builder, or agreements with each individual craftsman, and the purchase of part of the materials (particularly bricks or stone or timber) by the vestry or trustees. This was done in the case of the rebuilding of the nave of St John the Baptist, Gloucester in 1732–4. The main building contract was awarded to the Woodwards (except for the pews), but substantial quantities of timber and some bricks were bought directly by the church-wardens.[88] Of all these ways of organizing church and chapel building, separate contracts with the various craftsmen for both work and all or most of the materials were probably the most frequent method.

Why a particular approach was chosen is not normally known. An agreement with a single contractor to follow certain detailed plans and specifications for a fixed price under a surveyor's supervision enabled the trustees or churchwardens to know in advance the total cost, and if the tenders were too high to modify their original plans. In this case the work was usually offered for tender by newspaper advertisement. When the new Nicholas Street Congregational church in Weymouth was planned in 1802 it was agreed that 'to insert advertisements after obtaining plans elevations etc. for tenders to build by contract . . . [was] . . . most eligible, as by the adoption of this method, the aggregate of expence could be nearly ascertained, and as precluding many difficulties, arising in the progress of the building, from varieties of opinion among the gentlemen concerned'.[89] For the same reason it was judged by the building committee 'a salutary measure to have a surveyor to superintend the building in its progress and at the same time to see the execution exactly corresponded to the specifications to which the contractors were to be bound'.

The direct method of building by which the churchwardens or trustees advised by a surveyor purchased the materials and paid the various craftsmen enabled them to ensure that the price was fair for both sides and to make alterations in the original plan as work proceeded. The churchwardens may also have wished to avoid placing too much responsibility in the hands of one builder, who

Table 31   *Expenditure on free churches in provincial towns
1690–1805*

Chapel	Date	Amount spent
Ipswich meeting-house	1699–1700	£257[90]
Platt chapel, Manchester	1699–1700	£95[91]
Sandwich Congregational chapel (converted)	1705–6	c. £400[92]
Exeter Baptist church	1722–4	c. £600[93]
Chichester Baptist chapel	1728	£200[94]
Tiverton Baptist chapel	1730–2	£328 12s.[95]
Birmingham, Carr's Lane chapel (Presbyterian)	1748	c. £700[96]
Banbury Friends' meeting-house	1748–52	£144[97]
Plymouth Baptist chapel	1750–1	£450[98]
Exeter, George's chapel (Presbyterian)	1759–60	c. £2500–£3000[99]
Manchester, Cannon Street (Independents)	1761–2	£492[100]
Liverpool, Newington chapel	1777	£730[101]
Birmingham, Baptist chapel (enlarged)	1780	c. £800[102]
Birmingham, Methodist chapel	1782	£1200[103]
Birmingham, Bond Street Baptist chapel	1785–6	£540[104]
Gloucester Methodist chapel, Northgate	1787	£817 17s. 5d[105]
Wareham Congregational chapel	1789–90	£458 19s. 4d[106]
Birmingham, Calvinist Baptist chapel, Oxford Street	1790	£1100[107]
Liverpool, Paradise chapel	1790–1	£6749[108]
Newcastle, Particular Baptists (Tuthill Stairs)	1797–8	£1300[109]
Battle, Sussex, Particular Baptist chapel (wooden)	1798	£107 8s. 9d[110]
Kingston-upon-Thames Congregational chapel	1802–3	£996 16s.[111]
Plymouth Friends' chapel	1802–4	£1260[112]

might be incompetent, dishonest, or lack the financial resources or
credit to handle a substantial contract.

VI

During the eighteenth century spending on urban public building
was still very limited in comparison with the growing outlay on
housing, but both the number and variety of types of non-
residential building were increasing. Parish workhouses and
hospitals were being built for the poor. Theatres and assembly

rooms were being provided for leisure activities. There was a growing expenditure on commercial public buildings, particularly
market houses, and prison building was becoming important from
the 1770s. The revival of church building made a considerable
contribution to the rising aggregate expenditure on non-residential
construction. This may be illustrated by two local examples, from
Yorkshire and from Southern England.

In the West Riding a recent estimate by Dr Grady has suggested
that over 1.25 million pounds was spent on public building in the
twelve major towns, between 1700 and 1840, of which churches
took 42 per cent, compared with, for example, 16 per cent on
markets and commercial premises, and 8 per cent on schools and
colleges.[113] The importance played by churches in the development
of non-residential building may also be seen in Southampton in the
eighteenth century. Here a variety of public buildings were erected.
A new market house was built in 1771–3 for £4300 and at least £1400
was spent in 1786 on a new town gaol. New almshouses were built
and a workhouse under an act of 1773; the Free Grammar School
was enlarged in 1777–9. Barracks were erected in the town in the
1790s. Several assembly rooms were built in the course of the
century. Church building was considerable. Of the Nonconformist
churches, the Above Bar Congregational church was rebuilt in 1727
for about £287 and enlarged in 1802 for just over £1351. A small
Friends' meeting-house was built in 1704–5 for £176, and Baptist
chapels were erected in 1764 and 1801. Of the five surviving
Anglican churches, St Mary was rebuilt in 1711, and the construction of a new All Saints in the 1790s for £12,000 was a large
undertaking.[114] Although the outlay on church building in England
was modest in comparison with what was to come in the Victorian
period, in the eighteenth century new Anglican and Nonconformist
chapels were taking the lead among the new non-residential buildings which were an important new feature of provincial towns.

Some of the new public buildings were provided by local or
national taxes. County and borough quarter sessions largely paid
for prisons; court buildings were financed out of county rates, parish
workhouses out of the poor rates. This had the effect of spreading
the cost among all the more substantial inhabitants of town and
countryside; farmers, tradesmen and master craftsmen as well as
landowners, professional men and merchants. The frequent use of
loans to cover the initial building extended the payments over many
years. Private enterprise also played an important role in the

Part of the West side of North Gate Street Chester

Above   Street Market, Northgate Street, Chester, 1816

Below   Specialist shops, Bridge Street, Chester, 1816

Part of the West Side of Bridge Street

The exterior of All Saint's Church, Newcastle-upon-Tyne

The exterior and interior of the Unitarian Chapel, Bridport, Dorset

Above   The exterior of St John Baptist's Church, Gloucester

Below   The exterior of the Octagon Chapel, Norwich

erection of public buildings. The method usually employed was subscription. Subscriptions were raised for a wide range of purposes and in different forms during the eighteenth century. There were the usual small payments of perhaps one or two guineas made regularly as a contribution to a charity school or hospital or as a condition of membership of a club or society. There were also subscriptions in the form of a single, and usually considerable payment, varying between £20 and several hundred pounds. Hospital, charity schools, market buildings and exchanges, theatres and assembly rooms were erected by the subscriptions of numerous well-to-do townspeople and sometimes gentry from the neighbouring countryside. The Bristol Assembly Room, constructed between 1754 and 1755, was paid for by the sale of 120 tontine shares of £30 each.[115] In 1774 a published list of promised subscriptions for the Leeds White Cloth Hall building contained seventy-eight names of individuals or partnerships offering between a guinea and £200.[116] Thus, as in the case of subscriptions to churches and chapels the financial burden was spread among a large number of people.

Church building reflected both public and private enterprise in that it was based partly on taxation (in the form of church rates), and partly on voluntary contributions. Nonconformist chapel building was necessarily done on a subscription basis. Although a few churches and chapels were built largely or wholly with one wealthy person's money, again the chief characteristic of the financing of this type of building is the extent to which it was spread among local inhabitants and sometimes among congregations in various parts of the country. The reliance on church rates for many Anglican churches meant that as many as 100 to 200 parishioners might contribute to the building, sometimes over several decades if a loan had to be repaid. As we have seen, subscriptions involving the acquisition of pews were one means by which both Anglican and Nonconformist churches raised relatively small sums from numerous members of the congregation who could afford to pay for the privilege of listening to sermons in their own seats. There were also the donations from those who did not obtain pew rights. Money was also raised in tiny amounts of a few shillings or less from people up and down the country, through briefs in the case of Anglican churches and through personal appeals to other congregations by Nonconformist ministers and trustees. On occasions individual subscriptions or donations might reach as much as £1000, but most contributors to church building paid only small sums. As with other types of public building, church construction and improvement in the provincial towns of Hanoverian England never posed a serious burden on local inhabitants.

Notes and references

1   C. J. Abbey and J. H. Overton, *The English Church in the Eighteenth Century* (1896), p. 405; W. White, *Directory and Gazetteer of Leeds, Bradford, Halifax, Huddersfield, Wakefield and the Whole of the Clothing Districts of Yorkshire* (1853), p. 19; N. Pevsner, *Northamptonshire* (1973), p. 317. There was considerable interest in church furnishings and layout by the Arminians in the 1620s and 1630s.

2   E. G. W. Bill, *The Queen Anne Churches: a Catalogue of Papers in Lambeth Palace Library of the Commission for Building Fifty New Churches in London and Westminster 1711–1759* (1979), *passim*.

3   S. C. Carpenter, *Eighteenth Century Church and People* (1959), p. 172.

4   C. S. Davies, *A History of Macclesfield* (1961), pp. 325, 329–30, 334, 340, 342.

5   W. White, *History, Gazetteer, and Directory of Lincolnshire, and the City and Diocese of Lincoln* (1856), p. 86; F. Hill, *Georgian Lincoln* (1966), pp. 50, 63; Lincolnshire RO, St Botolph parish records 10/1, p. 14.

6   Southampton RO, PR5/1/2.

7   V. Green, *The History and Antiquities of the City and Suburbs of Worcester* (1796), p. 62.

8   A. Stark, *The History and Antiquities of Gainsborough* (1843), p. 378.

9   W. Ison, *The Georgian Buildings of Bristol* (1952), p. 67.

10   H. Owen and J. B. Blakeway, *A History of Shrewsbury* (1825), vol. 2 p. 249.

11   E. Hughes, 'The founding of Maryport', *Trans. Cumberland and Westmorland Antiquarian and Archaeol. Soc.*, 2nd series, **64** (1964), p. 307; Cumbria RO, D/Sen3/M. Chapel.

12   *Gore's Liverpool Directory* (1823), p. 144; J. Gnosspelius and S. Harris, 'John Moffat and St Peter's Church, Liverpool', *Trans. Historic Soc. of Lancashire and Cheshire*, **130** (1981), p. 4.

13   M. Whiffen, *Stuart and Georgian Churches* (1947–8), p. 25.

14   White, *Leeds*, p. 348; *The Stranger in Liverpool: or an historical and descriptive view of the Town of Liverpool and its Environs* (1815), p. 103.

15   Whiffen, *Stuart and Georgian Churches*, p. 52.

16   W. Ison, *The Georgian Buildings of Bath* (1948), p. 79; by the end of the century Anglican concern for the religious needs of the lower classes was growing as a result of the Evangelical movement.

17   J. Latimer, *Annals of Bristol in the Eighteenth Century* (1893), p. 479.

18 C. W. Chalklin, *The Provincial Towns of Georgian England: a Study of the Building Process 1740–1820* (1974), pp. 85–7.
19 Ison, *Bath*, p. 72.
20 S. G. Checkland, *The Gladstones: a Family Biography* (1971), p. 79.
21 H. S. Toy, *The History of Helston* (1936), pp. 334–6.
22 Lincolnshire RO, FAC 9/68.
23 Dorset RO, P63/CW 6, 9 and VE 2.
24 Ison, *Bristol*, pp. 70–1; Latimer, *Annals of Bristol*, p. 408.
25 Abbey and Overton, *The English Church*, pp. 411–14.
26 Southampton RO, 9/4/1/1.
27 A. T. Lee, *History of the Town and Parish of Tetbury* (1857), p. 111; there was also some plain seating for about eighty people, presumably in the corners of the church.
28 P. B. Chatwin, 'The rebuilding of St Mary's Church, Warwick', *Trans. Birmingham Archaeol. Soc.*, **65** (1949), p. 13.
29 Owen and Blakeway, *A History of Shropshire*, p. 249.
30 'The building and furnishing of St Mary's Church', *Cake and Cock-horse* (Banbury Hist. Soc. 1972), p. 64.
31 Davies, *A History of Macclesfield*, pp. 260, 313; R Richards, *Old Cheshire Churches* (1973), p. 213.
32 C. W. Bardsley, *Memoirs of St Ann's Church* (1877), p. 12; *The New Manchester Guide* (1815), pp. 111–13.
33 K. Kissack *Monmouth: the Making of a County Town* (1975), pp. 111–296.
34 Bodl., MS DD Par. Banbury *c.* 14.
35 Cumbria RO, D/Lons/W/Wh.Tn./67.
36 G. O. Rickword, 'The rebuilding of the church of St Mary-at-the-Walls, Colchester, 1713–14', *Trans. Essex Archaeol. Soc.*, **22** (1936–9), pp. 313, 319.
37 Norfolk RO, C38/2.
38 Cumbria RO, PR/110/1/288 pp. 1, 6.
39 E. MacKenzie, *A Discriptive and Historical Account of Newcastle* (1827), vol. 1, p. 303.
40 Kent AO, P243/4/1.
41 West Sussex RO, P243/4/38.
42 9 Geo.2 c.22 and 11 Geo.2 c.5.
43 Bristol RO, P/St.P/ChW4(b).
44 S. Pritchard, *The History of Deal* (1864), pp. 164–6.
45 Whiffen, *Stuart and Georgian Churches*, p. 25.
46 Cumbria RO, Lowther MSS letter book 1715–16 (18 September 1715).
47 Hill, *Georgian Lincoln*, p. 50.
48 Whiffen, *Stuart and Georgian Churches*, p. 31.
49 J. and S. Russell, *The History of Guildford* (1801), p. 52.
50 S. Lewis, *A Topographical Dictionary of England* (1831), vol. 2, p. 336.

51   W White, *History, Gazetteer and Directory of Devonshire* (1850), p. 700.
52   E. Baines, *Directory of Lancashire* (1836), p. 664.
53   *VCH*, Lancs., **4**, p. 99.
54   E. W. Brayley and J. Britton, *The Beauties of England and Wales* (1801), vol. 1 p. 282.
55   *VCH*, Warwicks., **8**, p. 531.
56   White, *Leeds*, p. 19.
57   *VCH*, Lancs., **4**, p. 100.
58   J. Rickman, (ed.), *Life of Thomas Telford* (1838), p. 33.
59   D. M. Butler, *Quaker Meeting Houses of the Lake Counties* (1978), p. 84.
60   A. Brockett, *Nonconformity in Exeter 1650–1875* (1962), pp. 54–5; *VCH*, York, p. 406.
61   J. Swaish, *Chronicles of Broadmead Church, Bristol* (1927), p. 81.
62   F. F. Bretherton, *Early Methodism in and around Chester, 1749–1812* (1903), p. 158.
63   H. Rowntree, *Early Quakerism in Guildford* (1952), pp. 53–6.
64   W. Hutton, *The History of Birmingham* (1835), p. 115.
65   F. Reynolds Levett, *A History of the Clapham Congregational Church* (1912), p. 86.
66   Dorset RO, N1/CO1.
67   F. F. Giraud and C. E. Donne, *A Visitor's Guide to Faversham* (1876), p. 82.
68   H. D. Roberts, *Matthew Henry and his Chapel 1662–1900* (1901), pp. 247–8.
69   Norfolk and Norwich RO, FC 13/1, 11.
70   MS J. Goodchild (Wakefield), 'The Building of Westgate Chapel, Wakefield' (1975).
71   *The Universal British Directory* (1790–8), vol. 5 pp. 364–6.
72   Dorset RO, N6/MC6.
73   Cumbria RO, Carlisle FCF 2/3, 3/3.
74   G. E. Evans, *A History of Renshaw Street Chapel* (1887), pp. 136–9.
75   F. Nicholson and E. Axon, *The Older Nonconformity in Kendal* (1915), pp. 499–50, 503–4.
76   J. T. Godfrey and J. Ward, *The History of the Friar Lane Baptist Chapel, Nottingham* (1903), pp. 2, 297–301.
77   Meadrow Unitarian Church, Godalming MSS.
78   Norfolk and Norwich RO, FC 18/14.
79   J. C. Cox and W. H. St John Hope, *The Chronicles of the Collegiate Church or Free Chapel of All Saints, Derby* (1881), pp. 61–5.
80   Dorset RO, N18 MC1 p. 27.
81   Southampton RO, D/ABC 7.
82   H. Colvin, *A Biographical Dictionary of British Architects, 1600–1840* (1978), pp. 914–15.

83 Owen and Blakeway, *A History of Shrewsbury*, p. 248.
84 C. E. Welch, 'The rebuilding of the churches of St Pancras and St Bartholomew, Chichester', *Sussex Notes and Queries*, **14** (1957), pp. 262–8.
85 Bristol RO, Bd/A1/2; for St Werburgh: Bristol RO, P/St.W./Ch.W/7.
86 Norfolk and Norwich RO, C38/2.
87 Rowntree, *Early Quakerism*, p. 56.
88 Gloucestershire RO, P154/9 CW2/1.
89 Dorset RO, N18 MC1 p. 27.
90 Suffolk RO, FK 4/1 2961.
91 B. Nightingale, *Lancashire Nonconformity* (1893), vol. 5, pp. 153–4.
92 R. W. Young, *History of the Sandwich Congregational Church* (1925), p. 13.
93 Brockett, *Nonconformity in Exeter*, p. 109.
94 T. G. Willis, *Records of Chichester* (1928), p. 293.
95 H. B. Case, *The History of the Baptist Church in Tiverton 1607 to 1907* (*c.* 1908), pp. 28–30.
96 Hutton, *The History of Birmingham*, p. 115.
97 *VCH*, Oxfordshire, **10**, p. 111.
98 H. M. Nicholson, *Authentic Records relating to the Christian Church, now meeting in George Street and Mutley Chapels, Plymouth, 1640 to 1870* (1904), p. 71.
99 Brockett, *Nonconformity in Exeter*, pp. 133–4.
100 T. Swindells, *Manchester Streets and Manchester Men* (1907), p. 75.
101 Information from Mrs Jane Longmore.
102 Hutton, *The History of Birmingham*, p. 116.
103 ibid., p. 118.
104 A. S. Langley, *Birmingham Baptists Past and Present* (1939), p. 82.
105 Gloucestershire RO, D3987.
106 Dorset RO, N6/MC 6.
107 Hutton, *The History of Birmingham*, p. 119.
108 H. D. Roberts, *Hope Street Chapel, Liverpool* (1909), pp. 247–8.
109 MacKenzie, *Newcastle*, p. 398.
110 R. F. Chambers, *The Strict Baptist Chapels of England* (1952), vol. 2, p. 70.
111 J. Waddington, *Surrey Congregational History* (1866), p. 238.
112 A. D. Selleck, 'Plymouth Friends: a Quaker history – Part II', *Trans. Devonshire Association*, **99** (1967), p. 217.
113 K. Grady, 'The provision of public buildings in the West Riding of Yorkshire, c.1600–1840' (unpublished PhD thesis, University of Leeds 1980), pp. 99–100.
114 A. T. Patterson, *A History of Southampton, 1700–1914* (1966), vol. 1, pp. 41, 52, 96, 105, 114; Southampton, RO, D/PM 5/3/7/2; Southampton RO, PR 5/1/2 and D/ABC 7; Southampton Meeting of Friends, *Quakers in Southampton 1660* (1975), p. 8; J. Silvester Davies,

A History of Southampton (1883), pp. 430–1; the figure of £12,000 is an approximate estimate based on the church MSS in Southampton RO., D/PM 9.

115 Ison, *Bristol*, p. 109.

116 H. Heaton, 'The Leeds White Cloth Hall', *Miscellanea VI* (Thoresby Soc., **22** 1915), p. 141.

10 The civic leaders of Gloucester 1580–1800

Peter Clark

Like present-day politicians the civic leaders of corporate towns in the early modern period were rarely popular or well-loved figures. Between 1600 and 1800 they were the target of repeated charges of corruption and malfeasance, with disaffected citizens accusing them of peculating funds, selling offices and acting unjustly. Criticism of this type was supported by the Municipal Corporation commissioners in the 1830s when they denounced the unreformed towns as 'not adapted to the present state of society; the corporate officers are not identified with the community'.[1] Later historians echoed their view. J. L. and B. Hammond declared that before 1835 the towns 'were for the most part in the hands of little oligarchies, seldom public spirited, and often corrupt'. Even the Webbs, who produced evidence of the responsible public actions of some closed corporations during the Hanoverian period, concluded that in general town rulers were uncontrolled, self-interested and myopic, preoccupied with local concerns.[2]

However, as Professor W. G. Hoskins pointed out a decade ago, the whole subject of the urban governing class in the pre-industrial period remains to be explored systematically. The old pessimistic view of the performance of civic fathers requires careful scrutiny. In the last few years David Palliser and one or two other writers have shed interesting light on the recruitment and wealth of certain town élites at particular times.[3] But a number of questions are still outstanding. How far did the pattern of civic rule change during the Stuart and Hanoverian periods? To what extent was the urban leadership of the pre-industrial era capable of adapting to new circumstances and pressures, especially in the eighteenth century? Was closed civic government a factor contributing, as some have thought, to the slower economic success of older corporate towns in the age of industrial revolution?

I

The aim of this paper is to illuminate at least some of these issues by a case study of Gloucester's civic leaders – its aldermen and common councillors – from the late sixteenth to the late eighteenth century, looking at the selection and composition of the ruling group and its impact on the urban community. It is not contended that our ruling caucus is synonymous with or necessarily representative of the urban élite as a whole. But there are serious logistical problems in defining membership of a wider urban élite, not least with the rise of new professions and other middle-class groups during the eighteenth century. By comparison, the civic ruling group is readily identifiable, enjoyed control over the essential levers of political power, and for most of our period embraced a high proportion of the economic and social *potentiores* in the community.[4]

Throughout the early modern period the city's rulers were a restricted group. Under the 1483 charter the common council was the main political body (with the membership by custom somewhat over forty) and from this were chosen the twelve aldermen (co-opted by the bench). The mayor was elected by the aldermen and senior councillors. A new charter in 1626–7 fixed the maximum size of the council at forty with a bench of twelve, but few other constitutional innovations occurred in the period.[5] From Table 32 we can see that ninety-one townsmen served on the corporation between 1580 and 1600; 115 held office in the period 1680–1700; and a smaller contingent of sixty-five in 1780–1800. Each group includes both men sitting at the start of the sample period and those subsequently elected. Civic leaders have been divided into ordinary 'councillors' and those who were or eventually became members of the bench (sometimes after the end of the sample period) – the 'aldermen'. There are methodological problems in this kind of study. However, by confining the examination to three cohorts we

Table 32   *Civic leaders: sample cohorts*

	1580–1600	1680–1700	1780–1800
Aldermen	40	48	34
Councillors	51	67	31
Total	91	115	65

avoid the danger of being overwhelmed by a cascade of names but preserve the ability to make comparisons over time. Apart from their temporal symmetry, the periods we have taken for our prosopographical snapshots have the merit of above average documentation. They also correspond with important phases in the city's development.[6]

At this point, it is important to say a few words about the urban context. Gloucester was fairly typical of the middle rank inland towns which formed the backbone of urban society in England for most of the early modern era. Settled by the Romans and enjoying considerable economic and political prominence during the Middle Ages, its population grew from nearly 4000 in the mid sixteenth century to about 5000 in the 1670s. After a period of demographic stability during the post-Restoration period, there was renewed growth in George III's reign with the total population reaching 7265 by 1801. Economically, the decades up to and including the Civil War were a time of difficulty. The city's staple trades of textiles and capping declined and its overseas commerce was poached by Bristol. Though the service sector – innkeeping and professional activity – was expanding, growth was sluggish. As a result Gloucester was heavily dependent on its marketing role, exchanging goods with the adjoining countryside and shipping grain and malt down the Severn to Bristol and the South-West. After the English Revolution a modest recovery took place. Like other cathedral cities Gloucester became a lively social arena with country gentry resorting there to preen themselves, plot party manoeuvres, consult lawyers and physicians, and indulge in a constellation of leisure pursuits from cock-fighting to choral music. By 1700 the city also had a second string to its bow. It was developing as a major centre for the pin-making industry, one of the many new consumer crafts prospering in post-Restoration England.[7] In 1712 we learn that 'the pin-making trade . . . is very considerable in this city and returns about £80 per week'. By 1781 the industry was said to return approximately £20,000 per annum from London, plus an extensive trade in the provinces. Thirty years later it employed 1500 people in and about the city, perhaps a quarter of Gloucester's working population, with exports going to America and Spain. On the other hand, Gloucester retained its important traditional functions as a distribution hub and purveyor of professional services, supplying the needs of a now flourishing farming region.[8] This was the community over which our civic leaders held sway.

II

Given that the late sixteenth century was a time of economic difficulty for Gloucester, with the main thrust of commercial activity derived from distribution and inland trade, it is not surprising perhaps that recruitment to the civic élite at this time was highly localized. Nearly four out of ten of the councillors and half the aldermen or future aldermen were natives of the city, with many of the remainder coming from the nearby county. Only one in five had arrived from outside Gloucestershire and the majority of these were from adjoining Worcestershire and Herefordshire. The pattern was more localized than for Gloucester's population as a whole. As for parental background (where known), the fathers of the late sixteenth-century cohort were almost invariably connected with a prosperous occupation: some were yeomen, others merchants or clothiers. At the same time there was no significant influx of the sons of gentlemen or professional men.

For those aspiring to civic office in the sixteenth century, family ties with established members of the ruling class were an obvious advantage, helping to ensure that they benefited from city funds for young masters and jumped the preliminary hurdles of the *cursus honorum* without difficulty. Approximately 14 per cent of the councillors and a quarter of the aldermen had kin ties with present or former members of the corporation. Local connections might also help, with a young man coming from the same village as a city elder.[9] Apprenticeship provided another key to civic office. Failure to become apprenticed or service to a minor master in a lesser craft effectively debarred a man from a civic career unless he had other cards up his sleeve. However, service to a leading master in an important trade might well be a political trump. Thus John Browne I, alderman from 1584 to 1593, was an apprentice of John Woodward, a mercer and clothier who had been mayor in 1566, while another aldermanic mercer, Lawrence Halliday, had served under Thomas Pury, mayor in 1560.[10]

Most of the élite group were literate. Some may have been educated as a condition of their apprenticeship; others probably went to a petty school or even one of the city grammar schools before they started work.[11] After the standard seven years or so as an apprentice, the typical young man often continued for a while with his old master, acquiring business experience and capital before he paid his freedom fine and set up on his own. At the same time, substantial numbers of apprentices never completed their term or took up the freedom afterwards, usually because of lack of money. Apprenticeship of course was not the only way to secure freeman status. At Gloucester it could also be gained through patrimony or purchase – though rising fines by 1600 made the last option less attractive. An average of twenty-three persons per annum were admitted to the freedom in the years 1534–64; by the middle of the next century the annual figure stood at thirty-six. Allowing for demographic growth, access to Gloucester's freemen body was probably close to the norm in provincial towns, less restrictive than at Exeter or Norwich, less open than at Chester.[12] For our embryonic alderman, the average age at this first stage of the traditional *cursus* was 26; for those on the way to becoming councillors it was 27; ordinary citizens took the freeman's oath rather later.

With this basic civic meal ticket in his pocket, qualifying him to trade in the community, the ambitious man had to get down to making a living. From Table 33 we can see that the late Elizabethan élite recruited heavily from the distributive trades. Roughly 40 per cent were mercers, drapers and goldsmiths. This compares with 17 per cent of the whole population listed as belonging to those trades in the 1608 muster return. The large cadre of mercers and the like on the bench testifies to the burgeoning importance of marketing at

Table 33 *Principal occupations of civic leaders*

| | 1580–1600 | | 1680–1700 | | 1780–1800 | |
	Ald. *per cent*	Counc. *per cent*	Ald. *per cent*	Counc. *per cent*	Ald. *per cent*	Counc. *per cent*
Gentlemen	7.5	7.8	16.6	5.9	17.6	3.2
Professional	5.0	9.8	18.7	11.9	20.6	29.0
Distributive	40.0	43.1	39.6	35.8	23.5	29.0
Food processors	25.0	7.8	8.3	20.8	5.9	3.2
Textile	10.0	9.8	0.0	4.4	2.9	9.6
Leather	5.0	5.8	4.2	2.9	0.0	0.0
Metalworkers	0.0	1.9	0.0	4.4	17.6	6.4
Miscellaneous other	7.5	14.0	12.6	13.9	11.9	19.6
Sample	37	44	42	58	30	25
Unknown	3	7	6	9	4	6

this time. A number were involved in the lucrative grain trade; others in distributing luxury goods imported *via* Bristol or South Wales. Direct trading abroad was limited. More vital was commerce with London. The mercer John Browne I was especially active, 'returning' sums to the capital for himself and other town leaders totalling over £20,000.[13]

But the dominance of this group of traders was also a comment on the dwindling significance of Gloucester's industrial sector. Only a handful of clothiers were on the corporation between 1580 and 1600 as most of the large cloth masters, once so important, departed the city. The leather trades were more buoyant in the late Tudor economy but like metalworking they produced few prosperous masters suitable for civic office.[14] The small representation of professional men and gentry is also noticeable. Though professional activity may have been less flourishing in the West Midlands than in the big cities and Home Counties, about thirty lawyers and medical men appear to have been practising in and about Gloucester between 1580 and 1600. But the great majority of the lawyers were small attorneys who frequently retained a country base; few seem to have resided in the city for any period. Those legal figures on the corporation were usually cathedral officials like Richard Hands and John Jones. The physicians and surgeons were likewise rather undistinguished.[15] In the case of the gentry a number lived within the liberties, including Sir William Guise and Sir William Cooke. However, most resided outside the walls in the inshire, the two hundreds of the county annexed to the city by the 1483 charter. From Elizabeth's reign the country gentry were busy disputing Gloucester's jurisdiction over the inshire and the city did its best to keep them off the corporation.[16]

Like business success, a good marriage was another stepping stone to civic office in late sixteenth-century Gloucester. Apart from the value of the dowry as working capital or security for loans, the wife's relatives could offer an éntree into the corporate establishment. Thomas Best, for instance, married the sister of alderman Thomas Machen in 1578 and over the next six years became a freeman, alderman and mayor; one of Machen's daughters wedded Thomas Rich who swiftly followed his father-in-law on to the bench.[17] The marital merry-go-round was accelerated by high mortality. A quarter of the councillors and a third of the bench are known to have married twice and three aldermen took three brides apiece. Marriage to widows was particularly popular because of their accumulated economic and social assets. In many instances brides came from Gloucester itself – emphasizing the local nature of the ruling class.

With the right trade and family ties, a healthy business and well-connected wife, the moderately ambitious citizen might expect co-option on to the common council by the time he was in his early 40s. There was also a faster track for high flyers with superior wealth or political support: future aldermen joined the council when they were about 35. Not that everyone jumped at the chance of elevation. From the 1550s repeated complaints were made of wealthy traders refusing to serve.[18]

Civic office imposed an increasingly heavy charge on the leading inhabitants of Tudor towns. There was often a succession of burdensome junior offices to fill before a man could attain political power. At Gloucester the new councillor was faced almost immediately with having to serve as one of the four stewards or treasurers, usually for a double term. Because of the city's financial problems, incoming stewards after the 1570s were obliged to lend the corporation large sums to cover the annual deficit. Little wonder that, having served as steward, substantial numbers of councillors declined to hold further office or resigned from the corporation. The stewardship in fact operated as an important filter, halting the advancement of men with limited means or commitment to civic affairs. However, the councillors who persevered might, after four or five years, be elected as one of the two city sheriffs. This post was more prestigious and less costly but with the growth of litigation it entailed the execution of large numbers of writs from national and local courts. This led several sheriffs to become entangled in prolonged lawsuits in London or before the Council of the Marches.[19]

By the last part of Elizabeth's reign, would-be aldermen were expected to serve as steward and sheriff twice before they were considered for promotion, though one term might be excused on payment of a hefty fine.[20] Even completion of the official circuit did not guarantee promotion. Often there were more qualified councillors than empty seats on the bench so that political favouritism generally determined who should be elevated. The usual period of conciliar service prior to membership of the bench was about thirteen years. Most city leaders had thus reached middle age – and the upper slopes of their business careers – when they joined the inner caucus. Once there election to the mayoralty was virtually automatic. Nearly three-quarters of our aldermen served twice; one in eight, three times. The mayoralty involved considerable expense, entertaining courtiers and county magnates, offering traditional hospitality to the freemen, supplying part of the petty cash for daily administration. In 1600 swingeing fines were levied on aldermen who sought to evade nomination.[21]

The *cursus honorum* lay at the heart of civic oligarchy before the Civil War. Gild office was of minor importance as a route to power, probably because of the accelerating decline of Gloucester's companies. Appointment to non-corporate posts tended to stem from promotion to the bench. More than half the aldermen acted as governors and assistants of the city's three main hospitals, disposing of a large amount of patronage – leases, almsplaces and contracts. Again the bench enjoyed a near monopoly of parliamentary representation with six of our aldermen elected by the freemen to Westminster.[22] By contrast, relatively few civic rulers are known to have held parish office.

Kin ties were more crucial in corporation politics, helping the advancement of aspiring citizens and consolidating their position once they were on the ruling body. At least 42 per cent of the élite were related, either by blood or marriage, to each other: among aldermen the proportion was 63 per cent. In several instances city fathers had up to four kinsmen sitting with them. Also helping to underpin élite authority was longevity. The average age of those leaving the bench was 66, but a number stayed until they were over 80. Advanced age created the image of the venerable urban patriarch. More important, it meant that an alderman knew the institutional ropes, ran an established network of followers, and had accumulated a string of political debts from other worthies.[23]

Unlike London, there was no formal financial qualification for aspirants to high office at Gloucester. But as we know recruitment was mostly from the more prosperous trades and only the well-off could survive the burdens of the stewardship and shrievalty. At the close of the Tudor period the city's political grandees were generally identical with the economic and social leaders of the community: to use the sociologists' term, they were a 'power élite'. Of the twenty-nine inhabitants taxed at more than £1 in the 1594 subsidy twenty-three were members of our civic cohort, plus the recorder and town clerk.[24] One or two aldermen were magnates by the modest standards of provincial towns. Thomas Machen was said to be worth £5000–6000 in land, sheep and money, and he held several leases of tithes. John Browne I died with an estimated £2000 in goods in 1593. But most of the town's rulers were much smaller men. The personal estate of the typical alderman was probably under £1000 and for councillors the figure was nearer £200 or £300. Their economic standing was probably comparable to that of civic worthies in other county towns.[25]

Part of élite wealth was inevitably tied up in trade. But property investment was also very important. At least half the councillors are known to have held property, leasehold and freehold, in the city; among aldermen the proportion was as high as 85 per cent, with holdings not confined to one parish but spread across the city. With the urban population and housing demand expanding, investment of this sort was profitable and reasonably safe. Rising rents in the countryside also had their attraction. A quarter of the councillors and more than 50 per cent of the aldermen held land or houses in the inshire, adjoining the city. John Browne II was charged with rack-renting during James I's reign.[26] But for most aldermen high rural rents were not the only concern. Country estates bestowed on them the cloak of gentility to outface the county gentry and helped them secure the city's control over the recalcitrant inhabitants of the inshire.

Gloucester's leaders acted together in grain shipments, property dealings and other business enterprises.[27] Élite solidarity was also strengthened by residential propinquity. Most of the councillors lived in three inner parishes adjoining the central market area, St Michael's, St John's and Holy Trinity, with others in the port district of St Nicholas; two-thirds of the aldermen resided in St Michael and St Nicholas. Here they celebrated their authority and success by building or rebuilding their houses in considerable style. Alderman John Browne I, for instance, built a large new four-storey mansion in Grace Lane on the site of several small tenements. Interior fittings were also increasingly costly.[28]

Occupying these large houses were substantial households with numbers of children and servants.[29] Children were often used by parents to consolidate their power in the community. Where we have information, the great majority of élite children married partners from the city – regularly from élite backgrounds. Of those boys with aldermanic fathers nearly half became distributive traders, though the professions (expanding in the seventeenth century) also attracted a number. But there was no exodus of these children into landownership. Rather they sought to follow their fathers on to the corporation. As many as fifteen of the sons of our aldermen became civic leaders in their turn.[30]

The general picture then at the end of the sixteenth century is of a ruling caucus which was very much home-grown. It recruited locally, mainly from the occupational groups associated with the localized market economy of the city. It controlled access to the inner sanctum of civic power through the arduous rock-climb of the *cursus honorum*. It cemented its position through kinship ties and longevity. In many ways it was a narrow, inward-looking élite. At the same time, it was not a ruling group that could boast great wealth (few were significant benefactors of the poor).

This created major political problems. For during the century or so after the Reformation, the administrative burdens of town leaders, particularly members of the bench, increased dramatically. The expanding central government imposed many new duties on magistrates. Preferring to work through small cliques of local worthies, the Crown placed growing emphasis on the aldermen acting as Justices of the Peace. Again the growth of population and myriad social problems created pressure within towns for greater official action by city rulers. Many problems required almost constant supervision by a standing committee of leading townsmen.[31]

By 1600 members of Gloucester's bench were meeting privately together once or more a week and exercising a powerful summary jurisdiction as JPs. In most areas of adminstration the aldermen took the initiative, granting leases and ordering expenditure with little reference to the common council. There were complaints that the mayor summoned meetings of the council when he knew members were out of town. The bench sought to control appointments which were customarily made by the council. In the latter part of Elizabeth's reign city finances were bailed out by loans from magistrates.[32]

A serious disjuncture thus arose between the new power and responsibilities of the principal city leaders and the type of men who were rising to the highest civic offices. The problem was widespread in medium-rank provincial towns. The repercussions for urban government were manifold. At Gloucester many aldermen endeavoured to compensate themselves for the burdens of office by selling city posts and alehouse licences, taking bribes for securing leases of town lands, and other profiteering. Political hanky-panky of some sort is a structural feature of local government in all periods, but the scale of corruption and abuse does seem to have worsened in the later decades of the sixteenth century.[33] Closely linked with it was an upsurge of political factionalism as city leaders fought over the limited pool of patronage. Gloucester from the late 1580s was riven by conflict between an establishment group led by alderman Thomas Machen and later his son-in-law, Thomas Rich, and a more populist party, headed by alderman Luke Garnons and the diocesan registrar John Jones, which appealed to the freemen and discontented inhabitants of the inshire. There were clashes over the appointment of a new recorder in 1587, the election of MPs in 1588, mismanagement of the corn stock in mid 1590s, and parliamentary elections in 1598 and 1604.[34] Charges of fraud and extortion were levelled against several mayors and though some were doubtless exaggerated, one has the impression that a number of the bench were behaving in an arbitrary and uncustomary way, exploiting the recent growth of oligarchic power for their own private ends; that city administration was starting to fall apart.[35]

In numerous provincial cities political dissension accelerated in the early Stuart period, with internal tension between magistrates and freemen compounded by growing gentry and Crown interference, especially in the 1620s and 1630s.[36] At Gloucester, however, the pattern was rather different. The initial years of James I's reign marked a turning point for the élite. Most of the city fathers, concerned at the damaging civic conflict, sought to put their house in order and to assert control over the community. There were moves to strengthen town government; record-keeping improved; the town clerk was required to be permanently based in the city; aldermanic control over the gilds was tightened. Leading townsmen who offended against city regulations were disciplined.[37] Also striking was the élite's growing commitment to moderate Puritanism, as I have argued elsewhere. By the 1610s the Puritan group on the corporation was clearly in the ascendancy, seeking to create the image of a godly commonwealth. In 1624 Thomas Prior preaching to the citizens cried rhetorically: 'Would thou . . . find sanctuary in a storm and a city of refuge against the pursuer?' and then adjured them to be 'numbered among the blessed'.[38]

At Gloucester the Puritan movement may have helped unify the ruling élite. It also served to buttress the magistrates' authority and encourage a sense of solidarity among the respectable citizenry. Not that such stabilizing effects were always apparent in other towns: Puritanism could also aggravate political conflict.[39] Crucial perhaps at Gloucester was that Puritanism also had a wider communal dimension, validating differences between the city and the outside world. From the 1590s Gloucester was under attack from county gentry and threatened with the loss of its inshire. The city fought back. In 1610 Sir William Cooke protested that the corporation 'profess hating to have a gentleman in any fellowship of government with them'. In the 1620s the magistrates beat off determined attempts by some of the inshire gentry to intrude into city government. The next decade the city rallied to resist the Crown's intervention in the community, particularly over the Puritan lecturer John Workman. In 1643 it was godly Gloucester which held out valiantly against the king's army when much of the country had subsided into royalism or neutrality. Despite this mounting conflict with outsiders, the civic leadership held together remarkably well. There were relatively few defections or expulsions during the Civil War or Interregnum.[40] But the price of localism and isolation was high. The city suffered badly as a result of the siege: the total damage and loss was assessed at £29,000 in 1646. No less serious was the decline of social traffic because of the loyalist sympathies of the county landowners. By the 1650s even the ruling fathers admitted their mounting concern at the severe economic and financial problems besetting the community.[41] The writing was on the wall for the old civic order.

III

The Restoration shattered the Puritan leadership which had developed out of the closed élite of the late sixteenth century. A number of leading radicals left the city for the safety of London. When the commissioners under the Corporation Act, mostly royalist gentry from the shire, visited Gloucester in 1662 they removed thirty members of the corporation (roughly three-quarters), with another four dismissed the following year. Soon after the city was deprived of its jurisdiction over the inshire, and its walls, monuments of the old godly commonwealth, were destroyed.[42] For all these reverses, however, the Puritan party (mostly Presbyterians) remained an influential force, and by 1670 had gained a fresh foothold on the corporation. Disputes over mayoral elections in 1670 and 1671 led to a new royal charter in 1672, which again purged the corporation, intruded a number of county gentry, and increased royal powers of supervision. Royal intervention in 1683 and 1687 caused further changes of personnel and a subsequent backlash.[43]

Successive purges of the corporation led to a greater number of people belonging to the late seventeenth-century civic élite. No less significant, the coherence of the old Puritan leadership gave way to an élite torn by conflict between Anglicans and dissenters or crypto-dissenters, Tories and Whigs. Recruitment to the élite remained heavily localized, as in Elizabeth's reign: 46 per cent of the councillors and 58 per cent of the aldermen had been born in Gloucester and virtually all the others came from the shire. On the other hand, the parental background of civic leaders was rather more rarefied. More than a quarter of the aldermen were the offspring of professional (mostly legal) families, and about the same proportion were the sons of gentlemen (though it has to be remembered that gentle status was declining in the later Stuart period). The children of distributive traders were also prominent. By contrast those from craft families were in decline.

As in the past substantial numbers of the élite had been apprenticed to a city master; at least half the councillors and a quarter of the aldermen. Virtually all were literate and some, particularly the gentry, may have enjoyed an advanced education: Sir Duncombe Colchester, for instance, had been to Charterhouse and academies in London and Oxford before going on to one of the Inns of Court.[44] Most prospective leaders continued to acquire the freedom in their 20s, though after the Restoration it became devalued as an economic and political privilege by the practice of enfranchising large numbers of people, inhabitants and outsiders, at parliamentary elections. The preliminary hurdle of the old *cursus honorum* was crumbling.

The changing character of the late seventeenth-century élite is apparent when we examine the occupational background of the councillors and aldermen (see Table 33). Distributive traders remained the largest single group on the corporation. Some of them had important wholesale businesses in the country or branch shops in the smaller market towns.[45] But there was also now an important contingent of gentlemen and professional men. A number of gentry, as we have said, were imposed on the city by royal fiat. One of the most widely travelled was Henry Norwood, a royalist captain during the Civil War who acted for the king in Virginia in 1650, plotted against the Parliamentary regime in 1654, and became in the 1660s deputy governor of Dunkirk and later governor of Tangier. An experienced hand at political survival, he retained his place on the Gloucester bench from 1671 to 1689. Other country gentry were welcomed on to the bench to strengthen the city's ties with county society. The Whig magnate Sir John Guise was elected councillor, alderman and mayor in 1690 after the overthrow of James II's nominees on the corporation.[46] William Cooke, descendant of the city's ancient enemy Sir William Cooke, became mayor three times in 1674, 1690 and 1699.

The professional contingent, mostly attorneys, demonstrated the growing importance of the service sector in post-Restoration Gloucester, as in other towns, catering for the landowners and farmers who flocked there for legal and medical advice. In the period 1680 to 1700 there were nearly sixty lawyers and medical practitioners resident in the city – over 50 per cent more than in the late sixteenth century. Many of the lawyers were quite substantial men, taking an active part in urban society. They also played an important role bringing together the city and county communities. As well as acting at law for country people, they served as manorial stewards and land surveyors, they arranged loans for landowners and others and invested money on behalf of people in the city and shire.[47] By contrast, craftsmen and manufacturers were unimportant on the later Stuart corporation. The civic élite was becoming more integrated, directly and indirectly, with the wider provincial world. Another sign of this was the geographical origin of spouses. Nearly a third of the women marrying our councillors came from outside the city or the adjoining countryside; quite a few aldermen's wives had been born outside Gloucestershire.

For those ambitious for high civic office, the traditional *cursus* had been short-circuited to some extent by the frequent royal nominations after 1672. Nearly one in eight of the late seventeenth-century élite had been elected as a result of the king's intervention; in some cases they became councillor, alderman and mayor on the same day. At least part of the old system prevailed however. In the majority of instances a man had to wait until he was in his mid or late 30s before election to the council; elevation to the bench came when he was about 50. It was still expected that councillors should serve as sheriff at least once, certainly if they sought to join the bench. But the most dangerous obstacle to civic promotion, the stewardship, disappeared after 1672, when city finances were reorganized and put in the hands of a single, semi-permanent chamberlain: Nicholas Webb, for example, was chamberlain from about 1685 until 1700, despite all the political upheavals in the city.[48] It has been argued that civic government may have been less oligarchic in the late seventeenth century. At Gloucester a lower proportion of aldermen held the mayoralty for two or more terms than in the earlier period and the average length of service of town rulers was shorter (twenty-five years compared with thirty years for the late Elizabethan élite). But most of this apparent liberalization was the result of government interference rather than any internal moves towards less restrictive rule.[49]

Despite the political turmoil of the late seventeenth century, the oligarchic inner circle, the bench, continued to dominate the corporation. Aldermanic power may have actually grown at this time, with the council meeting erratically and administrative initiative concentrated in the hands of the Justices of the Peace.[50] At the same time, and more interestingly, élite authority may have been less exclusively based on corporate office than before the Civil War. There was a proliferation of other posts held by civic leaders. Some, as before, were occupied *ex officio* by members of the bench – such as the governorships of the hospitals. But other offices were exercised more or less independently and were a separate source of political power. Thus the lawyers held a series of county appointments: alderman Robert Halford was a busy and unpopular under-sheriff in the shire; his colleague Benjamin Hyett succeeded him as under-sheriff and became clerk of the peace for Gloucestershire from 1678 to 1689.[51] A new development was the way that civic leaders crowded into parish offices, acting as churchwardens, overseers and auditors. Almost half of the later Stuart élite are known to have held a parish position, sometimes for several years in a row. This was particularly significant at a time when parish administration was increasingly crucial for urban order, providing generous poor relief and regulating through settlement controls lower class immigration to town.[52]

Kinship ties and age remained valuable supports of élite influence. Despite the greater turnover of personnel, 51 per cent of the élite are known to have had one or more relatives on the corporate body, though clusters of kinsmen are less common than in the late sixteenth century. Again the average age of aldermen leaving the bench was about 63 years, only slightly down on the earlier period; six stayed in office until they were 80 or over. More clearly than in the past, however, political power was strongly buttressed by economic and social status. By comparison with most of their Tudor predecessors, the rulers of late seventeenth-century Gloucester were wealthy figures with standing among the county's upper classes, as well as in the city. The gentry contingent included the major landowners Sir John Guise and Sir Duncombe Colchester. But even the local leaders were substantial men. Alderman John Price was said to have inherited most of the estate of a former mayor, John Woodward, valued at £16,000; his colleague the lawyer Benjamin Hyett was a leading money-lender, putting out up to £2000 a time on mortgage; councillor John Cromwell, a carrier turned pin-maker, was reputedly worth £5000 at one stage of his career. A small group of diocesan probate inventories reveal a range of personal wealth from over £2500 for the tanner William Nicholls to a more usual £300–400. But these figures understate the general personal wealth of our leaders since many had their estates proved in the London courts.[53]

Despite the presence of gentry on the corporation, the pattern of élite landholding outside the city remained broadly what it had been in the earlier period, reflecting perhaps the stagnation of rural rents by 1700. Investment in the urban property market also appears stable. But this may mask élite involvement in the piecemeal re-building of the city which was under way by 1700. A major development here was the erection of brick-built, more classical style houses, both to make up for the destruction caused by the siege of 1643 and to accommodate the growing numbers of fashion-conscious county gentry who came to town. Two of the élite, Anselm Fowler and Benjamin Hyett, both lawyers, are known to have occupied new brick-built houses in Marybone Park, while the mercer Joseph Ludlow rebuilt his house in Westgate about 1675. Within the houses furnishings became ever more lavish. Nathaniel Castle, a baker and councillor who died in 1702, had clocks, pictures, leather chairs and a great amount of plate in his recently enlarged house.[54]

Collectively and individually there was a move by the wealthier civic leaders to identify themselves more closely with county society. They boasted the landed titles of esquire and gentleman. Their children married more often with county families; 40 per cent of the children of councillors and 80 per cent of those of aldermen took partners from outside the city, usually the offspring of well-to-do Gloucestershire families. This new orientation of the civic élite was made inevitable by the collapse of the old city leadership at the Restoration. But it was also encouraged by the obvious economic advantages, evident throughout the seventeenth century, of the city exploiting the high prosperity of the county community and its gentry. Though dissent remained a significant force in Gloucester up to the 1720s, the religious particularism of the old city was submerged in a host of new entertainments and social events designed to appeal to gentle tastes: horse-races (sponsored as elsewhere by the city), assemblies, concerts, firework shows, and the Three Choirs Festival to name but a few.[55]

The most obvious symptom of the new alignment of the city with county society was the importation of party rivalries from the shire. As we noted earlier, after internal disputes in 1670–1, the new charter of 1672 brought the corporation firmly under loyalist control, with county Tories playing a prominent part in civic affairs. There was little trouble during the Exclusion Crisis when the city staunchly supported Charles II. But in 1687 the Tory magistrates ran foul of James II's plans for Toleration and there were several purges. The empty seats were taken by a sprinkling of Catholics and a number of dissenters. With William III's arrival the Jacobite interlopers were pushed out and the Tories returned. But in the early 1690s the Whigs, backed by support in the county and at Court, gained control of the bench, leaving the Tories to dominate the council. Most parliamentary elections were contested and there was considerable dissension in the corporation after 1700.[56]

At Gloucester, as in other towns, the corporation seemed overwhelmed by party conflict in the later Stuart period, but we have to see this conflict in perspective. In Gloucester, at least, it did not lead to any serious street disorder or breakdown of civic administration such as was threatened during the magisterial conflicts at the end of the sixteenth century. Only in 1688 was there a panic over the threat from Irish troops, and the civic leadership acted decisively to assert its control. One reason why party conflict was contained was because of the progressive institutionalization of city government – a development also seen elsewhere. Much of the routine administration was dealt with now by the town clerk and his posse of assistants and officials: in 1701 the offices of the town clerk near the Cross had to be enlarged to provide more space. From the 1670s town finances, as we know, were handled by a semi-permanent paid chamberlain and the chronic deficits of the past eventually receded, helped by declining prices and a more business-like attitude towards sources of revenue. In 1714 all city leases were examined with the aim of increasing rents (rental income rose by 50 per cent between 1715 and 1735).[57] Poor relief was mainly left to the parishes, where the élite were active as officials. But party politics did not invade the vestries. After 1702 Gloucester followed Bristol and numerous other provincial towns in centralizing some of the supervision of the poor under the control of a body of guardians which included, as well as members of the corporation, county gentry and represent-atives from city wards and the cathedral precincts. Though the scheme initially failed it was revived after 1727. Party politics was mostly confined to civic and parliamentary elections and the struggle for the spoils of traditional town patronage, notably the leases of hospital and charity lands (in 1712 the magistrates reportedly controlled property worth £60,000). The disruption of city government was limited.[58]

Overall the advent of a more county-orientated élite in the post-Restoration period may well have encouraged the city to expand its importance as a social and service centre, sharing in the wider affluence of the region. Modest economic success was buttressed by a new found governmental stability despite all the ritualized party strife. The advance remained precarious however. In the 1720s this new urban order was threatened for a while by party feuding erupt-ing out of its conventional strait-jacket. With the Tories taking both seats in Parliament in 1715 and 1722, the Whigs on the corporation launched a bitter counter-attack. Serious disorders broke out in 1727 when the Whig aldermen manufactured a huge number of freemen to swamp the poll at the parliamentary elections. Tory gangs attacked aldermen's houses. Upper-class fears were height-ened by riots and disorders in other Western towns about this time and by a county mob which marched into the city in 1734 and demolished the turnpike gates.[59]

Alarmed, Gloucester's leaders responded by concerted action. After 1734 parliamentary representation was usually shared by Whigs and Tories. Consensus became the rule: party conflict within the corporation was kept to the minimum. City administration became progressively dominated by its permanent officials – from 1738 the chamberlain was assisted by a salaried treasurer. There was energetic civic action as in the 1760s to deal with outbreaks of poverty and distress. Small scale improvement schemes were in-augurated. The middle decades of the century marked a sustained period of urban consolidation.[60]

IV

In the 1770s, however, we find growing political unrest in Gloucester. One reason was the deterioration in city finances as a result of the negligence and abuses of the treasurer, Gabriel Harris. Another was the down-turn in trade caused by the American war, at a time when the urban population was starting to expand again. A third reason was the mounting unpopularity of Lord North's government, with which a number of the élite old guard, including Harris and Alderman George Augustus Selwyn, the city's MP since 1754, were associated. There were calls for reform from within the élite: for the reorganization of city finances, a major programme of urban improvement and an attack on governmental corruption in London. By the end of the decade the reform agitation moved in close step with what was happening in the county, where supporters of the Association movement and administrative reform – county magnates like Sir George Onesiphorus Paul – held the stage.

It must be said at once that the emergence of an élite with a strong sense of civic responsibility was not the result of any radical liberal-ization of the city's political leadership in the late eighteenth century. The civic élite between 1780 and 1800 was significantly smaller than in the preceding periods with only sixty-five members. Lower rates of mortality were part of the explanation, but there also seems to have been a deliberate policy of leaving council seats vacant. Within the corporation the common council was now largely eclipsed by the bench: the reforms after 1779 did nothing to reverse this.

In certain respects recruitment to the élite also remained con-servative. 74 per cent of the councillors and 67 per cent of the aldermen originated in the city, with most of the rest coming from the shire: the bench in particular admitted few distant newcomers. Once again, as in the late seventeenth century, gentry, professional men and distributive traders were the favoured parents. However, the growing impact of industrial activity in the city is exemplified by the fact that nearly a quarter of the councillors and aldermen were the sons of pin-makers, textile masters and brush-makers. Given the localized pattern of entry it is not perhaps surprising that new-comers to the élite often had kin ties with former or present members: 26 per cent of the councillors and 35 per cent of the aldermen had such a connection, a higher proportion than in earlier periods. On the other hand, apprenticeship had largely disappeared as a stepping stone to power, with the final disintegration of Gloucester's gild companies after 1700. The education of our civic leaders was noticeably more catholic than in the past. At least a quarter had been to school in the city (mostly to the fashionable cathedral school which also attracted the sons of landowners);[61] one had been to Eton. Over 10 per cent had gone up to university, and five councillors and two aldermen had studied at the Inns of Court.

During the eighteenth century the freedom, conferred like confetti at election times, had lost most of its residual economic and political significance: certainly it was no barrier for aspirants to civic office. As in the past, the distributive trades, umbilically linked to Gloucester's continuing importance as a regional market and shopping centre, furnished substantial numbers of civic leaders (though markedly fewer than in the late sixteenth century). Some specialized in the wine trade, importing directly from abroad and selling in the city and the shire, helping perhaps to supply the cellars of the many well-to-do who resorted to Cheltenham from the 1780s. Most notable, however, was the major advance of professional men on the corporation. A number were attorneys like Thomas Commeline, the nephew of the leading county lawyer, Samuel Commeline, a great patron of Gloucester's infirmary (founded in 1755); and William Lane the reformist mayor in 1779. But others were barristers such as William Fendall and Thomas Hayward, working mainly at sessions and assizes, and reflecting the rise of the bar as a distinct professional group in the late eighteenth century. Another novel feature was the array of surgeons and assorted apothecaries on the corporation – a sign of the growing size and importance of the medical profession in the city centred around the infirmary.[62]

In several cases the professional men on Gloucester corporation, particularly the lawyers, had important links with substantial gentry families. Landed families also occupied some seats on the council and bench – though on a smaller scale than in the late seventeenth century. Thus Charles Howard, eleventh Duke of Norfolk, who had marriage ties with the Scudamores of Hempsted and was a strong Whig, joined the council in 1780 and became mayor in 1783, recorder in 1792 and high steward in 1811; his nephew Henry Howard of Thornbury was a councillor between 1790 and 1823 and MP from 1795. Links between gentry, lawyers and traders were consolidated by their joint involvement in banking: at least ten of the élite had major banking interests. The Gloucester Old Bank, established in 1716, was one of the earlier provincial banks, and by 1800 the city was an important banking centre, with four firms operating there. They channelled city and county capital into government funds, turnpikes, canals and other local investments;

some may have found its way into urban manufacturing.[63] There were more manufacturers, mostly pin-makers, on the bench in the late eighteenth century than at any previous time. Among them were John Box, mayor in 1777, and members of the Cowcher and Weaver families. A small group of wool-staplers also appeared on the corporation (several of them Unitarians), supplying the burgeoning cloth industry in the Stroud valley.[64]

Thus, despite the contraction of the civic élite, it was more closely linked with provincial and national society than earlier ruling groups. Further evidence is afforded by marriage patterns. Well over half the members of the élite married women from outside the city and its immediate hinterland. Councillors, like aldermen, increasingly chose their brides from beyond the county. At the same time, marriage was less crucial now as a vehicle for social advancement (as in society in general); about 12 per cent of the élite remained bachelors.[65]

New entrants to the corporation were younger than in the past: the average age for councillors was 32 and future aldermen 34. This was partly an indication of the shift away from a traditional gerontocratic society, partly a sign of the greater prosperity of late eighteenth-century civic recruits – they could take election in their stride somewhat earlier. But another factor was that newcomers were no longer called upon to undertake costly offices soon after their arrival on the council. The shrievalty was now largely honorific with the administrative work done by the town clerk. As before, however, promotion to the bench was reserved for those in early middle age (about 46). Once on the bench the mayoralty came swiftly, although only one or two individuals held it more than twice. Long service on the corporation was common: there was none of the fairly rapid turnover of personnel which occurred in the post-Restoration era. The mean span of service for aldermen was thirty-two years (over half the time on the bench); councillors acted for just over twenty years on average.

But corporation appointments were only part of the story by the late Hanoverian period. Continuing the trend already apparent before 1700, substantial numbers of civic leaders occupied other offices in and out of the city. Some, like the traditional hospital posts, came as usual after elevation to the bench. But there was now a multiplicity of additional offices – reflecting the more polycentric nature of town rule during the late eighteenth century. Members of the élite played a lively part in the Improvement Commission first set up in 1750 and re-established with wider powers in 1781. They also acted as governors and guardians of the poor, in charge of the city workhouse, although the proportion acting in a parish capacity was lower than in the later Stuart period. Town rulers are also found as officers of the new infirmary and county gaol as well as more mundane land tax and customs officials. With the final decay of the gilds none of our élite are known to have held gild office, but four were MPs.[66] No less important, one-third of this ruling cadre exercised offices of varying types in county society: as militia officers, manorial stewards, JPs, county sheriffs, canal treasurers, turnpike agents, and officers of the prestigious Severn Humane Society and the Gloucestershire Society, with its annual celebrations in London. This great diversity of posts helped both to sustain the civic authority of the ruling élite and to incorporate it firmly into provincial society.

Age and ramifying kinship ties continued to grace élite authority. 58 per cent of the corporation (a higher level than in the past) had kinsmen among their colleagues, and nearly two-thirds of the aldermen had one or more relatives in the élite. Aldermen often stayed on the bench until they were very old: the average age for departure was 65 years (as in the late sixteenth century), but one survived until he was 99. Less is known about élite wealth. Nevertheless, it seems likely that a number of town leaders in the late Georgian period were men with handsome estates. The banker James Wood, who joined the corporation a little after our sample period in 1808, and served as alderman from 1820, left nearly £900,000 at his death. Giles Greenaway, a former innkeeper who was mayor in 1791 and 1803, had estates estimated at over £20,000; John Olney, a wool-stapler and councillor after 1786, may have been worth over £50,000 at his death in 1836.[67] Several other civic leaders had assets of £10,000 or more. Again, a high proportion of the élite invested at least part of their wealth in property. But in addition to extensive holdings in the city itself, almost half the councillors and two-thirds of the aldermen held land in the county: one in six of the bench also owned or leased estates outside Gloucestershire, quite frequently in London. None the less, they had greater flexibility than before with new investment options open to them. Over a fifth had money tied up in government funds, and nearly half the élite had shares in canal companies, mainly the Gloucester to Berkeley project. Sir James Jelf was a backer of an early railway company and also of the Severn Tunnel Company.

Less speculative, money was also lent to the turnpike trusts. Clearly there was substantial support for improvements in the infrastructure of the regional economy.[68]

In the late sixteenth and seventeenth centuries the city fathers had tended to congregate in the more central parishes close to the heart of civic power, proclaiming their importance with rebuilt vernacular and later neo-classical style houses. By the late eighteenth century, however, many civic leaders were emphasizing their links with extra-urban society by taking up residence on the airy Cotswold slopes; if they kept a town house they lived in it for only part of the year. Other members of the corporation owned new and expensive villas in the expanding suburbs of Barton Street and Kingsholme.[69]

In spite of the continuing localized pattern of recruitment to the élite, the social world of Gloucester's civic leaders was far more outward-looking than in the past. Almost invariably now élite children selected their marriage partners from outside the city, indeed from outside the county. While the social status of spouses and their parents was generally upper class, there was no obvious urban bias. With the French war at its height at the end of the century, a considerable number of daughters of the élite followed the example of Jane Austen's Bennett girls and married naval or army officers. Of the boys, the largest group opted for the professions, not just the law and medicine, but the Church and universities. Even so, seven sons of councillors and eight sons of aldermen joined the corporation in due course, underlining the family stability of Gloucester's civic élite in the decades before the Municipal Reform Act.

There are some signs of an enhanced cultural sophistication about the city's leadership at the end of the eighteenth century. Charles Wilton, the son of the lawyer Henry Wilton, was sent to Italy for his musical training and on his return gave a number of recitals in his home town; the banker John Niblett built up an impressive collection of books, pictures and mathematical instruments; John Olney, who later retired from Gloucester, left many of his paintings to the National Gallery; William Lane, an attorney and reformer after 1779, owned an extensive library with numerous religious, historical and scientific books, and works on local history, together with prints of those radical heroes George Washington and Charles James Fox.[70] There were excursions by town leaders to the fashionable world at Bath and many regularly journeyed up and down to London – staying with relatives and friends there. They patronized the new scientific lectures and exhibitions that visited Gloucester. They also showed an interest in the wave of urban antiquarianism that affected the city. A close associate of several city leaders, John Washbourn, was involved in a scheme for publishing Civil War tracts on the city – applauding its godly past.[71]

Washbourn was a Unitarian, one of a small congregation that had descended after many internal conflicts from the powerful Puritan and Presbyterian party of the seventeenth century. Nine Unitarians or men with Unitarian connections sat on the corporation. They were not the important radical force we find at Nottingham, but they did provide part of the impetus for the reform movement in the city after 1779. Evangelicals were also influential on the corporation. William Lane, for instance, left £1000 in 1788 for the establishment of Sunday schools (Gloucester was an early centre of the Sunday school movement).[72]

Though there had been initial moves earlier in the decade, the reform campaign began in 1779 with an attack on two fronts. A wide-ranging improvement bill was sponsored. An act in 1777 had enabled some of Gloucester's principal streets to be paved and certain obstructions to be cleared, but the new measure was much more drastic. A fresh improvement commission was to be established with extensive powers to borrow money and to pull down old buildings; the city gates were to be demolished and the markets removed from the streets; the running of the city workhouse was to be reorganized and a new city gaol built. The Tory lawyer John Pitt orchestrated opposition to the scheme, mainly on the grounds of cost, and the measure was delayed in Parliament, although it was eventually passed in 1781. Meanwhile the reformers on the corporation led by William Lane, the surgeon William Crump, and Thomas Weaver, a pin-maker, managed to set up a committee of inquiry to investigate the state of city finances. It quickly discovered that outstanding rents totalled £2668, that some of the arrears owed to the city were up to 20 years old, and that part of the charity funds had disappeared for good. City Treasurer Harris was finally forced to resign in 1780.[73]

By then civic reform had been overtaken by parliamentary electioneering. Harris was the election agent for George Augustus Selwyn, the old-time Whig MP who had turned into a supporter of North. His almost equally long-service colleague Charles Barrow, formerly a Tory, was now an energetic opponent of the war and had

the strong support of the city reformers. Barrow played an important part in launching the Gloucestershire Association early in 1780
which followed Yorkshire in calling for an end to the American war
and for economical reform. Other members on the committee
included Giles Greenaway and John Webb, a member of an old
élite family. Gloucester itself petitioned Parliament for reform in
February 1780. Later that year Barrow and Webb stood against
Selwyn and his new running mate, the naval officer Sir Andrew
Hammond, in the parliamentary election for the borough. The
contest was fierce, with both sides trying to sway the large freeman
electorate with a barrage of polemic and circulars; the Selwyn
campaign was partly financed by the government. One broadsheet
cried: 'Is this respectable city to be treated as a Cornish borough?'.
The answer was a resounding no, with Selwyn and Hammond
forced to stand down to avoid a humiliating defeat.[74] Webb's
reformist record in the Commons was impeccable, voting for Parliamentary reform and Shelburne's peace. Webb and Barrow were
returned unopposed in 1784 but Gloucester's commitment to
national reform was more muted after the political disaster of the
Fox–North coalition. In 1789, on the death of Barrow, the Tory
John Pitt was elected after a long and bitterly fought struggle.[75]

However, reform measures were more successful in the city. In
1780 the duties of the two financial officers, the treasurer and
chamberlain, were carefully defined and detailed regulations introduced to control them. Expenditure on civic entertainment was
curbed and there was a move to phase out the old practice of long
leases for city lands. The city commons were enclosed in 1797. The
1781 Act was used to improve policing in the city. John Hemming
claimed in 1789 that 'no city in England is less infected with vagrants
and disorderly persons'.[76] The committee of inquiry continued to
meet into the 1790s, helping to plan and direct town improvement.
One scheme involved the enlargement of the docks and the remodelling of the bridge and main entrance to the city through
Westgate Street: the consequent rebuilding of St Bartholemew's
Hospital cost £2617. Another project to construct a grand purpose-
built market house in Eastgate Street in 1786 was financed by a
tontine or annuity arrangement which raised £4000. The corporation alone spent up to £10,000 on improvements between 1770 and
1800.[77] In addition, the city co-operated with county reformers like
Sir George Onesiphorus Paul, erecting a pioneering county gaol,
planning a lunatic asylum in the 1790s and raising a new shire hall in

Westgate. Civic leaders strongly supported the Gloucester–Berkeley canal, to link up with the Stroud navigation, and gave their backing to the Stourbridge and Hereford canals and canal projects as far away as Yorkshire.[78]

By 1800 Gloucester was the model of an improved, reformed town. The economy benefited from the expansion of marketing and the city's growth as a professional and banking centre; economic activity was further buoyed up by the pin-making industry. Gloucester had a reputation for religious and political tolerance. Joseph Priestley, the Birmingham Unitarian, acknowledged 'the liberality of the clergy and inhabitants' of the city, and one of his Unitarian friends found sanctuary for a while near Gloucester after his flight from Birmingham in the wake of the 1791 riots. Arguments for tolerance had been enunciated in the town since the 1760s by the influential reformer Josiah Tucker, Dean of Gloucester. And for numerous members of an increasingly enlightened, outward-looking élite, tolerance made good economic and social sense. In 1789, after the violent election campaign, leading Whigs and Tories got together and agreed to divide the parliamentary representation. It was this élite consensus which, together with the reforms of the previous decade, probably contributed to the absence of radical activity during the 1790s despite the vicissitudes of trade.[79]

Gloucester's rulers can hardly take all the credit for the city's prosperity by 1800. The flourishing state of the farming hinterland, the spread of industrial activity in the West Midlands which stimulated economic activity down the Severn, the general rise in demand for urban goods and services due to population increase, all contributed. But the élite's support for urban investment and improvement helped create a new mood of confidence, making the city more attractive to the rural well-to-do resorting there for trade, professional advice and social entertainment. Advances in communications, propelled by élite money and political support, boosted Gloucester as a manufacturing and commercial centre. The town leaders' closer ties with national society may have induced more flexible and tolerant attitudes in the community.

In conclusion, it is clear that oligarchic rule was a dominant theme of civic government at Gloucester (as in so many established towns) during the early modern period. Power was concentrated in the hands of a locally recruited, clannish and rather elderly ruling class. Indeed, oligarchic control grew pretty steadily over the whole period. On the other hand, the picture was less pessimistic than some critics have supposed. The civic leadership was not slumped incorrigibly in corruption and lethargy, unresponsive to outside change. After an irruption of factionalism and abuse in the corporation at the end of the sixteenth century, the early Stuart magistrates sought to reform and rally the city through an appeal to the idea of a godly commonwealth. Though this conservative, isolationist strategy proved an economic and political cul-de-sac, by the later Stuart era a more pluralistic ruling group was starting to establish a warmer relationship with the countryside, serving to integrate the city more closely with the provincial economy and providing a climate for recovery. At the close of the period city leaders presided over a significant phase of urban reform and resurgence.

How Gloucester's experience compares with that of other provincial towns is uncertain. At the important provincial capitals of York and Exeter before the Civil War, civic élites may have been recruited more widely than at declining Gloucester.[80] But in the post-Restoration period and after Gloucester probably followed in the mainstream of inland towns. In a number of communities like Stafford, Beverley and Exeter lawyers and later medical men became prominent élite figures as in Gloucester.[81] By the late eighteenth century two other developments were also more widely apparent: the consolidation of oligarchy and the growing commitment to civic improvement.[82] As for unchartered towns, little research has been done on the informal ruling groups of the rising industrial centres, but initial signs would suggest that these towns were not particularly open or radical in their recruitment patterns: small groups of professional men and landowners, as well as manufacturers, predominated in urban affairs.[83] Most towns seem to have become oligarchic in the pre-modern period as a function of their growing size: the same trend can be observed across the Atlantic in the larger colonial towns.[84] Certainly it is doubtful whether the openness or otherwise of the ruling cadre was a significant variable in the relative economic success of English provincial towns before 1800.

After the end of the Napoleonic wars Gloucester became a loser by big-city standards. The industrial sector sagged: pin-making disappeared in the 1830s; demographic growth was relatively sluggish; the city like numerous other cathedral or county towns enjoyed only modest expansion.[85] Most of this was due to structural changes in the national and regional economy into which the city had become progressively integrated during the eighteenth century and from which initially at least it had gained a great deal. It was affected by the rise of the Birmingham–Liverpool industrial–commercial axis and the general stagnation of Bristol and the South-West. But the response of the city's élite, with professional men in the ascendancy, may also have played a part. There is little sign of the antipathy to industry which Martin Wiener has seen as a characteristic of professional groups in Victorian England;[86] in the late eighteenth century these classes were often heavily engaged, directly or indirectly, in industrial activity. Rather, as manufacturing in some older centres like Gloucester came under pressure, the élite's ties with landed and farming activity made it easier to follow the sensible option of maximizing the towns' long-standing marketing and service sectors. It was not an heroic choice. But it did ensure a slow but long-term increase in prosperity at Gloucester during the nineteenth century.

Acknowledgements

Research for this project has been generously funded by grants from the Social Science Research Council. I am indebted to Drs Philip Morgan and Andrew Foster for their help in collecting the data. Mr Brian Frith provided valuable local advice.

Notes and references

1   Contemporary complaints are cited in P. Clark and P. Slack (eds.), *Crisis and Order in English Towns* (1972), p. 22; P. J. Corfield, *The Impact of English Towns 1700–1800* (1982), pp. 154–6. *PP*, 1835, **23**, *First Report of Commissioners . . . into Municipal Corporations of England and Wales [and] Appendix Part I*, p. 49.

2   J. L. and B. Hammond, *The Rise of Modern Industry* (9th edn. 1966), p. 225; see also W. Cunningham, *The Growth of English Industry and Commerce in Modern Times: Part Two* (1921), p. 807n; S. and B. Webb, *English Local Government from the Revolution to the Municipal Corporations Act: The Manor and the Borough: Part II* (1908), esp. pp. 723–33.

3   'Foreword' in Clark and Slack, *Crisis and Order*, p. vii; D. M. Palliser, *Tudor York* (1979), ch. 4; F. F. Foster, *The Politics of Stability: A Portrait of the Rulers in Elizabethan London* (1977); A. Dyer, *The City of Worcester in the Sixteenth Century* (1973), pp. 224–6; J. T. Evans, *Seventeenth-Century Norwich* (1979), pp. 30–60.

4   The Gloucester civic leadership meets most of R. A. Dahl's conditions for a ruling elite: 'Critique of the ruling elite model', *American Political Science Review*, **52** (1958), p. 466.

5   M. Weinbaum, *British Borough Charters 1307–1660* (1943), pp. 42–3; W. H. Stevenson (ed.), *Calendar of the Records of the Corporation of Gloucester* (1893), pp. 16–18, 40–1.

6   For some of the basic problems of collective biography including the inevitable patchiness and selectivity of the data see L. Stone, 'Prosopography', *Daedalus*, **100** (1971), pp. 57–65. In the present analysis all findings are based on substantial samples of civic rulers. The primary sources which were systematically trawled for biographical evidence included (1) at the Gloucestershire RO (hereafter GRO): corporation council minutes, financial and sessions papers and lease-books; dean and chapter rentals and other estate records; parish registers, poor rates and miscellaneous parochial collections; diocesan deposition books and visitation papers; probate wills and inventories; Gloucester infirmary records; Stroudwater canal papers; deposited family papers; (2) at Gloucester City Library (hereafter GCL): private and city collections; the *Gloucester Journal*; (3) at the PRO: the records of the principal London courts; parliamentary taxation listings; Privy Council and Home Office papers; probate wills and inventories. In addition, considerable use was made of printed materials, particularly in the *Transactions of the Bristol and Gloucestershire Archaeological Society* (1876–   ) (hereafter *TBGAS*) and *Gloucestershire Notes and Queries* (1881–1914).

7   For a more detailed account of the city's fortunes in the sixteenth and seventeenth centuries see P. Clark, ' "The Ramoth-Gilead of the Good": urban change and political radicalism at Gloucester 1540–1640', in P. Clark, A. G. R. Smith and N. Tyacke (eds.), *The English Commonwealth 1547–1640* (1979), pp. 168–76; and *VCH*, Gloucestershire, **4** (forthcoming).

8   R. Atkyns, *The Ancient and Present State of Glostershire* (1712) (reprinted 1974), p. 119; S. Rudder, *The History and Antiquities of Gloucester* (1781), p. 179; E. W. Brayley and J. Britton, *The Beauties of England and Wales V* (1803), pp. 560, 562–3; GCL, N.26.15.

9   Councillor David Wyatt said he had known John Maddock (councillor from 1595) since their childhood together, apparently in Herefordshire: GRO, GDR 57 (Maddock v. Ower).

10 For the problems of a Coventry apprentice without the right craft connection see R. Berger, 'Mercantile careers in the early 17th century: Thomas Atherall, a Coventry apothecary' (unpublished paper).

11 Evidence is available for thirty-eight rulers of whom five were subscriptionally illiterate; for school attendance (by councillor John Brook): GRO, GDR 32, pp. 108–9.

12   Freedom fines rose sixfold between the 1570s and 1630s (GRO, GBR 1376–7/1451–2). GBR 1300/1355; GBR 1466B. D. M. Woodward, 'Freemen's rolls', *Local Historian*, **9** (1970–1), p. 91.

13   E. A. Lewis (ed.), *The Welsh Port Books (1550–1603)*, (Cymmrodorion Record Series, **12** 1927); PRO, E 134/25 Eliz./H3; 27 Eliz./T1; 27, 28 Eliz./M17; REQ 2/275/13.

14   Clark, 'Ramoth-Gilead', pp. 170–1.

15   For activity by lawyers in Kent see P. Clark, *English Provincial Society from the Reformation to the Revolution* (1977), pp. 273–4, 279 *et seq.*; and medical activity at Norwich: C. Webster (ed.), *Health, Medicine and Mortality in the Sixteenth Century* (1979), pp. 207–26. Jones (*c.* 1558–1630) was diocesan registrar under eight bishops.

16   For the Guise family and conflict with the city: G. Davies (ed.), *Autobiography of Thomas Raymond and Memoirs of the Family of Guise. . .* (Camden Soc., 3rd series, **28** 1917), pp. 104, 167. Clark, 'Ramoth-Gilead', p. 180.

17   H. A. Machen, 'The Machen family, Gloucestershire', *TBGAS*, **64** (1943), p. 98; PRO, St Ch 8/4/9.

18   The earlier promotion of aldermen at York is noted by Palliser, *York*, pp. 71–2. GRO, GBR 1375/1450, fols. 56–7; 1376/1451, fols. 187v–8.

19   Clark, 'Ramoth-Gilead', p. 176; PRO: REQ 2/198/41; St Ch 8/52/11. Delegating routine work to an under-sheriff could cause further difficulties: GRO, GBR 1376/1451, vol. 103v.

20   For example, GRO, GBR 1376/1451, fol. 134v; PRO, E 134/3 James I/M3.

21   GRO, GBR 1889B, fol. 12; 1376/1451, fols. 187v–8.

22   GCL, MS 12120; PRO, E 134/ 11 Charles I/M45; GCL, NQ.12.1; W. R. Williams (ed.), *The Parliamentary History of the County of Gloucester . . . 1213–1898* (1898), pp. 190–4.

23   For example, Christopher Capel, councillor and later alderman, was related to John Baugh, Richard Handes and Lawrence and Thomas Singleton. cf. the similar gerontocratic pattern in other towns in K. Thomas, 'Age and authority in early modern England', *Proceedings of the British Academy*, **62** (1976), pp. 209–11.

24   P. Clark and P. Slack, *English Towns in Transition 1500–1700* (1976), p. 129; cf. C. Wright Mills, *The Power Elite* (New York 1956); PRO, E 179/115/430.

25   PRO: St Ch 8/4/9; REQ 2/118/59. For a comparable pattern of wealth at Worcester see Dyer, *Worcester*, pp. 224–5; the Leicester magnates were apparently smaller men: W. G. Hoskins, *Provincial England* (1965), p. 93.

26   PRO, C 2/James I/D 1/49.

27   PRO: E 134/36,37 Eliz./M14; REQ 2/54/77; E 134/30, 31 Eliz./M4; C 3/224/56.

28   PRO, E 134/40 Eliz./H9; REQ 2/43/43.

29   Some servants of civic leaders (those liable to militia service) are listed in the 1608 muster return: J. Maclean (ed.), *Men and Armour for Gloucestershire in 1608* (1902).

30   The picture was similar in a number of respects at York, though the greater wealth of élite families meant that rather more there entered the gentry (Palliser, *York*, pp. 98–9).

31   Clark and Slack, *English Towns in Transition*, pp. 128–32.

32   GRO, GBR 1376/1451, fols. 92–v, 108, 188, 196v; GBR, 1889B, fol. 16; PRO, St Ch 8/4/9.

33   PRO, St Ch: 8/4/8–9; 7/14/22; 8/254/23.

34   *APC*, 1586–7, pp. 321–2; 1587–8, pp. 17, 291–3; J. E. Neale, *The Elizabethan House of Commons* (1963), pp. 264–8; PRO, St Ch 8/254/23; GRO, GBR 1376/1451, fol. 174v; PRO, St Ch: 5/A 20/11; 8/228/30; 8/207/25.

35   PRO, St Ch: 8/4/9; 8/228/30; 8/207/25.

36   Clark and Slack, *English Towns in Transition*, pp. 135–6; Evans, *Norwich*, ch. 3; P. Clark, 'Thomas Scott and the growth of urban opposition to the early Stuart regime', *Historical Journal*, **21** (1978), pp. 11–24.

37   The important aldermanic sessions books start in 1609 (GRO, GBR 1453/1542 *et seq.*) and the city correspondence volumes date from 1619 (GBR 1420/1540 *et seq.*) GBR 1376/1451, fol. 268; *HMC*, 12th Report App. IX, pp. 416–18; 427–30, 526; GBR 1453/1542, fols. 16–v, 21–2v.

38   Clark, 'Ramoth-Gilead', pp. 182–4; T. Prior, *A Sermon at the Funeral of the Right Reverend Father in God, Miles, late Lord Bishop of Gloucester* (1632), pp. 297, 301.

39   *VCH*, Warwickshire, **8**, pp. 249, 265, 372–3 (Coventry); Clark, *English Provincial Society*, pp. 323, 340–1 (Sandwich, Dover).

40   PRO, SP 14/54/34; GRO, GBR 1878; Clark, 'Ramoth-Gilead', p. 184; J. K. G. Taylor, 'The civil government of Gloucester 1640–6', *TBGAS*, **67** (1946–8), p. 72.

41   F. A. Hyett, *Gloucester in National History* (1924), p. 124; GRO, GBR 1397/1502, p. 18; Davies, *Autobiography*, pp. 124–5; J. Dorney, *Certain Speeches made upon the day of the Yearly Election of Officers in the City of Gloucester* (1653), pp. 79–80. Some leading magistrates may have been adversely affected by the war themselves (for example, John Brewster: PRO C5/404/236).

42   GRO, GBR 1378/1453, pp. 224, 231; GBR 1470, fols. 6–8 *et passim*; GBR 1397/1502, p. 440. The city lost control of the inshire as a result of legislation in 1662 (*Lords Journals*, **11**, p. 473).

43   *CSPD*, 1670, pp. 35, 431; PRO, SP 29/278/123, 204; *CSPD*, 1671, pp. 411–12, 429 *et passim*; 1671–2, pp. 2–3, 7–8, *et passim*; PRO, SP 29/291/29, 52; 29/293/16, 113; 29/294/85, 128, 218; Stevenson, *Calendar*, pp. 46–8; GRO, GBR 1378/1453, pp. 449–50, 509, 839;

GBR 1379/1454, pp. 308, 322; GBR 1381/1456, fols. 174v–5, 205–v, 221v–2, 238–9.

44   GRO, D 36, A1, fols. 34v, 45v, 52; A2.

45   PRO, C 6/66/43; C 5/503/89.

46   For Norwood: GRO, D 303, F 40; for Guise's Whig connections see Davies, *Autobiography*, pp. 134–8.

47   For the activities of Gloucester lawyers see PRO, C 5/109/18; 5/264/6; C 6/277/76; 6/62/45. John Aubrey quotes a Gloucestershire attorney (1689) on the recent rise in the number of lawyers in the county (*Aubrey's Natural History of Wiltshire* (reprinted 1969), p. 118).

48   GRO, GBR 1398/1503.

49   J. T. Evans, 'The decline of oligarchy in seventeenth-century Norwich', *Journal of British Studies*, **14** (1974–5), pp. 49–76; R. O'Day, 'The triumph of civic oligarchy in the seventeenth century?', in *The Traditional Community under Stress* (Open University Urban History course 1977), p. 135.

50   GRO, GBR 1378/1453, p. 533, *et passim*; the median number of council meetings declined from 11.5 per annum in 1670–9 to 9.0 per annum 1700–9.

51   PRO, E 134/2 James II/E 21; F. A. Hyett, 'The Hyetts of Painswick' (1907) (typescript in GCL), pp. 25–9.

52   S. and B. Webb, *English Local Government: English Poor Law History: Part 1* (1927), p. 159 *et seq*.

53   GRO, D 326, F 13, 15 (Guise); D 36, F 8(34); PRO, C 6/119/29 (Colchester); C 5/71/35; 5/180/5 (Price); 5/205/48; 5/503/87; 5/329/17; (Hyett); C 7/585/20; 7/95/52 (Cromwell); GRO, GI 1693/170; also GW 1693/275 (Nicholls).

54   GRO, GBR 1398/1503; PRO, C 5/519/78; GRO, GI 1702/164; see also the inventory of councillor Henry Robins in C 6/131/219.

55   G. L. Turner (ed.), *Original Records of Early Nonconformity under Persecution and Indulgence* (1911), vol. 1, p. 600; vol. 2, p. 823; G. F. Nuttall, 'George Whitefield's "curate": Gloucestershire dissent and the revival', *Journal of Ecclesiastical History*, **27** (1976), pp. 371–5; Dr Williams Library, Evans MS 34. 4, pp. 42, 45. For example, *Gloucester Journal*, 10 September 1722, 29 October 1728 (horse-races); 30 November 1724, 7 July 1730 (assemblies); 10 September and 17 September 1722 (concerts); 17 October 1727 (firework shows). D. Lysons, *Origin and Progress of the Meeting of the Three Choirs* (1895).

56   Bodl., MS Addit. C.303, fols. 180, 225v–6; Stevenson, *Calendar*, pp. 46–8; *CSPD*, 1680–1, pp. 45–6; GRO, GBR 1378/1453, pp. 780, 787–90; GBR 1381/1456, fols. 174v–5, 221v–2, 238–9, 273v, 274; GBR 1382/1457, fol. 8, *et passim*; *HMC*, Portland MSS, **10**, pp. 76–8; GBR, 1383/1458, pp. 305, 429–30, 492; R. Sedgwick, *The House of Commons, 1715–1754* (1970), vol. 1, p. 246.

57   GRO, GBR: 1398/1503 (1688–9); 1381/1456, fols. 219v, 221v, 225; 1383/1458, p. 29; P. J. G. Ripley, 'The city of Gloucester, 1660–1740' (unpublished MPhil thesis, University of Bristol 1977), pp. 108–9, 329–31.

58   Rudder, *Gloucester*. pp. viii, 198–200; Atkyns, *Glostershire*, p. 119.

59   Sedgwick, *The House of Commons*, vol. 1, pp. 246–7; GRO, GBR Quarter Session Rolls Trinity 1727, Michaelmas 1727; GBR 1384/1459, fols. 214–15v; GCL, NX.10.2(20a). D. G. D. Isaac, 'A study of popular disturbances in Britain, 1714–54' (unpublished PhD thesis, University of Edinburgh 1953), pp. 57–66, 105–6; *Gloucestershire Notes and Queries*, **4** (1890), pp. 493–4.

60   P. Langford, *The Excise Crisis* (1975), pp. 136–7; Sedgwick, *The House of Commons*, vol. 1, p. 246–7; GRO, GBR 1384/1459, fols. 426–7; D. E. Williams, 'English hunger riots in 1766' (unpublished PhD thesis, University of Wales 1978), pp. 130, 180–1; GCL, NX.10.1; Rudder, *Gloucester*, pp. 32, 36.

61   *VCH*, Gloucestershire, **2**, pp. 332–3.

62   *Gloucester Journal*, 5 December 1791, 10 December 1795; *Gentleman's Magazine*, **57** (1787), p. 740; D. Duman, 'The English Bar in the Georgian era', in W. Prest (ed.), *Lawyers in Early Modern Europe and America* (1981), pp. 86–104; for links between the infirmary and the local medical profession see G. Whitcombe, *The General Infirmary at Gloucester* (1903), esp. p. 84 *et seq.*; GRO, Infirmary Records, General Court and Weekly Board Minutes; also D 303, C1–4.

63   G. L. Goodman, 'Pre-reform elections in Gloucester city, 1789–1831', *TBGAS*, **84** (1965), pp. 143–4; I. Gray, 'Jemmy Wood's journal', *TBGAS*, **90** (1971), p. 158.

64   For Box: PRO, PROB 11/1131; for the wool-stapler John Bush: *Gloucester Journal*, 4 June 1781; also 6 May 1782.

65   This contrasts with the finding of Wrigley and Schofield that celibacy rates in the national population were fairly low (E. A. Wrigley and R. S. Schofield, *The Population History of England 1541–1871* (1981), p. 260).

66   Rudder, *Gloucester*, pp. iii–vii, 199–200; Whitcombe, *General Infirmary*, p. 84 *et seq.*; Williams, *Parliamentary History*, pp. 210–13.

67   Gray, 'Wood's journal', p. 159; GRO, D 3117/1816 lists some of Greenaway's property; PRO, PROB 11/1859; also GRO, D 1018.

68   GCL, T. Hannam Clark Collection; A. S. Jelf, *James Jelf, 1763–1842* (privately printed 1938).

69   GCL, J. 3.24; J. Hemming, *The History and Chemical Analysis of the Mineral Water . . . of Gloucester* (1789), p. 11; for the general movement: T. R. Slater, 'Family society and the ornamental villa on the fringes of English country towns', *Journal of Historical Geography*, **4** (1978), pp. 129–44.

70   *Gloucester Journal*, 9 August 1784, 8 November 1784; PRO, PROB 11/1284; 11/1859; GCL, NF.28.1.

71   *Gloucester Journal*: 13 September 1790, 5 January, 12 January and 2 February 1795; 15 March 1790; Washbourn's work was eventually published as *Bibliotheca Gloucestrensis* (1825).

72   GCL, MS 10600(6); GRO, Barton Street Gloucester Unitarian Chapel, Dutton MSS. M. I. Thomis, *Politics and Society in Nottingham, 1785–1835* (1969), p. 128 *et seq. Gloucester Journal*, 4 January 1790; GRO, D 608/14/3; T. W. Laqueur, *Religion and Respectability: Sunday Schools and Working Class Culture 1780–1850* (1976), pp. 21–5.

73   GRO, GBR 1386/1461, fols. 260v–1, 264, 268v; Rudder, *Gloucester*, pp. iii–x; GBR 1500, pp. 5–6, 19, *et passim*.

74   GRO, GBR 1500, p. 113; GBR 1386/1461, fols. 265–7; E. Moir, 'The Gloucestershire Association for Parliamentary Reform', *TBGAS*, **75** (1956), pp. 180–5; GCL, NX.10.2(24); L. Namier and J. Brooke, *The House of Commons 1754–90* (1964), vol. 1, pp. 290–2: vol. 2, pp. 59–60; vol. 3, pp. 420, 614.

75   Namier and Brooke, *The House of Commons*, vol. 3, p. 614; vol. 1, pp. 290, 292; Goodman, 'Pre-reform elections', pp. 144–7.

76   GRO, GBR 1386/1461, fol. 339; GBR 1501; Hemming, *History*, p. 7.

77   GRO, GBR 1500, fol. 133; GBR 1501; GBR 1387/1462; GBR 1401/ 1506. Other major projects included the quay, the Gloucester– Berkeley canal and the Boothall (where the assizes were held).

78   E. Moir, 'Sir George Onesiphorus Paul' in H. P. R. Finberg (ed.), *Gloucestershire Studies* (1957), pp. 205, 209, 216; GRO, D 13165(4); Gray, 'Wood's journal', p. 167; GBR 1387/1462; GCL, JZ.14.3; *Gloucester Journal*, 28 December 1795.

79   GCL, J.3.24, pp. 263–4; T. Browne, *Supplicatory Addresses . . . from the Papers of the late William Russell* (1818), p. xviii; J. Tucker, *Religious Intolerance* (1774), pp. iii, 42; see also G. Shelton, *Dean Tucker and Eighteenth-Century Economic and Political Thought* (1981). *The Songs, Addresses, Squibs etc. etc. Published during the late Contest for the City of Gloucester* (n.d.), pp. 34–5, 37. In 1795 Robert Raikes wrote: 'in this city we are all quiet and have no symptoms of disorder but in the country around there is reason for alarm' (GCL, MS 17634).

80   Palliser, *York*, pp. 94–5, 106–7; W. T. MacCaffrey, *Exeter, 1540–1640* (1975), pp. 256–9.

81   K. R. Adey, 'Aspects of the history of the town of Stafford, 1590– 1710', (unpublished MA thesis, University of Keele 1971), p. 60; K. A. MacMahon (ed.), *Beverley Corporation Minute Books 1707–1835* (Yorkshire Archaeological Society, Record Series, **122** 1958), p. x; R. Newton, 'The membership of the Chamber of Exeter', *Devon and Cornwall Notes and Queries*, **33** (1977), pp. 282–3.

82 Thomis, *Nottingham*, pp. 115, 120; R. W. Greaves, *The Corporation of Leicester 1689–1836* (1970), pp. 10, 77, 105, 108; E. J. Dawson, 'Finance and the unreformed borough . . . 1660–1835' (unpublished PhD thesis, University of Hull 1978), p. 519 *et seq.*

83 C. Gill, 'Birmingham under the street commissioners, 1769–1851', *University of Birmingham Historical Journal*, 1 (1947–8) pp. 260–1; also at Sheffield (I am grateful here for discussions with Dr David Hey who is undertaking a major study of the eighteenth-century town).

84 E. M. Cook, *The Fathers of the Towns: Leadership and Community Structure in Eighteenth Century New England* (Baltimore 1976), pp. 33, 50, 62, 74, *et passim*; but see also B. C. Daniels, 'Democracy and oligarchy in Connecticut towns', *Social Science Quarterly*, **56** (1975), esp. pp. 474–5.

85 *PP, First Report Municipal Corporations*, app., p. 68. The population stood at 11,933 in 1831 and 17,572 in 1851, though it had risen to 36,552 by 1881. cf. at Exeter, R. Newton, *Victorian Exeter, 1837–1914* (1968).

86 M. J. Wiener, *English Culture and the Decline of the Industrial Spirit, 1850–1980* (1981), pp. 14–16.

Index

Gainsborough (Lincs.)   140, 287, 290, 294

Geertz, C.   243

gentry   19, 28, 29, 32, 39–42, 45, 103, 113, 115, 119, 120, 138, 139, 141, 144, 200, 206, 219, 232, 233, 238, 242, 262–3, 276–8, 292, 293, 314, 318, 319, 321, 322, 329, 335; political influence of   23, 36, 39, 40, 233–4, 321–4, 326–8, 330, 337; resident in   27, 29, 32, 34, 36, 43, 48, 86, 316; towns as social centres for   20, 22–3, 46, 201, 232–3, 249, 250, 272, 324, 327

George II   238, 239, 244

Germany   94

gilds   24, 101, 103, 110, 115, 118–21, 201–7, 217, 228, 229, 241, 249, 318, 321, 329, 332

Gladstone, John   289, 292

Glasgow   29

Glastonbury   137

Gloucester   19, 31, 150, 154; churches in   300, 302–3; economy   26, 33, 313–16, 319–20, 322, 328, 336–8; politics at   311–38; population of   16, 150, 152, 154, 313, 345n; religion at   321–3, 327, 336; ritual at   232

Gloucester, Dean of   336

Gloucestershire   122, 150, 314, 323–6, 332, 335

Gluckman, M.   242

Godalming (Surrey)   46, 299

Gosport (Hants.)   93, 298

Grady, K.   304

Grasmere   100, 129n

Gray, William   34

Greenaway, Giles   332, 335

Grew, Nehemiah   19

Guildford   295, 296, 302

guildhalls   *see* townhalls

Guise, Sir John   324, 326; Sir William   316

Halesowen (Worcs.)   171, 181

Halifax   20, 24

Hammond, Sir Andrew   335

Hammond, B. and J. L.   311

Hampshire   150, 298

Handel, George Frederick   232

Hargreaves, James   24

Harley, Lord   211

Harris, Gabriel   329, 334

harvest failure   27, 35; *see also* famine; subsistence crises

Harwich   19

Hawkshead (Lancs.)   100, 121, 122, 124

Hearth Tax   *see* taxation

Helston (Cornwall)   285, 289, 295

Hereford   241, 336

Herefordshire   314

Hinckley   149

Hogarth, William   234

Honiton   71

Horncastle   236

horse-racing   47, 172, 196, 233, 249–51, 261, 327

Hoskins, W. G.   64, 71, 311

housing   17, 18, 23, 34, 35, 41–3, 62–95, 172, 199, 249, 319, 326, 333; lower-class   43, 67; sub-division of   67, 92, 153; types   68–70, 74–92; *see also* building

Houston, R.   208

Howard, Charles, Duke of Norfolk   330

Howard, Henry   330

hucksters   26, 265, 269–70, 273–4

Huddersfield   20

Hull   15, 25, 29, 204

Hutton, William   185

improvement, town   16, 23, 27, 29, 33, 34, 38, 40–2, 44–6, 59n, 250, 284–306, 328–9, 331–2, 334–7, 344n; acts   40, 41, 334–5

incorporation   100, 103, 110, 122